1990

TIME AND NARRATIVE VOLUME 3

TIME AND
NARRATIVE VOLUME 3

PAUL RICOEUR

Translated by Kathleen Blamey and David Pellauer

The University of Chicago Press · Chicago and London

PAUL RICOEUR has been the dean of the faculty of letters and human sciences at the University of Paris X
(Nanterre) for many years and is currently the John Nu-
veen Professor Emeritus in the Divinity School, the
Department of Philosophy, and the Committee on Social Thought at the University of Chicago.

Originally published as *Temps et Récit,* vol. 3,
© Editions du Seuil, 1985

The University of Chicago Press, Chicago 60637
The University of Chicago Press, Ltd., London

Library of Congress Cataloging-in-Publication Data

Ricoeur, Paul.
  Time and narrative.

  Translation of: Temps et récit.
  Vol. 3: Translated by Kathleen Blamey and David
Pellauer.
  Bibliography: p.
  Includes index.
  1. Narration (Rhetoric).   2. Time in literature.
3. Mimesis in literature.   4. Plots (Drama, novel,
etc.).   5. History—Philosophy. I. Title.
PN212.R5213   1984   809'.923   83-17995
ISBN 0-226-71331-8 (v. 1)
ISBN 0-226-71333-4 (v. 2)
ISBN 0-226-71335-0 (v. 3)

Contents

PART IV
Narrated Time

Introduction

This fourth part of *Time and Narrative* is aimed at as complete an explication as possible of the hypothesis that governs our inquiry, namely, that the effort of thinking which is at work in every narrative configuration is completed in a refiguration of temporal experience. Following our schematism of the three-fold mimetic relation between the order of narrative, the order of action, and the order of life,[1] this power of refiguration corresponds to the third and last moment of mimesis.

This fourth part consists of two sections. The first is aimed at presenting an aporetics of temporality as what stands over against this power of refiguration. This aporetics generalizes the affirmation made in passing, in the course of our reading of Augustine, that there has never been a phenomenology of temporality free of every aporia, and that in principle there can never be one. This entry into the problem of refiguration by way of an aporetics of temporality calls for some justification. Others, desiring to attack directly what we might call the secondary narrativization of human experience, have legitimately approached the problem of the refiguration of temporal experience by narrative through the resources of psychology,[2] sociology,[3] genetic anthropology,[4] or the resources of an empirical inquiry aimed at detecting the influences of historical and literary culture (insofar as the narrative component is dominant in it) on everyday life, on self-knowledge and knowledge of others, and on individual and collective action. But, if it were to be something more than banal observations, such a study on my part would have required means of psychosociological inquiry and analysis that I do not possess. Aside from this incompetence, I would justify the order I follow in this volume by the philosophical consideration that actually motivated it. If the notion of temporal experience is to be worthy of its name, we must not confine ourselves to describing the implicitly temporal aspects of the remolding of behavior by narrativity. We need to be more radical and bring to light those experiences where time as such is thematized, something that cannot be done unless we introduce a third partner into the discussion between historiography and narratology, the phenomenology of time-consciousness. In fact, it is this consideration that has guided me ever since Part I, where I preceded my study of Aristotle's *Poetics* by an interpretation of the Augustinian conception of time. From that moment on, the course of the analyses in this fourth part was determined. The problem of the refiguration of temporal experience can no longer be confined within the limits of a psycho-sociology of the influences of narrativity on human behavior. We must assume the much greater risks of a specifically philosophical discussion, whose stake is whether—and how—the narrative operation, taken in its full scope, offers a "solution"—not a speculative one, but a poetic one—to the aporias that seemed inseparable from the Augustinian analysis of time. In this way, the problem of the refiguration of time by narrative finds itself brought to the level of a broad confrontation between an aporetics of temporality and a poetics of narrativity.

This formulation makes sense only if, as a prior question, we do not confine ourselves to what we learn from Book XI of Augustine's *Confessions,* but try to verify our thesis of the aporicity in principle of the phenomenology of time in terms of two canonical examples, Husserl's phenomenology of internal time-consciousness and Heidegger's hermeneutic phenomenology of temporality.

This is why an initial section will be entirely devoted to the aporetics of temporality. It is not that this aporetics must, as such, be assigned to one or the other of the phases of the mimesis of action (along with its temporal dimension). Such an aporetics is the work of a reflective and speculative form of thinking that, in fact, was developed without any regard for a specific theory of narrative. Only the reply of a poetics of narrative—as much historical as fictional—to the aporetics of time draws this aporetics into the gravitational space of threefold mimesis, at the moment when this mimesis crosses the threshold between the configuration of time *in* narrative and its refiguration *by* narrative. In this sense, it constitutes, to use the expression I deliberately introduced earlier, an entry into the problem of refiguration.

From this opening, as one says in playing chess, results the whole subsequent orientation of the problem of the refiguration of time by narrative. To determine the philosophical status of this refiguration requires an examination of the creative resources by which narrative activity responds to and corresponds to the aporetics of temporality. The second section of this volume will be devoted to such an exploration.

The five chapters of section 1 focus upon the main difficulty that the aporetics of temporality will reveal, namely, the irreducibility of one to the other, even the occultation of one by the other, of a purely phenomenological perspective on time and an opposed perspective that, to be brief, I will call the cosmological one. My aim will be to discover what resources a poetics of narrative possesses for, if not resolving, at least making this aporia work for us. We shall be guided by the dissymmetry that occurs between historical narrative and fictional narrative when we consider their referential implications, along with the truth-claim made by each of these two great narrative modes. Only historical narrative claims to refer to a "real" past, that is, one that actually happened. Fiction, on the contrary, is characterized by a kind of referring and a truth claim close to those I explored in my *Rule of Metaphor*.[5] This problem of relatedness to the real is unavoidable. History can no more forbid itself to inquire into its relationship to an actually occurring past than it can neglect considering, as was established in Part II of *Time and Narrative,* the relationship of explanation in history to history in narrative form. But if this problem is unavoidable, it may be reformulated in different terms than those of reference, which stem from a kind of investigation whose contours were established by Frege. The advantage of an approach that pairs history and fiction to confront the aporias of temporality is that it leads us to reformulate the classical problem of referring to a past that was "real" (as opposed to the "unreal" entities of fiction) in terms of refiguration, and not vice versa. This reformulation is not limited to a change in vocabulary, inasmuch as it marks the subordination of the epistemological dimension of reference to the hermeneutical dimension of refiguration. The question of the relation of history to the past no longer appears, then, on the same level of investigation as does the question of its relation to narrative, even when the epistemology of historical knowledge includes within its field the relation of explanation to eyewitness testimony, documents, and archives, and when it derives from this relation François Simiand's well-known definition of history as knowledge in terms of traces. The question of the meaning of this definition is posed by a second-order kind of reflection. History as a form of inquiry stops with the document as a given, even when it raises to the rank of document traces of the past that were not meant to serve as the basis for a historical narrative. The invention of documents, therefore, is still an epistemological question. What is no longer an epistemological question is the question about the meaning of the intention by which, in inventing documents (in the double sense of the word "invent"), history is conscious that it is related to events that "really" happened. The document becomes a trace for this consciousness, that is, as I shall make more explicit at the proper time, it is both a remains and a sign of what was but no longer is. It belongs to one form of hermeneutics to interpret the meaning of this ontological intention by which the historian, by taking a stand on documents, seeks to reach what was but no longer is. To put this question in more familiar terms, how are we to interpret history's claim, when it constructs a narrative, to reconstruct something from the past? What authorizes us to think of this construction as a reconstruction? It is by joining this question with that of the "unreality" of fictive entities that we hope to make progress simultaneously in the two problems of "reality" and "unreality" in narration. Let me immediately say that it is in terms of this framework that we shall examine the mediation brought about by reading between the world of the text and the world of the reader, announced at the end of Part I. It is along this path that we shall seek in particular for the true parallel to be given, on the side of fiction, to what we call historical "reality." At this stage of reflection, the language of reference, still preserved in *The Rule of Metaphor,* will have been definitively surpassed. The hermeneutic of the "real" and the "unreal" goes beyond the framework assigned by analytic philosophy to the question of reference.

The task of the following five chapters will be to reduce the gap between the respective ontological intentions of history and fiction in order to make sense of what, in volume 1, I was still calling the interweaving reference of history and fiction, an operation that I take to be a major stake, although not the only one, in the refiguration of time by narrative.[6] In my introduction to the second section of this volume I shall justify the strategy followed for bringing the largest gap between the respective ontological intentions of the two great narrative modes into fusion in the concrete work of the refiguration of time. Here I will confine myself to indicating that it will be by interweaving the chapters devoted respectively to history (chapters 4 and 6) and to fiction (chapters 5 and 7) that step-by-step I shall construct the solution to the stated problem of interweaving reference (chapter 8).

The final two chapters will be devoted to a broadening of the problem arising from a more intractable aporia than that of the discordance between the phenomenological and the cosmological perspectives on time, namely, the aporia of the oneness of time. Every phenomenology admits, along with Kant, that time is a collective singular, without perhaps really succeeding in giving a phenomenological interpretation of this axiom. So the question will be whether the problem, coming from Hegel, of a totalization of history does not respond, on the side of narrative, to the aporia of the oneness of time. At this stage of our investigation, the term "history" will cover not only recounted "history," whether in the mode of history or in that of fiction, but also history as made and undergone by human beings. With this question, the hermeneutics applied to the ontological intention of historical consciousness will take on its fullest scope. It will definitively surpass, while prolonging, our analysis of historical intentionality in Part II of this work.[7] That analysis still had to do with the aims of historical "research" as a procedure for acquiring knowledge. The question of the totalization of history has to do with historical consciousness, in the twofold sense of our consciousness of making history and our consciousness of belonging to history.

The refiguration of time by narrative will not have reached its end until this question of the totalization of history, in the broad sense of the term, will have been joined to that of the refiguration of time brought about conjointly by historiography and fiction.

Rereading the analyses carried out in the three volumes of *Time and Narrative* leads me to express one final reservation. Have we exhausted the aporetics of time by examining the conflict between the phenomenological and the cosmological perspectives on time, and with the complementary examination of phenomenological interpretations of the axiom of the oneness of time? Have we not on several occasions come close to another aporia of time, more deeply rooted than the preceding ones, without having made it the object of any direct treatment? And is not this aporia a sign pointing toward the internal and external limits of narrativity, which would not be recognized without a final confrontation between the aporetics of time and the poetics of narrative? I have added a conclusion in the form of a postscript dealing with this reservation.

Section I
The Aporetics of Temporality

I begin this last part by taking a position as regards the phenomenology of time, our third partner, along with historiography and fiction, in the three-way conversation concerning mimesis$_3$.[1] We cannot avoid this requirement since our study rests on the thesis that narrative composition, taken in its broadest sense, constitutes a riposte to the aporetic character of speculation on time. This was not sufficiently established by the single example of Book XI of Augustine's *Confessions*. What is more, our concern to reap the benefits of the central argument of the initial part of Augustine's valuable insight—that is, the discordant-concordant structure of time—did not permit us to take into account the aporias that are the price of this discovery.

To underscore the aporias of the Augustinian conception of time, before turning to those that arise in some of his successors, is not to deny the greatness of his discovery. On the contrary, it is meant to indicate, in terms of an initial example, the striking fact about the theory of time that any progress obtained by the phenomenology of temporality has to pay for its advance in each instance by the ever higher price of an even greater aporicity. Husserl's phenomenology, which is the only one with good reason to claim the title of being a "pure" phenomenology, will more than verify this disconcerting law. Heidegger's hermeneutic phenomenology, despite its radical break with the internal consciousness of time, will not escape this rule either, but instead will add its own difficulties to those of its two illustrious predecessors.

The Time of the Soul and the Time of the World
The Dispute between Augustine and Aristotle

The major failure of the Augustinian theory is that it is unsuccessful in substituting a psychological conception of time for a cosmological one, despite the undeniable progress this psychology represents in relation to any cosmology of time. The aporia lies precisely in the fact that while this psychology can legitimately be added to the cosmology, it is unable to replace cosmology, as well as in the further fact that neither concept, considered separately, proposes a satisfying solution to their unresolvable disagreement.[1]

Augustine did not refute Aristotle's basic theory of the primacy of movement over time, although he did contribute a lasting solution to the problem Aristotle left in abeyance concerning the relation between the soul and time. Behind Aristotle stands an entire cosmological tradition, according to which time surrounds us, envelops us, and dominates us, without the soul having the power to produce it. I am convinced that the dialectic of *intentio* and *distentio animi* is powerless to produce this imperious character of time and that, paradoxically, it helps conceal it.

Where Augustine fails is precisely where he attempts to derive from the distension of the mind alone the very principle of the extension and the measurement of time. We must, in this respect, pay homage to him for never having wavered in his conviction that measurement is a genuine property of time, as well as for refusing to lend any credence to what will later become Bergson's major doctrine in his *Essay on the Immediate Data of Consciousness,* namely, that time becomes measurable through its strange and incomprehensible contamination by space.[2] For Augustine, our division of time into days and years, as well as our ability to compare long and short syllables, familiar to the rhetoricians of antiquity, designate properties of time itself.[3] *Distentio animi* is the very possibility of so measuring time. Consequently, the refutation of the cosmological thesis is far from being a digression in Augustine's closely knit argument. Instead it constitutes one indispensable link in this argument. Yet this refutation is, from the start, misdirected. "I once heard a learned man say that time is nothing but the movement of the sun and the moon and the stars, but I did not agree."[4] By this overly simple identification of time with the circular movement of the two principal heavenly bodies, Augustine overlooks Aristotle's infinitely more subtle thesis that, without being movement itself, time is something that "has to do with movement" (*ti tès kinèséôs*).[5] In so doing, he is forced to see in the distension of the mind the principle for the extension of time. But the arguments by which he thinks he succeeds in doing so do not hold up. The hypothesis that all movement—that of the sun, just like that of the potter's wheel or the human voice—may vary, hence accelerate, slow down, even stop altogether, without the intervals of time being altered in any way, is unthinkable, not only for a Greek, for whom sidereal movements are absolutely invariable, but for us today, even though we know that the movement of the earth around the sun is not absolutely regular and even though we must continually extend our search for the absolute clock. Even the corrections that science continues to make in defining the notion of a "day"—as a fixed unit for computing months and years—attests that the search for an absolutely regular movement remains the guiding idea for any measurement of time. This is why it is simply not true that a day would remain what we call a "day" if it were not measured by the movement of the sun.

It is true that Augustine was unable to abstain entirely from referring to movement in order to measure the intervals of time. But he tried to strip this reference of any constitutive role and to reduce it to a purely pragmatic function. As in Genesis, the stars are only lights in the sky that mark times, days, and years (*Confessions,* XI, 23:29). Of course, we cannot say when a movement begins and when it ends if we have not marked (*notare*) the place where a moving body starts from and the place where it arrives. However, Augustine notes, the question concerning "how much time is needed" for a body to complete its movement between two points cannot find a reply in the consideration of the movement itself. So the recourse to the "marks" that time borrows from movement leads nowhere. The lesson Augustine draws from this is that time is something other than movement. "Time, therefore, is not the movement of a body" (24:31). Aristotle would have come to the same conclusion, but this would have constituted no more than the negative side of his main argument, namely, that time has something to do with movement, although it is not movement. But Augustine was unable to perceive the other side of his own argument, having limited himself to refuting the less refined thesis, the one where time is purely and simply identified with the movement of the sun, moon, and stars.

As a result he was forced to make the impossible wager that the principle of their measurement could be found in expectation and memory. Hence, according to him, we have to say expectation is shortened when what we are waiting for approaches and memory is extended when what we remember recedes. In the same way, when I recite a poem, as I move along through the present, the past increases by the same amount as the future diminishes. We must ask therefore what increases and what diminishes, and what fixed unit allows us to compare these variable durations.[6]

Unfortunately, the problem of comparing successive durations is only pushed back one step. It is not clear what direct access we can have to these impressions that are assumed to remain in the mind, nor how they could provide the fixed measure of comparison that he has refused to accord to the movement of the stars.

Augustine's failure to derive the principle for the measurement of time from the distension of the mind alone invites us to approach the problem of time from the other side, from that of nature, the universe, the world—expressions that we are temporarily taking as synonymous, knowing that we will subsequently have to distinguish them, as we shall also do for their antonyms, which for the moment we are terming indifferently soul, mind, consciousness. We shall later show how important it is for a theory of narrative that both approaches to the problem of time remain open, by way of the mind as well as by way of the world. The aporia of temporality, to which the narrative operation replies in a variety of ways, lies precisely in the difficulty in holding on to both ends of this chain, the time of the soul and that of the world. This is why we must go to the very end of the impasse and admit that a psychological theory and a cosmological theory mutually occlude each other to the very extent they imply each other.

In order to make apparent the time of the world, which the Augustinian analysis fails to recognize, let us listen to Aristotle, and also hear, behind him, the echoes of more ancient words, words whose meaning the Stagirite himself did not master.

The three-stage argument leading to the Aristotelian definition of time in Book IV of the *Physics* (219a34–35) needs to be followed through step by step.[7] This argument holds that time is related to movement without being identical with it. In this, the treatise on time remains anchored in the *Physics* in such a way that the originality belonging to time does not elevate it to the level of a "principle," an honor reserved for change alone, which includes local movement.[8] This concern not to tamper with the primacy of movement over time is evident in the very definition of nature at the beginning of Book II of the *Physics:* "nature is a principle [*arkhè*] or cause [*aitia*] of being moved and of being at rest in that to which it belongs primarily, in virtue of itself and not accidently" (192b21–23).

The fact that time, nevertheless, is not movement (218b21–219a10) was stated by Aristotle before Augustine.[9] Change (movement) is in every case in the thing that changes (moves), whereas time is everywhere in everything equally. Change can be rapid or slow, whereas time cannot include speed, under the threat of having to be defined in terms of itself since speed implies time.

In return, the argument holding that time is not without movement, which destroys Augustine's attempt to found the measurement of time in the distension of the mind alone, deserves our attention. "Now we perceive movement [more accurately: in (*hama*) perceiving movement] and time together . . . and not only that but also, when some time is thought to have passed, some movement also along with it seems to have taken place" (219a3–7). This argument does not place particular stress on the mind's activity of perception and discrimination, or, more generally, on the subjective conditions of time-consciousness. The term that is stressed is "movement." If there is no perception of time without the perception of movement, there is no possible existence of time itself without that of movement. The conclusion to this first phase of the overall argument confirms this. "It is evident, then, that time is neither movement nor independent of movement" (219a2).

This dependence of time with regard to change (movement) is a sort of primitive fact, and the task later will be to graft the distension of the soul in some way to this something that "belongs to movement." The central difficulty of the problem of time results from this. For we do not at first see how the distension of the soul will be able to be reconciled with a time that is defined essentially as something that "belongs to movement" (219a9–10).

The second phase in constructing the definition of time follows, namely, applying to time the relation of before and after, through the transfer of magnitude in general, passing by way of space and movement.[10] In order to lay the groundwork for this argument, Aristotle first posits the analogical relation that holds between the three continuous entities: magnitude, movement, and time. On the one hand, "the movement goes with [or better, obeys, *akoluthei*] the magnitude" (219a10), and on the other, the analogy extends from movement to time "for time and movement always correspond with each other" (219a17).[11] Now, what is continuity if not the possibility of dividing a magnitude an infinite number of times?[12] As for the relation between before and after, it consists in a relation of order resulting from a continuous division such as this. Thus the relation between before and after is in time only because it is in movement and it is in movement only because it is in magnitude. "Since then before and after hold in magnitude, they must also hold in movement, these corresponding to those. But also in time the distinction of before and after must hold, for time and movement always correspond with each other" (219a15–18). The second phase of the argument is completed. Time, we said above, has something to do with movement, but with what aspect of movement? With the before and after in movement. Whatever the difficulties in founding the before and after on a relation or order based on magnitude as such, and on the transfer by analogy from magnitude to movement and from movement to time, the point of the argument is not in doubt: succession, which is nothing other than the before and after in time, is not an absolutely primary relation. It proceeds by analogy from an ordering relation that is in the world before being in the soul.[13] Once again we here come up against something irreducible. Whatever the mind contributes to the grasping of before and after[14]—and we might add, whatever the mind constructs on this basis through its narrative activity—it finds succession in things before taking it up again in itself. The mind begins by submitting to succession and even suffering it, before constructing it.

The third phase of the Aristotelian definition of time is what is decisive for our purposes. It completes the relation between before and after by adding a numerical relation to it. And with the introduction of number the definition of time is complete: "For time is just this—number of motion in respect of 'before' and 'after'" (219b).[15] The argument, once again, rests on a feature of the perception of time, namely, the mind's ability to distinguish two end points and an interval. The soul, then, notes that there are two instants, and the intervals marked out by these instants can be counted. In a sense, the break formed by the instant, considered as an act of the intelligence, is decisive. "For what is bounded by the 'now' is thought to be time—we may asssume this" (219a-29). But the privilege accorded movement is not weakened in any way by this. If the soul is necessary in order to determine an instant—more exactly, to distinguish and count two instants—and to compare intervals on the basis of a fixed unit, this perception of differences is founded on the perception of the continuities of magnitude and movement, and on the relation of order between the before and after, which "follows" from the order of derivation between the three analogous continua. Hence Aristotle can specify that what is important for the definition of time is not counted but countable numbers, and this is said about movement before being said about time.[16] The result is that the Aristotelian definition of time—the "number of motion in respect of 'before' and 'after'" (219b2)—does not contain an explicit reference to the soul, despite drawing upon, at each phase of the definition, the operations of perception, discrimination, and comparison, which can only be those of the soul.

Below we shall discuss at what cost the phenomenology of "time-consciousness" that is implicit, if not in the Aristotelian definition of time, at least in the argumentation that leads up to it, can be brought to light, without thereby simply tipping the balance from Aristotle back to Augustine again. In truth, in one of the subsidiary treatises appended to his definition of time, Aristotle is the first to grant that the question of deciding whether "if the soul did not exist time would exist or not is a question that may fairly be asked" (223a21–22). Is not a soul, or better an intelligence, necessary in order to count, and first of all to perceive, discriminate, and compare?[17] To understand Aristotle's refusal to include any noetic determination in the definition of time, we must follow to the very end the requirements whereby the phenomenology of time, suggested by such noetic activity of the soul, is unable to displace the principal axis of an analysis that accords a certain originality to time, but only on the condition that it no longer question its general dependence with respect to movement.

What are these requirements? They are the prerequisites already apparent in the initial definition of change (and movement) that root it in *physis*—its source and its cause. It is *physis* that, by supporting the dynamism of movement, preserves the dimension of time over and above its human aspects.

In order to restore its fullness to *physis,* we must be attentive to what Aristotle retains from Plato, despite the advance his philosophy of time represents in relation to that of his teacher.[18] Moreover, we must lend an ear to the invincible word that, coming to us from far beyond Plato, before all our philosophy, and despite all our efforts to construct a phenomenology of time-consciousness, teaches that we do not produce time but that it surrounds us, envelops us, and overpowers us with its awesome strength. In this connection, how can we fail not to think of Anaximander's famous fragment on the power of time, where the alteration of generation and corruption is seen to be subject to the "arrangement of Time"?[19]

An echo of this word coming from antiquity can still be heard in Aristotle in some of the minor treatises that the redactor of the *Physics* joined to the major treatise on time. In two of these appended treatises, Aristotle asks what it means "to be in time" (220b32–222a9) and what things "are in time" (222b16–223a15). He strives to interpret these expressions of everyday language in a sense that is compatible with his own definition.

But we cannot say that he is completely successful in doing this. Certainly, he says, being in time means more than existing when time exists. It means "being in number." And being in number means being "contained" (*périékhétai*) by number, "as things in place are contained by place" (221a17). At first sight, this philosophical exegesis of everyday expressions does not go beyond the theoretical resources of the previous analysis. However the expression itself does go beyond the proposed exegesis. And what is at issue reappears, even more forcefully, a few lines further on in the following form: "being contained by time," which seems to give time an independent existence, superior to the things that are contained "in" it (221a28). As if carried along by the power of the words themselves, Aristotle admits that we can say that "a thing, then, will be affected by time" (221a30) and he accepts the saying that "time wastes things away, that all things grow old through time, and that people forget owing to the lapse of time" (221a31–32).[20]

Once again, he sets himself to solving the enigma. "For time is by its nature the cause rather of decay, since it is the number of change, and change removes what is" (221b1–2). But does he succeed? It is strange that he returns to the same enigma a few pages later, under another heading: "it is the nature of all change to alter things from their former condition [*ekstatikon*]. In time all things come into being and pass away; for which reason some called it the wisest of all things, but the Pythagorean Paron called it the most stupid, because in it we also forget; and his was the truer view" (222b16–20). In one sense, there is nothing mysterious in this. Indeed, it is necessary to do something for things to happen and develop. If nothing is done, things fall to pieces, and we then willingly attribute this destruction to time itself. All that is left of the enigma is a manner of speaking. "Still, time does not work even this change; but this sort of change too happens to occur in time" (222b25–26). But has this explanation removed time's sting? Only up to a point; for what does it mean to say that if an agent ceases to act, things fall apart? The philosopher may well deny that time as such is the cause of this decline, but immemorial wisdom seems to perceive a hidden collusion between change that destroys—forgetting, aging, death—and time that simply passes.

The resistance of this immemorial wisdom to philosophical clarity should make us attentive to two "inconceivable" elements that undermine the entire Aristotelian analysis of time. The first thing difficult to conceive is the unstable and ambiguous status of time itself, caught between movement, of which it is an aspect, and the soul that discerns it. Even more difficult to conceive is movement itself, as Aristotle himself confesses in Book III of the *Physics* (201b33). Does it not appear to be "something indefinite" (201b24) with respect to the available meanings of Being and Nonbeing? And is it not in fact undefinable, since it is neither power nor act? What do we understand when we characterize it as "the fulfillment of what is potentially, as such" (201a10–11)?[21]

These aporias that conclude our brief incursion into the Aristotelian philosophy of time are not intended to serve as an indirect apology on behalf of Augustinian "psychology." I maintain, on the contrary, that Augustine did not refute Aristotle and that his psychology cannot be substituted for, but can only be added to, a cosmology. Evoking the aporias proper to Aristotle is intended to show that he does not hold fast against Augustine owing to the strength of his arguments alone, but rather as a result of the force of the aporias undercutting his own arguments. For, over and above the anchoring of time in movement established by his arguments, the aporias these arguments run into indicate something about the anchoring of movement itself in *physis,* whose mode of being escapes the argumentative mastery that is so magnificently displayed in Book IV of the *Physics.*

Does this descent into the abyss, spurning the phenomenology of temporality, offer the advantage of substituting cosmology for psychology? Or must we say that cosmology is just as much in danger of blinding us to psychology as psychology is of blinding us to cosmology? This is the unsettling conclusion we are forced to draw despite our reluctance to take leave of the system-building approach.

If, indeed, the extension of physical time cannot be derived from the distension of the soul, the inverse derivation is just as impossible. What prevents it is quite simply the conceptually unbridgeable gap between the notion of the "instant" in Aristotle's sense and that of the "present" as it is understood by Augustine. To be thinkable, the Aristotelian "instant" only requires that the mind make a break in the continuity of movement, insofar as the latter is countable. This break can be made anywhere. Any instant at all is equally worthy of being the present. The Augustinian present, however, as we can say today following Benveniste, is any instant designated by a speaker as the "now" of his utterance. It does not matter which instant is chosen, the present is as singular and as determined as the utterance that contains it. This differential feature has two consequences for our own investigation. On the one hand, from an Aristotelian point of view, the breaks by means of which the mind is able to distinguish two "instants" are enough to determine a before and an after solely by reason of the orientation of movement from its cause to its effect. In this way, I can say that event A precedes event B and that event B follows event A, but I cannot for all this affirm that event A is past and event B future. On the other hand, from an Augustinian point of view, the future and the past exist only in relation to a present, that is, to an instant indicated by the utterance designating it. The past is before and the future after only with respect to this present possessing the relation of self-reference, attested to by the very act of uttering something. It follows from this Augustinian point of view that the before-and-after—that is, the relation of succession—is foreign to the notions of present, past, and future, and hence to the dialectic of intention and distension that is grafted to these notions.

This is the great aporia of the problem of time—at least before Kant. This aporia lies entirely within the duality of the instant and the present. Later we shall say in what way the narrative operation both confirms this aporia and brings it to the sort of resolution that we term "poetic." It would be useless to search in the solutions Aristotle contributes to the aporias of the instant for an indication of a reconciliation between the cosmological instant and the lived present. For Aristotle, these solutions remain within the sphere of a thought shaped by the definition of time as something having to do with movement. If they underscore the relative autonomy of time with respect to movement, they never lead to its independence.

The fact that the instant, the "now," constitutes a basic component of the Aristotelian theory of time is clearly stated in the passage cited above. "For what is bounded by the 'now' is thought to be time—we may assume this." For it is indeed the "now," the instant, that is the end of the before and the beginning of the after. And it is the interval between the two instants that is measurable and countable. In this respect, the notion of "instant" is perfectly assimilable to the definition of time as dependent on movement as regards its substratum. It expresses a potential break in the continuity that time shares with movement and with magnitude in virtue of the analogy between the three continua.

The autonomy of time, with respect to its essence, as this is confirmed by the aporias of the instant, never calls this basic dependence into question, and this is echoed in the minor appended treatises dealing with the instant.

How is it possible, we ask, that the instant is always in a sense the same and in a sense always other (219b12–22)? The solution draws upon the analogy between the three continua: time, movement, and magnitude. Thanks to this analogy, the fate of the instant "corresponds to" that of what "is carried along." This remains identical in its being, although it "is different in defini-tion." In this way, Coriscus is the same insofar as carried, but different when he is in the Lyceum and when he is in the marketplace. "And the body which is carried along is different, in so far as it is at one time here and another there. But the 'now' corresponds to the body that is carried along, as time corresponds to the motion" (219b22–23). The aporia thus contains a sophism only accidently. Nevertheless, the price to be paid is the absence of any reflec-tion on the features that distinguish the instant from a point.[22] However Aris-totle's meditation on movement, as an act of that which exists potentially, does lead to an apprehension of the "instant" that, without announcing the Augus-tinian present, does introduce a certain notion of the present related to the becoming that constitutes the actualization of potentiality. A certain "primacy of the present instant glimpsed in that of the moving body in act" does appear to make the difference between the dynamism of the "now" and the purely static character of the point, obliging us to speak of the present instant and, by implication, of the past and the future.[23] We shall see more of this below.

The second aporia concerning the instant raises an analogous problem. In what sense can we say that time "is both made continuous by the 'now' and divided at it"? (220a5)? The answer, according to Aristotle, requires nothing more than the simple relation of before and after—any break in a continuum distinguishes and unites. Thus the twofold function of the instant as break and as connection owes nothing to the experience of the present and derives wholly from the definition of the continuum by its endless divisibility. Never-theless, Aristotle was not unaware of the difficulty of maintaining here once again the correspondence between magnitude, movement, and time. Move-ment can stop, but time cannot. In this the instant "corresponds" to the point, but there is only a kind (*pos*) of correspondence (220a10). Indeed, it is only as potential that the instant divides. But what is a potential division that can never move into act? It is only when we consider time as a line, at rest by definition, that the possibility of dividing time becomes conceivable. There must therefore be something specific in the division of time by the instant; even more so, in its power to assure the continuity of time. In a perspective such as Aristotle's, where the main accent is placed on the dependence of time with respect to movement, the unifying power of the instant rests on a dy-namic unity of the body in motion that, although passing through a number of fixed points, remains one and the same moving body. But the dynamic instant that corresponds to the moving body's unity of movement calls for a specifically temporal analysis that goes beyond the simple analogy by virtue of which the instant in some way corresponds to a point. Is it not here that Augustine's analysis comes to the aid of Aristotle's? Must we not seek in the threefold present the principle of specifically temporal continuity and discontinuity?

In fact, the terms "present," "past," and "future" are not foreign to Aristotle's vocabulary, but he wants to see in them just a determination of the instant and of the relation of before and after.[24] The present, for him, is only an instant that is situated. This is the sort of present instant that the expressions used in ordinary language, as discussed in chapter 13 of Book IV of the *Physics,* refer to.[25] These expressions can be easily reduced to the logical structure of the argument that claims to resolve the aporias of the instant. The difference between the undifferentiated instant and the instant as situated or present is, for Aristotle, of no more relevance, in this respect, than the reference of time to the soul. Just as only an enumerated time really requires a soul to distinguish and actually to count the instants, so, too, only a determined instant can be designated as a present one. The same reasoning, which recognizes only what is countable in movement, which can exist without the soul, also recognizes only the undifferentiated instant, that is, precisely insofar as its "before and after" is countable (219b26–28).

Nothing, therefore, in Aristotle requires a dialectic between the instant and the present, unless it is the difficulty, which he admits, of maintaining to the end the correspondence between the instant and the point, in its twofold function of division and unification. It is on this very difficulty that an Augustinian style of analysis of the threefold present could be grafted.[26] Indeed, for such an analysis only a present heavy with the recent past and the near future can unify the past and the future, which at the same time it distinguishes. For Aristotle, however, to distinguish the present from the instant and the past-future relation from the relation of before and after would be to threaten the dependence of time on movement, the single, ultimate principle of physics.

It is in this sense that we were able to say that there is no conceivable transition between an Augustinian conception and an Aristotelian one. We must make a jump if we are to pass from a conception in which the present instant is simply a variant, in ordinary language, of the "now," which belongs wholly to the *Physics,* to a conception in which the present of attention refers first and foremost to the past of memory and the future of expectation. Not only must we make a jump to pass from one perspective on time to the other, it seems as though each is doomed to occlude the other.[27] And yet the difficulties peculiar to each perspective demand that these two perspectives be reconciled. In this respect, the conclusion to be drawn from our confrontation between Augustine and Aristotle is clear: the problem of time cannot be attacked from a single side only, whether of the soul or of movement. The distension of the soul alone cannot produce the extension of time; the dynamism of movement alone cannot generate the dialectic of the threefold present.

Our ambition will be to show below how the poetics of narrative contributes to joining what speculation separates. Our narrative poetics needs the complicity as well as the contrast between internal time-consciousness and objective succession, making all the more urgent the search for narrative mediations between the discordant concordance of phenomenological time and the simple succession of physical time.

2

Intuitive Time or Invisible Time?
Husserl Confronts Kant

The confrontation between the time of the soul in Augustine and the time of physics in Aristotle has not exhausted the whole aporetics of time. All the difficulties inherent in the Augustinian conception of time have not yet been brought to light. Our interpretation of Book XI of the *Confessions* has continually moved back and forth between bursts of insight and shadows of uncertainty. At times, Augustine exclaims, Here I know! Here I believe! At other times he asks, Did I actually just think I saw something? Do I really understand what I think I know? Is there some fundamental reason why time-consciousness cannot go beyond this oscillation between certainty and doubt?

If I have chosen to question Husserl at this stage of our inquiry into the aporetics of time, it is because of the principal ambition that appears to me to characterize his phenomenology of internal time-consciousness, namely, making time itself appear by means of an appropriate method and, in this way, freeing phenomenology of every aporia. This ambition of making time as such appear, however, runs up against the essentially Kantian thesis of the invisibility of time that, in the preceding chapter, appeared under the name of physical time and that returns in the *Critique of Pure Reason* under the name of objective time, that is, the time implied in the determination of objects. For Kant, objective time—the new figure of physical time in a transcendental philosophy—never appears as such but always remains a presupposition.

THE APPEARANCE OF TIME: HUSSERL'S LECTURES ON INTERNAL TIME-CONSCIOUSNESS

The Introduction to Husserl's *Phenomenology of Internal Time-Consciousness*, along with subsections 1 and 2, clearly states his ambition of submitting the appearance of time as such to a direct description.[1] Time-consciousness must thus be understood in the sense of "internal" (*inneres*) consciousness. And in this single adjective are conjoined the discovery and the aporia of the entire phenomenology of time-consciousness. The function of excluding (*Aus-*

schaltung) objective time is to produce this internal consciousness, which will be directly a time-consciousness (the German language clearly expresses, by means of the compound noun, *Zeitbewusstsein,* the absence of any gap between consciousness and time). But what is actually excluded from the field of appearing under the name of objective time? Precisely world time, which Kant showed is a presupposition of any determination of an object. If the exclusion of objective time is pushed by Husserl to the very heart of psychology as the science of psychic objects,[2] this is in order to lay bare time and duration (this term being taken in the sense of interval, or lapse of time), appearing as such.[3] Far from limiting himself to collecting first impressions, ordinary experience, Husserl is critical of the testimony they present. He may well call datum "the immanent time of the flow of consciousness" (p. 23), but this datum by no means constitutes anything immediate; or rather, the immediate is not given immediately. Instead, what is immediate must be conquered at great cost, at the cost of suspending "all transcendent presuppositions concerning existents" (p. 22).

Is Husserl capable of paying this price? We can answer this question only when we come to the end of Section 3 of the *Phenomenology of Internal Time-Consciousness,* which calls for an ultimate radicalization of the method of exclusion. It may be observed, nevertheless, that the phenomenologist cannot avoid admitting, at least at the start of his undertaking, a certain homonymy between the "flow of consciousness" and the "Objective flow of time"; or, again, between the "one after the other" of immanent time and the succession of objective time; or, yet again, between the continuum of the one and that of the other, as well as between their respective multiplicities. In what follows, we shall continually encounter comparable homonymies, as though the analysis of immanent time could not be constituted without repeated borrowings from the objective time that has been excluded.

The necessity for these borrowings can be understood if we consider that Husserl's aim is nothing less than to work out a "hyletics" of consciousness.[4] If this hyletics is not to be condemned to silence, among phenomenological data must be counted "the apprehension [*Auffassungen*] of time, the lived experiences in which the temporal in the Objective sense appears" (p. 24). These apprehensions are what allows discourse about the hyletic, the supreme wager of the phenomenology of internal time-consciousness. Concerning these apprehensions, Husserl holds that they express features of order in sensed time and that they serve as a basis for the constitution of objective time itself.[5] We may wonder, however, whether, in order to bring the hyletic out of silence, these apprehensions do not have to borrow from the determinations of objective time that are known before its exclusion.[6] Would we use the expression "sensed *at the same time*" if we knew nothing of objective simultaneity, of temporal distance, if we knew nothing of the objective equality between intervals of time?[7]

This question becomes particularly pressing when we consider the laws that, according to Husserl, govern the sensed temporal series. He in no way doubts that "a priori truths" (p. 29) belong to these apprehensions, which are themselves inherent in sensed time. And from these a priori truths derives the a priori of time, namely, "(1) that the fixed temporal order is that of an infinite, two-dimensional series; (2) that two different times can never be conjoint; (3) that their relation is a non-simultaneous one; (4) that there is transitivity, that to every time belongs an earlier and a later, etc. So much for the general introduction" (ibid.). Husserl's wager, therefore, is that the temporal a priori is capable of being clarified "by investigating *time-consciousness,* by bringing its essential constitution to light and, possibly, by setting forth the content of apprehension and act-characters pertaining specifically to time, to which content and characters the a priori laws of time are essentially due" (ibid., his emphasis).

The fact that the perception of duration never ceases to presuppose the duration of perception did not seem to trouble Husserl any more than did the general condition for all phenomenology, including that of perception; namely, that, without some prior familiarity with the objective world, the reduction of this world would itself lose its very basis. What is in question here is the general sense of this bracketing. It does not suppress anything at all; it is confined to the redirecting of our gaze, without losing sight of what is bracketed. The conversion to immanence, in this sense, consists in a change of sign, as is stated in *Ideas,* I, §32. This change of sign does not exclude our using the same words—unity of sound, apprehension, etc.—when our gaze moves from the sound that continues to its "how." [8] Nevertheless, the difficulty is compounded in the case of internal time-consciousness inasmuch as phenomenology performs its reduction on a perception that has already been reduced from the perceived to the sensed, in order to dig ever deeper into the innermost layers of a hyletics from which the yoke of the noetic has been removed. And yet we see no other way to develop a hyletic investigation except by way of such a reduction within the reduction. The reverse side of this strategy, however, is the proliferation of homonymies, ambiguities in terminology, maintained by the persistence of the problematic of the perceived object under the erasure of intentionality *ad extra.* Whence the paradox of an enterprise based upon the very experience it subverts.

This equivocal character seems to be the result not of an out-and-out failure of the phenomenology of internal time-consciousness but of the aporias that are the ever greater price to pay for an increasingly more refined phenomenological analysis.

Keeping these perplexities in mind, we now turn to the two great discoveries of the Husserlian phenomenology of time, the description of the phenomenon of retention and its symmetrical counterpart, protention, and the distinction between retention (or primary remembrance) and recollection (or secondary remembrance).

In order to begin his analysis of retention, Husserl provides himself with the support of the perception of an object that is as insignificant as possible, a sound—hence, something that can be designated by an identical name and that can be held to be actually the same: a *sound, a* sound.[9] This is something, therefore, that Husserl would like to consider not as a perceived object, placed before me, but as a sensed object. By reason of its temporal nature, the sound is no more than its own occurrence, its own succession, its own continuation, its own cessation.[10] In this respect, the Augustinian example of reciting a verse of the hymn *Deus creator omnium,* with its eight syllables alternating between long and short, would present, if we understand Husserl correctly, an object too complex to be held within the immanent sphere. The same thing can be said, with regard to Husserl himself, about the example of a melody, which he wastes no time in setting outside the scope of the analysis. To this minimal object—a sound that continues—Husserl gives the strange name *Zeitobjekt,* which Gérard Granel correctly translates as "tempo-object" in order to stress its unusual character.[11] So the situation is as follows. On the one hand, objective time is assumed to have undergone reduction and time itself is to appear as lived experience; on the other hand, if the discourse on the hyletic is not to be reduced to silence, the support of something perceived is necessary. The third section will say, whether, in order to go to the very end of this process of exclusion, the residual objective side of the tempo-object has to be bracketed. Until then, it is the tempo-object as a reduced object that provides its telos to the investigation. And it is this tempo-object that indicates what has to be constituted in the sphere of pure immanence, namely, duration, in the sense of the continuation of the same throughout the succession of other phases. We may deplore the ambiguity of this strange entity, yet we owe it an analysis of time that is straightway an analysis of duration in the sense of continuation, of "continuance considered as such" (*Verharren als solches*) (p. 43) and not simply of succession.

Husserl's discovery here is that the "now" is not contracted into a point-like instant but includes a transverse or longitudinal intentionality (in order to contrast it with the transcendent intentionality that, in perception, places the accent on the unity of the object), by reason of which it is at once itself and the retention of the tonal phase that has "just" (*soeben*) passed, as well as the protention of the imminent phase. It is this discovery that allows him to do away with any kind of synthetic function (even imagination, according to Brentano) added to a manifold. The "one after the other," which, as we shall see below, is formulated in Kant, is of course essential for the appearing of tempo-objects. By continuance, however, we are to understand the unity of duration (*Dauereinheit*) of the sound, assumed to be reduced to the status of a pure hyletic datum (beginning of §8). "It begins and stops, and the whole unity of its duration, the unity of the whole process in which it begins and ends, 'proceeds' to the end in the ever more distant past" (p. 44). There can be no doubt—the problem is that of duration as such. And retention, merely mentioned here, is the name of the solution that is sought.

Hereafter, the art of phenomenological description resides in shifting attention from the sound that endures to the mode of its continuance. Once again, the attempt would be in vain if the pure hyletic datum were amorphous and ineffable. In fact, I can call the consciousness of the sound at its beginning "now," can speak of "a continuity of phases as 'before' [*vorhin*]," and can speak of the whole duration "as an 'expired duration'" (*als abgelaufene Dauer*) (ibid.). If the hyletic is not to remain mute, we must take as a base, as does Augustine whenever he is combating the skeptics, the comprehension and communication of ordinary language, hence the received sense of words such as "begin," "continue," "end," and "remain," as well as the semantics of the verb tenses and the innumerable adverbs and conjunctions of time ("still," "as long as," "now," "before," "after," "during," and so forth). Unfortunately, Husserl does not stop to consider the irreducibly metaphorical character of the most important terms upon which his description is based: "flow" (*Fluss*), "phase," "expire" (*ablaufen*), "proceed" (*rücken*), "sink back" (*zurücksinken*), "interval" (*Strecke*), and in particular the pair "living-dead" applied as oppositional terms to the "productive point of the now" (p. 45) and to the expired duration, once it has sunk back into emptiness. The very term "retention" is metaphorical in that it signifies holding fast: "In this sinking back, I still 'hold' [*halte*] it fast, have it in a 'retention,' and as long as the retention persists the sound has its own temporality. It is the same and its duration is the same" (p. 44). Despite Husserl's silence on this point, we can perfectly well admit, as concerns the rich vocabulary applied to the very mode of duration, that ordinary language offers unsuspected resources for hyletic analysis, for the simple reason that people have never been limited to speaking only about objects but have always paid some attention, even if marginal and confused, to the modification of the appearing of objects while they are changing. Words are not always lacking. And when literal terms are missing, metaphor serves as a relay station, bringing with it the resources of semantic innovation. In this way, language offers apt metaphors for designating continuance in expiring duration. The very word "retention" is an unexcelled example of the relevance of ordinary language in its metaphorical usage.

This mixture of boldness and timidity in the process of excluding calls for an appropriate discussion, which we shall pursue in our detour by way of Kant. The homonymies and the ambiguities it tolerates—and perhaps even requires—are the price to be paid for the inestimable discovery of retention. Indeed, this discovery proceeds from a reflection on the sense to be given to the word "still" in the expression "the sound still resonates." "Still" implies both same and other. "The sound itself is the same, but 'in the way that' it appears, the sound is continually different" (p. 45). The reversal in perspective from the sound to the "mode of its appearing" (*der Ton 'in der Weise wie'*) (ibid.) brings the aspect of otherness into the foreground and transforms it into an enigma.

The first feature that this otherness presents, which is discussed at length in §9, concerns the twofold phenomenon of the diminishing clarity of the perception of expired phases and the fading or increasing piling up of the retained contents. "As the temporal Object moves into the past, it is drawn together on itself and thereby also becomes obscure" (p. 47). But what Husserl wants at all cost to preserve is the continuity in the phenomenon of passing away, of being drawn together, and of becoming obscure. The otherness characteristic of the change that affects the object in its mode of passing away is not a difference that excludes identity. It is an absolutely specific kind of alteration. Husserl's improbable wager is to have sought in the "now" a particular type of intentionality that is not directed toward a transcendent correlate but toward the now that has "just" expired. The entire advantage of this "now" is that it retains the now in such a way as to engender out of the now-point of the phase presently passing away what Granel calls "the big now" (*Le sens du temps,* p. 55) of the sound in its whole duration.

It is this longitudinal and nonobjectifying intentionality that ensures the very continuity of the duration and preserves the same in the other. Even if it is true that I could not become aware of this longitudinal intentionality, generating continuity, without the guideline of some unitary object, it is indeed this intentionality, and not the objectifying intentionality surreptitiously introduced in hyletic constitution, that ensures the continuation of the now-point in the extended present of the unitary duration. If this were not the case, retention would not constitute a specific phenomenon worthy of analysis. Retention is precisely what holds together the now-point (*Jetztpunkt*) and the series of retentions that are connected to it. In relation to the now-point, "the Object in its mode of appearing" is always other. The function of retention is to establish the identity of the now-point and the immanent non-point-like object. And retention poses a challenge to the very logic of the same and the other; this challenge is time. "Every temporal being 'appears' in one or another continually changing mode of running-off, and the 'object in the mode of running-off' is in this change always something other, even though we still say that the Object and every point of its time and this time itself are one and the same" (*Phenomenology of Internal Time-Consciousness,* p. 47). The paradox is not only in language—"even though we still say. . . ." The paradox is broader in the double sense that it is henceforth necessary to ascribe it to intentionality itself, depending on whether it designates the relation of consciousness to "what appears in its modal setting" or whether it designates the relation to what appears as such, the transcendent perceptual object (pp. 47–48).

This longitudinal intentionality marks the swallowing up of the serial aspect of the succession of nows, which Husserl calls "phases" (or "points"), in the continuity of the duration. We do know one thing about this longitudinal intentionality. "With regard to the running-off phenomenon, we know that it is a continuity of constant transformations which form an inseparable unity, not severable into parts which could be by themselves nor divisible into phases, points of the continuity, which could be by themselves" (p. 48). What gets emphasized is the continuity of the whole or the totality of the continuous, which the term duration (*Dauer*) itself designates. That something persists in change—this is what enduring means. The identity that results from this is therefore no longer a logical identity but precisely that of a temporal totality.[12]

The diagram included in §10 is intended only to help us visualize by means of a linear representation the synthesis of the otherness characteristic of simple succession and the identity of the continuance resulting from retention.[13] What is important in this diagram is not that the advance in time is illustrated by a line (OE) but that to this line—the only one Kant considers— must be added the diagonal line OE', which represents the movement "downward into the depths of the past," and especially the vertical line EE', which, in each point of the duration, joins the series of present instants to the downward movement. This vertical line represents the fusion of the present with its horizon of the past in the continuity of the phases. No line in itself represents retention; only the whole formed by these three lines presents a visual representation of retention. Husserl can thus state at the end of §10, "The figure thus provides a complete picture of the double continuity of modes of running-off" (p. 50).

The major drawback of this diagram is that it claims to give a linear representation of a nonlinear constitution. What is more, there is no way to draw the line of the advance of time while, simultaneously, presenting the successive nature of time and the position of every point of time on the line. To be sure, the diagram does enrich the linear representation by adding to it the slanted line of sinking down and the vertical line of the depth of each instant. In this way, the diagram as a whole, by completing the schema of succession, undercuts the privilege and the monopoly of succession in the figuration of phenomenological time. It remains true, however, that, by depicting a series of limit-points, the diagram fails to provide a figure of the retentional implication of source-points. In short, it fails to picture the identity of what is far away and what lies deep, through which the instants that have become other are included in a unique way in the thickness of the present instant. In truth, there is no adequate diagram of retention or of the mediation it performs between the instant and the duration.[14]

In addition, the vocabulary Husserl uses to describe retention is no less inadequate than the diagram, which we should perhaps quickly put out of our minds. Husserl, in fact, attempts to characterize retention in relation to the originary impression by use of the term "modification." The choice of this term is meant to indicate that the privileged status of the originary character of each new now extends to the series of instants that it retains in its depth despite their moving away. It follows that the line of difference is no longer to be drawn between the now-point and all that has already run off and expired, but between the recent present and the past properly speaking. This will have its full impact when the distinction between retention and recollection is made, which is the necessary counterpart to the continuity between initial impression and retentional modification. But even now it can be asserted that the present and the recent past mutually belong to each other, and that retention is an enlarged present that ensures not only the continuity of time but the progressively attenuated diffusion of the intuitive character of the source-point to all that the present instant retains in itself or under itself. The present is called a source-point (*Quellpunkt*) precisely because what runs off from it "still" belongs to it. Beginning is beginning to continue. The present itself is thus "a continuity, and one constantly expanding, a continuity of pasts" (p. 49). Each point of the duration is the source-point of a continuity of modes of running-off and the accumulation of all these enduring points forms the continuity of the whole process.[15]

The whole meaning of Husserl's polemic against Brentano lies here. There is no need to add an extrinsic connection—even that of imagination—to the series of "nows" to produce a duration. Every point contributes to this by expanding into a duration.[16]

This expansion of a point-source into a duration is what ensures the expansion of the originary character belonging to the impression characteristic of the point-source to the horizon of the past. The effect of retention is not just to connect the recent past to the present, but to pass on its intuitive aspect to this past. "Modification" thus receives a second meaning. Not only is the present modified into the recent present, the originary impression itself passes into the retention. "The tonal now is changed into one that has been. Constantly flowing, the *impressional* consciousness passes over into an ever fresh *retentional* consciousness" (p. 51). But the primal impression passes over into retention only in the form of gradually "shading off."[17] To this series should also be referred, I think, the expression "retention of retentions," as well as that of "a continuous series of retentions pertaining to the beginning point" (ibid.). Each new now, by pushing the preceding present into the recent past, makes it a retention that has its own retentions. This second-order intentionality expresses the unceasing recasting of earlier retentions by more recent ones, which makes up temporal fading away: "each retention is in itself a continuous modification which, so to speak, bears in itself the heritage (*Erbe*) of the past in the form of a series of shadings" (ibid.).[18]

If Husserl's aim in forging the notion of modification is indeed to extend the benefit of the original character belonging to the present impression to the recent past, the most important implication is that the notions of difference, otherness, and negativity expressed by the "no longer" are not primary, but instead derive from the act of abstraction performed on temporal continuity by the gaze that stops at the instant and converts it from a source-point into a limit-point. A grammatical feature of the verb "to be" confirms this view. It is in fact possible to conjugate the verb "to be" in the past tense (and in the future tense) without introducing negation. "Is," "was," "will be" are entirely positive expressions that mark in language the priority of the idea of modification over that of negation, at least in the constitution of primary remembrance.[19] The same thing is true of the adverb "still." Its use expresses in its own way the adhering of the "just past" to consciousness of the present. The notions of retention and intentional modification mean the same thing. Primary remembrance is a positive modification of the impression, not something different from it. In contrast to the representation of the past by images, primary remembrance shares with the living present the privilege of the originary, although in a continually weakening mode. "The intuition of the past itself cannot be a symbolization [*Verbildlichung*]; it is an originary consciousness" (p. 53).[20]

This does not exclude the fact that if in our thinking we stop the retentional flow, and if we isolate the present, the past and the present appear to exclude each other. It is then legitimate to say that the past is no longer and that "past" and "now" exclude each other. "Something past and something now can indeed be identically the same but only because it has endured between the past and now" (p. 57). This passage from "was" to "is no longer," and the way in which one overlaps the other, expresses the twofold meaning of the present, on the one hand as source-point, as initiating a retentional continuity, and on the other hand as a limit-point, abstracted from the infinite division of the temporal continuum. The theory of retention contributes to showing that the "no longer" proceeds from the "was" and not the contrary, and that modification precedes difference. The instant, considered apart from its power to begin a retentional series, is merely the result of abstracting from the continuity of this process.[21]

The distinction between primary remembrance and secondary remembrance, also called recollection (*Wiedererinnerung*), is the second properly phenomenological advance of the *Phenomenology of Internal Time-Consciousness*. This distinction is the counterpart required by the essential characterization of retention, namely, the adhering of the retained past to the now-point within a present that continues even while fading away. All that we understand by memory is not contained in this basic experience of retention. To speak in Augustinian terms, the present of the past means something other than the "just passed" past. What about that past that can no longer be described as the comet's tail of the present—that is, all our memories that no longer have a foothold, so to speak, in the present?

To resolve the problem, Husserl once again gives a paradigmatic example that, without having the bare-bones simplicity of the single continuing sound, presents, at first sight anyway, an extreme simplicity. We remember a melody that we have heard recently (*jüngst*) at a concert. This example is simple in the sense that, since the event recalled is recent, our memory aims to do no more than to reproduce a tempo-object. By this, Husserl no doubt thinks, all the complications connected to reconstructing the past, as would be the case for the historical past or even for far distant memories, are avoided. The example, however, is not entirely simple, since this time it concerns not a single sound but a melody that we can go over in our imagination by following the order of the first sound, then the second, and so on. No doubt, Husserl thought that his analysis of retention, applied to a single sound, could be transposed without major changes to the case of a melody, even though the composition of the latter was not taken into consideration in the discussion but only its manner of connecting up with the now-point. In this way, he allows himself the possibility of starting directly from the case of melody in this new stage of his description in order to focus attention on another feature of such a simple example, the fact that such a melody is no longer "produced" but "reproduced," no longer presented (in the sense of the extended present) but "re-presented" (*Repräsentation* or *Vergegenwärtigung*).[22] The presumed simplicity of the imagined example therefore concerns the "re-" (*wieder*) implied in the expression "re-collection" and in other related expressions that we shall come to below, in particular that of "re-petition" (*Wiederholung*), which will occupy an important place in the Heideggerian analysis, and concerning which I shall later show its importance for a theory of narrated time. This "re-" is thus described as a phenomenon of term-by-term "correspondence" in which, by hypothesis, difference lies not in the content—it is the same melody produced and then reproduced—but in the mode of accomplishment. The difference then falls between the melody perceived and the melody quasi-perceived, between hearing and quasi-hearing. This difference signifies that corresponding to the now-point is a quasi-present which, outside of its status "as if," presents the same features of retention and protention, hence the same identity between the now-point and its retentional train. The choice of a simplified example—the same melody re-collected—has no other purpose than to permit this transfer into the order of "as if" of this continuity between impressional consciousness and retentional consciousness, and all of the analyses relating to it.[23] The result is that any moment in the series of present instants can be re-presented in imagination as a source-point in the mode of "as if." This quasi-source-present will therefore possess a temporal halo (*Zeithof*) (p. 58) that will make it in each case the center of perspective for its own retentions and protentions. (Below, I shall show that this phenomenon is the basis of historical consciousness, for which every past that is retained can be set up as a quasi-present endowed with its own retrospections and anticipations, some of which belong to the [retained] past of the actual present.)

The first implication of the analysis of secondary remembrance is to reinforce, by contrast, the continuity, within a broadened perception, between retention and impression, at the expense of the difference between the now-point and the recent past. This struggle between the threat of rupture contained in the distinction, opposition, difference, and continuity between retention and impression is found in the earliest version of this subsection, dating from 1905.[24] The meaning of this struggle is clear. If the difference were not included in the continuity, there would be no temporal constitution, properly speaking. The continuous passage from perception to nonperception (in the strict sense of these terms) is temporal constitution, and this continuous passage is the work of the apprehensions, which we said above belonged to the same stratum as the hyletic data. The oneness of the continuum is so essential to grasping tempo-objects that it can be said that the true "now" of a melody comes only when the final note has sounded. It is then the ideal limit of the "continuum of gradations" constituting the tempo-object taken as a whole. In this sense, the differences that Husserl calls the differences of time (*die Unterschiede der Zeit,* p. 62) are themselves constituted in and through the continuity unfolded by tempo-objects in a lapse of time. There is no better way to stress the primacy of continuity with respect to difference, without which there would be no sense in speaking of either tempo-object or lapse of time.

It is precisely this continuous passage from the present to the past that is missing in the global opposition between presentation and representation. The "as if" is in no way assimilated to the continuous passage constituting presentation through the modification of the present into the recent past.[25]

Thus the before and the after must be constituted in primary remembrance, that is, in broadened perception. The "quasi" character of re-presentation can only reproduce its sense but cannot produce it in an original manner. The union of impression and retention alone, prior to any "quasi," holds the key for what Husserl, challenging Aristotle and Kant, calls "the temporally creative acts of the now and the past" (*der zeitschaffende Jetztakt und Vergangenheitsakt*) (p. 64). Here we are indeed at the heart of the constitution of internal time-consciousness.

This primacy of retention finds further confirmation in the unbridgeable aspect of the break that separates re-presentation from presentation. Only the latter is an original self-giving act. "Not to be self-giving is precisely the essence of phantasy" (p. 68). The "once again" has nothing in common with the "still." What might mask this phenomenological difference is that major feature of retentional modification that, in fact, transforms the original or reproduced "now" into a past. But the continuous fading-away characteristic of retention must not be confused with the passage from perception to imagination that constitutes a discontinuous difference. Nor is the decreasing clarity of representation to be confused with the progressive fading-away of primary remembrance. These are two different types of lack of clarity and they must not be mistaken for each other (§21). It is the deep-rooted prejudice of the point-like present that continually gives rise to the illusion that the extension of the present is the work of the imagination. The gradual fading away of the present in retention is never the equivalent of a phantasy. The phenomenological gap is unbridgeable.

Is this to say that recollection is called upon only to reinforce the primacy of retention in the constitution of time? It is not inconsequential that I can represent to myself an earlier lived experience. Our freedom of representation is not a negligible component in the constitution of time; representation alone, according to Kant, can be compared to *Selbstaffektion*. Recollection, with its free mobility and its power of recapitulation, provides the stepping back of free reflection. Reproduction then becomes "a free running-through" (*Durchlaufen*) that can give the representation of the past a variable tempo, articulation, and clarity.[26] This is why the phenomenon that seems on the whole to Husserl to be the most remarkable is that in which a "coincidence" (*Deckung*) occurs between the past that is simply retained in the aura of the present and reproduction that goes back over the past. "Then the pastness [*Vergangenheit*] of the duration is given to me *simpliciter* as just is the 're-givenness' [*Wiedergegebenheit*] of the duration" (p. 66). (Below we shall discuss what a reflection on the historical past can receive from this *Wiedergegebenheit* stemming from the "coincidence" between a past that is retained passively and a past that is represented spontaneously.) The identification of one and the same temporal object seems to depend in large part on this "re-turn" (*Zurückkommen*) in which the *nach* of *Nachleben*, the *wieder* of *Wiedergegebenheit*, and the *züruck* of *Zurückkommen* coincide in the "re-" of re-collection. But the "I can" (of "I can recollect") cannot by itself ensure continuity with the past, which in the final analysis rests on the retentional modification that lies in the order of affection rather than in that of action. In any case, the free reiteration of the past in recollection is of such great importance for the constitution of the past that the phenomenological method itself rests on this power of repeating—in the double sense of making something come back and of reiterating—the most foundational experience of retention. This repeating follows the "lines of similarity" that make possible the gradual coincidence between the same succession as it is retained, then recollected. This "coincidence" itself precedes any reflective comparison, the resemblance between the retained and the recollected depending, for its part, on an intuition of resemblance and of difference.

If "coincidence" plays such an important role in the analysis of recollection, this is because it is intended to compensate for the break between retention, which still belongs to the present, and representation, which no longer belongs to it. The question that haunts Husserl therefore is this: if the way in which recollection presentifies the past differs fundamentally from the presence of the past in retention, how can a representation be faithful to its object?

This faithfulness must be that of an adequate correspondence between a present now and a past one.[27]

A new problematic is opened up by the distinction between imagination and recollection. This distinction had to be bracketed in the earlier analyses, which were centered on the difference between the retained past and the represented past. We even, unconcernedly, took as synonymous "represented" and "imagined," as mentioned above. However, this question arises "How does the reproduced now come to represent something past?"[28] but in another sense of the word "represent" that corresponds to what today we would call a truth claim. What is important is no longer the difference between recollection and retention but the relation to the past that passes through this difference. Recollection must now be distinguished from imagination by the positional value (*Setzung*) attached to recollection but absent from imagination. In truth, the notion of the coincidence between the reproduced past and the retained past foreshadows that of the positing of the reproduced now. However the identity of the same content, despite the difference between "once again" and "still," involved more than the intention directed at the current now that makes remembrance represent this content, in the sense that it posits it as having been. It is not enough to say that the flow of representations is constituted in just the same way as the flow of retentions, with the same play of modifications, retentions, and protentions. We must arrive at the idea of a "second intentionality" (p. 75) that makes it a representation *of;* second, in the sense that it is the equivalent of a replica (*Gegenbild*) of the transverse intentionality constituting retentions and generating the tempo-object. In its form of a flow of lived experience, recollection does present the same features of retentional intentionality as does primary resemblance. In addition, it intentionally aims at this primary intentionality. This intentional reduplication of the intentionality characteristic of retention ensures the integration of recollection into the constitution of internal time-consciousness, which might have been lost from sight as a result of our concern with distinguishing recollection from retention. Recollection is not only a present "as if"; it intends the present and, in this way, posits it as having been. (Like the operation of coinciding, the operation of positing is essential to the understanding of the historical past, something we shall return to again below.)

To complete the insertion of recollection into the unity of the current of lived experience, we must also consider that memory contains intentions of expectation, the fulfillment of which leads to the present. In other words, the present is both what we are living and what realizes the expectations of a remembered past. In turn, this realization is inscribed in memory; I remember having expected what is now realized. This realization is henceforth part of the meaning of the remembered expectation. (This feature is of great value to an analysis of the historical past. In this sense, the present is the actualization of the future of what is remembered. The realization, or lack of realization, of an expectation related to a remembered event acts upon the memory itself and retroactively gives a particular coloring to the reproduction.) We shall return to and develop this theme at the appropriate moment. For now, let us simply say this: the possibility of turning to a memory and of sighting in it the expectations that were or were not realized later, contributes to inserting the memory within the unitary flow of lived experience.

We can now speak of a "temporal series" in which each event receives a different place. The sort of weaving together that we have described between retention and recollection indeed allows us to join them together in a single temporal course. Intending the place of a remembered event in terms of this single series constitutes a supplementary intentionality that is added to the internal order of recollection, held to reproduce that of retention. This intending of a "place" in the temporal series is what allows us to characterize, as past, present, or future, durations presenting different contents but occupying the same place in the temporal series—and hence of giving a formal sense to the characteristic: past, present, or future. But this formal sense is not an immediate datum of consciousness. We do not deal with events as specifically past, future, and present except in relation to the second intentionality of recollection, in intending an event's place independently of its content and duration. This second intention is inseparable from the retroaction by which a recollection receives a new meaning from the fact that its expectations have found their actualization in the present. The abyss separating recollection and retentional consciousness is thus bridged through the intertwining of their intentions, without thereby doing away with the difference between re-production and retention. There has to be a split in the intentionality of recollection that separates the place from the content. This is why Husserl calls the intending of place a nonintuitive, "empty" intention. The phenomenology of internal time-consciousness strives here, through a complex interplay of superimposed intentionalities, to account for the pure form of succession. This form is no longer a presupposition of experience, as for Kant, but the correlate of the intentions directed toward the temporal series apart from the remembered contents. This series is thus intended as the obscure "surroundings" of what is currently remembered, comparable to the spatial background of perceived things. Henceforth, every temporal thing seems to stand out against the background of the temporal form in which it is inserted by the interplay of intentionalities we have described.

We may be surprised that Husserl favored memory to such an extent at the expense of expectation. Several reasons seem to have contributed to this apparent imbalance. The first one has to do with Husserl's major preoccupation, which is to resolve the problem of the continuity of time without resorting to a synthetic operation like that of Kant or Brentano. The distinction between retention and recollection suffices to resolve the problem. Besides, the distinction between future and past supposes that a formal meaning has been given to the characteristic of being future or past. The double intentionality of recollection solves this problem, if we are prepared to introduce, through anticipation, expectation into memory itself as the future of what is remembered. Husserl, consequently, does not believe that he can treat expectation thematically (§26) until he has established the double intentionality of recollection (§25). It is in the temporal surroundings of the present that the future takes its place and that expectation can be integrated as an empty intention. More fundamentally, it does not seem that Husserl conceived of the possibility of dealing directly with expectation. It cannot be the counterpart of memory, which "reproduces" a present experience, both intentional and retentional. In this sense, expectation is "productive" in its own way. In the face of this "production" Husserl seems helpless, no doubt owing to the primacy of the phenomenology of perception, which the exclusion of objective time suspends without abolishing. Only Heidegger's philosophy, anchored directly in care and not in perception, will be able to do away with the inhibitions that paralyze the Husserlian analysis of expectation. Husserl conceives of expectation as little more than an anticipation of perception. "It pertains to the essence of the expected that it is an about-to-be-perceived" (p. 80). And when the expected perception occurs, hence becomes present, the present of the expectation has become the past of this present. From this angle, the question of expectation leads back to that of primary memory, which remains the major guideline of the *Phenomenology of Internal Time-Consciousness*.[29]

The insertion (*Einordnung*) of reproduction in the series of internal time thus adds a decisive rectification to the opposition between the "quasi" character of reproduction and the originary character of the unity constituted by perception and retention. The more we stress the thetic nature of memory in order to oppose it to figurative consciousness (§28), the more we insert it into the same temporal current as retention. "In contrast to this figurative consciousness, reproductions have the character of self-presentation (*Selbstvergegenwärtigung*) in the sense of what is past" (p. 82). Even if we do not lose sight of the formal nature of this insertion, the characteristic of "past," henceforth common to reproduction and retention, is inseparable from the constitution of internal time, as the unitary series of all lived experience. The thetic character of the reproduction of the past is the most effective agent of this aligning of secondary remembrance and primary remembrance under the aegeis of the past.

This is perhaps why reproduction is itself also called a modification, in the same way as retention. In this sense, the opposition between "quasi" and "originary" is far from being the last word concerning the relation between secondary and primary remembrance. It was first necessary to oppose them in order better to tie together retentional consciousness and impressional consciousness, against Kant and Brentano. It was then necessary to bring them back together in order better to ensure their common insertion in the single temporal flow, however formal this unitary series might be. Nor should we forget that this formal character itself derives from the second intentionality of recollection which preserves the concrete character of "environmental intention" (*Umgebungsintention*) (p. 84) belonging to this formal series.

The final question raised here concerns whether, as a counterpart to the bracketing of objective time, the *Phenomenology of Internal Time-Consciousness* has contributed anything to the constitution of objective time.

The success of this constitution would be the only verification of the well-foundedness of the initial procedure of reduction. We find in the *Phenomenology*—at least in the final subsections (§§30–33) of Section Two—no more than the beginning steps of this demonstration. Below, when we examine the third section of this work, we shall say why Husserl did not continue on in this direction.

Inserting retention and re-production (when the latter adds a thetic character to the pure "as if") in the series of internal time is the basis upon which time, in the objective sense of the word, is constructed as a serial order indifferent to the contents that fill it. The notion of a temporal position (*Zeitstelle*) is the key concept in this passing from the subjective to the objective or, to put it a better way, from the "material" of lived experience to its temporal "form." This "temporal position" is what permits us to apply the characteristic of present, past, or future to materially different "lived experiences." But if Husserl performs the reduction of time in one fell swoop, he nevertheless proceeds prudently in objectifying the formal aspects of temporality. He begins by opposing the formal objectivity of temporal positions to the material objectivity of the contents of experience. The two phenomena are actually the inverse of each other and their contrast constitutes a good introduction to the problem that is posed. On one side, the same objective intention—aiming at an identical object—is preserved despite the modification that causes the impression, shoved aside by the newness of a new present, to lose its now-character and to fade away into the past. On the other side, the same temporal position is attributed to the contents of lived experience, despite their material differences. It is in this sense that the extra-temporal identity of the contents, in one case, and the identity of the temporal position of materially different contents, in the other, work to opposite effect. On the one hand, the same *Bestand* but a temporal "sinking away"; on the other hand, the same temporal position but a different *Bestand*. Husserl even speaks in this regard of an apparent antinomy (at the beginning of §31). It is in fact a question here of a contrasted individuation, by the identity of the object and by the identity of temporal position.

It is by disentangling the identity of the temporal position from the identity of the object that we reach the problematic of objective time. This consists, in effect, in the devolution of "a fixed position in time" (p. 88). This operation poses a problem to the extent that it stands in contrast to the descent by which the present tone sinks back into the past. By this detour of the question of the identity of temporal position, we encounter an eminently Kantian problem. "Time is motionless and yet it flows. In the flow of time, in the continuous sinking away into the past, there is constituted a non-flowing, absolutely fixed, identical Objective time. This is the problem" (p. 89). Retentional modification, it seems, allows us to understand the sinking back into the past but not the fixedness of the position in time. It does not seem that the identity of sense, in the flow of temporal phases, can supply the answer we are seeking, since it has been shown that the identity of content and the identity of place themselves form a contrast, and since we have admitted that the second is the key to the first. It seems that Husserl holds as an essential law that the sinking back of one and the same sound into the past implies a reference to a fixed temporal position. "It is part of the essence of the modifying flux that this temporal position stands forth as identical and necessarily identical" (p. 90). Of course, unlike what has to do with an a priori of intuition in Kant, the form of time is not superimposed on pure diversity, since the interplay of retentions and representations constitutes a highly structured temporal fabric. It remains nonetheless that this very interplay requires a formal moment that it does not seem capable of generating. In the final pages of Section Two, Husserl strives to bridge this gap.

He tries to demonstrate that the temporal position of an impression, one first present then become past, is not extrinsic to the very movement of fading back into the past. It is by modifying its distance with respect to the present that an event takes its place in time. Husserl himself is not entirely satisfied by his attempt to connect the temporal position to the sinking back as such, that is, to the increasing distance from the source-point. "With the preservation of the individuality of the temporal points in their sinking back into the past, we still do not have, however, consciousness of unitary, homogeneous Objective time" (p. 94). The preceding explanation is based upon retention alone, which involves only a limited temporal field. Instead it is recollection that must be appealed to and, more precisely, the power to transpose every instant, shoved back in the retention process, into a zero point, into a quasi-present, and to do this repeatedly. What is reproduced in this way is the positing of the zero point as the source-point for new cases of this sinking back, by a second-order distancing. "Theoretically, this process is to be thought of as capable of being continued without limit, although in practice actual memory soon breaks down" (p. 95). This statement is of the highest interest for the shift from the time of remembrance to historical time, which goes beyond the memory of each individual. A transition is assured by recollection, thanks to the transposition of any given point in the past into a quasi-present; and this is an endless process. The question remains, it seems to me, however, whether this imaginary extension of the temporal field, through the mediation of an end-less series of quasi-instants, can take the place of a genesis of "the one Objective time with the one fixed order" (ibid.).

The same requirement increases in strength, that is, the requirement for a linear order in which "every temporal interval, no matter which—even the external continuity with the actual temporal field reproduced—must be a part of a unique chain, continuing to the point of the actual now" (p. 96). Whenever we attempt to derive objective time from internal time-consciousness, the relation of priority is inverted. "Even every arbitrarily phantasied time is subject to the requirement that if one is able to think of it as real time (i.e., as the time of any temporal Object) it must subsist as an interval within the one and unique Objective time" (ibid.). Husserl takes refuge here behind "some a priori temporal laws" (the title of §33) that make the datum of temporal position something immediately evident; for example, the fact that two impressions have "identically the same temporal position" (ibid.). It is part of the a priori essence of this state of affairs that these two impressions are simultaneous and involve one and the same now.

It seems that Husserl hoped to obtain from the notion of temporal position, closely related to the phenomena of retention and recollection, the assurance of the constitution of objective time that would not presuppose in every case the result of the constituting operation.[30]

The true sense of the Husserlian enterprise appears only in Section Three. Here it is a matter of attaining, by going through the different degrees of constitution, the third level, that of absolute flux. The first level included the things experienced in objective time; this is what was bracketed at the start of the work and what he attempted to constitute at the end of Section Two. The second level was that of the immanent unities, the order of tempo-objects; and the subsequent analysis took place on this level. In relation to the third level, the unities that stand out here are still constituted unities. The third level is that of the "absolute, temporally constitutive flux of consciousness" (p. 98).[31]

Saying that all tempo-objects should be considered as constituted unities is the consequence of the numerous presuppositions that the earlier analysis had temporarily to accept as given: that tempo-objects endure, that is, preserve a specific unity throughout the continuous process of temporal modification; that changes in objects are more or less rapid with reference to the same duration. In contrast, if the absolute flux of consciousness has some sense, we must give up the attempt to base our construction on any sort of identity whatsoever, even that of tempo-objects, and so must stop speaking as well of relative speed. Here we no longer have "something" that endures. We begin to see the audacity of this undertaking: taking as a basis only the modifications as such through which the "continuity of shading" (p. 99) constitutes a flux. We can also see the great difficulty in this. "For all this, names are lacking" (p. 100). Either we name the constituting—the flux—after what is constituted (the present phase, the continuity of pasts in retention, etc.), or we rely on metaphors: flux, source-point, springing up, sinking back, and so on. It was already difficult enough to go beneath the transcendent object and to remain on the level of appearing, that of the immanent object or the tempo-object. The task is now to go beneath the immanent object and to place ourselves on the level where consciousness is flux, where all "consciousness of . . ." is a "moment of the flux." The question is whether we are not simply reduced to a mere shift in vocabulary, in which the same analyses, carried out once in terms of appearing, would be done a second time in terms of consciousnesss: perceptual consciousness, retentional consciousness, reproductive consciousness, etc. Otherwise, how would we know that immanent time is one, that it implies simultaneity, durations of unequal length, and a determinability according to before and after (p. 101)?

Three problems are posed: the form of the unity that connects the various fluxes into a single flux; the common form of the now (the origin of simultaneity); and the continuity of the modes of running-off (the origin of succession).

Concerning the unity of the flux, all we can say is that "immanent time is constituted as one for all immanent Objects and processes. Correlatively, the consciousness of time of immanent things is single [*eine Alleinheit*]" (p. 102). But what distinct access do we have to this "all-together" (*Zusammen*), this "all-at-once" (*Zugleich*), this "all-embracing," by which the running-off of any object and of any process constitutes "a homogeneous, identical form of running-off for the entire all-together" (p. 103)? The question is the same concerning the form of the now, identical for a group of primal sensations, and concerning the identical form of running-off that transforms, without difference or distinction, any now-consciousness into a consciousness of a before. Husserl limits himself to saying, "But what does this mean? Here, one can say nothing further than: 'See'" (p. 103). It seems that the formal conditions of experience that Kant held to be presuppositions are considered simply as intuitions. The originality of the third level thus lies in bracketing the tempo-objects and formalizing the relations among point-source, retention, and protention, without regard for the identities, even the immanent ones, constituted here; in short, in formalizing the relation between the originary "now" and its modifications. Can this occur without appealing to some constituted objectivity?

Husserl was not unaware of this problem: "how [is it] possible to have knowledge [*wissen*] of a unity of the ultimate constitutive flux of consciousness?" (pp. 105–6). The answer is to be sought in a split in intentionality at the very heart of the phenomenon of retention. An initial intentionality is turned toward the tempo-object, which, although immanent, is already a constituted unity; the second is turned toward the modes of originarity, retention, and recollection. We are therefore dealing with two analogous and contemporaneous processes. ("It is the one unique flux of consciousness in which the immanent temporal unity of the sound and also the unity of the flux of consciousness itself are constituted" [p. 106].) Husserl is not insensitive to the paradoxical character of this statement. "As startling (if not at first sight even contradictory) as it may appear to assert that the flux of consciousness constitutes its own unity, it is still true, nevertheless" (ibid.). It is still within an eidetics that we can perceive the difference between a gaze directed toward what is constituted throughout the phases of running-off, and a gaze that has shifted to the flux. All of the earlier analyses of retention, of the retention of retentions, etc., can then be reexamined in terms of this flux rather than in terms of some tempo-object. In this, the intentionality of the self-construction of the flux itself is distinguished from the intentionality that, through the co-inciding of phases, constitutes the sound as a tempo-object. This double intentionality had, in fact, been foreseen as early as Section Two, when the identity of the temporal position was distinguished from the identity of the content and, more fundamentally, when the mode of running-off of the duration was distinguished from the unity of the tempo-object that is constituted there.

At the same time, we may wonder what real progress is made by passing to this third stage, if the two intentionalities are inseparable. Passing from the one to the other lies in a shift in our regard rather than in a clear bracketing as when we pass from the first stage to the second one. In this shift in regard, the two intentionalities continually refer back and forth to each other. "Consequently, like two aspects of one and the same thing, there are in the unique flux of consciousness *two* inseparable, homogeneous *intentionalities* which require one another and are interwoven with one another" (p. 109; his emphases); in other words, in order to have something that endures, there must be a flux that constitutes itself. To do this, the flux must appear in person. Husserl well perceived the aporia that is dawning on the horizon here, that of an infinite regress. Does not the flux's appearing in person require a second flux in which it appears? No, he says, reflection does not require this sort of doubling up, "qua phenomenon it [the flux] constitutes itself" (p. 109; translation modified). The enterprise of a pure phenomenology is completed with this self-constitution. Husserl claims the same self-evidence in its regard as his phenomenology grants to internal perception. There is even a "self-evident consciousness of duration" (p. 112), just as indubitable as that of immanent contents. The question remains, however, whether the self-evident consciousness of duration can be sufficient to itself without relying in any way on that of a perceptual consciousness.

Two points in Husserl's argument concerning the self-evidence of the duration deserve to be emphasized. The first concerns the self-evidence of the major feature of the flux—its continuity. In one and the same breath Husserl asserts the self-evidence of the unity of the flux and that of its continuity. The unity of the flux is an unbroken unity; the difference between two lapses of time is precisely a distinction, not a separation (*ver-schieden,* not *ge-schieden*) (ibid.). "Discontinuity presupposes continuity, be it in the form of changeless duration or of continuous alteration" (p. 113). This assertion deserves to be noted because of the way it echoes in the contemporary discussion about the discontinuity of paradigms or epistemes. For Husserl, there can be no doubt, discontinuity can be thought only against the background of continuity, which is time itself. But the question recurs, how do we know it, outside of the mixture of transcendent intentionality (toward the object) and longitudinal intentionality (toward the flux)? It is not by chance that he is forced to draw support once again from the continuity of the unfolding of a tempo-object, such as a sound. The argument must thus be understood in the following way. Discontinuity cannot be distinguished at one point in experience unless the continuity of time is attested to by some other experience that has no break. Difference can only be, so to speak, local, situated where the coincidence between originary consciousness and intentional consciousness is lacking. At the very most we can say that continuity and discontinuity are interwoven in the consciousness of the unity of the flux, as if the split arose out of continuity and vice versa.[32] However, for Husserl, continuity encompasses the differences. "In every case, however, not merely in that of continuous acceleration, the consciousness of otherness, of difference, presupposes a unity" (p. 114).

The second point that must now draw our attention concerns the self-evidence of another major feature of the flux: the primacy of the present impression in relation to reproduction in the order of the originary.[33] In a sense we already know this. The entire theory of reproduction rests on the difference between the "as if" and the originarily present. Taking up the same problem once again on a more fundamental level is not without significance. At the price of a certain contradiction with the earlier analysis, which stressed the spontaneity and the freedom of reproduction, what is underscored now is its receptive and passive character. This comparison on the receptive level, adding to the term-by-term correspondence between re-production and production, opens the way for an assertion carrying a much weightier implication, that re-presentation is in its own way an impression and a present impression. "In a certain sense, then, all lived experiences are known through impressions or are impressed" (p. 116).[34] It is the conversion of the entire analysis from the second level to the fundamental level of consciousness that allows us to say that the return of a memory to the surface is a present return and, in this sense, an impression. The difference between re-production and production is not abolished, but it loses its aspect of being a "break." Re-presentation "presupposes primary consciousness in which we are impressionally aware of it" (p. 117).

The thesis of the continuity of the flux is at the same time reinforced by the omnipresence of impressional consciousness. The unity of the transcendent thing (level one) is built upon that of thing-appearances and immanent apprehensions (level two); this, in turn, is founded upon the unity of impressional consciousness (level three). "An impression . . . is to be grasped as a primary consciousness which has no further consciousnesss behind it in which we are aware of it" (ibid.). The hierarchy of object (level one), thing-appearance (level two), and impression (level three) refers to what is ultimate: the absolute flux. The "immanent unities are constituted in the flux of multiplicities of temporal shading" (p. 119).

Time itself has finally to be considered on three levels: objective time (level one), the objectified time of tempo-objects (level two), and immanent time (level three). "The primal succession of moments of appearance, by virtue of the time-founding retentions, and the like, constitues appearance (altered or unaltered) as phenomenological-temporal unity" (p. 122).

The question is whether "the analogy between the constitution of immanent and transcendent unities" reasserted in concluding (p. 121) does not condemn the entire enterprise to circularity. The phenomenology of internal time-consciousness ultimately concerns immanent intentionality interwoven with objectifying intentionality. And the former, in fact, rests on the recognition of something that endures, which the latter alone can provide for it. This is, as we shall see, the very presupposition that Kant articulates in the series of his three "Analogies of Experience" under the titles of permanence, ordered succession, and reciprocal action.

THE INVISIBILITY OF TIME: KANT

I do not expect that a return to Kant will provide a refutation of Husserl, any more than I demanded from Aristotle that he take the place of Augustine. To begin with, I want to find in Kant the reason for the repeated borrowings made by the phenomenology of internal time-consciousness with respect to the structure of objective time, which this phenomenology claims not only to bracket but actually to constitute. In this regard, what the Kantian method refutes are not Husserl's phenomenological analyses themselves but their claim to be free of any reference to an objective time and to attain, through direct reflection, a temporality purified of any transcendent intention. In return, I intend to show that Kant himself is unable to construct the presuppositions concerning a time which itself never appears as such, without borrowing from an implicit phenomenology of time, which is never expressed as such because it is hidden by his transcendental mode of reflection. This twofold demonstration repeats on a different level what we observed above using the resources of Augustinian psychology and Aristotelian physics. In conclusion, we shall say what a modern dialectic, which sets into action the relation between subjectivity and objectivity, adds to the ancient dialectic, which sets into opposition to each other a time of the soul and a time of motion.

What most obviously opposes Kant to Husserl is the assertion of the indirect nature of all assertions about time. Time does not appear. It is a condition of appearing. This style of reasoning, diametrically opposed to the Husserlian ambition to make time per se appear, is complete only in the "Analytic of Judgment," and particularly in the "Analogies of Experience." Nevertheless, the outlines of this argument can be found in the "Transcendental Aesthetic."

We would be mistaken to believe that, by assigning the status of a priori intuitions to space and time, Kant also conferred upon his assertion of this status an intuitive character. In this respect, ascribing time to inner sense must not lead us astray; throughout the first edition of the *Critique of Pure Reason,* and to an even greater extent in the second edition, inner sense always falls short of the ability to constitute itself as a source of self-knowledge.[35] If some phenomenological implication can be made out here, it is to be found in the reference, which itself is never thematized, to the *Gemüt.*[36] The very first definition of intuition as an immanent relation to objects as given is linked up with the notion that the mind (*Gemüt*) "is affected in a certain way" (A19, B33). The definition that follows—"The capacity (receptivity) for receiving representations [*Vorstellungen*], through the mode in which we are affected by objects, is called *sensibility [Sinnlichkeit]*"—is not without phenomenological overtones. In the same way, both external sense and inner sense rest on an *Eigenschaft unseres Gemüts* (A22, B37). However, the phenomenological core of the initial definitions in the "Aesthetic" is quickly introduced in the distinction—an ancient one, to be sure—between matter, which becomes the "manifold," and form, of which it is merely said that it "must lie ready for the sensations a priori in the mind [*Gemüt*]" (A20, B34). The method of double abstraction by which sensibility is first isolated from thought by means of the concept and, a second time, on the level of sensibility itself, when the form is separated from the manifold, makes no appeal to self-evidence but instead receives its indirect justification from the *Critique* as a whole.

In the "Transcendental Aesthetic" this justification takes the form of an argument that is essentially a refutation. In this way, the question that opens the "Aesthetic," an eminently ontological one—"What, then, are space and time?" (A23, B37)—allows for just four possibilities: substances, accidents, real relations, or relations involving the subjective constitution of our *Gemüt.* The fourth solution follows from the elimination of the first three, on the basis of arguments taken from the ancients or from Leibniz.[37] This refutational style explains the form of reductio ad absurdum that the argument takes in favor of the fourth solution, that of Kant. "If we depart from the subjective condition under which alone we can have outer intuition, namely, liability to be affected by objects, the representation of space stands for nothing whatsoever" (A26, B42). And further on, concerning time: "If we abstract from our mode of inwardly intuiting ourselves—the mode of intuition in terms of which we likewise take up into our faculty of representation all outer intuitions—. . . then time is nothing" (A34).

The nonintuitive character of the properties of time considered as an a priori intuition is particularly underscored by the priority given in the "Aesthetic" to the study of space in relation to time. We can see why. Space affords a "transcendental exposition" that has no equal on the side of time, by reason of the weight of geometry, for which space constitutes a setting for possible constructions. It is because geometry is a science of relations that space can be neither a substance nor an accident, but rather a relation of externality. What is more, it is because geometry rests on properties that are not demonstrable analytically that propositions about space (and by analogy about time) must consist of synthetic and not analytic judgments. The constructive character of geometry and its axiomatic nature go hand in hand and tend to constitute a single argument. On the other hand, the intuitive nature of space is inseparable from arguments concerning proof by construction in geometry.[38]

This is the core of the transcendental exposition of the concept of space, which is indisputably nonintuitive. "I understand by a transcendental *exposition* [*Erörterung*] the explanation of a concept as a principle from which the possibility of other a priori synthetic knowledge can be understood" (A25, B40). The transcendental exposition of time is constructed exactly on the model of that of space, as this is summed up in this simple sentence from the second edition: "Thus our concept of time explains the possibility of that body of a priori synthetic knowledge which is exhibited in the general doctrine of motion, and which is by no means unfruitful" (B49).

The metaphysical exposition that precedes the transcendental exposition rests on the rigorous parallel between the properties of space and time, and the argument offers, in both cases, a strictly refutational style. The first two arguments establish the nonempirical status of time and space. The first argument, which G. Martin has called "Platonizing," establishes the nonempirical character of both time and space. We would not perceive two events as simultaneous or successive if the representation of time did not serve as the ground for the apprehension of these temporal predicates of perceptual experience. A new argument, more "Aristotelian" this time, owing to the fact that it establishes an order of preference, posits that time could be emptied of all its events, just as space can be emptied of all its contents, without for all that eliminating time itself. Its preeminence with respect to events is justified by this thought-experiment. According to the third argument, space and time cannot be discursive concepts, that is, generic concepts. Just as we can represent to ourselves only a single space of which diverse spaces are no more than parts (not different kinds assembled under one concept), in the same way different times can only be successive. This axiom, positing the unidimensionality of time, is not produced by experience but instead is presupposed by it. The intuitive and nondiscursive character of time results from this. If indeed different times are only parts of the same time, time does not behave as a genus in relation to different species—it is a collective singular. In the fourth argument time, like space, is a given, infinite magnitude. Its infinity implies nothing other than the necessity of considering every determined time, every lapse of time, as a limitation of the one, unique time.

Regardless of what we may say about the phenomenology implicit in this reasoning—and we shall return to this point in a moment—the main accent is placed on the presuppositional character of any assertion about time. This character is inseparable from the relational and purely formal status of time and space. More specifically, "time is the formal a priori condition of all appearances whatsoever." It is immediate with respect to all internal phenomena and mediate for all external phenomena. This is why the discourse of the "Aesthetic" is that of presupposition and not that of lived experience. The regressive argument always wins out over direct vision. This regressive argument, in turn, assumes the privileged form of an argument from absurdity. Time "is nothing but the form of our inner intuition. If we take away from our inner intuition the peculiar condition of our sensibility, the concept of time likewise vanishes; it does not inhere in the objects, but merely in the subject which intuits them" (A37).[39]

That an inchoative phenomenology is both implied and repressed by the transcendental reasoning is attested to by a few remarks in the 1770 *Dissertation,* remarks that are not mere replicas of the analysis of space.[40] It is not an accident, in this regard, if in the *Dissertation* the discussion of time (§14) precedes that of space.

Even if the mode of argumentation by presupposition already prevails here, as will also be the case in the "Transcendental Aesthetic," it retains a phenomenological cast, which our passage by way of Husserl makes all the more evident.[41] Thus the presupposition of a temporal order defined by the perception of all things as either simultaneous or successive is accompanied by the following comment. Succession does not "engender" (*gignit*) the notion of time but rather "appeals to it" (*sed ad illam provocat*). We understand what is meant by the word "after" (*post*) through the prior (*praevio*) concept of time. This idea of an "appeal" addressed by experience to a prior concept deserves more thorough examination. It implies, according to J. N. Findlay, a "vague vision of the indefinitely temporal order" (p. 88). As for the second thesis of the *Dissertation,* concerning the singularity of time (which will become the fourth and fifth arguments of the "Aesthetic"), it too possesses a certain phenomenological cast. Do we not understand without any further argument that it is one thing for sensuous contents to be "posited in time" (*in tempore posita*), and another thing again to be contained under a general notion "in the manner of a common mark" (*tanquam nota communi*)? We are thus inclined to say that this "common mark," which is prior to all sensation, is itself intuitively apprehended insofar as this form of coordination is integrated into all sensuous contents and has to be filled with sensorial contents without being dependent on them.[42] And this experience of a horizon, which seems to support the argument for the pure nature of the intuition of time, is, in fact, phenomenologically speaking, neither a conceptual generality nor a determined sensuous content.[43]

Taking this latent, or inchoative, phenomenology in the *Dissertation* for our guide, let us return to the arguments concerning time presented in the "Transcendental Aesthetic." Above we stressed only the symmetry between the transcendental properties of time and space. What is there to say about the dissymmetry between them? Can it be reduced to the difference between the sciences that are made possible by each of these forms? That is to say, finally, between sciences with a one-dimensional content and sciences with a three-dimensional content? Is there not implicit in the idea of succession the recognition of a specific feature, namely, the necessity that any progress of thought proceed phase by phase, fragment by fragment, without ever having the object in its entirety before its gaze at the same time? In order to compensate for the fragmentary character of all experience in time, is it not necessary to introduce the experience of a temporal "horizon," underlying both the "Platonic" argument which holds that the idea of time precedes all temporal experience and the "Aristotelian" one which rests on the reflective experience of a time emptied of all its event-contents? Even the idea that time is singular—that there is only one time of which all times are merely parts, not species—is this not guided by the experience of such a horizon?[44] A certain preunderstanding of its inclusive character, added to the fragmentary character of our temporal experience, seems in this way to accompany the axiomatic status of the "Transcendental Aesthetic." Its function, according to the words of the *Dissertation,* is to "call for" the concept of time, without having the power to generate it.

The paradox of the *Critique,* in sum, is that its particular argumentative mode has to hide the phenomenology implicit in the thought-experiment that governs the demonstration of the ideality of space and time.

This is confirmed in the "Analytic," where the main reason for the nonphenomenality of time per se is presented. For it is in the "Analytic" that the necessity of the detour by way of the constitution of the object for any new determination of the notion of time is demonstrated.

There is no point in expecting that the theory of the schematism will confer on time the appearing that was refused to it by the "Transcendental Aesthetic." It is certainly true that the new determinations of time are related to the use of the schematism. For example, we speak of "the *time series,* the *time content,* the *time order,* and lastly, the *scope of time* in respect of all possible objects" (A145, B184). However, this "transcendental determination of time" acquires meaning only when it is supported by the initial a priori synthetic judgments, or "principles" (*Grundsätze*), that make the schemata explicit. These principles have no other function than to posit the conditions for the objectivity of the object. It follows from this that time cannot be perceived in itself, but that we have only an indirect representation of it through simultaneously intellectual and imaginative operations applied to objects in space. Time, once again does not appear but remains a condition for objective appearing, and this is the theme of the "Analytic." In this respect, giving a figure to time by means of a line, far from constituting a basis extrinsic to the representation of time, is an integral part of its indirect way of manifesting itself in the application of a concept to the object by means of the imagination.

In addition to this, the representation of time, on the level of schemata and principles, is always accompanied by a determination of time, that is, by a particular lapse of time, a determination that adds nothing to the presupposition of an infinite time of which all times are the successive parts. It is in the determination of particular successions that this indirect character of the representation of time becomes clearer.

This twofold nature of the representation of time—at once indirect and determined—is the principal reason for the nonphenomenality of time on the level of the "Analytic." Hence Kant's warning concerning the schematism is extended to all the determinations of time corresponding to the schematism. These determinations share with the latter the fact of being "a universal procedure [*Verfahren*] of imagination in providing an image for a concept" (A140, B179). But, for this very reason, they must, like the schema, stem from "an art concealed in the depths of the human soul, whose real modes of activity nature is hardly likely ever to allow us to discover and to have open to our gaze" (A141, B180–81). Does not this solemn declaration contain a clear warning against any attempt to "lift out" new phenomenological features that these transcendental determinations of time may possesss, which are part of the mediating function called, depending on the point of view, subsumption, application, or restriction? The paradox is that it is this very tie between time and the schema that moves us one step farther from an intuitive phenomenology of time. It is only in the operation of schematizing the categories that the corresponding temporal property is discovered. And the schematization of the categories, in turn, takes shape only through the "principles"—axioms of intuition, anticipations of perception, analogies of experience, principles of modality—for which the schemata serve in each instance as abbreviated names.

It is under this very restrictive condition that we can legitimately attempt to elicit some information concerning time as such. But let us first note that if this information enriches our notion of time as succession, it does so without ever involving the relation of a lived present to the past and the future through memory or expectation, or, as in Husserl's attempt, through retention and protention.

The "Analogies of Experience" that discursively employ the schemata of substance, cause, and coexistence are the richest in observations concerning the transcendental determination of time as order. Even if, once again, these observations require a detour by way of a determined representation in a time which is itself determined, "the general principle," we read in the first edition, is that all "appearances are, as regards their existence, subject a priori to rules determining their relations to one another in one time" (A127). "In one time," hence in a determined lapse of time. We must, therefore, connect these two expressions: the representation of a necessary connection in our perceptions, and their relation in one time. It is this detour by way of representation in a determined time that gives a meaning to the statement, one of the utmost importance for our principal argument, that "time cannot be perceived in itself" (A183, B226), but that we perceive only objects "in" time (ibid.). This major reservation must not be lost sight of as we examine each of the analogies of experience.

The most important of the remarks on time concerns the principle of permanence (the first analogy). It is the first time, in fact, that Kant observes that the "three modes of time are *duration, succession,* and *coexistence*" (A177, B219), to which correspond the three rules of all the relations of time in phenomena. Up to now we have spoken only of succession and coexistence (or simultaneity). Is permanence a "mode" similar to the other two? This does not seem to be the case.

What does it mean "to persist," not only for the existence of a phenomenon but for time itself? This feature is said, precisely, to designate time "in general" (A183, B226). In order that two phenomena be held to be successive or simultaneous, they must be given "an underlying ground which exists *at all times,* that is, something *abiding* and *permanent,* of which all change and coexistence are only so many ways (modes of time) in which the permanent exists" (ibid.). (We can see why above Kant spoke of three modes and not of three relations.) Here we touch on something quite profound. "For change does not affect time itself, but only appearances in time" (ibid.). But since time itself cannot be perceived, it is only by way of the relation between what persists and what changes, in the existence of a phenomenon, that we can discern this time that does not pass and in which everything passes. This is what we call the duration (*Dauer*) of a phenomenon, that is, a quantity of time during which changes occur in a substratum, which itself remains and persists. Kant stresses this point. In mere succession, hence without reference to permanence, existence only appears and disappears without ever possessing the slightest quantity. If time is not to be reduced to a series of appearances and disappearances, it must itself remain. This feature, however, can only be recognized by observing what remains in phenomena, which we determine as substance when we put into relation what remains and what changes.[45]

The principle of permanence thus contributes a preciseness to the axiom in the "Aesthetic" that there is just one time of which all other times are merely parts. To the oneness of time it adds the totality characteristic of time. But the permanence of substance, upon which this description is based, takes nothing away from the invisibility essential to time. Permanence remains a presupposition—an "indispensable something"—of our ordinary perception and of the apprehension by science of the order of things. "The schema of substance is permanence of the real in time, that is, the representation of the real as a substrate of empirical determination of time in general, and so as abiding while all else changes" (A143, B183). In a single move thought posits time as immutable, the schema as the permanence of the real, and the principle of substance. "To time itself non-transitory and abiding, there corresponds in the [field of] appearance what is non-transitory in its existence, that is, substance" (ibid.). So there is a correspondence between the determination of time (immutability), the determination of appearances in accordance with the schema (the permanence of the real in time), and the principle that concerns the first instance, the principle of the permanence of substance. This is why there is no perception of time as such.

The second analogy, called in the second edition, "Principle of the Succession of Time, in Accordance with the Law of Causality" (B233), confers on the notion of the order of time a well-known specification, tied to that of regular succession. There is no point in returning to the classic discussion concerning the synthetic character of causality.[46]

However it is important to separate out from this discussion the remarks that concern the very notion of the order of time. It is stated again that "time cannot be perceived in itself" (B233).[47] This implies that I can know the transcendental determination of time—itself resulting from "a synthetic faculty of imagination, which determines the inner sense in respect of the time-relation" (B233)—only by taking as a basis objective causal relations. I can do this only by making a distinction in my representations between two sorts of succession, one that rests on an objective relation between appearances, as in the observation of a boat sailing down a river, and another that admits of a subjective arbitrariness, as in the description of a house, a description that I can pursue in any direction. It is in this work of distinguishing between two kinds of succession—objective and subjective—that I glimpse obliquely, as an invisible presupposition, the transcendental determination of time as order. This work of distinguishing constitutes the core of the "proof" of the principle of production or of succession in time in accordance with a rule. Once again, the "proof" brings the arguments of the "Transcendental Aesthetic" to a close on the level of presuppositions. What causality sets into relief is not succession as such but the possibility of making the division between a succession that would be "a merely subjective play of my fancy [*Einbildung*] . . . a mere dream" (A202, B247), and a succession that gives meaning to the notion of event (*Begebenheit*) in the sense of something "as actually happening" (A201, B246). So the second analogy in fact depends on the sense of the word "to happen" (*Geschehen*) following the initial formulation of the second analogy: "Everything that happens, that is, begins to be, presupposes something upon which it follows according to a rule" (A189). Before this is specified, we have only a succession without events. There are no events unless an ordered succession is observed in an object. It is therefore on the basis of the relational character of a Newtonian nature that I see the ordered character of time.

The principle of coexistence or community (in the third analogy of experience) gives rise to similar remarks. I can indeed say—echoing in this the "Aesthetic"—that "coexistence is the existence of the manifold in one and the same time" (B257). And further on: "Things are coexistent so far as they exist in one and the same time" (B258). The coexistence of things, however, is perceived only through reciprocal action. It is thus not an accident that Kant repeats, once again, that "time itself cannot be perceived, and we are not, therefore, in a position to gather, simply from things being set in the same time, that their perceptions follow each other reciprocally" (B257). Only by presupposing a reciprocal action of things in relation to one another can coexistence (simultaneity) be revealed to be a relation of order: "only on this condition can these substances be empirically represented as *coexisting*" (A212, B259).

In conclusion, the three dynamic relations of inherence, consequence, and composition, by organizing appearances in time,[48] determine, by implication, the three relations of temporal order that define duration as a quantity of existence, regularity in succession, and simultaneity in existence.

It is not surprising therefore that time which, already in the "Aesthetic," was attained only by argument and not by intuition (to which must be added the antinomies and the mutual reductio ad absurdum of thesis and antithesis) can receive further determination only by the detour of the *Grundsätze,* accompanied by their "proofs" or their "clarifications."

We may say that, through its transcendental determinations, time determines the system of nature. But time, in turn, is determined by the construction of the axiomatic system of nature. In this sense we can speak of a reciprocal determination of the axiomatic system constitutive of the ontology of nature and of the determination of time.

This reciprocity between the process of constituting the objectivity of the object and the emergence of new determinations of time explains why the phenomenological description that these determinations could give rise to is systematically repressed by the critical argument. For example, the permanence of time, following the first analogy, tacitly appeals to the conviction that our power of pursuing ever further our exploration of time has as its counterpart, to use Findlay's expression, the integration of all the phases of this movement "into a vast space-like map" (p. 165), without which, as Kant himself notes, time would unceasingly vanish and begin anew at every instant. Does not the argument by reductio ad absurdum—as is always the case in Kant— also point to the empty place reserved for a phenomenology of retention and protention based, not on the notion of an instant, but on the experience of the lived present?

The second analogy of experience poses an identical problem. What is ultimately at stake here is the irreversibility of time. Yet the meaning that we ascribe to the orientation of time is far from being exhausted by the transcendental "proof" given by Kant, to wit, the distinction in our imagination between two kinds of succession, one whose organization would be arbitrary because it would be purely subjective, the other whose orientation would be necessary because I could oppose to "the representations of my apprehension," "an object distinct from them" (A191, B236). In order to distinguish between an arbitrarily reversible succession and a necessarily irreversible succession, have we available to us no more than the formal criterion of the causal relation, itself held to be a priori? Without going into the new problems posed by modern physics concerning the "arrow of time," or into the crisis of the principle of causality, connected to that of the Kantian a priori as a whole, we may wonder whether the transcendental argument does not betray an unawareness of a distinction that was highlighted in our confrontation between Augustine and Aristotle, namely, the distinction between a succession of instants and the relation between a past and a future connected to a present that is the instant of its own utterance. In a theory of time in which succession has no point of reference other than the instant, the distinction between subjective succession and objective succession must, in fact, be based on a criterion external to succession as such, which Kant sums up in the opposition between the object of successive apprehensions and these apprehensions themselves as simply represented. However it is only in relation to a present, irreducible to an instant that is indistinguishable from any other that the dissymmetry between past and future is itself revealed to be irreducible to the principle of order provided by causal regularity alone. In this sense, the notion of an event, that is, of something that happens, as this figures in the statement of the second analogy (also called a "principle of production" [*Erzeugung*]), is also not exhausted by the notion of ordered succession. It can have two meanings depending on whether time is reduced to simple succession, that is, the relation of before and after of indistinguishable instants, or whether it rests on the irreversible relation between the before of the present—or the past—and the after of the present—or the future.

In this regard, the third analogy merely reinforces the duality of these two approaches. The simultaneity of indistinguishable instants based on reciprocal action, according to the Kantian principle of reciprocity or coexistence, is one thing; the contemporaneousness of two or several courses of experience, created by a reciprocity of an existential order, according to the innumerable modes of "living together," is something else again.

Widening the debate beyond the discussion of the analogies of experience, the phenomenologist willingly asserts that the determinations of time would not maintain their role of "restriction" in the use of the categories if they did not display their own specific phenomenological properties. Must not the determinations of time be comprehensible in themselves, at least implicitly, if they are to serve as means of discrimination with respect to the meaning of the categories; that is, with respect to their use value? The phenomenologist may draw some comfort from the following consideration. In the order of exposition, Kant goes from the category to the schema, then to the principle. In the order of discovery, is there not first the schematization of the category with its temporal determination, then, by abstraction, the category? Heidegger's reading of Kant follows this line. But this reversal of priority between the category and the schema/time pair changes nothing with respect to the more fundamental question that Kant poses to all phenomenology. In the pair schema/time, the correspondence between temporal determination and the development of the schema in its principle is what prevents the constitution of a pure phenomenology of this temporal determination. At the very most we can assert that the notion of the determination of time must contain the lineaments of an implied phenomenology, if in the reciprocity between temporalization and schematization the former is to contribute something to the latter. But this phenomenology cannot be disentangled without breaking the reciprocal connection between the constitution of time and the constitution of the object, a break that is consummated, precisely, by the phenomenology of internal time-consciousness.

Two important texts in the second edition of the *Critique* bring to light the ultimate reasons why a critical perspective and a phenomenological one cannot help but occlude each other.

The first text seems, at first sight, to give the most support to a phenomenology freed from the tutelage of the critique. It is the famous text on *Selbstaffektion* that Kant placed in an appendix to the theory of figurative synthesis in §24 of the second Transcendental Deduction (B152–57).

If we recall the framework of this discussion, Kant has just said that the application of categories to objects in general requires that the understanding "as spontaneity, is able to determine its inner sense" (B150). He takes this opportunity to settle definitively the problem of the relations between time and our inner sense. He does not hesitate to present the problem as a "paradox," left in abeyance since §6 of the "Aesthetic." The paradox is the following. If our inner sense in no way constitutes an intuition of what we are as a soul, hence as a subject in itself, but "represents to consciousness even our own selves only as we appear to ourselves, not as we are in ourselves" (B152–53), then we must say that we have no intuition of our acts themselves but only of the way in which we are internally affected by our acts. Only in this way do we appear to ourselves as an empirical object, just as external objects result from our being affected by things unknown in themselves. These two affections are strictly parallel, and the inner sense has nothing more to do with the power of apperception, which it has entirely dethroned.[49] Whence the paradox resulting from this drastic solution: how can we behave passively (*leidend*) in relation to ourselves?

The answer is ready—"affecting" is still "determining." By affecting my-self, I determine myself, I produce mental configurations capable of being described and named. But how can I so affect myself by my own activity, if not by producing determined configurations in space? It is here that the detour by way of figurative synthesis is shown to be the necessary mediation between myself as affecting (unknown) and myself as affected (known).[50] It is therefore not surprising that the example of "drawing the line" returns precisely here, in the explanation of the paradox of *Selbstaffektion*. The act of drawing a line—along with that of describing a circle, or that of constructing a tri-angular figure—is first of all one example among others of the determination of the inner sense by means of the transcendental act of the imagination. But it adds to the representation of the line, the circle, the triangle, an act of atten-tion bearing on "the act of the synthesis of the manifold whereby we suc-cessively determine inner sense, and in so doing attend to the succession of this determination in inner sense" (B154). In this way, the act of drawing a line certainly does not constitute the intuition of time but does cooperate in its representation.

There is no confusion here between space and time, contrary to what Bergson thought, but the movement from the intuition (unobservable as such) of time to the representation of a determined time, through reflection on the operation of drawing a line. Among all the determinations of space, the line has the advantage of conferring an external character of representation ("the outer figurative representation of time" [B154]). But the core of the argument is that the synthetic activity of the imagination has to be applied to space— drawing a line, tracing out a circle, extending three perpendicular axes all starting from the same point—so that, reflecting on the operation itself, we discover that time is implied here. By constructing a determined space I am conscious of the successive character of the activity of understanding.[51] But I know it only to the extent that I am affected by it. Thus we know ourselves as an object—and not as we are—insofar as we represent time by a line. Time and space mutually generate one another in the work of the synthetic imagina-tion: "we cannot obtain for ourselves a representation of time, which is not an object of outer intuition, except under the image of a line, which we draw, and that by this mode of depicting it alone could we know the singleness [*Einheit*] of its dimension" (B156). It is in every case a question of determination— whether of figures in space or of length of time or epoch. These are deter-minations that we produce together: "the determinations of inner sense have therefore to be arranged as appearances in time in precisely the same manner in which we arrange those of outer sense in space" (ibid.). Of course, what is important to Kant in this argument is that self-affection is strictly parallel to affection from outside: "so far as inner intuition is concerned, we know our own subject only as appearance, not as it is by itself" (ibid.).

For us, although we are not interested here in the division into transcenden-tal subject, absolute self, and phenomenological ego, but just in the new determinations of time that are revealed by *Selbstaffektion,* this very roundabout investigation provides considerable food for thought. Not only is the unobservable character of time as such reaffirmed, but the nature of the indirect representation of time is made more specific. Far from being a matter of the contamination of time by space, the mediation performed by the spatial operations reveals in a single stroke the connection, at the very heart of the experience of time, between passivity and activity. We are temporally affected insofar as we act temporally. Being affected and producing constitute one and the same phenomenon. "The understanding does not, therefore, find in inner sense such a combination of the manifold, but produces it, in that it affects the inner sense" (B155). Kant was not wrong in calling this self-affecting of the subject by its own acts a paradox.[52]

The ultimate warning against any attempt to make time as such appear can be read in the text Kant added to the second edition of the *Critique* following the second postulate of the theory of modality—the postulate of reality—under the title "Refutation of Idealism" (B274–79). Regardless of the polemical reasons that motivated the urgency of this addition,[53] the point of the argument is evident: "our inner experience, which for Descartes is indubitable, is possible only on the assumption of outer experience" (B275). It is noteworthy that Kant's thesis takes the form first of a theorem, then of a proof. The theorem states, "The mere, but empirically determined, consciousness of my own existence proves the existence of objects in space outside of me" (ibid.). Let us be clear about what is at stake. It is a question of existence and of consciousness of my existence, in a noncategorical sense of existence, the opposite of that given in the transcendental deduction. Whereas the latter grants the "I am" of the "I think" only the status of an empirically undetermined existence (§24), here it is a matter of the empirically determined consciousness of my own existence. It is this determination that, as in the rest of the "Analytic," requires that we cease to juxtapose, as was the case in the "Aesthetic," time and space and that we even abandon the effort to base the nominal definition of the schemata on the determinations of time alone. This determination requires, instead, that we closely connect determination in time and determination in space. This connection is no longer made, as it was in the analogies of experience, on the level of representation but on that of the "consciousness of existence" either of myself or of things (whatever the consciousness of existence can signify in a transcendental philosophy that nevertheless continues in its own way to be an idealism). The connection between space and time is thereby linked to the deepest level of experience, at the level of the consciousness of existence. The "proof" consists expressly in taking up again on this more radical level the argument of permanence, employed in the first analogy of experience on the level of the simple representation of things. The first analogy of experience, in effect, taught us that the determination of time as permanent is based on the relation that we bring about in external representation between what changes and what remains. If we transpose this argument from representation to existence, we must say that the immediate character of the consciousnesss of existence of other things outside me is proved by the nonimmediate nature of the consciousness that we have of our existence as determined in time.

If this argument bearing on existence can say anything distinct from the argument of the first analogy of experience bearing on representation, this can only be inasmuch as it subordinates affection by ourselves to affection by things. For, it seems to me, only our reflection on affected being is capable of being carried to the level of the consciousness of existence, both in us and outside us.

It is at this radical level, reached only by a very indirect path[54] that the possibility of an intuitive phenomenology of internal time-consciousness, tacitly admitted by Augustine and explicitly claimed by Husserl, is called into question.

Our confrontation of Husserl and Kant has led us to an impasse comparable to the one revealed by our confrontation of Augustine and Aristotle. Neither the phenomenological approach nor the transcendental one is sufficient unto itself. Each refers back to the other. But this referral presents the paradoxical character of a mutual borrowing, on the condition of a mutual exclusion. On the one hand, we can enter the Husserlian problematic only by bracketing the Kantian problematic; a phenomenology of time can be articulated only by borrowing from objective time, which, in its principal determinations, remains a Kantian time. On the other hand, we can enter the Kantian problematic only on the condition of abstaining from all recourse to any inner sense that would reintroduce an ontology of the soul, which the distinction between phenomenon and thing in itself has bracketed. Yet the determinations by which time is distinguished from a mere magnitude must themselves be based on an implicit phenomenology, whose empty place is evident in every step of the transcendental argument. In this way, phenomenology and critical thought borrow from each other only on the condition of mutually excluding each other. We cannot look at both sides of a single coin at the same time.

To conclude, let us say a word about the relation between the conclusion of this chapter and those of the preceding one. The polarity between phenomenology, in Husserl's sense, and critical philosophy, in Kant's, repeats, on the level of a problematic where the categories of subject and object—or more precisely of subjective and objective—predominate, the polarity between the time of the soul and the time of the world, on the level of a problematic introduced by the question of the being or nonbeing of time.

The filiation relating Augustine and Husserl is easier to recognize. It is admitted and claimed by Husserl himself in the opening lines of the *Phenomenology of Internal Time-Consciousness*. Hence we can see in the phenomenology of retention and in that of primary and secondary recollection a subtle form of the dialectic of the threefold present and of that of *intentio/distentio animi*, and even the phenomenological resolution of certain paradoxes in the Augustinian analysis.

A connection between Kant and Aristotle is more difficult to perceive, or to accept. By asserting the transcendental ideality of space and of time in the "Aesthetic," is Kant not closer to Augustine than to Aristotle? Does not transcendental consciousness mark the fulfilment of a philosophy of subjectivity, for which Augustine had paved the way? Given this, how can Kantian time lead us back to the time of Aristotle? But this would be to forget the meaning of the transcendental in Kant, for its entire function lies in establishing the conditions of objectivity. The Kantian subject, we may say, is wholly taken up in making the object be there. The "Aesthetic" already stresses the fact that the transcendental ideality of space and time has as its other side their empirical reality. And this reality is articulated by the sciences that are related to it. When the "Transcendental Aesthetic" proclaims that time and space inhere originarily in the subject, this cannot hide the other side of the problem and prevent us from asking the question, what sort of empirical reality corresponds to transcendental ideality? More fundamentally, what sort of object is structured by the categorial apparatus of the critique?

The answer is contained in the analytic of principles. The objectivity of the object, which is guaranteed by the transcendental subject, is a nature for which physics is the corresponding empirical science. The analogies of experience provide the conceptual apparatus, whose network articulates this nature. The theory of modalities adds the principle of closure that excludes from the real any entity that falls outside this network. The representation of time is entirely conditioned by this network, by the very reason of its indirect character. It results from this that time, despite its subjective character, is the time of a nature whose objectivity is wholly defined by the categorical apparatus of the mind.

It is by this detour that Kant leads us back to Aristotle; not, certainly, to the pre-Galilean physicist but to the philosopher who places time on the side of nature. Nature, after Galileo and Newton, is, to be sure, no longer what it was before them. But time has not ceased to be on the side of nature rather than on that of the soul. In truth, with Kant, the side of the soul is no more. The death of the inner sense, the assimilation of the conditions under which internal phenomena can be known objectively to the conditions to which external phenomena are themselves submitted, allows just one nature to be known.[55]

Have we, then, actually moved as far as it may seem from the subordination of Aristotelian time to physics? Here again time "has something to do with motion." Of course, a soul is required to count, but the numerable is first of all to be found in motion.

This comparison suddenly places the relation between Kant and Husserl in a new light. The opposition between the intuitive character of Husserlian time and the invisible nature of Kantian time is not merely formal. It is material as well, the opposition between a time that, like the *distentio animi* in Augustine, requires a present capable of both separating and uniting a past and a future, and a time that has no point of reference in the present, because it is, in the final analysis, only the time of nature. Once again, each of the two doctrines discovers its field of application only by occluding the other. The price of the Husserlian discovery of retention and secondary remembrance is that nature is forgotten, yet succession is presupposed by the very description of the internal consciousness of time. But is not the price of critical philosophy a blindness reciprocal to that of Husserl? By tying the fate of time to a determined ontology of nature, has not Kant prevented himeslf from exploring properties of temporality other than those required by his Newtonian axiomatic system—succession, simultaneity (and permanence)? Has he not shut off access to other properties resulting from the relations of the past and the future to the actual present?

3

Temporality, Historicality, Within-Time-Ness
Heidegger and the "Ordinary" Concept of Time

Now that we are about to consider the Heideggerian interpretation of time in *Being and Time,* we must counter a biased objection that is leveled against any reading that would isolate *Being and Time* from Heidegger's later work, which, in the eyes of the majority of his disciples, constitutes at one and the same time the hermeneutic key to *Being and Time,* its critique, and even its denial.[1] This objection stresses two points. On the one hand, it states that to separate the temporality of *Dasein* from the understanding of Being, which is truly revealed only in the works following Heidegger's reversal or turn, his *Kehre,* is fatally to confine *Being and Time* to a philosophical anthropology that ignores its real intention. Heidegger himself perhaps saw the inevitability of this misunderstanding when he left *Being and Time* unfinished and abandoned the path of the analytic of Dasein. On the other hand, if we lose sight of the theme of the destruction of metaphysics, which, as early as *Being and Time,* accompanies the recovery of the question of Being, we run the risk of misunderstanding the meaning of the critique aimed, on the level of phenomenology, at the primacy of the present, by failing to perceive the connection between this critique and that of the primacy accorded by metaphysics to vision and presence.

We should not, I think, be intimidated by this warning.

It is perfectly legitimate to treat *Being and Time* as a distinct work, because this is the way it was published, once we propose a reading that respects its unfinished character, or even that stresses its problematic aspect. *Being and Time* deserves this sort of reading on its own merits and to pay proper tribute to it.

Are we thereby forced into the error of an anthropological interpretation? It is, after all, the object of *Being and Time* to attempt an approach to the question of the meaning of Being by way of an existential analysis that establishes the very criteria for approaching this question. Are we in danger of failing to apprehend the antimetaphysical point of its phenomenological critique of the present and of presence? On the contrary, a reading that is not too quick to see a metaphysics of presence in a phenomenology of the present may become attentive to those features of the present that do not reflect the alleged errors of an intuitive metaphysics directed toward some intelligible world. To this apology, which is still too defensive, for a distinct reading of *Being and Time,* I would like to add an argument that is more directly related to the theme of my own investigation. If we do not allow Heidegger's later works to overpower the voice of *Being and Time,* we give ourselves an opportunity to perceive, on the level of this hermeneutic phenomenology of time, tensions and discordances that are not necessarily those that led to the incompletion of *Being and Time,* because they do not have to do with the overall relation of the existential analytic to ontology, but have to do rather with the meticulous, extraordinarily well-articulated detail of the analytic of Dasein. These tensions and discordances, as we shall see, can be related to those that have already caused difficulty in the two preceding chapters, can shed new light on them, and perhaps, can reveal their true nature, owing, precisely, to the kind of hermeneutic phenomenology practiced in *Being and Time,* restored through our reading to the autonomy its author conferred upon it.

A HERMENEUTIC PHENOMENOLOGY

As regards the aporias of time in Augustinian and Husserlian thought, we might say that *Being and Time* resolves them, or rather dissolves them, inasmuch as, as early as the Introduction and Division One, the ground upon which these aporias took shape is left behind in favor of a new kind of questioning. How then can we still oppose a time of the soul, in Augustinian terms, to a time that would essentially have "something to do with movement," hence be related to physics, after the manner of Aristotle? For one thing, the existential analytic has as its referent not the soul but Dasein, being-there; that is, the being that we are. But, at the same time, "Dasein is an entity which does not just occur among other entities. Rather it is ontically distinguished by the fact that in its very Being, that Being is an *issue* for it" (*Being and Time,* p. 32). The relationship of Dasein "in its Being . . . towards that Being" (ibid.), which belongs to the constitution of the Being of Dasein, is not presented as a simple ontic distinction between the psychological and the physical regions. What is more, for an existential analysis, nature cannot constitute an opposite pole, or much less an alien theme, in the consideration of Dasein, inasmuch as "the 'world' itself is something constitutive for Dasein" (p. 77). As a result, the question of time—to which the second division of Part One of *Being and Time* (the only part published) is devoted—can come, following the thematic order of this work, only after that of Being-in-the-world, which reveals the fundamental constitution of Dasein. The determinations related to the concept of existence (of my own existence) and to the possibility of authenticity and inauthenticity contained in the notion of mineness "must be seen and understood *a priori* as grounded upon that state of Being which we have called '*Being-in-the-world.*' An interpretation of this constitutive state is needed if we are to set up our analytic of Dasein correctly" (p. 78). In fact, almost two hundred pages are devoted to Being-in-the-world, to the world-hood of the world in general, as though it were first necessary to allow our-selves to be permeated by the sense of the surrounding world, before having the right—before being entitled—to confront the structures of "Dasein . . . as such": situation, understanding, explication, discourse. It is not without importance that, in the thematic order followed by *Being and Time,* the question of the spatiality of Being-in-the-world is posed not only before that of temporality but as an aspect of "environmentality," hence of worldhood as such. How then could anything remain of the Augustinian aporia of a *distentio animi* robbed of cosmological support?

The opposition between Augustine and Aristotle seems therefore to have been superseded by the new problematic of Dasein, which overturns the received notions coming from physics and psychology.

Must not the same thing be said with respect to the Husserlian aporia of internal time-consciousness? How could the slightest trace remain of the antinomy between internal time-consciousness and objective time in an analytic of Dasein? Does not the structure of Being-in-the-world destroy the problematic of subject and object just as surely as it destroys that of the soul and nature?

What is more, the Husserlian ambition of making time itself appear is discounted from the first pages of *Being and Time* by the assertion that Being has been forgotten. If it is true that "only as phenomenology is ontology possible" (p. 60), phenomenology itself is possible only as hermeneutics, inasmuch as, owing to this forgetfulness, hiddenness is the first condition of any effort at finally showing something.[2] Released from its tie to direct vision, phenomenology becomes part of the struggle against dissimulation. "Covered-up-ness is the counter-concept to 'phenomenon'" (p. 60). Beyond the dilemma of the visibility or invisibility of time, the path of a hermeneutical phenomenology opens up where seeing steps aside in favor of understanding or, to use another expression, in favor of a "discovering interpretation," guided by the anticipation of the meaning of the Being that we are, and bent on exposing (*freilegen*) this meaning, that is, on freeing it from forgetfulness and hiddenness.

This mistrust as regards any shortcut that would allow time itself to emerge within the field of appearing is evident in the strategy of postponement that marks the thematic treatment of the question of time. We must first pass through the long Division One—termed "preparatory" (*vorbereitende*)—before we can reach the problematic of Division Two, "Dasein and Temporality." And in Division Two, the various stages that will be discussed below must be traversed before we reach, in §65, the first definition of time. "This phenomenon has the unity of a future which makes present in the process of having been; we designate it as '*temporality*'" (p. 374). We can, in this respect, speak of a retreat of the question of time in Heidegger.

Is this to say that the attempt to escape the dilemma of direct intuition or indirect presupposition can lead only to a kind of hermeticism, considered as a form of mystification? This would be to neglect the labor of language that gives *Being and Time* a greatness that no subsequent work will eclipse. By a labor of language, I mean, first and foremost, the effort to articulate in an appropriate manner the hermeneutic phenomenology that ontology enlists in its own behalf. This is attested to by the frequent use of the term "structure." In addition, I mean the search for basic concepts that can be used to support the proposed structuring. *Being and Time,* in this respect, represents an immense construction site where the existentials that are to Dasein what categories are to other entities are formed.[3] If hermeneutic phenomenology can claim to escape the alternative of a direct, but silent, intuition of time or an indirect, but blind, presupposition of it, this is indeed thanks to the labor of language that makes the difference between interpreting (*auslegen,* §32) and understanding. Interpreting is, in fact, developing understanding, ex-plicating the structure of a phenomenon as (*als*) this or that. In this way, we can bring to language, and hence to the level of assertion (*Aussage,* §33) the understanding that we always already possess of the temporal structure of Dasein.[4]

I would like to summarize in a few pages the breakthrough this hermeneutic phenomenology brings about in the understanding of time, in relation to the discoveries that must be credited to Augustine and Husserl. Below, we shall have to admit how much greater a price must be paid for this audacious interpretation.

To Heidegger, we owe three admirable discoveries. The first one says that the question of time as a whole is enveloped, in a manner that remains to be explicated, by the basic structure of "Care." The second one says that the unity of the three dimensions of time—future, past, and present—is an ecstatic unity in which the mutual exteriorization of these ecstases proceeds from their very entanglement with one another. Finally, the unfolding of this ecstatic unity reveals, in turn, a constitution of time that may be said to be layered, a hierarchization of the levels of temporalization, which requires distinct denominations: temporality, historicality, and within-time-ness. We shall see how these three discoveries are interrelated and how the difficulties generated by the first discovery are taken up and multiplied by the second and third discoveries.

CARE AND TEMPORALITY

To connect the authentic structure of time to that of Care is, immediately, to remove the question of time from the theory of knowledge and to bring it to the level of a mode of being that (1) retains the scar of its relation to the question of Being; (2) has cognitive, volitional, and emotional aspects, without itself being reduced to any one of these, or even being situated on a level where the distinction between these three aspects is pertinent; (3) recapitulates the major existentials such as projection, thrownness into the world, and fallenness; and (4) provides a structural unity for these existentials that straightaway posits the requirement of "Being-a-whole" (*Ganzsein*) that leads directly to the question of temporality.

Let us pause and look at this last feature, which governs all that follows.

Why is it necessary to get into the question of temporality by way of the question of the "possibility of Being-a-whole" or, as we could also say, of "Being-integral"? At first sight the notion of Care does not appear to require this; it even seems at odds with it. The very first temporal implication that is unfolded is indeed that of Being-ahead-of-itself (*das Sichvorweg*), which includes no closure but, on the contrary, remains incomplete due, precisely, to Dasein's potentiality-for-Being (*Seinskönnen*). If the question of Being-a-whole has, nonetheless, a certain privilege, this is insofar as the hermeneutic phenomenology of time has as its stakes the articulated unity of the three moments of the future, the past, and the present. Augustine made this unity arise from the present by means of triplification.[5] But the present, according to Heidegger, cannot assume this function of articulation and dispersion because it is the temporal category least apt to receive an originary and authentic analysis, by reason of its kinship with the fallen forms of existence, namely, the propensity of Dasein to understand itself in terms of things present-at-hand (*vorhanden*) and ready-to-hand (*zuhanden*) that are the object of its present care, of its preoccupation. Here already, what seems closest in the eyes of a direct phenomenology turns out to be the most inauthentic phenomenon, while the authentic is what is most concealed.

If therefore we admit that the question of time is first of all the question of its structural wholeness, and if the present is not the modality appropriate for this search for totality, it remains for us to find in Care's Being-ahead-of-itself the secret of its completeness. It is here that the idea of Being-towards-the-end (*zum-Ende-sein*) offers itself as the existential that bears the mark of its own internal closure. Being-the-end is remarkable in that it "belongs" (p. 276) to that which remains in abeyance and in suspension in Dasein's potentiality-for-Being. The " 'end' of Being-in-the-world is death" (pp. 276–77); " 'ending,' as dying, is constitutive for Dasein's totality" (p. 284).[6]

This entrance into the problem of time through the question of Being-a-whole and this alleged connection between Being-a-whole and Being-towards-death pose an immediate difficulty, which will not be without effect on the other two phases of our analysis. This difficulty lies in the unavoidable interference, at the heart of the analytic of Dasein, between the existential and the "existentiell."

Let us say a word about this problem in its most general and most formal aspects. In principle, the term "existentiell" characterizes the concrete choice of a way of Being-in-the-world, the ethical commitment assumed by exceptional personalities, by ecclesiastical and other communities, by entire cultures. The term "existential," on the other hand, characterizes any analysis that aims at explicating the structures that distinguish Dasein from all other beings and, therefore, that connect the question of the meaning of the Being of the entity that we are to the question of Being as such, to the extent that, for Dasein, the meaning of its Being is an issue for it. But this distinction between the existential and the existentiell is obscured by its interfering with the distinction between the authentic and the inauthentic, which itself is caught up in the search for the primordial (*ursprünglich*). This latter overlapping is inevitable as soon as the degraded and fallen state of the concepts available to a hermeneutic phenomenology reflects the state of forgetfulness in which the question of Being lies, and when this fallen state requires the labor of language referred to above. The conquest of primordial concepts is thus inseparable from a struggle against inauthenticity, which itself is practically identified with everydayness. But this search for the authentic cannot be carried out without a constant appeal to the testimony of the existentiell. Commentators, it seems to me, have not sufficiently stressed this core of the entire hermeneutical phenomenology of *Being and Time*. This phenomenology is continually obliged to provide an existentiell attestation for its existential concepts.[7] This is not due to the need to reply to some epistemological objection coming from the human sciences, despite the words "criterion," "assurance," "certainty," "guarantee." The need for attestation results from the very nature of that potentiality-for-Being in which existence lies. Existence, in fact, is free, either for the authentic or the inauthentic, or even for some undifferentiated mode. The analyses of Division One had constantly relied on average everydayness and are therefore themselves confined to this indistinct, even frankly inauthentic, sphere. This is why a new demand is imposed: " Existence' means a potentiality-for-Being—but also one which is authentic" (p. 276). However, since an inauthentic being can well be less than whole (*als unganzes*), as is verified by the attitude of fleeing in the face of the possibility of death, it must be admitted that "*our existential analysis of Dasein up till now cannot lay any claim to primordiality*" (ibid.). In other words, without the guarantee of authenticity, the analysis also falls short of insuring primordiality.

The necessity of basing existential analysis on existentiell testimony has no other origin. A striking example of this can be found at the beginning of *Being and Time* in the relation established between Being-a-whole and Being-towards-death.[8] Clear confirmation of this can then also be found in the testimony anticipatory resoluteness makes concerning the entire analysis. The reign of inauthenticity never ceases, in fact, to reopen the question of the criterion of authenticity. Conscience (*Gewissen*) is supposed to provide this confirmation of authenticity.[9] Chapter 2, which is devoted to this analysis, is entitled "Dasein's Attestation [*Bezeugung*] of an Authentic Potentiality-for-Being, and Resoluteness" (p. 312). This chapter, which again seems to postpone the decisive analysis of temporality, has an irreplaceable role. Ordinary language, in fact, has already said everything there is to say about death: everyone dies alone, death is certain but its hour is uncertain, etc. Hence we have not finished with the gossip, deceit, dissimulation, and covering-up that infect everyday discourse. This is why it is necessary to call upon nothing less than the attestation of conscience, and the appeal addressed, through its voice, by the self to itself, in order to establish Being-towards-death at its highest level of authenticity.[10]

So the testimony given by conscience about resoluteness belongs in an organic manner to the analysis of time as the totalization of existence. It places the seal of authenticity on the primordial. This is why Heidegger does not try to move directly from the analysis of Care to that of time. Temporality is accessible only at the intersection point of the primordial, reached in part by the analysis of Being-towards-death, and the authentic, established by the analysis of conscience. This is perhaps the most decisive reason for the strategy of postponement that we have opposed to the strategy of taking a shortcut adopted by Husserl, with its exclusion of objective time and the description of objects as minute as a sound that continues to resonate. Heidegger allows himself a series of delays before approaching temporality thematically. First, there is the long "preparatory" treatise (the entire first division of *Being and Time*) dealing with the analysis of Being-in-the-world and with the "there" of Being-there, of Dasein, which is crowned by the analysis of Care. Next, there is the short treatise (the first two chapters of Division Two) that, by joining together the themes of Being-towards-death and resoluteness in the complex notion of anticipatory resoluteness, assures the overlapping of the primordial by the authentic. To this strategy of postponement will correspond, after the thematic analysis of temporality, a strategy of repetition, announced in the introductory section to Division Two (§45). It will be the task of Chapter 4 of Division Two to undertake a recapitulation of all the analyses of Division One, in order to glean, after the fact, their temporal meaning. This recapitulation is announced in the following terms. "The existential-temporal analysis of this entity needs to be confirmed [*Bewährung*] concretely. . . . by thus recapitulating [*Wiederholung*] our preparatory fundamental analysis of Dasein, we will at the same time make the phenomenon of temporality itself more transparent [*durchsichtiger*]" (pp. 277–78). We can consider as an additional postponement the long "recapitulation" (*Wiederholung*) of Division Two of *Being and Time* (pp. 380–81), inserted between the analysis of temporality properly speaking (Chapter 3) and that of historicality (Chapter 4), with the clearly defined intention of finding in the reinterpretation in temporal terms of all the moments of Being-in-the-world covered in Division One a "confirmation [*Bewährung*] of its constitutive power [*seiner konstitutiven Mächtigkeit*]" (p. 380). Chapter 4, dealing with the "temporal interpretation" of the features of Being-in-the-world, can thus be placed under the same heading of an attestation of authenticity as was the case in Chapter 2 with respect to the resolute anticipation. What is new here is that the sort of confirmation provided by this review of all the analyses of Division One is addressed to the modes derived from fundamental temporality, as is already indicated by the title of this intermediary chapter, "Temporality and Everydayness." When we say everydayness (*Alltäglichkeit*), we say day (*Tag*), that is, a temporal structure the meaning of which is put off until the final chapter of *Being and Time*. In this way, the authentic character of the analysis is attested to only by its capacity to account for the derived modes of temporality. Derivation is here the equivalent of attestation.

The price to be paid, however, is now the lack, so feared and so strongly denied, of a distinction between the existentiell and existential. This lack of a distinction presents two major drawbacks.

We can first of all ask whether the entire analysis of temporality is not tied to the personal conception that Heidegger has of authenticity, on a level where it competes with other existentiell conceptions, those of Pascal and of Kierkegaard—or that of Sartre—to say nothing of that of Augustine. It is not, in fact, within an ethical configuration, strongly marked by a certain Stoicism, that resoluteness in the face of death constitutes the supreme test of authenticity? More important, is it not within a categorial analysis, heavily influenced by the recoil-effect of the existentiell on the existential, that death is held to be our utmost possibility, even our ownmost potentiality, inherent in the essential structure of Care? I myself consider just as legitimate an analysis such as Sartre's, which characterizes death as the interruption of our potentiality-for-Being rather than as its most authentic possibility.

We can also ask ourselves whether this very peculiar existentiell mark, placed from the outset on the analysis of temporality, will not have extremely serious consequences on the effort to hierarchize temporality in the last two chapters of the division on Dasein and time. Despite the desire to derive historicality and within-time-ness from radical temporality, a new dispersion of the notion of time will, in fact, emerge from the incommensurability of mortal time, which temporality is identified with by the preparatory analysis, historical time, which historicality is supposed to ground, and cosmic time, which within-time-ness leads to. The perspective of a concept of time broken up in this way, which will reawaken the aporias Augustine and Husserl ran into, can become clearer only when the notion of "derivation" has itself been examined as it is applied to the interconnection of the three levels of temporalization. And it is by this examination that we shall conclude our own presentation.

If we withdraw from mortality the capacity to determine by itself alone the level of radicalness on which temporality can be thought, we do not thereby weaken the mode of questioning that guides the investigation of temporality (Chapter 3). Quite the opposite. If the potentiality of Dasein to be a whole— or as we might say, its capacity for being integral—ceases to be governed solely by the consideration of Being-towards-the-end, the potentiality-of-Being-a-whole can once again be carried back to the power of unification, articulation, and dispersion belonging to time.[11] And if the modality of Being-towards-death seems instead to result from the recoil-effect of the other two levels of temporalization—historicality and within-time-ness—on the most original level, then the potentiality-for-Being constitutive of Care can be revealed in its purest state, as Being-ahead of itself, as *Sichvorweg*. The other features that, together, make up resolute anticipation are not weakened either, but are strengthened by the refusal to give a preference to Being-towards-death. In this way, the attestation provided by the silent voice of conscience, and the guilt that gives this voice its existentiell force, is addressed to our potentiality-for-Being in its barest form and its fullest scope. In the same way, thrown-Being is just as fully revealed by the fact of being born one day, and in a particular place, as by the necessity of having to die. Fallenness is attested to no less by old promises that are not kept as by the fact of fleeing in the face of death. Endebtedness and responsibility, which are designated by the same word in German, *Schuld,* themselves constitute a powerful appeal to every person to choose according to their ownmost possibilities, making them free for their task in the world, when Care recovers its original impetus through carefreeness with respect to death.[12]

So there is thus more than one existentiell way of accepting, in all its existential force, Heidegger's formula defining temporality: "*Temporality gets experienced in a phenomenally primordial way in Dasein's authentic Being-a-whole, in the phenomenon of anticipatory resoluteness*" (p. 351).[13]

TEMPORALIZATION: COMING-TOWARDS, HAVING-BEEN, AND MAKING-PRESENT

As we have said, it is only at the end of Chapter 3 of Division Two, §§65–66, that Heidegger deals with temporality thematically in its relation to Care. In these extremely dense pages, he attempts to go beyond the Augustinian analysis of the threefold present and farther than the Husserlian analysis of retention and protention, which, as we saw above, takes place in the same phenomenological space. Heidegger's originality lies in his effort to seek in Care itself the principle of the pluralizing of time into future, past, and present. From this shift toward what is more primordial will result the promotion of the future to the place occupied up to now by the present, and a complete reorientation of the relations between the three dimensions of time. This will require that the very terms "future," "past," and "present" be abandoned, terms that Augustine never felt obliged to question, out of respect for ordinary language, despite his audacity in speaking of the present *of* the future, the present *of* the past, and the present *of* the present.

What we are looking for, it is stated at the beginning of §65, is the meaning (*Sinn*) of Care. It is a question not of vision but of understanding and of interpretation. Taken strictly, meaning "signifies the 'upon-which' [*voraufhin*] of the primary projection of the understanding of Being." " 'Meaning' signifies the 'upon-which' [*das Voraufhin*] of a primary projection in terms of which something can be conceived in its possibility as [*als*] that which it is" (p. 371).[14]

Between the internal organization of Care and the threefold nature of time we find, therefore, a quasi-Kantian relation of conditionality. But the Heideggerian "making possible" differs from the Kantian condition of possibility in that Care "possibilizes" all human experience.

These considerations on possibilization, inherent in Care, already announce the primacy of the future in the analysis of the articulated structure of time. The intermediary link in the reasoning is provided by the preceding analysis of resolute anticipation, itself resulting from the meditation on Being-towards-the-end and Being-towards-death. This is more than the primacy of the future. It involves the reinscription of the term "future," borrowed from everyday language, in the idiom appropriate to hermeneutic phenomenology. An adverb, more than a noun, serves as a guide here, namely, the *zu* in *sein-zum-Ende* and *sein-zum-Tode,* which can be applied to the *zu* of the expression *Zu-kunft* (to-come, coming-towards). With this, *kommen*—to come— also takes on a new aspect by joining the power of the verb to that of the adverb, in place of the substantive form "the future." In Care, Dasein aims at coming toward itself in accordance with its ownmost possibilities. Coming-towards (*Zukommen*) is the root of the future. "This letting-itself-*come-towards*-itself [*sich auf sich zukommen-lassen*] . . . is the primordial phenomenon of the *future as coming towards* [*Zukunft*]" (p. 372). This is the possibility included in resolute anticipation. "Anticipation [*Vorlaufen*] makes Dasein *authentically* futural, and in such a way that the anticipation itself is possible only in so far as Dasein, *as being,* is always coming towards itself—that is to say, in so far as it is futural [*zukünftig*] in its Being in general" (p. 373).[15]

This new signification given to the future allows us to distinguish some overlooked relations of close mutual implication among the three dimensions of time.

Heidegger starts with the implication of the past by the future, thereby postponing a consideration of their relation to the present, which was at the center of both Augustine's and Husserl's analyses.

The passage from the future to the past no longer constitutes an extrinsic transition because "having-been" appears to be called for by the future as "coming-towards," and in a sense, to be contained within it. There is no recognition in general without the recognition of debt and responsibility, once resoluteness itself implies that we ourselves assume the fault and its moment of thrownness (*Geworfenheit*). "But taking over thrownness signifies *being*

Dasein authentically *as it already was* [*in dem, wie es je schon war*]" (p. 373). The important thing here is that the imperfect tense of the verb "to be"— "was"—and the adverb that stresses it—"already" are not separate from Being; instead "as it already was" bears the mark of the "I am," as one can say in German "*ich bin gewesen,*" "I-am-as-having-been" (ibid.). It can then be said, "As authentically futural, Dasein *is* authentically as '*having-been*'" (ibid.). This summing up is in fact the turning back upon the self inherent in any act of taking responsibility. In this way, having-been stems from coming-towards. "Having-been," not "the past," if by "past" we are to understand the past of past things that we oppose, on the level of given presence and things that are present-at-hand, to the openness of future things. Do we not take as self-evident the fact that the past is determined and the future open? This asymmetry separated from its hermeneutical context does not permit us to apprehend the intrinsic relation between the past and the future, however.[16]

As for the present, far from engendering the past and the future by multiplying itself, as in Augustine, it is the mode of temporality possessing the most deeply concealed authenticity. There is, of course, a truth of everydayness in its dealings with things ready-to-hand and present-at-hand. In this sense, the present is indeed the time of concern. But it must not be thought of following the model of the presence-at-hand of the things of our concern, but rather as an implication of Care. It is through the intermediary of the situation which is in each case offered to resoluteness that we can rethink the present in its existential mode. We must then speak of "enpresenting" in the sense of "making present" rather than of being present.[17] "Only as the Present [*Gegenwart*] in the sense of making present, can resoluteness be what it is: namely, letting itself be encountered undisguisedly by that which it seizes upon in taking action" (p. 374).

Coming-towards and turning back upon itself are thus incorporated in resoluteness, once the latter is placed in a situation by making it present, by "enpresenting" it.

Temporality is then the articulated unity of coming-towards, having-been, and making-present, which are thereby given to be thought of together. "This phenomenon has the unity of a future which makes present in the process of having been; we designate it as '*temporality*'" (ibid.). We see in what sense this kind of deduction of the three modes of temporality, from each other, corresponds to the concept of "making-possible" mentioned above. "Temporality makes possible [*ermöglicht*] the unity of existence, facticity, and falling" (p. 376). This new status of making-possible is expressed in the substitution of the verb for the nominal form. "Temporality 'is' not an *entity* at all. It is not, but it *temporalizes* itself" (p. 377).[18]

If the invisibility of time as a whole is no longer an obstacle to thinking, once we think of possibility as making possible and of temporality as temporalizing, what remains just as obscure in Heidegger as it was in Augustine is the triplicity internal to this structural wholeness. The adverbial expressions—the towards of coming-towards, the already of having-been, and the alongsideness of concern—indicate on the very level of language itself the dispersion that undermines the unitary articulation from within. The Augustinian problem of the threefold present is simply carried over to temporalization taken as a whole. It seems that we can only point toward this intractable phenomenon, designate it by the Greek term *ekstatikon,* and state that "*Temporality is the primordial 'outside-of-itself' [Ausser-sich] in and for itself*" (p. 377).[19] At the same time, it is necessary to complete the idea of the structural unity of time by adding that of the differences among its ecstases. This differentiation is intrinsically implied by temporalization insofar as it is a process that gathers together in dispersing.[20] The passage from the future to the past and to the present is at one and the same time unification and diversification. Here, all at once, we see the enigma of the *distentio animi* reintroduced, although it is no longer based on the present. And for similar reasons, we recall, Augustine was careful to account for the extensible character of time that makes us speak of a long time or a short time. For Heidegger, too, what he considers to be the ordinary conception of time—that is, the succession of "nows" external to one another—finds a secret ally in the primordial exteriorization with regard to which the ordinary conception is but the expression of a leveling off. This leveling off is the leveling off of this aspect of exteriority. We shall be in a position to consider this leveling off only after we have spread out before ourselves the hierarchical levels of temporalization: temporality, historicality, and within-time-ness, inasmuch as what this leveling off actually affects is the mode whose derivation makes it the furthest removed from primordial temporality, within-time-ness. Nevertheless, it is possible to perceive in the *Ausser-sich* of primordial temporality the principle of all the subsequent forms of exteriorization and of the leveling off that will affect it. The question then arises whether the derivation of the least authentic modes does not conceal the circularity of the entire analysis. Is derived time not already anticipated in the *Ausser-sich* of primordial temporality?

HISTORICALITY (GESCHICHTLICHKEIT)

There is no way I can measure my debt as regards the ultimate contribution of Heidegger's hermeneutic phenomenology to the theory of time. The most valuable discoveries in it give rise to the most disconcerting perplexities. The distinction between temporality, historicality, and within-time-ness (which occupies the last two chapters with which *Being and Time* breaks off, it can be said, more than concludes) can be added to its two other remarkable discoveries—the recourse to Care as that which makes temporality possible and the plural unity of the three ecstases of temporality.

The question of historicality is introduced by the formulation of a scruple (*Bedanken*), one which is now familiar to us. "Have we indeed brought the whole of Dasein, as regards it authentically Being-a-whole, into the fore-having [*Vorhabe*] of our existential analysis?" (p. 424).[21] Temporality is lacking in one aspect that would make it a whole. This aspect is *Erstreckung, stretching along*, between birth and death. But how could this have been considered in an analysis that has up to now disregarded birth and, along with it, the between-birth-and-death? Now, this between-the-two is the very stretching-along of Dasein. If nothing has been said of this earlier, it was out of the fear of falling back into the web of ordinary thinking concerning the things present-at-hand and ready-to-hand. What could be more tempting than to identify this stretching-along with a measurable interval between the "now" of the beginning and that of the end? But, have we not, at the same time, neglected to consider human existence in terms of a concept, familiar to many thinkers at the beginning of this century, including Dilthey, that of the "connectedness of life" (*Zusammenhang des Lebens*), conceived of as an ordered sequence of experiences (*Erlebnisse*) "in time"? It cannot be denied that something important is stated here, but something that is perverted by the defective categorization imposed by the ordinary representation of time. For indeed it is within the framework of simple succession that we place not only connectedness and sequence but also change and permanence (all of which, let us note, are concepts that hold the highest interest for narration). Birth then becomes an event of the past that no longer exists, just as death becomes a future event that has not yet taken place, and the connectedness of life a lapse of time framed by the rest of time. It will only be by connecting to the problematic of Care the legitimate investigations centered on the concept of the "connectedness of life" that we shall be able to restore to the notions of stretching-along, movement (*Bewegheit*), and self-constancy (*Selbständigkeit*) their ontological dignity, which the ordinary representation of time places in line with the constancy, change, and permanence of things present-at-hand. Reconnected to Care, the between-life-and-death ceases to appear as an interval separating two nonexistent end-points. On the contrary, Dasein does not fill up an interval of time but, by stretching-along, constitutes its true being as this very stretching-along, which envelops its own beginning and its own end, and gives meaning to life as "between." We could not find ourselves any closer to Augustine than in this observation.

It is to indicate clearly this derivation of the stretching-along of Dasein starting from primordial temporalization that Heidegger attempts to renew the meaning of the old German word *Geschehen* and to put it on an equal footing with the ontological problematic of between-life-and-death. The choice of this word is apt inasmuch as *Geschehen* ("historize" in the English translation of *Being and Time*) is a verb homologous to *Zeitigen*, which indicates the temporalizing operation.

In addition, thanks to its semantic kinship with the substantive form *Geschichte*—history—the verb *geschehen* leads to the threshold of the epistemological question, so important to us, whether it is due to historiographical science that we think historically, or whether it is not because Dasein historizes itself that historical research has a meaning. Later we shall give this debate between the ontology of historicality and the epistemology of historiography the attention it fully deserves. For the moment, our problem is more radical. It concerns the nature of the "derivation" by which we pass from temporality to historicality on the ontological level.

This is less of a one-way derivation than Heidegger seems to announce.

On the one hand, historicality owes its ontological tenor to this derivation. Stretching along, movement, and self-constancy can be lifted out of their degraded representation only by referring the whole problematic of historicality to that of temporality.[22] We are even incapable of giving a satisfactory meaning to the relations between movement and self-constancy so long as we think of them in terms of the opposing categories of change and permanence.

On the other hand, historicality adds a new dimension—an original, equiprimordial dimension—to temporality, toward which all the ordinary expressions of cohesion, change, and self-constancy point despite their degraded state. If common sense did not have a certain preconception, the question of readjusting these expressions to the ontological discourse of Dasein would not even arise. We would not even ask the question of the historical becoming of Dasein, if we had not already raised, within the framework of inappropriate categories, the questions of change and self-constancy, akin to the question of Dasein's stretching along between life and death. The question of self-constancy, in particular, imposes itself on our reflection as soon as we ask ourselves about the "who" of Dasein. We cannot avoid this question once the question of the self returns to the foreground with the question of resoluteness, which itself goes along with the self-reference of promising and guilt.[23]

It is therefore quite true that although it is derived, the notion of historicality adds to that of temporality, on the existential level itself, those features signified by words "stretching along," "movement," and "self-constancy." We must not forget this enrichment of the primordial by the derivative when we ask in what way historicality is the ontological ground of history, and, reciprocally, in what way the epistemology of historiography is a discipline grounded on the ontology of historicality.[24]

We must now explore the resources provided by this innovative derivation—if we may call it so. Heidegger's main concern in this regard is to resist two tendencies found in all historical thinking. The first one consists in thinking of history straightaway as a public phenomenon, for is history not the history of all people? The second leads to separating the past from its relation to the future and to construing historical thought as pure retrospection. These two tendencies go hand in hand, for it is indeed public history that we are trying to understand after the fact, in the mode of retrospection, even of retrodiction.

To the first temptation, Heidegger opposes the primacy of the historicality of each "factical" Dasein in relation to all research concerning world history, in the sense that Hegel ascribes to this term. "Dasein factically has its 'history', and it can have something of the sort because the Being of this entity is constituted by historicality" (p. 434). And it is indeed this first sense of the word "history" that is prescribed by an investigation that takes Care as its guide and that sees in Being-towards-death—solitary and untransferable—the touchstone for any authentic attitude toward time.[25]

As for the second temptation, Heidegger confronts it head-on with the full weight of the preceding analysis, which gives priority to the future in the mutual genesis of the three temporal ecstases. This analysis, however, cannot simply be continued in the same way, if we are to take into consideration the new features added by historicality (stretching-along, movement, and self-constancy). This is why the movement of coming-towards in the direction of having-been must be rethought in such a way as to account for the reversal by which the past seems to regain priority over the future. The decisive moment in the argument is as follows. There is no impetus toward the future that does not turn back toward the condition of finding itself already thrown into the world. Now this returning back upon itself is not limited to returning to the most contingent and most extrinsic circumstances of our imminent choices. In a more essential manner, it consists in grasping hold of the innermost and most permanent possibilities held in reserve in what appears to constitute no more than the contingent and extrinsic occasion for action. In order to state this close relationship between anticipation and fallenness, Heidegger ventures to introduce the kindred notions of heritage, transfer, and transmission. The term heritage—*Erbe*—was chosen for its particular connotations. For everyone, in fact, fallenness—being thrown—presents the singular configuration of a "lot" composed of possibilities that are neither chosen nor fettering, but that are handed down and transmitted. In addition, a heritage is what can be received, taken over, assumed by someone. The French language, unfortunately, does not have the semantic resources of German to reconstitute the network of verbs and prefixes that knit together this idea of a heritage that is handed down, carried over, and assumed.[26]

This key notion of a heritage that is handed down and assumed constitutes the pivot point of this analysis. It enables us to see how every turning backwards comes from a resoluteness that is, in its essence, turned toward the future.

The distinction between the transmission of potentialities that are my own self, as having-been, and the fortuitous transfer of a fixed set of circumstances, opens up in turn the path for an analysis that rests on the kinship between the three concepts that the semantics of German groups together: *Schiksal, Geschick,* and *Geschichte*—which we translate by "fate," "destiny," and "history."

The first term certainly reinforces the monadic character of the analysis, at least in its beginnings. What I hand down, I hand down to myself, just as I receive myself as a heritage of potentialities. This is my fate. If indeed we construct all of our projects in light of Being-towards-death, then all that is fortuitous falls away. What remains in our lot, that share that we are, in the destitution of our mortality. Fate: "This is how we designate Dasein's primordial historizing, which lies in authentic resoluteness and in which Dasein *hands* itself *down* to itself [*sich . . . überliefert*], free for death, in a possibility which it has inherited and yet has chosen" (p. 435). At this level, constraints and choices merge together, as do powerlessness and all-powerfulness in the overdetermined concept of fate.

Is it true, however, that a heritage is handed down from the self to itself? Is it not always received from someone else? Yet Being-towards-death, it seems, excludes everything that is transferrable from one person to another. To which conscience adds the personal tone of a silent voice addressed from the self to itself. The difficulty is compounded when we pass from individual historicality to common history. It is then the notion of *Geschick*—common destiny—that is called upon to assure the transition, to make the leap.

The abrupt passage from an individual fate to a common destiny is made intelligible by resorting to the existential category of *Mitsein,* Being-with, which is done only too infrequently in *Being and Time.* I say only too infrequently because, in the section devoted to *Mitsein* (§§25–27), it is for the most part the deteriorated forms of everydayness that are emphasized under the category of the "they." And the conquest of the self always takes place against the background of this "they," without taking into consideration the authentic forms of communion or mutual assistance. At least the recourse to Being-with at this critical point of the analysis does authorize us to link together *Mitgeschehen* and *Geschehen,* co-historicality and historicality. This is precisely what defines a common destiny. It is, in fact, noteworthy that Heidegger, continuing here his polemic against the philosophies of the subject—and also those of intersubjectivity—contests the claim that the historicality of a community, a people (*Volk*), can be formed on the basis of individual fates. This is a transition as unacceptable as that which would conceive of Being-with-one-another as "the occurring together [*Zusammenvorkommen*] of several Subjects" (p. 436). Everything indicates that Heidegger here confines himself to suggesting the idea of a homology between communal destiny and individual fate, and to indicating the transfer of the same observations from one place to the other—the heritage of a ground of potentialities, resoluteness, etc. In so doing, he is prepared, if need be, to point to the empty place to be filled by categories more specifically suited to Being-with: struggle, combative obedience, loyalty.[27]

Setting aside these difficulties, to which we shall return in a later chapter, the central line of the entire analysis of historicality begins from the notion of stretching-along (*Ersktreckung*), follows the chain of the three semantically related concepts—history (*Geschichte*), fate (*Schicksal*), and common destiny (*Geschick*)—and then culminates in the concept of repetition (or recapitulation) (*Wiederholung*).

I should like to stress in particular the contrast between the initial term of stretching-along and the final one of repetition. It coincides exactly with the Augustinian dialectic of *distentio* and *intentio*, which I have often transcribed into the vocabulary of discordance and concordance.

Repetition (or recapitulation) is not a concept unknown to us at this stage of our reading of *Being and Time*. The analysis of temporality as a whole is, as we have seen, a repetition of the entire analytic of Dasein developed in Division One. In addition, the dominant category of temporality has received, in Chapter 4 of Division Two, a specific confirmation in its ability to repeat, feature by feature, each of the moments of the analytic of Dasein. Now we find that repetition is the name given to the process by which, on the derived level of historicality, the anticipation of the future, the recovery of fallenness, and the moment of vision (*augenblicklich*) in tune with "its time" reconstitute their unity. In one sense, the reciprocal engendering of the three ecstases of temporality, beginning with the future, contained an outline of repetition. However, inasmuch as historicality brought with it new categories stemming from *Geschehen,* and especially inasmuch as the entire analysis is shifted from the anticipation of the future toward the recovery of the past, a new concept for relating the three ecstases is required, based on the explicit theme of historicality, namely, the handing down of possibilities that are inherited and nevertheless chosen. "*Repeating is handing down explicitly*—that is to say, going back into the possibilities of the Dasein that has-been-there" (p. 437).[28]

The cardinal function of the concept of repetition is to reestablish the balance that the idea of a handed-down heritage tipped to the side of having-been, to recover the primacy of anticipatory resoluteness at the very heart of what is abolished, over and done with, what is no longer. Repetition thus opens potentialities that went unnoticed, were aborted, or were repressed in the past.[29] It opens up the past again in the direction of coming-towards. By sealing the tie between handing-down and resoluteness, the concept of repetition succeeds at once in preserving the primacy of the future and in making the shift toward having-been. This secret polarization between the heritage handed down and anticipatory resoluteness can even make repetition into a rejoinder (*erwidern*), which can go so far as to be a disavowal (*Widerruf*) of the grip of the past on the present.[30] Repetition does even more. It puts the seal of temporality on the entire chain of concepts constitutive of historicality—heritage, handing down, taking over, history, co-historicizing, fate, and destiny—and brings historicality back to its origin in temporality.[31]

The time seems to have come to pass from the theme of historicality to that of within-time-ness, which, in fact, has been continually anticipated in the preceding analyses. We must, however, pause here and take into account a quarrel that is far from marginal in relation to the overall project of *Being and Time*. This quarrel concerns the status of historiography, and more generally of the *Geisteswissenschaften*—in other words, the human sciences—in relation to the existential analytic of historicality. The place this debate occupies in German thought, principally under the influence of Dilthey, is well known. It is also well known that this problem preoccupied Heidegger before he wrote *Being and Time*. In this sense, we could say that the refutation of the claim made by the human sciences to be constituted on an autonomous basis, equal to the natural sciences, belongs to the formative core of *Being and Time,* even though the thesis that the epistemology of the human sciences is wholly subordinated to the existential analytic seems to constitute only a sort of enclave (cf. §§72, 75–77) within the general problematic of the derivation of the levels of temporalization.

Rapidly stated, the reproach leveled at a simple epistemology of the human sciences (Dilthey being the most noteworthy craftsman in this regard) is that such an epistemology grants itself an unfounded concept of pastness, by failing to ground this concept in the having-been of historicality, which makes intelligible its relation to coming-towards and making-present.[32]

Whoever does not understand "historizing," in the hermeneutical sense, does not understand "historical," in the sense of the human sciences.[33]

In particular, scholars do not understand what should be an enigma to them: that the past, which is no longer, has effects, exerts an influence, an action (*Wirkung*) on the present. This after-effect (*Nachwirkende*), which may be said to be declared only subsequently or after the fact, ought to surprise us. More precisely, our puzzlement should be directed to the notion of the remains of the past. Do we not say, of what remains of a Greek temple, that it is a "fragment of the past," that it is "still present"? The paradox of the historical past in its entirety lies here. On the one hand, it is no longer; on the other, the remains of the past hold it still present-at-hand (*Vorhanden*). The paradox of the "no longer" and the "not yet" returns with a vengeance.

It is clear that the understanding of what is meant by remains, ruins, antiquities, old equipment, and so on escapes an epistemology that has no basis in Dasein. Its past character is not written on the face of a remainder, even when it has deteriorated. Quite the opposite; however transitory it may be, it has not yet passed away, it is not yet past. This paradox attests to the fact that there is no historical object except for a being that already possesses the sense of historizing. We then come back to the question: what were, at another time, the things that we now see before us, deteriorated and yet still visible?

There is but a single solution. What is no longer is the world to which these remains belonged. But the difficulty seems only to be pushed farther back. For what does being-no-longer signify for the world? It is not stated that the "world is only in the manner of *existing* Dasein, which *factically* is as Being-in-the-world" (p. 432)? In other words, how can Being-in-the-world be conjugated in the past tense?

Heidegger's reply leaves me puzzled. According to him, the paradox strikes only those beings that fall under the category of the *vorhanden* and the *zu-handen,* concerning which we cannot understand how they can be "past," that is, no longer yet still present. However the paradox does not strike what involves Dasein because Dasein escapes the only categorization for which the past poses a problem. "A Dasein which no longer exists, however, is not past [*vergangen*], in the ontologically strict sense; it is rather 'having-been-there' [*da-gewesen*]" (ibid.). The remains of the past are remains of the past because they were equipment that belonged "to a world that has been (*da-gewesen*)— the world of a Dasein that has been there" (ibid.). Once this distinction has been made between "past" and "having-been," and once the past has been ascribed to the order of equipment, given and ready-to-hand, the path is clear for the well-known analysis of historicality, which we discussed above.

We may nevertheless wonder whether historiography has found a grounding in historicality, or whether, instead, its own problems have been simply avoided. Certainly, Heidegger was not unaware of this difficulty, and we can agree with him when he says that what is past in historical remains is the world to which they belonged. But as a result, he was forced to shift his emphasis to the term "world." It is the world of a Dasein that is said to have been there. By this shift of emphasis, the equipment we encounter in the world itself becomes historical, in a derivative sense.[34] In this way, Heidegger is led to forge the expression *weltgeschichtlich,* world-historical, to designate those beings other than Dasein that are called "historical," in the sense of historizing, due to their belonging to the world of Care. Heidegger thinks that by this he has done away with the claims of Diltheyian epistemology. "World-historical entities do not first get their historical character, let us say, by reason of a historiological Objectification; they get it rather *as those entities* which they are in themselves when they are encountered within-the-world" (p. 433).

What appears to me to be shunted aside here is precisely the problematic of the trace, in which the very characterization as historical—in the existential sense of the term—is based upon the persistence of a thing that is given and ready to hand, that is, of a physical "mark" capable of guiding a return toward the past.[35] Along with the trace, Heidegger also challenges the idea that increasing distance in time is a specific feature of history, making oldness per se the criterion of history. The notion of temporal distance too is set aside as having no primordial significance. According to Heidegger, every characterization as historical proceeds exclusively from the temporalizing of Dasein, with the reservation that the emphasis be placed on the side of the world in Being-in-the-world and that the encounter with equipment be incorporated into such Being-in-the-world.

The only way of justifying the ontological priority of historicality over historiography would be, it seems to me, to show convincingly how the latter proceeds from the former. Here we run into the greatest difficulty for any thinking about time that refers every derivative form of temporality to one primordial form, the mortal temporality of Care. This poses a major obstacle to any historical thinking. I cannot see how the repetition of possibilities inherited by each of us as a result of being thrown into the world can measure up to the scope of the historical past. Extending the notion of historizing to co-historizing, what Heidegger calls destiny (*Geschick*) provides, of course, a wider basis for having-been. But the gap between having-been and the past remains, insofar as what, in fact, opens the way for an inquiry into the past are visible remains. Everything still has to be done if this past indicated by the trace is to be integrated with the having-been of a community with a destiny. Heidegger lessens the difficulty only by attributing to the idea of the source or origin (*Herkunft*) of the derivative forms the value, not of a gradual loss of meaning, but of an increase of meaning. This enrichment, as we shall see, owes a debt to what the analysis of temporality—which is nevertheless overly marked by its reference to the most intimate feature of existence, namely, our own mortality—has borrowed from the analyses made in Division One of *Being and Time,* where the emphasis was placed on the world-pole of Being-in-the-world. This return in force of worldliness at the end of the work is not the least of the surprises to be found in the Heideggerian analytic of temporality.

This is confirmed by what follows in the text in the passage from historicality to within-time-ness.

The final sections (§§75–77) of the chapter on historicality, directed against Dilthey,[36] are too ostensibly concerned with stressing the subordination of historiography to historicality to shed any new light on the inverse problem of the passage from having-been to the historical past. The main emphasis is on the inauthenticity of the preoccupation that inclines us to understand ourselves in relation to the objects of our Care and to speak the language of the "they." To this, says Heidegger, we must obstinately reply, with all the seriousness of the hermeneutic phenomenology of Care, that the "*historizing of history is the historizing of Being-in-the-world*" (p. 440) and that with "*the existence of historical Being-in-the-world, what is ready-to-hand and what is present-at-hand have already, in every case, been incorporated into the history of the world*" (ibid.). That the historizing of equipment makes such entities autonomous deepens the enigma of pastness and of the past, for lack of any support in the historicality of Being-in-the-world, which includes the being of equipment. However, this autonomy, which gives a sort of objectivity to the processes that affect equipment, works, monuments, and the like can be understood phenomenologically through the genesis of preoccupation starting from Care, *"without being grasped historiologically"* (p. 441). The structures of fallenness, of everydayness, of anonymity, that stem from the analytic of Dasein are sufficient, Heidegger believes, to account for this misunderstanding by which we ascribe a history to things. The call to authenticity wins out over the concern to take the step from ontology to epistemology, even though the necessity to do so is not contested.[37]

However, can we inquire into "the existential source of historiology" (p. 444), can we assert that it is rooted in temporality, without traversing the path that connects them *in both directions?*

WITHIN-TIME-NESS (INNERZEITIGKEIT)

Let us close the parenthesis of this long-standing quarrel concerning the ground of the human sciences and again take up our guideline of the problematic dealing with the levels of temporalization, which forms the heart of Division Two of *Being and Time.*

By unfolding the new meanings that the phenomenological concept of time has acquired by passing from the level of pure temporality to that of historicality, have we given to temporality itself the concrete fullness that it has continually lacked since the start of our analyses?[38] Just as the analysis of temporality remains incomplete without the derivation—which itself creates new categories—that leads to the idea of historicality, so too historicality has not been completely thought out so long as it has not in turn been completed by the idea of within-time-ness, which is, nonetheless, derived from it.[39]

The chapter entitled "Temporality and Within-time-ness as the Source of the Ordinary Conception of Time" (p. 456) is, in fact, far from constituting a pale echo of the existential analysis of temporality. It too shows a philosopher with his back to the wall. Two distinct questions are raised: in what way is within-time-ness—that is, all of the experiences through which time is designated as that "in which" events occur—still connected to fundamental temporality? In what way does this derivation constitute the origin of the ordinary concept of time? As closely related as they may be, these questions are distinct. One raises the problem of derivation, the other that of leveling off. What is at stake in both questions is whether the duality between the time of the soul and cosmic time (our Chapter 1) and the duality between phenomenological time and objective time (our Chapter 2) are finally overcome in an analytic of Dasein.

Let us concentrate our attention on the aspects of within-time-ness that recall its source (*Herkunft*), starting from primordial temporality. The pivotal expression used by Heidegger to indicate the double aspect of dependence and innovation with respect to this source is that of "reckoning with [*Rechnen mit*] time," which has the advantage of announcing the leveling off by means of which the idea of reckoning (*Rechnung*) will win out in the ordinary representation of time and contain within itself traces of its phenomenological origin, which are still accessible to existential interpretation.[40] As we go over these traces, they will progressively reveal the originality of this mode of temporalization and, at the same time, pave the way for the thesis concerning the leveling off of within-time-ness in the common representation of time, in that the most original features of within-time-ness, apparently, are simply those that possess a more deeply concealed origin.

With respect to an initial group of features, the source is easy to discern. "Reckoning with" is first of all to highlight the world-time that was already mentioned in discussing historicality. World-time moves to the foreground once we shift our emphasis to the mode of being of the things we encounter "in" the world: present-at-hand (*vorhanden*), ready-to-hand (*zuhanden*). One whole side of the structure of Being-in-the-world in this way reminds analysis that the priority accorded to Being-towards-death was in danger of tipping the balance to the side of interiority. It is time to recall that if Dasein does not know itself in accordance with the categories of presence-to-hand and readiness-to-hand, Dasein is in the world only through the commerce it maintains with these things, and their categorization must not be forgotten in turn. Dasein exists alongside (*bei*) the things of the world, just as it exists with (*mit*) others. This Being-alongside, in turn, recalls the condition of thrownness that constitutes the reverse side of every project and underscores the primordial passivity against which all understanding stands out, an understanding that is always "in a given situation." In fact, the dimension of being-affected was never sacrificed in the earlier analyses to that of being-projected, as the deduction of the three ecstases of time amply demonstrated. The present analysis underscores the legitimacy of this demonstration. Shifting the emphasis to "thrownness alongside" has as its corollary the importance attributed to the third temporal ecstasis, upon which the analysis of time as the time of a project, hence as future, cast a sort of suspicion. Being alongside the things of our concern, is to live Care as "preoccupation" (*besorgen*). With preoccupation, what predominates is the ecstasis of the present or rather of enpresenting, in the sense of making present (*gegenwärtigen*). With preoccupation, the present is finally given its due. Augustine and Husserl started from it, Heidegger ends up there. At this point, consequently, their analyses intersect. Heidegger by no means denies that, on this level, it is legitimate to reorganize the relations among the three ecstases of time around the pivot point of the present. Only someone who says "today" can also speak of what will happen "then" and of what has to be done "before," whether it is a matter of plans, of impediments, or of precautions; only this being can speak of what, having failed or escaped attention, took place "before" and must succeed "now."

Simplifying a great deal, we can say that preoccupation places the accent on the present, just as primordial temporality placed it on the future and historicality on the past. However, as the deduction of each of the ecstases of temporality from the others has shown, the present is understood existentially only last of all. We know why. By restoring the legitimacy of the within-the-world surroundings of Dasein, we risk yoking the understanding of Dasein once again to the categories of what is present-at-hand and what is ready-to-hand, categories under which, according to Heidegger, metaphysics has always tried to classify things, up to the distinction between the psychical and the physical. We are all the more in danger of doing just this when the swing of the scale that shifts the emphasis to the "world" of Being-in-the-world makes the things of our concern outweigh Being-in-Care.

This is where the leveling off, which we shall discuss below, begins.

After this group of descriptive features, whose "source" is relatively easy to uncover, the analysis moves to a group of three characteristics that are precisely those that the ordinary conception of time has leveled off. They therefore occupy a key position in the analysis, at the intersection point of the problematic of the source and the problematic of derivation (§80).

Given the framework of the discussion that will follow, we cannot be too attentive to the innovation in meaning that gives this derivation a productive character.

The three characteristics in question are named: datability, lapse of time, and publicness.

Datability is connected to "reckoning with time," which is said to precede actual calculation. It is likewise affirmed here that datability precedes the assigning of dates; in other words, actual calendar dating. Datability proceeds from the relational structure of primordial time, when it is referred to the present, forgetting the primacy of the reference to the future. Every event is datable, once it is located in relation to a "now." We can then say either that it has "not yet" occurred and that it will occur "later," "then," or that it exists "no longer" and occurred "earlier." In contrast to what we may believe, this relational structure—the same one on which the Augustinian analysis of the threefold present and the Husserlian analysis of retention-protention are based—is not understandable in and of itself. We must move from the "now" as absolute in some sense to the "now that . . . ," to which are added the "when" and the "before," in order to find the phenomenological meaning of this interplay of relations. In short, we must return to the Being-alongside that connects preoccupation to the things of the world. When we speak of time as a system of dates organized in relation to a point of time taken as an origin, we quite simply forget the work of interpretation by which we moved from making-present, including all that it awaits and all that it retains, to the idea of an indifferent "now." The task of hermeneutic phenomenology, in speaking of datability rather than of dates, consists in reactivating this work of interpretation that is concealed and is itself annihilated in the representation of time as a system of dates.[41] By reactivating this work, the existential analytic restores both the ecstatic character of the "now," that is, its belonging to the network of coming-towards, having-been, and making-present, and its character of having a horizon, that is, the reference of "now that . . ." to the entities encountered in the world by reason of the constitution of being-alongside, which is characteristic of preoccupation. Dating "always" occurs in relation to the beings encountered by reason of the opening of the "there."

The second original feature of within-time-ness is the consideration of the laspe of time, of the interval between a "since then" and an "until," generated by the relations between "now," "then," and "before" (an interval that, in turn, produces a second-order datability: "while . . ."). "During" this lapse of time, things have their time, do their time, what we ordinarily call "lasting" or "enduring." What we find again here is the stretching-along (*Erstrecktheit*) characteristic of historicality, but interpreted in the idiom of preoccupation. By being connected to datability, stretching-along becomes a lapse of time. In turn, the notion of an interval, referred back to that of a date, produces the idea that we can assign a temporal extension to every "now," to every "then," to every "before," as when we say "during the meal" (now), "last spring" (before), "next fall" (then). The question of the extension of the present, which is so troublesome for psychologists, finds its origin, and the origin of its obscurity, here.

It is in terms of a lapse of time that we "allow" an amount of time, that we "employ" our day well or poorly, forgetting that it is not time that is used up, but our preoccupation itself, which, by losing itself among the things of its concern, loses its time as well. Anticipatory resoluteness alone escapes the dilemma: always having time or not having time. It alone makes the isolated now an authentic instant, a moment of vision (*Augenblick*), which does not claim to control things but contents itself with "constancy" (*Ständigkeit*). From this constancy comes the self-constancy (*Selbst-Ständigkeit*) that embraces future, past, and present, and fuses the activity expended by Care with the original passivity of a Being-thrown-in-the-world.[42] The final original feature is that the time of preoccupation is a public time. Here again we are misled by false appearances. In itself, time has nothing public about it; behind this feature is concealed everyday understanding—the average understanding of being-with-one-another. Public time results then from an interpretation that is grafted on this everyday understanding which, in a sense, "publicizes" time, "makes it public," to the extent that the everyday condition no longer reaches making-present except through an anonymous and commonplace "now."

It is on the basis of these three features of within-time-ness—datability, lapse of time, and public time—that Heidegger attempts to rejoin what we call time and to lay the groundwork for his final thesis concerning the leveling off of the existential analysis in the ordinary conception of time.[43] This is the time of preoccupation, but interpreted in terms of the things alongside which our concern makes us reside. In this way, reckoning and measuring, valid for things present-at-hand and ready-to-hand, come to be applied to this datable, extended, public time. For example, reckoning astronomical and calendar time arises from dating in relation to repeated occurrences of our environment. The anteriority that this reckoning appears to have in relation to the public datability of within-time-ness can be explained once again by the thrownness that permeates Care.[44] It is therefore insofar as we are affected that astronomical and calendar time appear autonomous and primary. Time then swings back to the side of beings other than the one that we are, and we begin to wonder, as did ancient thinkers, whether time *is,* or, as do modern ones, whether it is subjective or objective.

The reversal that appears to give an anteriority to time in relation to Care itself is the final link in a chain of interpretations that are but so many misinterpretations. First, the prevalence of preoccupation in the structure of Care; next, the interpretation of the temporal features of preoccupation in terms of the things alongside which Care stands; finally, forgetting this interpretation itself, which makes the measurement of time appear to belong to things present-at-hand and ready-to-hand themselves. The quantifying of time then appears to be independent of the temporality of Care. The time "in" which we ourselves are is understood as the receptacle of things present-to-hand and ready-to-hand. What is particularly forgotten is the condition of thrownness, as a structure of Being-in-the-world.

It is possible to catch sight of the moment when this is first forgotten, and of the reversal that results from it, in the relation that circumspection (another name for preoccupation) maintains with visibility and that visibility maintains with the light of day.[45] In this way, a sort of secret pact is concluded between the sun and Care, in which light serves as the intermediary. We say, "As long as daylight remains," "for two days," "for the past three days," "in four days."

If the calendar is the computation of days, the clock is that of hours and their subdivisions. But the hour is not tied in such a visible way to our preoccupation as the day is, and through this preoccupation to our thrownness. The sun does in fact appear on the horizon of things present-at-hand. The derivation of the hour is thus more indirect. Yet it is not impossible, if we keep in mind that the things of our concern are in part things ready-to-hand. The clock is the thing ready-to-hand that permits us to add a precise measurement to exact dating. In addition, this measurement completes the process of making time public. The need for such precision in measuring is inscribed in the dependence of preoccupation with respect to what is ready-to-hand in general. The analyses at the beginning of *Being and Time* devoted to the worldhood of the world have prepared us to seek in the structure of significance that connects our instruments together, and that connects all of them to our preoccupation, a reason for the proliferation of artificial clocks on the basis of natural ones. In this way, the connection between scientific time and the time of pre-occupation becomes ever more tenuous and more deeply concealed, until the apparently complete autonomy of the measurement of time in relation to the fundamental structure of Being-in-the-world constitutive of Care is affirmed. If hermeneutic phenomenology has nothing to say about the epistemological aspects of the history of the measurement of time, it does take an interest in the direction this history has taken in loosening the ties between this measurement and the process of temporalization in which Dasein is the pivot point. At the end of this emancipation, there is no longer any difference between following the course of time and following the movement of the hands on the face of a clock. "Reading the hour" on clocks that are more and more precise seems no longer to have any connection with the act of "saying now"—an act itself rooted in the phenomenon of reckoning with time. The history of the measurement of time is that of forgetting all the interpretations traversed by making-present. At the end of this forgetting, time itself is identified with a series of ordinary and anonymous nows.[46]

In this way, we have followed the derivation of within-time-ness—in other words, we have brought to light its origin (*Herkunft*)—up to the point where the successive interpretations, quickly changed into misinterpretations, give time a transcendence equal to that of the world.[47]

Before taking up the polemic leveled by the existential interpretation of within-time-ness against the ordinary representation of time, I want to acknowledge the advance that Heidegger's hermeneutic phenomenology has made over those of Augustine and Husserl.

In one sense, the debate between Husserl and Kant is rendered obsolete—in the same sense that the opposition between subject and object is. On the one hand, world-time is more "objective" than any object, in that it accompanies the revelation of the world as world. As a result, it is no more tied to psychical beings than to physical ones. " 'Time' first shows itself in the sky" (p. 471). On the other hand, it is more "subjective" than any subject because of its being rooted in Care.

The debate between Augustine and Aristotle appears even more obsolete. On the one hand, in contrast to Augustine, the time of the soul is also a world-time, and its interpretation requires no refutation of cosmology. On the other hand, in contrast to Aristotle, it is no longer a troublesome question to ask whether time can exist if there is no soul to distinguish between two instants and to count the intervals.

However new aporias are born from this very advance in hermeneutic phenomenology.

They are revealed by the failure of the polemic against the ordinary concept of time, a failure that, by a recoil-effect, helps to bring to light the aporetic character of this hermeneutic phenomenology itself, stage by stage, and as a whole.

The Ordinary Concept of Time

Heidegger places his polemic against the ordinary concept of time under the heading of "leveling off," never to be confused with the discussion of the "source," even if this leveling off is induced by forgetting the source. This polemic constitutes a critical point, much more dangerous than Heidegger might have thought, preoccupied as he was during this period with another polemic over the human sciences. In this way, he can claim, without qualms, not to distinguish the scientific concept of universal time from the ordinary concept of time that he is criticizing.

His argumentation directed against ordinary time makes no concessions. Its ambition is no less than a genesis without remainder of the concept of time as it is employed in all the sciences starting from fundamental temporality. This genesis is a genesis progressing by leveling off, taking its point of departure in within-time-ness, but one whose far-off origin lies in the failure to recognize the tie between temporality and Being-towards-death. Starting from within-time-ness has the obvious advantage of making the ordinary concept of time first appear in greatest proximity to the last decipherable figure of phenomenological time. But, more importantly, it has the advantage of organizing the ordinary concept of time around the pivotal notion whose kinship with the principal characteristic of within-time-ness is still apparent. This pivotal notion is the point-like "now." As a consequence, ordinary time can be characterized as a series of point-like "nows," whose intervals are measured by our clocks. Like the hand moving across the face of the clock, time runs from one now to another. Defined in this way, time deserves to be called "now-time." "The world-time which is 'sighted' in this manner in the use of clocks, we call the 'now-time' [*Jetzt-Zeit*]" (p. 474).

The genesis of the point-like "now" is clear. It is merely a disguise of the making-present that awaits and withholds, that is, the third ecstasis of temporality, which preoccupation brought to the fore. In this disguise, the instrument of measurement, which is one of the things ready-to-hand upon which we fix our circumspection, has eclipsed the process of making-present that had made measurement desirable.

Starting from here, the three major features of within-time-ness are subjected to an identical leveling off. Datability no longer precedes the assigning of dates but rather follows it; the lapse of time, which itself arises from the stretching out characteristic of historicality, no longer precedes the measurable interval but rather is governed by it; and, above all else, the character of making-public, founded in the "being-with" relating mortals to one another, gives way to the allegedly irreducible characteristic of time, its universality. Time is held to be public because it is declared to be universal. In short, time is defined as a system of dates only because dating takes place on the basis of an origin that is an indistinguishable "now." It is defined as a series of intervals. Universal time, in the end, is only the sequence (*Folge*) of these point-like "nows" (*Jetztfolge*).

Other features of the ordinary concept of time only appear, however, if we retrace the genesis of a contemporary failure to recognize the most original temporality. As we know, phenomenology must be hermeneutic because what is closest to us is also what is most covered over. The features we are going to look at all have in common the fact that they serve as symptoms, in the sense that they allow us to glimpse an origin at the same time that they attest to the failure to recognize this origin. Consider the infinity of time. It is because we have erased from our thoughts originary finiteness, imprinted on time to come by Being-towards-death, that we hold time to be infinite.[48] In this sense, infinity is but a fallen state of the finiteness of the future attested to by anticipatory resoluteness. Infinity is non-mortality; but what does not die is the "they." Thanks to this immortality of the "they," our thrownness among things present-at-hand and ready-to-hand is perverted by the idea that our life span is only a fragment of this time.[49]

One indication that this is how things are is that we say of time that it "flies." Is this not because we fly from ourselves, in the face of death, because the state of loss in which we sink, when we no longer perceive the relation between thrownness, fallenness, and preoccupation, makes time appear as a flight and makes us say that it passes away (*vergeht*)? Otherwise, why would we notice the fleeing of time rather than its blossoming forth? Is this not something like a return of the repressed, by which our fleeing in the face of death is disguised as the fleeing of time? And why do we say that we cannot stop time? Is this not because our fleeing in the face of death makes us want to suspend the course of time, by an understandable perversion of our anticipation in its least authentic form? "*Dasein knows fugitive time in terms of its 'fugitive' knowledge about its death*" (p. 478). And why do we consider time to be irreversible? Here again leveling off does not prevent some aspect of the originary from showing through. Would not a neutral stream of "nows" be able to be reversed? "The impossibility of this reversal has its basis in the way public time originates in temporality, the temporalizing of which is primarily futural and 'goes' to its end ecstatically in such a way that it 'is' already towards its end" (p. 478).

Heidegger by no means denies that this ordinary representation is valid in its own right, to the very extent that it proceeds by leveling off the temporality of a thrown and fallen Dasein. This representation belongs, in its own way, to the everyday mode of Dasein and to the understanding that is appropriate to it.[50] The only thing unacceptable is the claim that this representation be held to be the true concept of time. We can retrace the process of interpretation and of misunderstanding that leads from temporality to this ordinary concept. The opposite route, however, cannot be traveled.

My doubts begin precisely at this point. If, as I believe, human temporality cannot be constituted on the basis of a concept of time considered as a series of "nows," is not the opposite path, from temporality and Dasein to cosmic time, in accordance with the preceding discussion, just as impracticable?

In the preceding analysis, one hypothesis was excluded from the outset by Heidegger: that the process held to be a phenomenon of the leveling off of temporality was also, and simultaneously, the separating out of an autonomous concept of time—cosmic time—that hermeneutic phenomenology never completely follows through on and with which it never manages to come to terms.

If Heidegger excludes this hypothesis from the beginning, it is because he never tries to vie with contemporary science in its own debate over time, and because he takes it for granted that science has nothing original to say that has not been tacitly borrowed from metaphysics, from Plato to Hegel. The role assigned to Aristotle in the genesis of the ordinary concept of time (p. 473) bears witness to this. Aristotle is supposed to be the first one guilty of this leveling off, confirmed by the entire subsequent history of the problem of time, through the definition given in *Physics* IV, 11, 218b29–219a6, which we examined above.[51] His assertion that the instant determines time is said to have begun the series of definitions of time as a sequence of "nows," in the sense of indistinguishable instants.

Even given the—highly debatable—hypothesis that the entire metaphysics of time might be contained *in nuce* in the Aristotelian conception of it,[52] the lesson we have drawn from our reading of the famous passage in Aristotle's *Physics* is that there is no conceivable transition—either in one direction or the other—between indistinguishable, anonymous instants and the lived-through present. Aristotle's strength lies precisely in the fact that he describes the instant as any instant whatsoever. And the instant is anonymous precisely in that it precedes from an arbitrary break in the continuity of local motion, and more generally of change, and indicates the occurrence (lacking the quality of the present) in each movement of the imperfect act constituted by the act of power. Movement (change) belongs, as we have seen, to the principles of physics, which do not include in their definition a reference to a soul that discriminates and counts. What is essential, therefore, is, first, that time have "something to do with movement," without ever measuring up to the constitutive principles of nature; next, that the continuity of time "accompanies" that of movement and of magnitude, without ever freeing itself entirely from them. The result is that, if the noetic operation of discrimination by which the mind distinguishes two "nows" is sufficient to distinguish time from movement, this operation is grafted onto the sheer unfolding of movement whose numerable character precedes the distinctions relative to time. The logical and ontological anteriority that Aristotle assigns to movement in relation to time seems to me to be incompatible with any attempt at derivation through the leveling off of so-called ordinary time, starting from the time of concern. Having something to do with movement and something to do with Care seem to me to constitute two irreconcilable determinations in principle. "World-historicizing" merely hides the gap between the present and the instant. I fail to understand either how or why the historicality of the things of our concern should free itself from that of our Care, unless the world-pole of our Being-in-the-world developed a time that was itself the polar opposite of the time of our Care, and unless the rivalry between these two perspectives on time, the one rooted in the worldhood of the world, the other in the there of our way of Being-in-the-world, gave rise to the ultimate aporia of the question of time for thinking.

This equal legitimacy of ordinary time and phenomenological time at the heart of their confrontation is confirmed with particular emphasis if, instead of just confining ourselves to what philosophers have said about time—following Aristotle or not—we lend an ear to what the scientists and epistemologists most attentive to modern developments in the theory of time have to say.[53] The very expression "ordinary time" then appears ridiculous compared to the scope of problems posed to science by the orientation, continuity, and measurability of time.[54] In light of this increasingly more technical work, I am led to wonder whether a single scientific concept can be opposed to the phenomenological analyses, which are themselves multiple, received from Augustine, Husserl, and Heidegger.

If, first of all, following Stephen Toulmin and June Goodfield, we limit ourselves to classifying sciences according to the order of the discovery of the "historical" dimension of the natural world, we find that it is not only a progressive extension of the scale of time beyond the barrier of six thousand years, assigned by a petrified Judeo-Christian tradition, that the natural sciences have imposed on our consideration, but also an increasing differentiation of the temporal properties characteristic of each of the regions of nature open to an ever more stratified natural history.[55] This feature—the extension of the scale of time from six thousand to six billion years—is certainly not to be neglected if we consider the unbelievable resistance that had to be overcome for it to be recognized. If breaking this barrier of time was the source of so much consternation, this was because it brought to light a disproportion, easily translated in terms of incommensurability, between human time and the time of nature.[56] At first, it was the discovery of organic fossils in the final decades of the seventeenth century that, in opposition to a static conception of the earth's crust, imposed a dynamic conception of geological change, whose chronology dramatically pushed back the barrier of time. With the acknowledgment of such geological changes and the explanation of their temporal sequence, "the earth acquires a history."[57] On the basis of material traces, fossils, strata, faults, it became possible to infer the succession of the "epochs of nature," to borrow the title used by Buffon. The science of stratification, invented at the beginning of the nineteenth century, decisively transformed geology into a "historical" science, on the basis of inferences made from the witness of things. This "historical" revolution, in turn, opened the way, through the intermediary of paleontology, for a similar transformation in zoology, crowned in 1859 by Darwin's great work *Origin of Species*. We can only dimly imagine the enormous mass of received ideas that was to be dislodged by the simple hypothesis of an evolution of species, to say nothing of the degree of probability of the theory as such, whether we consider the mode of acquisition, or of transmission, or of accumulation of specific variations. What is important for our discussion is that, with Darwin, "life acquires a genealogy." [58] For the Darwinian or neo-Darwinian biologist, time is indistinguishable from the very process of descent, marked by the occurence of favorable variations and sealed by natural selection. The whole of modern genetics is inscribed within the major assumption of a history of life. This idea of a natural history was further to be enriched by the discoveries of thermodynamics, and, above all, by the discovery of subatomic processes—in particular, quantum processes—on the other end of the great chain of beings. To the extent that these phenomena are in turn responsible for the formation of heavenly bodies, we can speak of "stellar evolution" [59] to account for the life cycle assigned to individual stars and galaxies. A genuine temporal dimension was thereby introduced into astronomy, one that authorizes us to speak of the age of the universe counted in light-years.

However this first feature—the breaking of the temporal barrier accepted for thousands of years and the fabulous extension of the scale of time—must not mask a second feature, one of even greater philosophical significance, namely, the diversification in the meanings attached to the term "time" in the regions of nature we have just referred to and in the sciences that correspond to them. This phenomenon is masked by the previous one to the extent that the notion of a scale of time introduces an abstract factor of commensurability that takes into account only the comparative chronology of the processes considered. The fact that this alignment along a single scale of time is ultimately misleading is attested to by the following paradox. The length of time of a human life, compared to the range of cosmic time-spans, appears insignificant, whereas it is the very place from which every question of significance arises. [60] This paradox suffices to call into question the presumed homogeneity of time-spans projected along a single notion of a natural "history" (whence our constant use of quotation marks in this context). Everything occurs as if, through a phenomenon of mutual contamination, the notion of history had been extrapolated from the human sphere to the natural sphere, while, in return, the notion of change, specified on the zoological level by that of evolution, had included human history within its perimeter of meaning. Yet, before any ontological argument, we have an epistemological reason for refusing this reciprocal overlapping of the notions of change (or evolution) and history.

This criterion is the one we expressed in Part II of this study, namely, the narrative criterion, itself patterned on that of praxis, every narrative being ultimately a mimesis of action. On this point, I unreservedly ascribe to Collingwood's thesis drawing a line between the notions of change and evolution on the one hand, and history on the other.[61] In this respect, the notion of the "testimony" of human beings concerning events of the past and the "testimony" of the vestiges of the geological past does not go beyond the mode of proof; that is, the use of inferences in the form of retrodiction. Misuse begins as soon as the notion of "testimony" is severed from the narrative context that supports it as documentary proof in service of the explanatory comprehension of a course of action. It is finally the concepts of action and narrative that cannot be transferred from the human sphere to the sphere of nature.

This epistemological hiatus is, in turn, but the symptom of a discontinuity on the level that interests us here, that of the time of the phenomena considered. Just as it seemed impossible to generate the time of nature on the basis of phenomenological time, so too it now seems impossible to proceed in the opposite direction and to include phenomenological time in the time of nature, whether it is a question of quantum time, thermodynamic time, the time of galactic transformations, or that of the evolution of species. Without deciding anything about the plurality of temporalities appropriate to the variety of epistemological regions considered, a single distinction—an altogether negative one—is sufficient, that between a time without a present and a time with a present. Regardless of the positive aspects included in the notion of a time without a present, one discontinuity is of the utmost importance to our discussion of phenomenological time, the very one that Heidegger tried to overcome by gathering together under the heading of "ordinary time" all the temporal varieties previously aligned under the neutral concept of the scale of time. Whatever the interferences between the time with a present and the time without a present, they presuppose the fundamental distinction between an anonymous instant and a present defined by the instance of discourse that designates this present reflexively. This fundamental distinction between the anonymous instant and the self-referential present entails that between the pair before/after and the pair past/future, the latter designating the before/after relation as it is marked by the instance of the present.[62]

The outcome of this discussion is that the autonomy of time with respect to movement (to employ a vocabulary that is Kantian as well as Aristotelian) constitutes the ultimate aporia for the phenomenology of time—an aporia that only the hermeneutical conversion of phenomenology could reveal in its radicality. For it is when the phenomenology of time reaches those aspects of temporality that are most deeply hidden, even though they are closest to us, that it discovers its external limit.

For someone who is attracted wholly to the polemic that Heidegger has undertaken, by designating ordinary time the universal time of astronomy, the physical sciences, biology, and, finally, the human sciences, and by attributing the genesis of this alleged ordinary time to the leveling off of the aspects of phenomenological time, for this sort of reader *Being and Time* appears to end in failure—the failure of the genesis of the ordinary concept of time. This is not, however, how I should like to conclude. This "failure," in my opinion, is what brings the aporetic character of temporality to its peak. It sums up the failure of all our thinking about time, and first and foremost that of phenomenology and of science. But this failure is not without value, as the rest of this work will attempt to show. And even before it refuels our own meditation, it reveals something of its fruitfulness insofar as it serves to uncover what I will call the work of the aporia active within the existential analysis itself.

I will group my remarks on this work of the aporia around four poles.

1. It is first of all the "ordinary" concept of time that, from the outset, exerts a sort of attraction-repulsion on the whole existential analysis, forcing it to unfold, to distend itself, to stretch itself out until it corresponds, by an ever-increasing approximation, to its other which it cannot generate. In this sense, as it were, the external aporia that develops in the concept of time, due to the disparity among perspectives on time, is what provokes, at the very heart of the existential analysis, the greatest effort at internal diversification, to which we owe the distinction between temporality, historicality, and within-time-ness. Without being the origin of this diversification, the scientific concept acts as a sort of catalyst for it. The admirable analyses of historicality and within-time-ness then appear as an almost desperate effort to enrich the temporality of Care, centered first on Being-for-death, with ever more worldly features, so as to offer an approximate equivalence of sequential time within the limits of existential interpretation.

2. In addition to the constraint exerted from outside by the ordinary concept of time on the existential analysis, we can speak of a mutual overlapping between one mode of discourse and the other. This borderline exchange takes on the extreme forms of contamination and conflict, with the whole parade of intellectual and emotional nuances that can be produced by these interferences of meaning.

Contamination has more particularly to do with the overlappings on the level of within-time-ness. These phenomena of contamination are what served to legitimate the idea that the border was crossed as a result of leveling off alone. We anticipated this problem when we discussed the relations between the three major phenomena of datability, lapse of time, publicness, and the three conceptual features of actual dating, the measurement of intervals by fixed units of duration, and simultaneity, which serves as a criterion for all co-historicality.[63] In all these cases, we may speak of an overlapping of the existential and the empirical.[64] Between thrownness and fallenness, which constitute our fundamental passivity with regard to time, and the contemplation of the stars, whose sovereign revolution is not subject to our mastery, a complicity is established, one so close that the two approaches become indiscernible to feeling. This is attested to by the expressions "world-time" and "Being-in-time," which compound the strength of both discourses on time.

In return, the effect of conflict, stemming from the interference between our two modes of thinking, can be more easily distinguished at the other end of the scale of temporality; it is the conflict between the finitude of mortal time and the infinity of cosmic time. In truth, it was to this aspect that ancient wisdom was most attentive. Elegies on the human condition, ranging in their modulations from lamentation to resignation, have never ceased to sing of the contrast between the time that remains and we who are merely passing. It is only the "they" that never dies? If we hold time to be infinite, is this only because we are concealing our own finitude from ourselves? And if we say that time flies, is this simply because we are fleeing the idea of our Being-towards-the-end? Is it not also because we observe in the course of things a passage that flees us, in the sense that it escapes our hold, to the point of being unaware, as it were, even of our resolution to pay no attention to the fact that we have to die? Would we speak of the shortness of life, if it did not stand out against the immensity of time? This contrast is the most eloquent form that can be taken by the twofold movement of detachment whereby the time of Care, on the one hand, tears itself away from the fascination with the carefree time of the world and, on the other hand, astronomical and calendar time frees itself from the goad of immediate concern and even from the thought of death. Forgetting the relation between the ready-to-hand and concern, and forgetting death, we contemplate the sky and we construct calendars and clocks. And suddenly, on the face of one of them, the words *memento mori* stand out in mournful letters. One forgetfulness erases another. And the anguish of death returns once more, goaded on by the eternal silence of infinite spaces. We can thus swing from one feeling to the other: from the consolation that we may experience in discovering a kinship between the feeling of Being-thrown-into-the-world and the spectacle of the heavens where time shows itself, to the desolation that unceasingly reemerges from the contrast between the fragility of life and the power of time, which is more destructive than anything else.

3. In turn, the difference between these two extreme forms of a borderline exchange between the two perspectives on time makes us attentive to the polarities, the tensions, even the breaks inside the domain explored by hermeneutic phenomenology. If the derivation of the ordinary concept of time by means of leveling off appeared problematical, the derivation by means of their source, which ties together the three figures of temporality, also deserves to be questioned. We have not failed to emphasize, at the transition from one stage to the next, the complexity of this relation to the "source," which is not confined to a gradual loss of authenticity. By their supplement of meaning, historicality and within-time-ness add what was lacking in the meaning of fundamen-

tal temporality for it to be fully primordial and for it to attain its wholeness, its *Ganzheit.* If each level arises from the preceding one by reason of an interpretation that is at the same time a misinterpretation, a forgetting of the "source," it is because this "source" consists not in a reduction but in a production of meaning. The world-time through which hermeneutic phenomenology approaches astronomical and physical science is revealed by a final surplus of meaning. The conceptual style of this creative source leads to a certain number of consequences that accentuate the aporetical character of the part dealing with temporality in *Being and Time.*

First consequence: when the accent is placed on the two end-points in this increase in meaning, Being-towards-death and world-time, we discover a polar opposition, paradoxically concealed throughout the hermeneutical process directed against all concealment: mortal time on the one side, cosmic time on the other. This faultline, which runs through the entire analysis, in no way constitutes a refutation of it; it merely makes the analysis less sure of itself, more problematic—in a word, more aporetic.

Second consequence: if, from one temporal figure to the next, there is both a loss of authenticity and an increase in primordiality, could not the order in which these three figures are examined be reversed? In fact, within-time-ness is continually presupposed by historicality. Without the notions of datability, lapse of time, and public manifestation, historicality could not be said to unfold between a beginning and an end, to stretch along in this in-between, and to become the co-historizing of a common destiny. The calendar and the clock bear witness to this. And if we follow historicality back to primordial temporality, how could the public character of the historizing fail to precede in its own manner the most radical temporality, inasmuch as its interpretation itself comes out of language, which has always preceded the forms of Being-towards-death reputed to be untransferrable? Even more radically, does not the *Ausser-sich* of originary temporality indicate the recoil-effect of the structures of world-time on those of originary temporality through the intermediary of the stretching-along characteristic of historicality?[65]

Final consequence: if we are attentive to the discontinuities that mark the process of the genesis of meaning throughout the section on time in *Being and Time,* we may ask whether hermeneutic phenomenology does not give rise to a deep-rooted dispersion of the figures of temporality. By adding to the break, on the level of epistemology, between phenomenological time on the one hand and astronomical, physical, and biological time on the other, the split between mortal time, historical time, and cosmic time attests in an unexpected way to the plural, or rather pluralizing, vocation of this hermeneutic phenomenology. Heidegger himself paves the way for this interrogation when he states that the three degrees of temporalization are equiprimordial, expressly taking up again an expression he had earlier applied to the three ecstases of time. But if they are equiprimordial, the future does not necessarily have the priority that the existential analysis of Care confers on it. The future, the past, and the present each has a turn to predominate when we pass from one level to another. In this sense, the debate between Augustine, who starts from the present, and Heidegger, who starts from the future, loses much of its sharpness. What is more, the variety of functions assumed by our experience of the present warns us against the arbitrary restrictions of a too one-sided concept of the present. Despite the one-way filiation that Heidegger proposes, moving from the future toward the past and toward the present, and also despite the apparently univocal descending order governing the source of the least authentic figures of temporality, the process of temporalization appears at the end of the section on time to be more radically differentiated than it seemed to be at the start of the analysis. For it is in fact the differentiation of the three figures of temporalization—temporality, historicality, and within-time-ness—that displays and makes more explicit the secret differentiation by virtue of which the future, the past, and the present can be called the ecstases of time.

4. The attention paid to the aporias that are at work in the section on temporality in *Being and Time* warrants our casting one last look at the place of historicality in the hermeneutic phenomenology of time.

The position of the chapter on historicality between the chapter on fundamental temporality and the one on within-time-ness is the most obvious indication of a mediating function that far surpasses the convenience of a didactic exposition. The range of this mediating function is equal to that of the field of aporias opened up by the hermeneutic phenomenology of time. By following the order of the questions raised above, we may first ask ourselves whether history is not itself constructed on the fracture line between phenomenological time and astronomical, physical, and biological time—in short, whether history is not itself a fracture zone. But if, as we have also suggested, the overlappings of meaning compensate for this epistemological break, is not history the place where the overlappings due to the contamination and the conflict between the two orders of thinking are most clearly manifested? On the one hand, the exchanges due to contamination appeared to us to predominate on the level of within-time-ness between the phenomena of datability, lapse of time, and publicness as they are brought out by the existential analysis, and the astronomical considerations that governed the construction of calendars and clocks. This contamination cannot help but affect history to the extent that it gathers together the characteristics of historicality and those of within-time-ness. On the hand, exchanges due to conflict appeared to us to predominate on the level of primordial temporality, as soon as Being-towards-death is cruelly contrasted with the time that envelops us. Here again, history is indirectly involved to the extent that, in it, the memory of the dead clashes with the investigation of institutions, structures, and transformations that are stronger than death.

However, the median position of the historical between temporality and within-time-ness is more directly a problem when we pass from the borderline conflicts between phenomenology and cosmology to the discordances within phenomenological hermeneutics itself. What are we to say, finally, about the position of historical time, set between mortal time and cosmological time? It is in fact when the continuity of the existential analysis is questioned that historicality becomes the critical point of the entire undertaking. The greater the distance between the compass points marking the two poles of temporalization, the more the place and role of historicality become problematical. The more we inquire into the differentiation that disperses, not just the three major figures of temporalization, but the three ecstases of time, the more the site of historicality becomes problematical. From this perplexity springs a hypothesis: if within-time-ness is the point of contact between our passivity and the order of things, then might historicality not be the bridge that is erected within the phenomenological field itself between Being-towards-death and world-time? It will be the task of the chapters that follow to clarify this mediating function by taking up once more the three-cornered conversation among historiography, narratology, and phenomenology.

At the end of these three confrontations I would like to draw two conclusions. The first one has been anticipated a number of times; the second may have remained unperceived.

Let us first say that, if the phenomenology of time can become one privileged interlocutor in the three-way conversation we are about to undertake among phenomenology, historiography, and literary narratology, this is a result not just of its discoveries but also of the aporias it gives rise to, which increase in proportion to its advances.

Let us next say that in opposing Aristotle to Augustine, Kant to Husserl, and everything scholarship ties to the "ordinary" concept of time to Heidegger, we have undertaken a process that is no longer that of phenomenology, the process the reader may have expected to find here, but rather a process that is one of reflective, speculative throught as a whole in its search for a coherent answer to the question: what is time? If, in stating an aporia, we emphasized the phenomenology of time, what emerges at the end of this chapter is a broader and more balanced insight—namely, that we cannot think about cosmological time (the instant) without surreptitiously appealing to phenomenological time and vice versa. If the statement of this aporia outruns phenomenology, this aporia thereby has the great merit of resituating phenomenology within the great current of reflective and speculative thought. This is why I did not title this first section of this volume "The Aporias of the Phenomenology of Time," but rather "The Aporetics of Temporality."

Section 2
Poetics of Narrative
History, Fiction, Time

The time has come to test out the major hypothesis of Part IV, namely, that the key to the problem of refiguration lies in the way history and fiction, taken together, offer the reply of a poetics of narrative to the aporias of time brought to light by phenomenology.

In our sketch of the problems placed under the aegis of mimesis$_3$, we identified the problem of refiguration with that of the interweaving reference between history and fiction, and said that human time stems from this interweaving in the milieu of acting and suffering.[1]

In order to respect the dissymmetries between the respective intentions of history and fiction, we shall take up these intentions in terms of a resolutely dichotomous apprehension of them. Therefore it is first to the specificity of the reference of historical narrative, then to that of fictional narrative, that we shall attempt to do justice in the first two chapters of this second section of Part IV. It is necessary to proceed in this way so the conjunction between history and fiction in the work of the refiguration of time will preserve its paradoxical aspect to the very end. My thesis here is that the unique way in which history responds to the aporias of the phenomenology of time consists in the elaboration of a third time—properly historical time—which mediates between lived time and cosmic time. To demonstrate this thesis, we shall call on procedures of connection, borrowed from historical practice itself, that assure the resinscription of lived time on cosmic time: the calendar, the succession of generations, archives, documents, and traces. For historical practice, these procedures raise no problem. Only their being brought into relation with the aporias of time, by reflection on history, makes the poetical character of history appear in relation to the difficulties of speculation.

To this reinscription of lived time on cosmic time, on the side of history, corresponds, on the side of fiction, a solution opposed to the same aporias in the phenomenology of time, namely, the imaginative variations that fiction brings about as regards the major themes of this phenomenology. So, in chapters 4 and 5, the relation between history and fiction, as regards their respective power of refiguration, will be marked by an opposition between them. However, the phenomenology of time will be the common standard of measure without which the relation between fiction and history would remain absolutely undecidable.

Next, in chapters 6 and 7, we shall take a step in the direction of the relation of complementarity between history and fiction, by taking as our touchstone the classical problem of the relation of narrative, be it historical or fictional, to reality. Restating this problem and its solution will justify the change in terminology which has led us henceforth to prefer the term "refiguration" to that of "reference." Approached from the side of history, the classical problem of reference was, in effect, knowing what is meant when we say that historical narrative refers to events that really happened in the past. It is precisely the signification attached to the word "reality," when applied to the past, that I hope to revive. We shall already have begun to have done so, at least implicitly, by tying the fate of this expression to the invention (in the twofold sense of creation and discovery) of the historical third-time. However the kind of security that the reinscription of lived time on cosmic time gives rise to vanishes as soon as we confront the paradox attached to the idea of a past that has disappeared yet once was—was "real."

This paradox was carefully set aside in our study of historical intentionality in volume 1 thanks to an artifice of method.[2] Confronted with the notion of an event, we chose to separate the epistemological criteria of the event from its ontological ones, so as to remain within the boundaries of an investigation devoted to the relation between historical explanation and configuration by emplotment. It is these ontological criteria that return to the front rank with the concept of a "real" past. Indeed, this notion is supported by an implicit ontology, in virtue of which the historian's constructions have the ambition of being reconstructions, more or less fitting with what one day was "real." Everything takes place as though historians knew themselves to be bound by a debt to people from earlier times, to the dead. It is the task of philosophical reflection to bring to light the presuppositions underlying this tacit "realism," which does not succeed in abolishing the most militant forms of "constructivism" of most historians who reflect upon their epistemology. We shall give the name "standing-for" (or "taking the place of") to the relations between the constructions of history and their vis-à-vis, that is, a past that is abolished yet preserved in its traces. The paradox attached to this notion of standing-for (or taking the place of) suggested to me submitting the naive concept of a "real" past to the test of some "leading kinds" freely suggested by Plato's *Sophist:* the Same, the Other, and the Analogous. Let me immediately say that I do not expect the dialectic of standing-for to resolve the paradox that affects the concept of a "real" past, only that it should render problematic the very concept of "reality" applied to the past.

Does there exist, on the side of fiction, some relation to the "real" that we could say corresponds to that of standing-for? At first sight, it seems as though this relation has to remain without a parallel on the side of fiction inasmuch as the characters, events, and projected plots of fictional narratives are "unreal." Between the "real" past and "unreal" fiction, the abyss seems unbridgeable. A closer investigation cannot stay at the level of this elementary dichotomy between "real" and "unreal," however. In chapter 6, we shall learn at the price of what difficulties the idea of a "real" past may be preserved, and what dialectical treatment it has to undergo. The same thing applies, symmetrically, to the "unreality" of fictive entities. By calling them "unreal," we merely characterize these entities in negative terms. But fictions also have effects that express their positive function of revelation and transformation of life and customs. Therefore it is through a theory of effects that we shall have to pursue our inquiry. We covered half this path when, at the end of volume 2, we introduced the notion of a world of the text, in the sense of a world we might inhabit and wherein we can unfold our ownmost potentialities.[3] But this world of the text still constitutes just a form of transcendence in immanence. In this regard, it remains part of the text. The second half of our path lies in the mediation that reading brings about between the fictive world of the text and the actual world of the reader. The effects of fiction, effects of revelation and transformation, are essentially effects of reading.[4] It is by way of reading that literature returns to life, that is, to the practical and affective field of existence. Therefore it is along the pathway of a theory of reading that we shall seek to determine the relation of application that constitutes the equivalent of the relation of standing-for in the domain of fiction.

The last step in our investigation of the interweavings of history and fiction will lead us beyond the simple dichotomy, and even the convergence, between the power of history and that of fiction to refigure time, that is, it will bring us to the heart of the problem that, in volume 1, I designated by the phrase the "interwoven reference" of history and fiction.[5] For reasons that have been indicated a number of times already, I now prefer to talk of an interwoven refiguration to speak of the conjoint effects of history and fiction on the plane of human acting and suffering. To reach this final problematic, we must enlarge the space of reading to include everything written, historiography as well as literature. A general theory of effects will be the result, one that will allow us to follow to its ultimate stage of concretization the work of refiguring praxis through narrative, taken in its broadest sense. The problem then will be to show how the refiguration of time by history and fiction becomes concrete thanks to the borrowings each mode of narrative makes from the other mode. These borrowings will lie in the fact that historical intentionality only becomes effective by incorporating into its intended object the resources of fictionalization stemming from the narrative form of imagination, while the intentionality of fiction produces its effects of detecting and transforming acting and suffering only by symmetrically assuming the resources of historicization presented it by attempts to reconstruct the actual past. From these intimate exchanges between the historicization of the fictional narrative and the fictionalization of the historical narrative is born what we call human time, which is nothing other than narrated time. Chapter 8 will underscore how these two interweaving movements mutually belong to each other.

The question has yet to be raised concerning the nature of the process of totalization that still allows us to designate time so refigured by narrative as a collective singular reality. This question will be the issue in the last two chapters of *Narrated Time*.

The question will be to know what, on the side of narrative, whether fictional or historical, answers to the presupposition of the oneness of time. A new sense of the word "history" will appear at this stage, one that exceeds the distinction between historiography and fiction, and one that takes as its best synonyms the terms "historical consciousness" and "historical condition." The narrative function, taken in its full scope, covering the developments from the epic to the modern novel, as well as those running from legends to critical history, is ultimately to be defined by its ambition to refigure our historical condition and thereby to raise it to the level of historical consciousness. This new meaning of the word "history" at the end of our inquiry is attested to by the very semantics of the word, which has designated for at least two centuries, in a great many languages, both the totality of the course of events and the totality of narratives referring to this course of events. This double sense of the word "history" in no way is the result of some regrettable ambiguity of language, rather it attests to another presupposition, underlying the overall consciousness we have of our historical consciousness; namely, that, like the word "time," the term "history" also designates some collective singular reality, one that encompasses the two processes of totalization that are under way at the level of historical narrative and at that of actual history. This correlation between a unitary historical consciousness and an equally indivisible historical condition thus becomes the final issue at stake in our inquiry into the refiguration of time by narrative.

The reader will no doubt have recognized the Hegelian accent in this formulation of the problem. This is why I did not think it possible to forgo the obligation of examining the reasons for passing through Hegel along with the even stronger reasons for finally renouncing his position. This will be the object of our penultimate chapter.

If it is necessary, as I believe, to think of our historical condition and historical consciousness as a process of totalization, we need also to say what kind of imperfect mediation between the future, the past, and the present is capable of taking the place of Hegel's total mediation. This question stems from a hermeneutics of historical consciousness, that is, from an interpretation of the relation that historical narrative and fictional narrative taken together stand in, with regard to each of us belonging to actual history, whether as an agent or a sufferer. This hermeneutics, unlike the phenomenology and personal experience of time, aims at directly articulating on the level of common history the three great ecstases of time: the future under the sign of the horizon of expectation, the past under the sign of tradition, and the present under the sign of the untimely. In this way, we can preserve the impetus Hegel gave to the process of totalization, without giving in to the temptation of a completed totality. With the interplay of references among expectation, tradition, and the untimely upheaval of the present, the work of refiguring time by narrative is completed.

I shall reserve for the concluding chapter the question whether the correlation between narrative and time is just as adequate when narrative is taken in terms of its function of totalization in the face of the persupposition of the oneness of time as when it is considered from the point of view of the interweaving of the respective referential intentions of historiography and fiction. This question will arise out of a critical reflection on the limits encountered by my ambition of responding to the aporias of time by a poetics of narrative.

4

Between Lived Time and Universal Time
Historical Time

In the current state of the discussion about a philosophy of history, it is usually taken for granted that the only choice is between speculation regarding universal history, in a Hegelian form, or an epistemology of the writing of history, as in French historiography or English-language analytic philosophy of history. A third option, arising from our rumination on the aporias of the phenomenology of time consists in reflecting upon the place of historical time between phenomenological time and the time phenomenology does not succeed in constituting, which we call the time of the world, objective time, or ordinary time.

History initially reveals its creative capacity as regards the refiguration of time through its invention and use of certain reflective instruments such as the calendar; the idea of the succession of generations—and, connected to this, the idea of the threefold realm of contemporaries, predecessors, and successors; finally, and above all, in its recourse to archives, documents, and traces. These reflective instruments are noteworthy in that they play the role of connectors between lived time and universal time. In this respect, they bear witness to the poetic function of history insofar as it contributes to solving the aporias of time.

However, their contribution to the hermeneutics of historical consciousness only appears at the end of a reflective inquiry that no longer stems from the epistemology of historical knowledge. For historians, these connectors are, as I said, just intellectual tools. They make use of them without inquiring into their conditions of possibility—or rather, their conditions of significance. These conditions are revealed only if we relate the functioning of these connectors to the aporias of time, something historians as historians need not consider.

What these practical connectors of lived and universal time have in common is that they refer back to the universe the narrative structure I described in Part II of this work. This is how they contribute to the refiguration of historical time.

CALENDAR TIME

The time of the calendar is the first bridge constructed by historical practice between lived time and universal time. It is a creation that does not stem exclusively from either of these perspectives on time. Even though it may participate in one or the other of them, its institution constitutes the invention of a third form of time.

This third form of time, it is true, is in many ways only the shadow cast over historians' practice by a vastly larger entity which can no longer appropriately be designated by the name "institution," and even less by that of "invention." This entity can only be designated broadly and in an approximate fashion by the title "mythic time." Here we are bordering upon a realm that I said we would not enter when I took as the starting point of our investigation into narrative first epic and then historiography. The split between these two narrative modes has already occurred when our analysis begins. Mythic time takes us back before this split, to a point in the problematic of time where it still embraces the totality of what we designate as, on the one hand, the world and, on the other hand, human existence. This mythic time was already present in outline in Plato's conceptual labors in is *Timeaus* as well as in Aristotle's *Physics*. We have also referred to its presence in Anaximander's well-known aphorism.[1] We rediscover this mythic time at the origin of the constraints that preside over the constituting of every calendar. We must move back, therefore, before the fragmentation into mortal time, historical time, and cosmic time, a fragmentation that has already taken place when our meditation begins, in order to recall, as myth does, the idea of a "great time" that envelops, to use the word still preserved by Aristotle in his *Physics,* all reality.[2] The primary function of this great time is to order the time of societies and of human beings who live in society in relation to cosmic time. This mythic time, far from plunging thought into a night where all cows are black, initiates a unique, overall scansion of time, by ordering in terms of one another cycles of different duration, the great celestial cycles, biological recurrences, and the rhythms of social life. In this way, mythic representations contributed to the institution of calendar time.[3] Still less should we neglect, in speaking of mythic representation, the conjunction between myth and ritual.[4] Indeed, it is through the mediation of ritual that mythic time is revealed to be the common root of world time and human time. Through its periodicity, a ritual expresses a time whose rhythms are broader than those of ordinary action. By punctuating action in this way, it sets ordinary time and each brief human life within a broader time.[5]

If we must oppose myth and ritual, we may say that myth enlarges ordinary time (and space), whereas ritual brings together mythic time and the profane sphere of life and action.

It is easy to see what reinforcement my analysis of the mediating function of calendar time receives from the sociology and the history of religions. Yet at the same time, we do not want to confuse these two approaches, taking a genetic explanation as equivalent to understanding a meaning, at the price of doing injustice to both of them. Mythic time concerns us as regards certain expressly limiting conditions. Of all its functions, which are perhaps heterogeneous ones, we shall retain only its speculative function bearing on the order of the world. And from the relay station of rituals and festivals, we shall retain only the correspondence they set up, on the practical level, between the order of the world and that of ordinary action. In short, we shall retain from myth and ritual only their contribution to the integration of ordinary time, centered upon the lived experience of active, suffering individuals, into the time of the world outlined by the visible heavens. It is the discernment of the universal conditions of the institution of the calendar that guides our use of information gathered by the sociology and the comparative history of religions, in exchange for the empirical confirmation that these disciplines bring to the slow discerning of the universal constitution of calendar time.

This universal constitution is what makes calendar time a third form of time between psychic time and cosmic time. To sort out the rules of this constitution I will take as my guideline what Emile Benveniste says in his essay "Le language et l'expérience humaine." [6] The invention of calendar time seems so original to Benveniste that he gives it a special name, "chronicle time," as a way of indicating, through the barely disguised double reference to "time," that "in our view of the world, as in our personal existence, there is just one time, this one" (p. 70). (Note as well the reference to both the world and personal existence.) What is most important for a reflection that might be called transcendental in order to distinguish it from genetic inquiry is that "in every form of human culture and in every age, we find in one way or another an effort to objectify chronicle time. This is a necessary condition of the life of societies as well as of the life of individuals in a society. This socialized time is that of the calendar" (p. 71).

There are three features common to every calendar. Together they constitute the computation of, or division into, chronicle time.

1. A founding event, which is taken as beginning a new era—the birth of Christ or of the Buddha, the Hegira, the beginning of the reign of a certain monarch—determines the axial moment in reference to which every other event is dated. This axial moment is the zero point for computing chronicle time.

2. By referring to the axis defined by the founding event, it is possible to traverse time in two directions: from the past toward the present and from the present toward the past. Our own life is part of the events our vision passes over in either direction. This is why every event can be dated.

3. Finally, we determine "a set of units of measurement that serve to designate the constant intervals between the recurrence of cosmic phenomena"

(ibid.). Astronomy helps us determine, although not to enumerate, these cosmic intervals. For example, the day as based on measuring the interval between the rising and setting of the sun, the year as a function of the interval defined by one complete revolution of the sun and the seasons, the month as the interval between two conjunctions of the moon and the sun.

In these three distinctive features of calendar time, we can recognize both an explicit relationship to physical time, which was recognized in antiquity, and implicit borrowings from lived time, which were not very well thematized before Plotinus and Augustine.

The relationship of calendar time to physical time is not difficult to see. Calendar time borrows from physical time those properties that Kant as well as Aristotle saw in it. It is, as Benveniste puts it, "a uniform, infinite continuum, segmentable at will" (p. 70). Drawing upon Kant's "Analogies of Experience," as well as Aristotle's *Physics,* I would add that insofar as physical time is segmentable at will, it is the source of the idea of an instant in general, stripped of any meaning as the present moment. And as connected to movement and causality, it includes the idea of a direction in the relations of before and after, but pays no attention to the opposition between past and future. It is this directional aspect that allows an observer to regard time in two directions. In this sense, the two-dimensional aspect of observing time presupposes the single direction of the course of events. Finally, as a linear continuum, physical time allows for measurement, that is, it includes the possibility of establishing a correspondence between numbers and equal intervals of time, which are related to the recurrence of natural phenomena. Astronomy is the science that furnishes the laws for such recurrences, through an increasingly exact observation of the periodicity and regularity of astral movement, in particular of the sun and the moon.

But if the computation of calendar time is based [*étayé*][7] upon astronomical phenomena that give meaning to the idea of physical time, the principle governing the division of calendar time is not reducible to either physics or astronomy. As Benveniste rightly says, the features common to every calendar "proceed" from the determination of the zero point of some computation.

The borrowing here is from the phenomenological notion of the present as distinct from the idea of any instant in general, which itself is derived from the segmentable character of physical time owing to its status as a uniform, infinite, linear continuum. If we did not have the phenomenological notion of the present, as the "today" in terms of which there is a "tomorrow" and a "yesterday," we would not be able to make any sense of the idea of a new event that breaks with a previous era, inaugurating a course of events wholly different from what preceded it. The same thing applies as regards the bidirectionality of calendar time. If we did not have an actual experience of retention and protention, we would not have the idea of traversing a series of events that have already occurred. What is more, if we did not have the idea of a quasi-present—that is, the idea that any remembered instant may be qualified as present, along with its own retentions and protentions, in such a way that recollection which Husserl distinguished from mere retention or the recent past (become a retention of retentions), and if the protentions of this quasi-present did not interweave with the retentions of the actual present—we would not have the notion of a traversal in two directions, which Benveniste very aptly speaks of as "from the past toward the present or from the present toward the past" (p. 70). There is no present, and hence neither past nor future, in physical time as long as some instant is not determined as "now," "today," hence as present. As for measurement, it is grafted onto the experience Augustine describes so well as the shortening of expectation and the lengthening of memory, and whose description Husserl takes up again with the help of metaphors such as falling away, flowing, and receding, which convey the qualitative differences between near and far away.

However, physical time and psychological time provide only the dual basis of chronicle time. This form of time is a genuine creation that surpasses the resources of both physical and psychological time. The axial moment—from which the other characteristics of chronicle time are derived—is not just an instant in general, nor is it a present moment, even though it does encompass both these things. It is, as Benveniste says, "such an important event that it is taken as giving rise to a new course of events" (p. 71). The cosmic and psychological aspects of time get a new significance from this axial moment. On the one hand, every event acquires a position in time, defined by its distance from the axial moment—a distance measured in years, months, days—or by its distance from some other moment whose distance from the axial moment is known—for example, thirty years after the storming of the Bastille. . . . On the other hand, the events of our own life receive a situation in relation to these dated events. "They tell us in the proper sense of the term *where* we are in the vast reaches of history, what our place is in the infinite succession of human beings who have lived and of things that have happened" (p. 72, his emphasis). We can thus situate the events of interpersonal life in relation to one another. In calendar time, physically simultaneous events become contemporary with one another, anchor points for all the meetings, the mutual efforts, the conflicts that we can say happen at the same time, that is, on the same date. It is also as a function of such dating that religious or civil gatherings can be called together ahead of time.

The originality that the axial moment confers on calendar time allows us to declare this the form of time "external" to physical time as well as to lived time. On the one hand, every instant is a possible candidate for the role of axial moment. On the other hand, nothing about any particular calendar day, taken by itself, says whether it is past, present, or future. The same date may designate a future event, as in the clauses of a treaty, or a past event, as in a chronicle. To have a present, as we have also learned from Benveniste, someone must speak. The present is then indicated by the coincidence between an event and the discourse that states it. To rejoin lived time starting from chronicle time, therefore, we have to pass through linguistic time, which refers to discourse. This is why any date, however complete or explicit, cannot be said to be future or past if we do not know the date of the utterance that pronounces it.

The externality attributed to the calendar in relation to physical time and lived time expresses the specificity of chronicle time and its mediating role between the other two perspectives on time on the lexical plane. It cosmologizes lived time and humanizes cosmic time. This is how it contributes to reinscribing the time of narrative into the time of the world.

These are the "necessary conditions" that all known calendars satisfy. They are brought to light by a transcendental reflection that does not exclude our taking up a historical or a sociological inquiry into the social functions the calendar exercises. Furthermore, so as not to substitute a kind of transcendental positivism for a genetic empiricism, I have tried to interpret these universal constraints as creations exercising a mediating function between two heterogeneous perspectives on time. Transcendental reflection on calendar time thereby finds itself taken up into our hermeneutic of temporality.

THE SUCCESSION OF GENERATIONS
CONTEMPORARIES, PREDECESSORS, AND SUCCESSORS

The second mediation suggested by historians' practice is that of the succession of generations. With it, the biological basis of the historical third-time succeeds the astronomical one. In return, the idea of a succession of generations finds its sociological projection in the anonymous relationship between contemporaries, predecessors, and successors, to use Alfred Schutz's apt formula.[8] If the idea of a succession of generations enters the historical field only when it is put in terms of the network of contemporaries, predecessors, and successors, the same idea, conversely, indicates the basis for this anonymous relationship among individuals considered in terms of its temporal dimension. My goal is to disengage from this complex of ideas the new temporal operator that draws its significance from its relation to the major aporia of temporality, to which it replies on another level than that of the calendar. The Heideggerian analytic of Dasein gave us the opportunity to formulate this aporia in terms of an antinomy between mortal and public time.[9] The notion of a succession of generations provides an answer to this antinomy by designating the chain of historical agents as living people who come to take the place of dead people. It is this replacement of the dead by the living that constitutes the third-time characteristic of the notion of a succession of generations.

Recourse to the idea of a generation in the philosophy of history is not new.

Kant made use of this notion in his "Idea for a Universal History with a Cosmopolitan Intent" (1784).[10] It appears precisely at the turning point from the teleology of nature, which disposes human beings toward sociability, to the ethical task that requires the establishment of a civil society. "What will always seem strange," Kant says in discussing his third thesis, "is that earlier generations appear to carry out their laborious tasks only for the sake of later ones, to prepare for later generations a step from which they in turn can raise still higher the building that nature had in view—that only the most recent generations should have the good fortune to live in the building on which a long sequence of their forefathers (though certainly without any intention of their own) worked, without being able themselves to partake of the prosperity they prepared the way for" (p. 31). There is nothing surprising about this role played by the idea of a generation. It expresses how the ethico-political task is anchored to nature and it connects the notion of human history to that of the human species, which Kant takes for granted.

The enrichment that the concept of a generation brings to the concept of actual history, therefore, is greater than we might have suspected. Indeed, the replacement of the generations underlies in one way or another historical continuity and the rhythm of tradition and innovation. Hume and Comte enjoyed imagining what a society or a generation would be either as replacing another society or generation all at once, instead of doing so by continually replacing the dead with the living, or as something that would never be replaced because it was eternal. According to Karl Mannheim, these two thought experiments, implicitly or explicitly, have always served as a guide in evaluating the phenomenon of the succession of generations.[11]

How does this phenomenon affect history and historical time? From a positive—if not positivist—point of view, the idea of a generation expresses several brute facts about human biology: birth, aging, death. One result of these is another fact, that of the average age for procreation—let us say thirty years—which, in turn, assures the replacement of the dead by the living. This measurement of the average duration of life is expressed in terms of the units of our regular calendar: days, months, years. But this positive point of view, linked to just the quantitative aspects of the notion of a generation, did not seem sufficient to the interpretative sociologists Dilthey and Mannheim, who were especially attentive to the qualitative aspects of social time.[12] They asked what we have to add to the undeniable facts of human biology in order to incorporate the phenomenon of generations into the human sciences. We cannot derive a general law concerning the rhythms of history directly from a biological fact; for example, that youth are progressive by definition and older people conservative, or that the thirty-year figure for the replacement of generations automatically determines the tempo of progress in linear time. In this sense, the simple replacement of generations, in quantitative terms—whereby we count eighty-four generations between Thales and the time when Dilthey was writing—is not equivalent to what we mean by a succession (*Folge*) of generations.

Dilthey, who came first, was particularly interested in those characteristics that make the concept of a generation an intermediary phenomenon between the "external" time of the calendar and the "internal" time of our mental lives.[13] He distinguishes two uses of the term. On the one hand, that individuals belong to the "same generation"; on the other, the "succession of generations," a phenomenon that has to be interpreted in terms of the preceding one if it is not to be reducible to the purely quantitative phenomena derived from the notion of an average life-span.

According to Dilthey, contemporaries who have been exposed to the same influences and marked by the same events and changes belong to the same generation. The circle he outlines is thus wider than that of the we-relation but narrower than that of anonymous contemporaneity. This form of belonging together is a whole that combines something acquired and a common orientation. When set within time, this combination of influences received and influences exercised explains what accounts for the specificity of the concept of a "succession" of generations. This is a "chain" or a series arising out of the interlacing of the transmission of what is acquired and the opening of new possibilities.

Karl Mannheim undertook to refine this notion of belonging to the same generation by adding to its biological criteria a sociological criterion of a dispositional kind, which included disinclinations as well as propensities to act, feel, and think in a certain way. All contemporaries, in fact, are not submitted to the same influences nor do they all exercise the same influence.[14] In this sense, the concept of a generation requires us to distinguish the kind of belonging together that comes from the localization of belonging to an age class (*verwandte Lagerung*) from merely belonging to a concrete social "group," in order to designate those more subtle affinities that are undergone more than they are intentionally and actively sought. And we must characterize the connection between generations (*Generationszusammenhang*) by prereflective participation in a common destiny as much as by real participation in its recognized directive intentions and formative tendencies.

The notion of a succession of generations, which is the real object of our interest here, ends up enriched by the precisions applied to the notion of belonging to the same generation. Already for Dilthey, this notion constitutes an intermediary structure between physical externality and the psychic internality of time, and makes history a "whole bound together by continuity" (p. 38). So we rediscover on the intermediary level of the succession of generations the historical equivalent of the interconnectedness (*Zusammenhang*), taken in the sense of a motivational connection, that is the major concept of Dilthey's comprehensive psychology.[15]

Mannheim, in turn, saw how social dynamics depended upon the modes of interconnecting the generations, taken at the level of potential "localizations" in social space. Some fundamental features of this successive interconnection were the focus of his attention. First, the constant arrival of new bearers of culture and the continual departure of others; two features that, taken together, create the conditions for a compensation between rejuvenation and aging. Next, the stratification of age classes at a given moment. The compensation between rejuvenation and aging thus takes place in each temporal division of the period defined arithmetically through the average life-span. A new concept, an "enduring" concept, of a generation follows from this combination of replacement (which is successive) and stratification (which is simultaneous). Whence the character of what Mannheim called the dialectic of the phenomena included in the term "generation"—not just the confrontation between heritage and innovation in the transmitting of the acquired culture but also the impact of the questions of youth on older people's certainties, acquired during their own youths. Upon this retroactive compensation, this remarkable reciprocal action, rest, in the final analysis, the continuity in the change of generations, along with all the degrees of conflict this change gives rise to.

The idea of the "realm of contemporaries, predecessors, and successors," introduced by Alfred Schutz, constitutes, as I have said, the sociological complement to the idea of the succession of generations, which, in return, gives the former term a biological basis. What is important about this is how it allows us to discern the significance of the anonymous time that is constituted at the turning point between phenomenological and cosmic time.

The great merit of Alfred Schutz's work is his having considered simultaneously the work of both Edmund Husserl[16] and Max Weber[17] and to have drawn an original sociology from social existence in its anonymous dimension.

The major interest of a phenomenology of social existence lies in exploring the transitions leading from the direct experience of the "we" to the anonymity characteristic of the everyday social world. In this sense, Schutz interweaves the genetic phenomenology and the phenomenology of intersubjectivity which were poorly tied together in the work of Husserl. Phenomenological sociology, for Schutz, is largely a genetic constitution of anonymity, instituted on the basis of an underlying instituting intersubjectivity—from the "we," as directly experienced, to the anonymous, which mostly escapes our awareness. The progressive enlargement of the sphere of direct interpersonal relationships to include anonymous relationships affects every temporal relation between past, present, and future. In fact, the direct relationship of the I to the Thou and to the We is temporally structured from its very beginning. We are oriented, as agents and sufferers of actions, toward the remembered past, the lived present, and the anticipated future of other people's behavior. Applied to the temporal sphere, the genesis of the meaning of "anonymity" will therefore consist in deriving from the triad of present, past, and future, characteristic of the direct interpersonal relationship, the triad of the realm of contemporaries, the realm of predecessors, and the realm of successors. It is the anonymity of this threefold realm that provides the mediation we are seeking between private and public time.

As regards the first figure of anonymous time, the realm of contemporaries, the originary phenomenon is that of a simultaneous development of several temporal streams. The "simultaneity or quasi-simultaneity of the other self's consciousness with my own" (Schutz, p. 143) is the most basic presupposition of the genesis of meaning of the historical field. Here Schutz proposes a particularly apt expression: we share "a community of time," "we are growing old together" (p. 163). Simultaneity is not something purely instantaneous. It brings into relationship two enduring individuals (if, with Spinoza, we understand duration as "the indefinite continuance of existence").[18] One temporal stream accompanies another, so long as they endure together. The experience of a shared world thus depends on a community of time as well as of space.

Upon this simultaneity of two distinct streams of consciousness is built up the anonymous contemporaneity characteristic of everyday social existence, a contemporaneity that extends well beyond the field of interpersonal, face-to-face relations. The genius of Schutz's phenomenology is that it traces out the transitions leading from "growing old together" to this anonymous contemporaneity. If, in the direct we-relation, the symbolic mediations are weakly thematized, the passage to anonymous contemporaneity indicates an increase in them in inverse proportion to the decrease in immediacy.[19] Interpretation thus appears as a remedy for the increasing loss of immediacy: "We make the transition from direct to indirect social experience simply by following this spectrum of decreasing vividness" (p. 177). This mediation includes Max Weber's ideal-types: "when I am They-oriented, I have 'types' for partners" (p. 185). In fact, we only reach our contemporaries through the typified roles assigned to them by institutions. The world of mere contemporaries, like that of our predecessors, is made up of a gallery of characters who are not and who never will be individuals. At best, the post-office employee, for example, reduces to a "type," a role which I respond to while expecting her to distribute the mail correctly. Contemporaneity here has lost its aspect of being a shared experience. Imagination entirely replaces the experience of mutual engagement. Inference has replaced immediacy. The contemporary is not given in a pre-predicative mode.[20]

The conclusion as regards our own inquiry is that the very relation of contemporaneity is a mediating structure between the private time of individual fate and the public time of history, thanks to the equations encompassing contemporaneity, anonymity, and understanding based on ideal-types. "My mere contemporary . . . is one whom I know coexists with me in time but whom I do not experience immediately" (p. 181).[21]

It is regrettable that Schutz does not pay as much attention to the world of predecessors as he does to the world of contemporaries.[22] There are a few comments, however, that do allow us to take up again what was said above concerning the succession of generations. In fact, the frontier is not so easy to trace as it might seem between individual memory and that past before any memory which is the historical past. Absolutely speaking, my predecessors are those people none of whose experiences are contemporary with my own. In this sense, the world of predecessors is one that existed before my birth, and I cannot influence it by any form of interaction taking place in a common present. Nevertheless, there does exist a partial overlapping between memory and the historical past that contributes to the constitution of an anonymous time, halfway between private time and public time. The canonical example in this regard is that of a narrative received from the mouth of one of our ancestors. My grandfather might have told me during my youth of events concerning people whom I could never have known. Here the frontier that separates the historical past from individual memory is porous, as can be seen in the history of the recent past—a slippery genre to be sure—which blends together the testimony of surviving witnesses and documentary traces detached from their authors.[23] An ancestor's memory partly intersects with his descendants' memories, and this intersection is produced in a common present that itself can present every possible degree, from the intimacy of a we-relationship to the anonymity of a newspaper clipping. In this way, a bridge is constructed between the historical past and memory by the ancestral narrative that serves as a relay station for memory directed to the historical past, conceived of as the time of people now dead and the time before my own birth.

If we proceed along this chain of memories, history tends to become a we-relationship, extending in continuous fashion from the first days of humanity to the present. This chain of memories is, on the scale of the world of predecessors, what the retention of retentions is on the scale of individual memory. But it must also be said that a narrative told by an ancestor already introduces the mediation of signs and thus leans toward the side of the silent mediation of the document and the monument that makes knowledge of the historical past something completely different than a giant-sized memory, just as the world of contemporaries is distinguished from the we-relationship through the anonymity of its mediations.[24] This feature authorizes the conclusion that "the stream of history includes anonymous events" (p. 231).

To conclude, I would like to draw two consequences from the connecting role that the idea of a succession of generations, joined to that of the network of contemporaries, predecessors, and successors, plays between phenomenological time and cosmological time.

The first has to do with the place of death in the writing of history. In history, death bears an eminently ambiguous signification that mixes together the intimacy of each person's death and a reference to the public character of the replacement of the dead by the living. These two references meet in the idea of anonymous death. Under the saying "they die," the historian recognizes death obliquely and only to go immediately beyond it.

Death is so intended, for example, in the sense that the replacement of generations is the euphemism by which we signify that the living take the place of the dead. Thanks to this oblique intention, the idea of a generation is the insistent reminder that history is the history of mortals. But death is also thereby superseded. For history, there are only roles always left in escheat and then assigned to new actors. In history, death, as the end of every individual life, is only dealt with by allusion, to the profit of those entities that outlast the cadavers—a people, nation, state, class, civilization. Yet death cannot be eliminated from the historian's field of attention if history is not to lose its historical quality.[25] Thus we have the mixed, ambiguous notion of anonymous death. Is this not an unbearable concept? Yes, if we deplore the inauthenticity of the "they." No, if we discern in the anonymity of death the very mark of that anonymity, not just postulated but established by historical time at the sharpest point of the collision between mortal and public time. Anonymous death is, as it were, the central point of the whole conceptional network that includes the notions of contemporaries, predecessors, successors, and, as a background to them, a succession of generations.

The second, even more noteworthy consequence will not take on its full meaning until it is helped along by the following analysis of the trace. It has less to do with the biological side of the idea of the succession of generations than with the symbolic side of the related idea of the realm of contemporaries, predecessors, and successors. Ancestors and successors are others, infused with an opaque symbolism whose figure comes to occupy the place of an Other, wholly Other, than mortals.[26] One thing that bears witness to this is the representation of the dead, not just as absent from history, but as shadows haunting the historical present. Another thing is the representation of future humanity as immortal, as can be seen in numerous Enlightenment thinkers. For example, in Kant's "Idea for a Universal History with a Cosmopolitan Intent" (1784), the commentary already partially cited earlier on the third thesis ends with the following affirmation, which we are asked to accept "no matter how puzzling this is." It is "nonetheless equally as necessary once one assumes that one species of animal should have reason and that as a class of rational beings—each member of which dies, *while the species is immortal*— it is destined to develop its capacities to perfection."[27] This representation of an immortal humanity, which Kant here raises to the rank of a postulate, is the symptom of a deeper symbolic function through which we intend a more human Other, whose lack we fill through the figure of our ancestors, the icon of the immemorial, along with that of our successors, the icon of hope. It is this symbolic functioning that the notion of a trace has to make more clear.

ARCHIVES, DOCUMENTS, TRACES

The notion of a trace constitutes a new connector between the temporal perspectives that speculation arising out of phenomenology, especially Heideggerian phenomenology, dissociates. A new connector, perhaps the final one. In fact, the notion of a trace becomes thinkable only if we can succeed in discovering in it what is required by everyone of those productions of the historian's practice that reply to the aporias of time for speculation.

That the trace, for historical practice, is such a requirement can be shown if we examine the thought process that begins with the notion of archives, moves on to that of a document (and, among documents, eyewitness testimony), and then reaches its final epistemological presupposition: the trace. Our reflection on historical consciousness will begin its own second-order investigation from this final requirement.

What do we mean by archives?

If we open the *Encyclopaedia Universalis* and the *Encyclopaedia Britannica* to this term "archives," in the former we read, "archives are constituted by the set of documents that result from the activity of an institution or of a physical or moral person." [28] The latter says that "the term archives designates the organized body of records produced or received by a public, semipublic, institutional, business or private entity in the transaction of its affairs and preserved by it, its successors or authorized repository through extension of its original meaning as the repository for such materials." [29]

These two definitions and their development in these two encyclopedia articles allow us to isolate three characteristics: first, the reference to the notion of a document (or "record"). Archives are a set, an organized body of documents. Next, comes the relationship to an institution. Archives are said, in the one case, to result from institutional activity; in the other, they are said to be produced by or received by the entity for which the documents in question are the archives. Finally, putting documents produced by an institution (or its juridical equivalent) into archives has the goal of conserving or preserving them. The *Encyclopaedia Universalis* adds in this regard that, unlike libraries, archives constituted of gathered-together documents, "are only conserved documents," although it modifies this distinction by adding that some discrimination is unavoidable—what should be conserved, what thrown away?— even if this choice is made only in terms of the presumed usefulness of the documents, and hence of the activity they stem from. The *Encyclopaedia Bri-*

tannica says, in a similar sense, that conservation makes archives an "authorized deposit" through the stipulations that spell out the definition of the goals of the institution under consideration.

Therefore the institutional character of archives is affirmed three times. Archives constitute the documentary stock of an institution. It is a specific activity of this institution that produces them, gathers them, and conserves them. And the deposit thereby constituted is an authorized deposit through some stipulation added to the one that sets up the entity for which the archives are "archives."

A sociological interpretation might legitimately be grafted to this institutional character, denouncing, if the need should arise, the ideological character of the choice that presides over the apparently innocent operation of conserving these documents and that betrays the stated goal of this operation.

However, this is not the direction in which our investigation leads us. Instead we must turn toward the notion of a document (or record) contained in the initial definition of archives and to the notion of a trace implicitly contained in the notion of a deposit.

In the notion of a document the accent today is no longer placed on the function of teaching which is conveyed by the etymology of this word—it is derived from the Latin *docere,* and in French there is an easy transition from *enseignement* (teaching) to *renseignement* (information); rather the accent is placed on the support, the warrant a document provides for a history, a narrative, or an argument. This role of being a warrant constitutes material proof, what in English is called "evidence," for the relationship drawn from a course of events. If history is a true narrative, documents constitute its ultimate means of proof. They nourish its claim to be based on facts.[30]

Criticism of this notion of a document may take place on several levels. At an elementary epistemological level, it has become banal to emphasize that any trace left by the past becomes a document for historians as soon as they know how to interrogate its remains, how to question them. In this respect, the most valuable traces are the ones that were not intended from our information. Historians' interrogations are guided by the theme chosen to guide their inquiries. This first approach to the notion of a document is a familiar one. As I said in Part II, in volume 1,the search for documents has continued to annex zones of information more and more distant from the type of documents lying in already constituted archives; that is, documents that were conserved because of their presumed usefulness. Anything that can inform a scholar, whose research is oriented by a reasonable choice of questions, can be a document. Such critical inquiry at this first level leads to the notion of involuntary testimony, Marc Bloch's "witnesses in spite of themselves." Rather than calling into question the epistemological status of documents, it enlarges their field.[31]

A second level of criticism for the notion of a document is contemporaneous with the quantitative history discussed in volume 1. The relationship between documents and monuments has served as the touchstone of this criticism. As Jacques Le Goff reminds us in an insightful article in the *Enciclopedia Einaudi,* archives were for a long time designated by the term "monument." [32] For example, the *Monumenta Germaniae Historica,* which date from 1826. The development of positivist history at the end of the nineteenth and the beginning of the twentieth centuries marked the triumph of the document over the monument. What makes a monument suspect, even though it often is found *in situ,* is its obvious finality, its commemoration of events that its contemporaries—especially the most powerful among them—judged worthy of being integrated into the collective memory. Conversely, the document, even though it is collected and not simply inherited, seems to possess an objectivity opposed to the intention of the monument, which is meant to be edifying. The writings in archives were thus thought to be more like documents that like monuments. For criticism directed against ideology, which prolongs the criticism mentioned above concerning the setting up of archives, documents turn out to be no less instituted than monuments are, and no less edifying as regards power and those in power. A criticism is born that takes as its task to discover the monument hiding behind the document, a more radical form of criticism than the critique of authenticity that assured the victory of the document over the monument. This new form of criticism directs its attack against the conditions of historical production and its concealed or unconscious intentions. In this sense we must say with Le Goff that once its apparent meaning is demystified, "the document is a monument" (p. 46).

Must we, then, give up seeing in contemporary historiography, with its data banks, its use of computers and information theory, its constituting of series (using the model of serial history), an enlargement of our collective memory? [33] This would be to break with the notions of a trace and the testimony of the past. However difficult the notion of a collective memory may be, particularly when it does not openly carry its credentials with it, to reject it would be to announce the suicide of history. In fact, the substitution of a new science of history for our collective memory rests upon an illusion about documents that is not fundamentally different from the positivist illusion it thinks it is combating. The data in a data bank are suddenly crowned with a halo of the same authority as the document cleansed by positivist criticism. The illusion is even more dangerous in this case. As soon as the idea of a debt to the dead, to people of flesh and blood to whom something really happened in the past, stops giving documentary research its highest end, history loses its meaning. In its epistemological naiveté, positivism at least preserved the significance of the document, namely, that it functions as a trace left by the past. Cut off from that significance, the datum becomes truly insignificant. The scientific use of data stored in and manipulated by a computer certainly gives birth to a new kind of scholarly activity. But this activity constitutes only a long methodological detour destined to lead to an enlargment of our collective memory in its encounter with the monopoly exercised over speech by the powerful and the clerisy. For history has always been a critique of social narratives and, in this sense, a rectification of our common memory. Every documentary revolution lies along this same trajectory.

If therefore neither the documentary revolution nor the ideological critique of the document/monument reaches the actual basis of the function of the document as informing us about the past and enlarging the scope of our collective memory, the source of the authority of the document, as an instrument of this memory, is the significance attached to the trace. If archives can be said to be instituted, and their documents are collected and conserved, this is so on the basis of the presupposition that the past has left a trace, which has become the monuments and documents that bear witness to the past. But what does it mean "to leave a trace"?

Here historians put their trust in common sense, and, we are about to see, they are not wrong in doing so.[34] Littré gives as the first sense of the word "trace": "vestige that a human being or an animal has left on the place where it passed."[35] Then he notes the more general usage: "any mark left by a thing." Through generalization, the vestige becomes a mark. At the same time, the origin of a trace is extended from a human being or an animal to anything whatever. On the other hand, the idea of being past has disappeared. All that remains is the remark that the trace is "left behind." Here is the heart of the paradox. On the one hand, the trace is visible here and now, as a vestige, a mark. On the other hand, there is a trace (or track) because "earlier" a human being or an animal passed this way. Something did something. Even in language as we use it, the vestige or mark "indicates" the pastness of the passage, the earlier ocurrence of the streak, the groove, without "showing" or bringing to appearance "what" passed this way. Note the apt homonymy between "passed" [être passé] (in the sense of having passed a certain place) and "past" [être passé] (in the sense of having happened). This is not surprising. Augustine's *Confessions* have made us familiar with the metaphor of time as a passage: the present as an active transit and a passive transition; once the passage has taken place, the past falls behind. It passed this way. And we say that time itself passes. Where then is the paradox? In the fact that the passage no longer is but the trace remains. Recall Augustine's perplexity over the idea of the vestigial image as something that remains (*manet*) in the mind.

Historians confine themselves to this preunderstanding familiar to ordinary language, which J. L. Austin so admired because he saw in it a storehouse for the most appropriate forms of expression.[36] More precisely, historians stand halfway between the initial definition of a trace and its extension to a thing. People from the past left these vestiges. However they are also the products of their activities and their work, hence they are those things Heidegger speaks of as subsisting and at hand (tools, dwellings, temples, tombs, writings) that have left a mark. In this sense, to have passed this way and to have made a mark are equivalent. "Passage' is a better way of speaking about the dynamics of a trace, while "mark" is a better way of indicating its static aspect.

Let us explore the implications of this first sense as they profit history. Someone passed by here. The trace invites us to pursue it, to follow it back, if possible, to the person or animal who passed this way. We may lose the trail. It may even disappear or lead nowhere. The trace can be wiped out, for it is fragile and needs to be preserved intact; otherwise, the passage did occur but it did not leave a trace, it simply happened. We may know by other means that people or animals existed somewhere, but they will remain forever unknown if there is not some trace that leads to them. Hence the trace indicates "here" (in space) and "now" (in the present), the past passage of living beings. It orients the hunt, the quest, the search, the inquiry. But this is what history is. To say that it is a knowledge by traces is to appeal, in the final analysis, to the signifi- cance of a passed past that nevertheless remains preserved in its vestiges.

The implications of the broader meaning—the sense of a mark—are no less suggestive. It first suggests the idea of a harder, more durable support than the transitory activity of human beings. In particular, it is because humans worked, and committed something to stone, or bone, or baked clay tablets, or papyrus, or paper, or recording tape, or a computer's memory, that their works outlive their working. People pass, their works remain. But they remain as things among other things. This "thing-like" character is important for our investiga- tion. It introduces a relationship of cause to effect between the marking thing and the marked thing. So the trace combines a relation of significance, best discerned in the idea of a vestige, and a relation of causality, included in the thing-likeness of the mark. The trace is a sign-effect. These two systems of relations are interwoven. On the one hand, to follow a trace is to reason by means of causality about the chain of operations constitutive of the action of passing by. On the other hand, to return from the mark to the thing that made it is to isolate, among all the possible causal chains, the ones that also carry the significance belonging to the relationship of vestige to passage.

This double allegiance of the trace, far from betraying an ambiguity, consti- tutes the trace as the connection between two areas of thought and, by im- plication, between two perspectives on time. To the same extent that the trace marks the passage of an object or a quest in space, it is in calendar time and, beyond it, in astral time that the trace marks a passage. This is the condition for the trace, as conserved and no longer in the process of being laid down, to become a dated document.

This connection between trace and dating allows us to take up again the problem left unresolved by Heidegger of the relationship between the funda- mental time of Care, the temporality directed toward the future and toward death, and "ordinary" time, conceived of as a succession of abstract instants.

I would like to show that the trace brings about this relationship, which phenomenology seeks in vain to understand and to interpret relying only on the temporality of Care.

It ws not, as we have seen, that Heidegger was unaware of the problem. His criticism of Dilthey's claim to give the human sciences an autonomous epistemological status not grounded in the ontological structure of historicality begins precisely from the inability of historiography to account for "pastness" as past.[37] Furthermore, the phenomenon of the trace is explicitly taken by Heidegger as the touchstone for the enigma of pastness. However, the answer he proposes to this enigma redoubles it rather than resolves it. Heidegger is certainly correct when he states that what no longer is, is the world within which these "remains" once belonged, as equipment. As he says, "That *world* is no longer. But what was formerly *within-the-world* with respect to that world, that which is *now* still present at hand can belong nevertheless to the '*past*'."[38] This text defines adequately what we mean by "remains of the past," or, in other words, by a trace. But what do we gain by refusing the predicate "past" (*vergangen*) to Dasein, limiting it to those beings qualified as subsistent and manipulatable, while reserving for the Dasein of earlier times the predicate "having-been-there" (*da-gewesen*)? Recall Heidegger's unambiguous statement in this regard: "A Dasein which no longer exists, however, is not past [*vergangen*], in the ontologically strict sense; it is rather 'having-been-there' [*da-gewesen*]" (ibid.). What, we shall ask, are we to understand by a Dasein—a "being-there"—that had been there previously? Is it not precisely on the basis of the "remains" of the past that we assign this qualification to the being we ourselves are? Heidegger glimpses something of this mutual relationship when he adds an important corrective to his clear distinction between *da-gewesen* and *vergangen*. Indeed, it is not sufficient just to distinguish these two terms, we have to sketch the genesis of the meaning of the second beginning from the first. We must say that the historical character of Dasein is in a way transferred to some subsisting, manipulatable things so that they count as traces. The aspect of being an implement that is still attached to these remains of the past is then said to be historical in a secondary sense.[39] We have only to forget this filiation of the secondary sense of "historical" to form the idea of something that would be "past" as such. "Historical" in the primary sense preserves the relation to the future and the present. For "historical" in the secondary sense this fundamental structure of temporality is lost sight of and we begin to pose unsolvable questions concerning the "past as such." Furthermore, the restitution of this filiation of meaning allows us to account for what Heidegger calls the "world-historical" (*weltgeschichtlich*). The remains of the past, with their equipment-like character, constitute the leading example of what is world-historical. In fact, these remains are themselves what seem to be the carriers of the signification "past."

But can we avoid anticipating the problematic of within-time-ness at the very heart of the problem of historicality if we are to account for this derived form of historicality? These anticipations would indicate some progress in our interpretation of the phenomenon of the trace only if, as I suggested in my analysis of *Being and Time,* we can give the idea of the "origin" (*Herkunft*) of the derived forms of temporality the value not of a decrease but of an increase in meaning. This at least seems to be what is implied by the introduction of the notion of the world-historical at the very heart of the analysis of historicality.

The phenomenon of the trace—along with the phenomena of ruins, remains, and documents—thus finds itself displaced from the historical toward the intratemporal, that which is "within-time."

Would we then have a better account of the trace if we took account of the surplus of meaning "within-time-ness" brings to historicality? There can be no doubt that the notions of datable, public, and extensive time are essential to deciphering the "traces" of the past. To follow a trace, to retrace it, is to bring into play in one way or another each of the characteristics of witin-time-ness. This is surely the stage where Heidegger would have wished to situate this operation. However I do not think he would have succeeded in doing so without making further loans from "ordinary time," taken as a simple leveling off of within-time-ness. Indeed, it does not seem to me that he could ever account for the significance of the trace without associating ordinary time and within-time-ness. The time of the trace, it seems to me, is homogeneous with calendar time.

Heidegger comes close to recognizing this when he suggests that "remains, monuments, and records that are still present-at-hand, are *possible* 'material' for the concrete disclosure of the Dasein which has-been-there" (p. 446; his emphasis). But nothing more is said about the status of this "material" other than the reiterated affirmation that only its world-historical character allows such material to exercise a historiographical function. We cannot make more progress in our analysis of the trace unless we show how the operations proper to the historian's practice, relative to monuments and documents, contribute to forming the notion of "the Dasein which has been there." This bringing about of the convergence of a purely phenomenological notion with historiographical procedures, all of which can be referred to the act of following or retracing a trace, can only be carried out within the framework of a historical time that is neither a fragment of stellar time nor a simple aggrandizement of the communal dimensions of the time or personal memory; this is a hybrid time, issuing from the confluence of two perspectives on time—the phenomenological perspective and that of ordinary time, to use the Heideggerian terminology.

If, however, we are to give equal rights to the time of Care and to universal time, we have to renounce seeing in the latter a "leveling off" of the least authentic forms of temporality.

This composite constitution of the significance of a trace finally allows us to give a less negative twist to Heidegger's estimation of the categories of history. If he gave up completing his thesis about the subordination of historiography to historicality by an inverse analysis of the procedures by which historiography provides the "material" of historicality, it was because, for him, in the last analysis, historiography is situated on the fault line between within-time-ness and ordinary time. He can even concede that "the ordinary representation of time has its natural justification" (p. 478), but the mark of fallenness stamped upon it by hermeneutic phenomenology is an indelible one.[40] Historiography, in this sense, must always be poorly grounded.

This would no longer be the case if the operators that historiography brings into play—whether the calendar or the trace—were dealt with as actual creations, stemming from the interweaving of the phenomenological perspective and the cosmic perspective on time, perspectives that cannot be coordinated with each other on the speculative level.

The idea of a connection stemming from historians' actual practice allows us to go even further than this simple assertion of a mixture of attraction and repulsion between these two perspectives, as I indicated at the end of my inquiry into the Heideggerian conception of time. These connectors add the idea of a mutual overlapping or even of a mutual exchange that makes the fault line upon which history is established a line of sutures. This exchange along the frontiers of our two perspectives on time can take on the extreme forms of either a negotiated collision or a rule-governed mutual contamination. If the calendar illustrates the first form, the trace stems from the second one. Let us begin by considering the calendar again. If we abstract from the immense labor that goes into the constituting of the calendar, we are left with the collision resulting from the heterogeneity of our two perspectives on time. The oldest forms of human wisdom call this to our attention. Elegies about the human condition, modulating between lamentation and resignation, have always sung of the contrast between time which remains and we who pass on. Would we so deplore the brevity of life if it did not appear against the background of the immense scope of time? This contrast is the most moving form that the mutual movement of separation can take, thanks to which, on the one hand, the time of Care tears itself away from the fascination of a time impervious to our mortality, and, on the other hand, the time of the stars turns us toward contemplating the sky rather than thinking about the sting of our immediate preoccupations and even our own death. Yet the construction of the calendar is then completed by the making of clocks. These govern all our meetings, which come about owing to our common concerns, on the basis of measures of time that show no care for us. This does not prevent some of our clocks, however, from having written on their faces a mournful *memento mori*. With this reminder and this warning, forgetfulness of one figure of time brings to mind the forgetfulness of the other figure.

The trace illustrates the inverted form of the exchange between the two figures of time, that of a mutual contamination. We had a presentiment of this phenomenon in our discussion of the three major features of within-time-ness: datability, the lapse of time, and its public character. Recall that I already suggested there the idea of an "overlapping" of the existential and the empirical.[41] The trace consists in this overlapping.

In the first place, to follow a trace is one way of "reckoning with time." How could the trace left in space refer back to the passage of the sought-for object without our calculations concerning the time that passed between them, that is, between the passage and the trace it left? Immediately then, datability with its "now," "then," "earlier," and so on, is brought into play. However, no hunters or detectives would limit themselves to these vague references. Datability without a specific date is of no interest to them. Rather it is with watch in hand that they follow the trace—or with a calendar in their bag that they retrace it. Next, to follow a trace, to retrace it, is to decipher, in space, the "stretching along" of time. How can we do this, though, unless right away we calculate and measure the lapse of time? The trajectory of the passage, like the tracing of the trace, is relentlessly linear. The significance of the trace has to be reconstituted in terms of successive time, even if it is not contained in some pure succession. Finally, the trace, as visible to everyone, even if it can only be deciphered by a few, projects our preoccupation, as illustrated by our hunt, search, or inquiry, into public time which makes our private durations commensurate with one another. The seriousness of our preoccupation—so well expressed by the term "circumspection"—does not betray any failure here that would further aggravate the dereliction that our thrownness has already brought us to. On the contrary, if we are willing to be guided by the trace, we must be capable of that letting-go, that abnegation that makes care about oneself efface itself before the trace of the other. However we must always take the inverse trajectory too. If the significance of the trace depends on the computations inscribed in ordinary time, just as the trace itself is inscribed in geometrical space, this significance is not exhausted by the relations of successive time. As I said above, this significance consists in the reference back from the vestige to the passage, a reference that requires the quasi-instantaneous synthesis of the print left here and now, and the event that occurred.

That this significance, in turn, distances us from Heidegger's critique of ordinary time, I willingly grant—and all the more so because I have borrowed the very expression "the significance of the trace," not from Heidegger but from Emmanuel Lévinas, in his noteworthy essay on this topic.[42] However, my borrowings from Lévinas can be only indirect and must appear biased to him. He speaks of the trace in the context of the epiphany of the face. His interrogation, therefore, is not directed at the historian's past but at, if I may put it this way, the past of the moralist. What, he asks, is the past before history, the past of the Other, for which there is no unveiling, no manifestation, not even an icon? Is the trace, the significance of the trace, what assures Entry and Visitation without revelation? This significance escapes the alternation of unveiling and concealment, the dialectic of revealing and hiding, because the trace for Lévinas signifies something without making it appear. It is compelling but not revealing. Lévinas's perspective, therefore, is very different from my own as regards the trace. And yet. . . .

Yet I cannot overestimate how much my investigation of the role of the trace in the problematic of the role of reference in history owes to this magnificent meditation. Essentially, it owes to it the idea that a trace is distinguished from all the signs that get organized into systems, because it disarranges some "order." The trace is "this disarrangement expressing itself" (p. 63). The trace left by a wild animal disarranges the vegetation of the forest: "the relationship between signified and signification, in the trace, is not one of correlation but one of unrightness" (p. 59). I am aware that in saying this Lévinas places the absent outside of any memory, assigning it to an immemorial past. The impact of his meditation on my analysis, however, is that it underlines the strangeness of the trace which "is not a sign like others" (p. 60), inasmuch as it is always a passage that it indicates, not some possible presence. His remark also holds for the historian's trace/sign: "hence taken as a sign, the trace still has this as exceptional about it in relation to other signs: it signifies beyond any intention of giving a sign and beyond every project for which it may have been the intended object" (ibid.). Is this not what Marc Bloch designated as "witnesses in spite of themselves"?

I do not wish to bring down to the level of historical immanence this meditation on the trace wholly dedicated to a "past that has absolutely taken place," "a past more distant than any past and any future which are still ordered in terms of my own time . . . toward the past of the Other where eternity is indicated, an absolute past that reunites every time" (p. 63). I would rather leave open the possibility that in the last analysis there is a relative Other, a historical Other; that in some way the remembered past is meaningful on the basis of an immemorial past. Perhaps this is the possibility that literature holds open when some "tale about time" points to some form of eternity.[43] Who knows what underground connections may attach this literature to the infinity of the absolute Other, in Lévinas's sense, an absolute Other whose trace appears in the visage of other people? However that may be, the connection between my analysis and Lévinas's meditation may be summed up as follows: the trace signifies something without making it appear.

The trace is thus one of the more enigmatic instruments by means of which historical narrative "refigures" time. It refigures time by constructing the junction brought about by the overlapping of the existential and the empirical in the significance of the trace. Indeed, historians, as historians, do not know what they are doing when they constitute signs as traces. With regard to such traces, they stand in a relationship of usage. It is in frequenting archives and consulting documents that historians look for the trace of the past as it actually occurred. The problem of what the trace as such signifies is not the historian's but the philosopher's.

5

Fiction and Its Imaginative Variations on Time

Our task here is to think of the world—or rather the worlds—of fiction in counterpoint to the historical world, insofar as this relates to the resolution of the aporias of temporality brought to light by phenomenology.

In volume 2 I introduced the concept of imaginative variations, which will guide our analyses in this chapter, to characterize in terms of one another the diverse fictive experiences of time set forth in our discussions of *Mrs. Dalloway, Der Zauberberg,* and *A la recherche du temps perdu.* But there we confined ourselves to using this concept without being able to analyze it. This was so for two reasons. First, we still lacked a fixed term of comparison in relation to which the fictive experiences of time are imaginative variations, not just in relation to one another but simply as fictions. This fixed term was recognized only at the end of our analysis of the constitution of historical time through the reinscription of phenomenological time on cosmic time. This phenomenon of reinscription is the invariant with respect to which our tales about time appear as imaginative variations. In addition, this contrast lacked the background against which it could stand out, namely, the aporetics of time, which provided the opening for this third volume. I want to stress the role of this third partner in our three-way conversation. It is not enough to oppose, term by term, such imaginative variations on time to the fixed constitution of historical time; we must also be able to say to what common aporias the variable constitution of fictive time and the invariable constitution of historical time provide a different response. Without this common reference to the aporias of temporality, historical time and the imaginative variations produced by our tales about time would remain disconnected from one another and strictly speaking would be incomparable with one another.

The Neutralization of Historical Time

The most visible but not necessarily the most decisive feature in the opposition between fictive time and historical time is the emancipation of the narrator—whom we are not confusing with the author—with respect to the major obligation imposed on the historian, namely, the need to conform to the specific connectors acting to reinscribe lived time upon cosmic time. Having said this, we are still just giving a negative characterization of the freedom of the artisan of fiction and, by implication, of the unreal status of fictive temporal experience. Unreal characters, we might say, have an unreal experience of time. Unreal, in the sense that the temporal marks of this experience do not have to be connected to the single spatial-temporal network constitutive of chronological time. For the same reason, they do not have to be connected to one another like geographical maps set side by side. The temporal experience of a particular hero has no need to be referred to the one system of dating and the single chart of all possible dates for which the calendar serves as the frame of reference. In this sense, from the epic to the novel, by way of tragedy and the ancient and modern forms of comedy, the time of fictional narrative has been freed from the constraints requiring it to be referred back to the time of the universe. The search for connectors between phenomenological time and cosmological time—the institution of the calendar; the time of contemporaries, predecessors, and successors; the replacement of generations; documents and traces—thus seems, at least as a first approximation, to lose all reason for existing. Each fictive temporal experience unfolds its world, and each of these worlds is singular, incomparable, unique. Not just plots, but also the worlds of experience they unfold, are—as are Kant's segments of a unique successive time—limitations belonging to a unique imaginary world. Fictive temporal experiences cannot be totalized.

This negative characterization of the freedom of the artisan of fiction does not, however, constitute the last word. Removing the constraints of cosmological time has as its positive counterpart the independence of fiction in exploring the resources of phenomenological time that are left unexploited or are inhibited by historical narrative, owing to its constant concern to connect historical time to cosmological time through the reinscription of historical time upon cosmological time. These hidden resources of phenomenological time, and the aporias which their discovery gives rise to, form the secret bond between the two modalities of narrative. Fiction, I will say, is a treasure trove of imaginative variations applied to the theme of phenomenological time and its aporias. To show this, I propose to combine the analysis made at the end of volume 2 of our three tales about time with the principal results of our discussion of the phenomenology of time.[1]

VARIATIONS ON THE SPLIT BETWEEN LIVED TIME AND WORLD TIME

In order to stress the parallel and the contrast between the imaginative variations produced by fiction and the fixed time constituted by the reinscription of lived time on world time on the level of history, I will go directly to the major aporia revealed—and to a certain extent produced—by phenomenology, namely, the split [*faille*] opened up by reflective thinking between phenomenological time and cosmic time. It is in their manner of relating to this split that history and fiction begin to differ.[2]

We find a basic indication of the way in which the fictive experience of time relates in its own way lived temporality and time perceived as a dimension of the world in the fact that the epic, the drama, and the novel never fail to mix together historical characters, dated or datable events, and known geographical sites with invented characters, events, and places.[3]

For example, the plot of *Mrs. Dalloway* is clearly situated after the First World War, more precisely in 1923, and unfolds within the monumental framework of what was still the capital of the British Empire. Likewise, the adventures of Hans Castorp in *The Magic Mountain* clearly belong to the pre-war years and explicitly lead into the 1914 catastrophe. Finally, the episodes of *Remembrance of Things Past* can be divided into those that occur before and after World War I; developments in the Dreyfus affair provide easily identifiable chronological markers, and the description of Paris during the war is inserted within an explicitly dated time.

Nevertheless, we would be sorely mistaken if we were to conclude that these dated or datable events draw the time of fiction into the gravitational field of historical time. What occurs is just the opposite. From the mere fact that the narrator and the leading characters are fictional, all references to real historical events are divested of their function of standing for the historical past and are set on a par with the unreal status of the other events. More precisely, the reference to the past, and the very function of standing-for, are preserved but in a neutralized mode, similar to the one Husserl uses to characterize the imaginary.[4] Or, to use a different vocabulary, borrowed this time from analytical philosophy, historical events are no longer denoted, they are simply mentioned. In this way, World War I, which serves in each case as a reference point for the events recounted in all three novels, loses the status of a common reference and is reduced instead to that of an identical quotation within temporal universes that cannot be superimposed upon one another, that cannot communicate with one another. It must also be said that World War I, as a historical event, is in each case fictionalized in a different way, as are all the historical characters included in each novel. So these novels take place within heterogeneous temporal spheres. All the specific connectors set in place by history can also be neutralized and simply mentioned: not only calendar time but the succession of generations, archives, documents, and traces. The entire range of tools serving the relation of standing-for can be fictionalized in this way and considered as the work of the imaginary.

The question is to know in what way a segment of world events is incorporated within the temporal experience of the fictional characters. Fiction re-

plies to this question by unfolding the range of imaginative variations that respond to the major aporia of phenomenology.

For example, the entire dynamics of Virginia Woolf's novel was derived in
our analysis from the antagonism between what I called mortal time and
monumental time. But what gives the novel a wealth infinitely superior to the
statement of a merely speculative antinomy lies in the fact that the narrator
does not bring into confrontation two entities, two categories—even if these
be existentials in the Heideggerian sense of the term—but rather two limit-
experiences, between which lies the entire range of individual experiences the
narrator has chosen to put on stage. One of these limit-experiences, that of
Septimus Warren Smith, signifies, to be sure, the impossible reconciliation
between the hours struck by Big Ben and the unfortunate hero's incommuni-
cable dream of personal wholeness. However, Septimus's suicide also marks
the embodiment of the existential Being-towards-death in a singular existentiell experience, an experience closer to the invitation to despair Gabriel Marcel sees as ineluctably following from the spectacle presented by the world
than, for example, to the resolute anticipation that Heidegger holds to be the
most authentic testimony to the primordial character of Being-towards-death.
The same can be said as regards cosmological time. This novel points to it
only through the trappings of the monumental, only as it is incarnated in figures of authority, of "proportion" and intolerance, the accomplices of established order. Given this twofold concretization, the chimes struck by Big Ben
by no means punctuate a neutral and common time but, in each case, possess
a different meaning for each of the characters whose experience stretches between the two limits marking the boundaries of the space opened up by the
novel. Common time does not bring together, it divides. Caught between two
extremes, Clarissa's privileged experience does not constitute a mediation, in
the sense of a speculative mixture, but a singular variant, marked by an essential conflict between her secret role as Septimus's "double" and her public role
as the "perfect hostess." The gesture of defiance by which the heroine goes
back to her party—"she must assemble"—itself expresses a singular existentiell modality of resolution in the face of death: that of a fragile and perhaps
inauthentic compromise (but it is not the task of fiction to preach authenticity)
between mortal time and monumental time.

The Magic Mountain poses the problem of the confrontation between lived
time and cosmic time in entirely different terms. To begin with, the concrete
constellations revolving around the two poles are not the same. Those "below" enjoy no privilege with respect to the monumental; they are people
caught up in everydayness; only a few of their emissaries recall the figures of
authority in Mrs. Dalloway, and they remain the representatives of ordinary
time. As for those "above," they differ radically from the hero of internal time
found in Mrs. Dalloway. Their time is globally and unremittingly a morbid
and decadent time where even eroticism is tainted with the stigmata of corrup-

tion. This is why, in the Berghof, there is no Septimus who kills himself because he cannot bear the rigor of clock-time. There is instead an entire population at the sanatorium that is slowly dying for having lost all measure of time. In this respect, Mynheer Peeperkorn's suicide differs radically from that of Septimus. His is not a challenge addressed to those "below," it is a capitulation uniting him with those "above." From this radically original manner of positing the problem results an equally novel solution. Unlike Clarissa Dalloway, who is searching for a compromise between two extremes, Hans Castorp attempts to resolve the antinomy by abolishing one of its terms. He will go as far as possible in his effort to erase chronological time, to abolish the measures of time. What is at stake, then, is knowing what apprenticeship, what elevation—what *Steigerung*—can result from such an experiment with time, cut off as it is from the very thing that gives it a size, a magnitude. The answer to this question will illustrate another point of correlation between the phenomenology of time and our tales about time. Let us confine ourselves for the moment to this: in place of the reinscription of lived time upon cosmic time by history, *The Magic Mountain* proposes a particularly perverse imaginative variation. Its attempt to erase the traces of cosmic time is still a way of relating to cosmic time, something like the clever doctor who gives his uncooperative patients a thermometer with no markings on it. Like a "silent sister," ordinary time continues to accompany the hero's spiritual adventure.

In *Remembrance of Things Past,* we find another highly unusual variation on the polarity between the time of consciousness and the time of the world. The figure in which the time of the world appears is that of the various domains in which there operates what we have termed, along with Gilles Deleuze, the apprenticeship to signs: signs of the social world, signs of life, signs of sensuous impressions, signs of art. However, because these four domains are never represented except through their signs, apprenticeship to them also involves the world and consciousness. Another cleavage results from this, opposing time lost to time regained. Lost, first of all, is past time, prey to the universal decay of things. In this sense, *Remembrance of Things Past* is an exhausting struggle against the effacement of traces, against forgetfulness. (I shall discuss below the remythicizing of time that is entailed by the narrator's speculations as he reflects upon the universal erosion of all things.) Lost also is the time dissipated among signs not yet recognized as such, destined to be reintegrated within the great work of recapitulation. Lost, finally, is dispersed time, like the places in space, symbolized by the two "ways," Méséglise and Guermantes. We might speak in this regard of the intermittence of time, as one speaks of the intermittence of the heart. Actually, the meaning of the expression "time lost" remains in suspension as long as it has not yet become the very thing that is to be regained. Before the point of conjunction between quest and illumination, between apprenticeship and visitation, *Remembrance of Things Past* does not know where it is headed. And it is indeed this disorientation, and the disenchantment it produces, that defines time as lost, as long as *Remembrance of Things Past* has not been instilled with the great design of creating a work of art. However, the lesson that the phenomenology of time can receive from this conjunction between the apprenticeship to signs and ecstatic experience no longer has to do with the initial aporia we have just examined, that to which historical time provides an answer.

In this initial retracing of the path from *Mrs. Dalloway* to *The Magic Mountain* to *Remembrance of Things Past,* we have seen fiction propose diverse responses to one and the same aporia while varying the very manner of posing the problem, to the point of shifting the initial place of difficulty. In doing this, fiction removes the partitions between problems that the aporetics of time had carefully separated—beginning with the distinction, which now appears more didactic than substantive, between the enigmas acknowledged by phenomenology as belonging to internal time-constitution and those generated by the very gesture that inaugurates phenomenology, the reduction of cosmic, objective, ordinary time. It is because of this shift in the problematic itself that we are carried back from the, so to speak, peripheral aporias to the core aporias of the phenomenology of time. At the very heart of the opposition between the imaginative variations produced by our tales about time and the fixed term of the reinscription by history of lived time upon world time, it appears that the major contribution of fiction to philosophy does not lie in the range of solutions it proposes for the discordance between the time of the world and lived time but in the exploration of the nonlinear features of phenomenological time that historical time conceals due to the very fact that it is set within the great chronology of the universe.

Variations on the Aporias Internal to Phenomenology

We are now going to examine the stages of this liberation of phenomenological time beyond the constraints of historical time. We shall be considering, in succession, (1) the problem of unifying the temporal flow, which Husserl sees as resulting from the phenomenon of "coincidence" in the horizontal constitution of time and which Heidegger derives from the phenomenon of "repetition" in the herarchical constitution of the levels of temporalization; (2) the reawakening of the Augustinian theme of eternity in certain tightly concentrated limit-experiences of temporality; and finally (3) the modalities of re-mythicizing time, which are no longer the province of phenomenology but which fiction alone has the power to evoke, in the strong sense of this word.

1. Our new review of the three tales about time that have captured our attention will take as its starting point the analyses by means of which Husserl thought he had solved the Augustinian paradox of the threefold present: the present of the past, the present of the future, the present of the present. This

solution is composed of two phases. It first grants a certain thickness to the lived-through present that distinguishes it from the point-like instant by connecting it to the recent past, retained within the present, and the imminent future, which constitutes a zone of protention corresponding to the zone of retention in the present. However the price to pay for this extension of the present is the break between retention (or primary remembrance), included in its own way within the living present, and recollection (or secondary remembrance), excluded from the living present. Husserl then sees the unity of the flux of time as being constituted by the endless coincidence of the retentions (and of retentions of retentions) that constitute the "comet's tail" of the living present with the series of quasi-presents into which I transport myself freely through my imagination, and which each unfold their own system of retentions and protentions. So the unification of the temporal flux stems from the sort of "tiling" effect that results from the overlap of various systems of retentions and protentions flowing from the living present and from any other quasi-present, the retention of one present overlapping the protention of another.

The same process of coinciding returns in another form and with another name in Heidegger's hermeneutic phenomenology, more attentive, it is true, to the internal hierarchization of the levels of temporality than to the continuity of the unitary temporal flux. This is why "repetition" appeared to us as the nodal point of all his analyses of temporality. By joining together having-been, coming-towards, and making-present on the level of historicality, repetition links together on this median plane the deep level of authentic temporality and the superficial level of within-time-ness, where the worldhood of the world wins out over the mortality of Dasein. This same overlapping structure of time is not just described, it is set into operation—in many different ways—by the imaginative variations of fiction.

For example, Virginia Woolf's novel appeared to us to be at once pulled ahead by the anticipation of Clarissa's party and pulled back by each of the protagonists' excursions into the past, billows of memories continually rising up in the midst of the action. Virginia Woolf's art here lies in interweaving the present, with its stretches of the imminent future and the recent past, and a recollected past, and so making time progress by slowing it down. Furthermore, the time-consciousness of each of the main characters is ceaselessly polarized between the lived present, leaning toward the imminence of the near future, and a variety of quasi-presents that hold a particular radiating capacity for each individual. For Peter Walsh, and to a lesser degree for Clarissa, it is the memory of unrealized love, of a refusal of marriage, of the happy days at Bourton. Septimus is no less torn out of the living present by his memories of the war, to the point of being prevented from living in the present by the vision of his dead friend, who returns to haunt his delirium. As for Rezia, her past as a small-time milliner remains for her the anchorage point for her regrets amidst the shipwreck of her incongruous marriage. Each character thus has the task of generating his or her own flow of time, by making the protentions arising out of the quasi-presents belonging to the past, which is no more, "coincide" with the retentions of retentions belonging to the living present. And, if it is true that the time of *Mrs. Dalloway* is made up of the overlapping of individual time-spans, with their "private caves," the coincidence by means of "tiling" that produces the time of the novel is continued from one stream of consciousness to the next, thanks to the suppositions that each character makes about the ruminations of the other, the protentions of the one turning toward the retentions of the other. The narrative techniques we studied in Part III are placed by the narrator in the service of these meaning-effects, in particular those devices that play the role of tunnels between the various streams of consciousness.

The Magic Mountain holds, perhaps, fewer lessons about the constitution of the flow of time through "coincidence." The weight of this novel lies elsewhere, as shall be explained below. Nevertheless, at least two features of it do concern the present analysis. First, the return to the past which occurs in Chapter 2 gives the experience of the present the density of an unfathomable past, a few emblematic memories of which continue to exist in the mind, such as the grandfather's death and, in particular, the episode of the pencil that is borrowed and later taken back by Pribislav. Under the time of succession, the measurements of which are gradually erased, persists a time of great density, an almost immobile time, whose life-giving springs break through the surface of clinical time. Thus recollection, irrupting into the actual present, confers upon the character of Clavdia Chauchat her uncanniness, first in the daydream of the *verträumte Intermezzo,* then, in particular, in the famous episode of *Walpurgisnacht.* It is Pribislav's pencil that Clavdia lends and takes back. Clavdia is Pribislav. Discordant concordance is overcome in a coincidence pushed to the point of identification. The other side of this magic indistinguishability is that the eternity it confers on the instant is itself but the eternity of a dream, a carnival eternity.

It is in *Remembrance of Things Past* that the Husserlian term "coincidence" passes over into the Heideggerian term "repetition." Let me repeat: fiction does not illustrate a pre-existing phenomenological theme; it actualizes the universal meaning of this theme in a singular figure.

To be sure, we can speak again in this connection of coincidence, in characterizing the interplay between the perspective of the hero, who advances toward his uncertain future through the apprenticeship to signs, and that of the narrator, who forgets nothing and anticipates the overall meaning of the adventure. The narrator we might say is caught up in a sort of overlapping of time spans by incorporating the reminiscences of the hero in the course of a search that moves forward, giving the narrative the form of a "future in the past." The play of narrative voices, however, reaches other depths. The narrator performs an authentic repetition when he relates the Quest constituted by the apprenticeship to signs to the Visitation prefigured in moments of happiness and culminating in the great meditation on art as redemptive which takes place in the prince of Guermantes's library. The Proustian formula for redemption is the regaining of time lost. We have pointed out three equivalents here: stylistic, in the figure of metaphor; optical, in the guise of recognition; and, finally, spiritual, under the patronage of the impression regained. Under different titles, repetition thus proves to be something entirely different from a reawakening. What is more, it is when the direct short-circuit between two similar sensations, obtained in happy moments, is supplanted by the long meditation on the work of art, that repetition takes on its full signification, which appeared to me to be summed up in the admirable expression of distance traversed. In happy moments, two similar instants were miraculously brought together. Through the mediation of art, this fleeting miracle is stabilized in an enduring work. Time lost is equated with time regained.

2. By accompanying the movement by which the Husserlian problematic of coincidence passes over into the Heideggerian problematic of repetition in this way, fiction takes phenomenology at the same time into a region it had ceased to frequent after Augustine. Indeed, our three tales about time possess the remarkable character of daring to explore, with the figurative power we have recognized, what in volume 1 I termed the upper limit on the hierarchization process of temporality. For Augustine, this upper limit is eternity. And for the current in Christian tradition that incorporated the teachings of Neoplatonism, time's approximation of eternity lies in the stability of a soul at rest. Neither Husserlian phenomenology nor the Heideggerian hermeneutic of Dasein has continued this line of thinking. Husserl's *Phenomenology of Internal Time-Consciousness* is silent on this point, inasmuch as the discussion is limited to the passage from transverse intentionality (directed toward the unity of the noematic object) to longitudinal intentionality (directed toward the unity of the temporal flux). As for *Being and Time,* its philosophy of finitude seems to substitute thinking about Being-towards-death for meditating on eternity. I myself asked the question: "Are these two irreducible ways of guiding the most extensive duration back toward the most tensive duration? Or is this disjunction only apparent?" [5]

The answer to this question can be sought on several levels. On the properly theological level, it is not certain that the conception of eternity is summed up in the idea of rest. We will not discuss here the Christian alternatives to the equating of eternity with rest. But on the formal level of a philosophical anthropology—the level where Heidegger still situates himself in the period of *Being and Time*—it is possible to distinguish between the existential and the existentiell components in the pair that constitutes Being-towards-death and anticipatory resoluteness in the face of death. The function of attestation ascribed to the latter with respect to the existential "Being-towards-death" allows us to think that this existential of universal mortality leaves open a vast range of existentiell responses, including the quasi-Stoic resoluteness affirmed by the author of *Being and Time*. For my part, I have unhesitatingly held mortality to be a universal feature of the human condition. Nor have I hesitated to speak of mortal time, contrasting it with public time and cosmic time. But I left hanging the question whether the existential component of Being-towards-death, and perhaps even that of anticipatory resoluteness, leaves room for existentiell modalities other than the Stoic tone given by Heidegger to resolution, including the modalities of Christian hope stemming in one way or another from faith in the Resurrection. It is in this interval between the existential and the existentiell that a meditation on eternity and on death can be conducted.

Our tales about time make their own contributin to this meditation. And this contribution continues to lie in the imaginative variations that attest to the fact that eternity—like being, according to Aristotle—can be said in many different ways.

This theme is not absent from *Mrs. Dalloway*. Despite its extreme ambiguity, Septimus's suicide at the very least makes us see that time is an absolute obstacle to the complete vision of cosmic unity. It is no longer, we said, time that is mortal but rather eternity that brings death. The calculated ambiguity of this message lies, on the one hand, in the confused mixture of rationalizations and madness in Septimus himself and, on the other hand, in the quasi-redemptive effect of his suicide on Clarissa, who draws from it the courage to face the conflicts of life.

The Magic Mountain is quite obviously the fiction richest in variations on the theme of eternity and death. Here it is no longer some ambiguity but rather the narrator's irony in reflecting on the spiritual experience of the hero that makes the work's message hard to decipher. In addition, this novel deploys a large number of variants on this theme. The eternity of identity in *Ewigkeitssuppe* is one thing; the dream-like eternity, the carnival eternity of *Walpurgisnacht* is something else again; still another thing is the immobile eternity of stellar revolutions; and yet another, the joyful eternity of the *Schnee* episode. Whatever affinity there may be between these disparate eternities may well be provided by the malevolent charm of the "magic mountain." In this case, an eternity that, instead of crowning the most intensive, the most concentrated temporality, is constructed upon the refuse of the most distended temporality, in the state of the greatest decomposition, might perhaps be simply a lure. For otherwise, why does the brutal irruption of large-scale history into the secluded world of the Berghof take on the figure of a "thunderbolt"?

It is fascinating to place *The Magic Mountain*'s variations on eternity alongside those of *Remembrance of Things Past*. Attaining the "extra-temporal" realm of aesthetic essences in the great meditation on time regained might be no less a source of deception and illusion than Hans Castorp's ecstasy in the *Schnee* episode, if the decision "to make a work of art" did not intervene to fix the fleeting illumination and to provide as its sequel the reconquest of time lost. There is no need for history to come to interrupt a futile experience of eternity. By sealing the writer's vocation, eternity transforms itself from a bewitchment into a gift; it confers the power of "bringing back days gone by." The relation between eternity and death is not abolished, however. The *memento mori* of the spectacle of the death-like figures seated around the table of the prince de Guermantes at the dinner party following the great revelation introduces its funereal echo into the very core of the decision to write. Another interruption threatens this experience of eternity; it is not the irruption of great history, as in *The Magic Mountain*, but that of the death of the writer. The combat of eternity and death thus continues in other guises. Time regained through the grace of art is still only an armistice.

3. One final resource of fiction deserves recognition. Fiction is not restricted to the successive exploration by means of its imaginative variations, first, of the aspects of discordant concordance connected to the horizontal constitution of the temporal flux, then of the varieties of discordant concordance related to the hierarchization of the levels of temporalization, and, finally, of the limit-experiences that mark the boundaries of time and eternity. Fiction has, in addition, the capacity of exploring another boundary, the one marking the borderline between fable and myth. On this theme, even more than on the preceding one of time and eternity, our phenomenology is silent. And its sobriety is not to be held against it. Fiction alone, because it remains fiction even when it projects and depicts experience, can allow itself a little inebriation.

For example, in *Mrs. Dalloway,* the hours struck by Big Ben have a resonance that is more than merely physical, psychological, or social. They have an almost mystical resonance: "The leaden circles dissolved in the air," the narrative voice says repeatedly. Likewise, the refrain of Shakespeare's Cymbeline—"Fear no more the heat o' the sun/Nor the furious winter's rages"— secretly unites the twin fates of Septimus and Clarissa. But only Septimus knows how to hear, beyond the noise of life, the "immortal ode to Time." And, in death, he takes with him "his odes to Time."

Nor does the ironic tone of *The Magic Mountain* prevent a certain mythicizing of time, ineluctably tied to the elevation of time to the level of a distinct content of experience, which fiction makes appear as such. This remythicizing is not for the most part to be sought in the moments of speculative suspension, when the narrator does not hesitate to accompany the hero, and even leads him on in his babblings. The most significant moment in this regard is instead perhaps the moment when internal time, freed from chronological constraints, collides with cosmic time, exalted by this contrast. The effacing of measurements makes a nonmeasurable time border on an incommensurable time. The immemorial can no longer be inscribed within any experience, whether temporal or external, except the silent spectacle of the revolutions of the heavens. The entire work, moreover, unfolds a secretly hermetic dimension, which eludes all our previous analyses. The experiments tinged with spiritualism, appearing toward the end of the novel, give free rein for a moment to this exaltation, kept in check the rest of the time.

Of the three works we have discussed, *Remembrance of Things Past* certainly goes the farthest in remythicizing time. The strangest thing is that in its own fashion the myth repeats fiction's imaginative variations on time and eternity, inasmuch as it presents two antithetical faces of time. There is destructive time; and there is "Time, the artist." Both are active: one moves hastily, the other "works very slowly." But, under both appearances, time needs a body in order to exernalize itself, to make itself visible. In the case of destructive time, it is the "dolls" of the macabre dinner party; for "Time, the artist," it is the daughter of Gilberte and Robert de Saint-Loup, in whom are joined together the two sides, Méséglise and Guermantes. Everything happens as though the visibility that phenomenology is incapable of according to time, without falling into error, fiction is able to confer upon it at the price of a materialization, comparable to the personifications of time in ancient prosopopoeia.[6] While time thus finds bodies "in order to cast its magic lantern upon them" (magic like *The Magic Mountain* or in some other way?), these incarnations take on the phantasmatic dimension of emblematic beings.[7]

So myth, which we wished to set outside our field of investigation, has, in spite of us, made two appearances: once at the outset of our investigation of historical time, in connection with calendar time, and a second time here at the end of our investigation of the time of fiction. However, long before us, Aristotle had vainly tried to push this intruder outside his sphere of discourse. The murmuring of mythical language has continued to resonate under the *logos* of philosophy. Fiction gives it a more sonorous echo.

Imaginative Variations and Ideal Types

The first stage of our confrontation between the modalities of the refiguration of time that belong respectively to history and to fiction has upheld the dissymmetry between the two great narrative modes. This dissymmetry results essentially from the difference between the solutions contributed by each of them to the aporias of time.

In order to dissipate an important misconception, I would like to conclude this chapter with a reflection on the relation I establish between what I am calling a solution here and what, above, I called an aporia. I was able to do without this reflection in the corresponding chapter dealing with historical time because the solution contributed to these aporias by historical time consists finally in an appeasement, a reconciliation that tends to blunt their cutting edge, even to make them fade into irrelevance and insignificance. The same is not true of our tales about time, which possess the principal virtue of revivifying these aporias and even of sharpening their sting. This is why I have so often been led to say that resolving the aporias poetically is not so much to dissolve them as to rid them of their paralyzing effect and to make them productive.

Let us attempt to clarify the meaning of this poetic resolution with the help of the preceding analyses.

We return to the Husserlian theme of the constitution of a single temporal field through the overlapping of the network of retentions and protentions of the living present with the network of the retentions and protentions stemming from the multiple quasi-presents into which recollection is transported. The imaginative variations applied to this constitution through coincidence uncover something that remains unsaid in phenomenology. What is left unsaid is precisely what we suspected when we repeatedly stated that the advances and discoveries of phenomenology carried the cost of increasingly more radical aporias. But what more is there to say about the status of these discoveries and the tie between discovery and aporia? The answer is supplied by the imaginative variations of fiction. They reveal that, under the same name, phenomenology designates both the aporia and its ideal resolution; I would even venture to say, the ideal type (in Weber's sense of the term) of its resolution. What indeed do we mean when we state that a field of consciousness constitutes its unity through coincidence, if not that coincidence is the *eidos* under which phenomological reflection places the imaginative variations relating to the ideal type of the fusion of islands of memories, more or less well coordinated, and the effort of primary remembrance to gather together, through the retention of retentions, the entire past in the comet-tail of the living present? Our hypothesis, moreover, is strict Husserlian orthodoxy. It is by means of imaginative variations that every *eidos* is revealed as an invariant. The paradox in the case of time is that the same analysis reveals an aporia and conceals its aporetic character under the ideal type of its resolution, which is brought to light, as the *eidos* governing the analysis, only through imaginative variations on the very theme of the aporia.

We can consider as exemplary the case of the constitution of the unity of the temporal flux through the coincidence of the expansion of the living present in accordance with the force lines of retention and protention, and the recentering of scattered memories in terms of the various quasi-presents that the imagination projects behind the living present. This constitution is the model for all the discordant concordances encountered in our work. It allows us to move back to Augustine and ahead to Heidegger.

What does the dialectic of *intentio/distentio* signify if not a rule for interpreting the recitation of a poem as well as the unity of a vaster story, extended to the dimensions of an entire life, even to that of universal history? Discordant concordance was already the name of a problem to be solved and of its ideal solution. This is what I meant when I said a moment ago that the same analysis discovers the aporia and hides it under the ideal type of its resolution. The study of the interplay of imaginative variations will have the task of clarifying this relation of the aporia to the ideal type of its resolution. In fact, it is principally in fictional literature that the innumerable ways in which *intentio* and *distentio* combat each other and harmonize with each other are explored. In this, literature is the irreplaceable instrument for the exploration of the discordant concordance that constitutes the cohesiveness of a life.

This same relation between the aporia and the ideal type of its resolution can be applied to the difficulties we encountered in reading *Being and Time,* when it accounts no longer for the horizontal constitution of a temporal field but for its vertical constitution through the hierarchization of the three levels of temporalization named temporality, historicality, and within-time-ness. It is, in fact, a new sort of discordant concordance, one more subtle than the Augustinian *distentio/intentio* or the Husserlian coincidence that is revealed by this strange derivation, aimed both at respecting the "source" of the modes derived, starting from the mode held to be the most primordial and the most authentic, and at accounting for the emergence of new meanings, revealed by the very process of the derivation of historicality and within-time-ness at the heart of fundamental temporality.

This kinship is confirmed by the stubborn manner in which Heidegger returns, chapter after chapter, to the lacerating question that agitates the second division of *Being and Time,* the question of Being-a-whole (*ganzsein*); more precisely, the Being-a-whole of our potentiality-for-Being. This demand for Being-a-whole is threatened by the potentiality for dispersion expressed by the ecstatic structure of temporality. This is why the conditions for authentic Being-a-whole, for a truly primordial totalization, are perhaps never satisfied. Indeed, hermeneutic phenomenology distinguishes itself from Husserlian-style intuitive phenomenology in that what is most proximate remains most deeply hidden. Is it not then the function of fiction to wrest the conditions for totalization from their concealment? Even more, is it not stated that these conditions stem less from transcendental possibility than from existential making-possible? What mode of discourse is better suited to articulate this making-possible than the mode that plays on the imaginative variations of a fictive experience?

The twofold character of aporia and ideal-type belonging in this way to the complex process of totalization, diversification, and hierarchization described by *Being and Time* is nowhere better expressed in concrete terms than in the imaginative variations applied by our tales about time to the oscillations of an existence torn between the sense of its mortality and the silent presence of the immensity of the time enveloping all things.

The role Heidegger assigns to repetition in the economy of time seems to me to reinforce these views on the exchanges between phenomenology's quest for authenticity and fiction's exploration of the paths for making this authenticity possible. Repetition occupies a strategic position in hermeneutic phenomenology entirely comparable to that occupied by the dialectic of intention and distention in Augustine and that of coincidence in Husserl. Repetition in Heidegger replies to the stretching-along of Dasein, as does *intentio* in Augustine to *distentio,* and as does coincidence in Husserl to the disparity between retention and recollection. In addition, repetition is asked to reestablish the primacy of anticipatory resoluteness over thrownness and in this way to open up the past again in the direction of coming-towards. We can even say that the pact among heritage, handing-down, and taking up again is at one and the same time an aporia to resolve and the ideal-type of its resolution. Nothing is more suitable than our tales about time for exploring the space of meaning opened up by the demand for an authentic taking up again of the heritage that we are for ourselves in the projection of our ownmost possibilities. Illuminated after the fact by our tales about time, Heideggerian repetition reveals itself to be the emblematic expression of the most deeply concealed figure of discordant concordance, the one that holds together, in the most improbable manner, mortal time, public time, and world time. This ultimate figure sums up all the modalities of discordant concordance accumulated by the phenomenology of time since Augustine. This is why it also proves to be the one most apt to serve as a guideline in the interpretation of those fictive temporal experiences whose ultimate stakes are "the interconnectedness of a life." [8]

One last consequence stands out at the end of our analysis. It takes us from Heidegger back to Augustine. Fiction is not confined to illustrating concretely the themes of phenomenology, nor even to revealing the ideal-types of resolution concealed under an aporetic description. It also shows the limits of phenomenology, which are those of its eidetic style. The renewal of the theme of eternity in our three tales about time constitutes in this respect a limited but exemplary test case. Not that they offer a single model of eternity. On the contrary, they offer the imagination a vast field of possibilities of making-eternal, all of which share but one common feature, that of being paired with death. Our tales about time thus lend support to what I had to say above about the legitimacy of the Heideggerian analysis of Being-towards-death. I proposed then distinguishing in Being-towards-death and in resoluteness in the face of death an existentiell component and an existential one. It is precisely the work of the imaginative variations deployed by tales about time to open up the field of existentiell modalities capable of authenticating Being-towards-death. The limit-experiences that, in the realm of fiction, confront eternity and death serve at the same time to reveal the limits of phenomenology, and to show that its method of reduction leads to privileging subjective immanence, not only with respect to external transcendence but also with respect to higher forms of transcendence.

6

The Reality of the Past

With this chapter we move to a new stage in our investigation of the refiguration of time by intersecting references. In our opening step the emphasis was on the dichotomy between the intentions of each narrative mode, a dichotomy that is summed up in the overall opposition between the reinscription of lived time on the time of the world and the imaginative variations having to do with the way these two forms of time are related to each other. Our second step is indicative of a certain convergence between, on the one hand, what we have called from the beginning of this section the function of standing-for exercised by historical knowledge as regards the "real" past and, on the other hand, the function of significance that clothes fictional narrative when reading brings into relation the world of the text and the world of the reader. It goes without saying that it is on the basis of our first determination of intersecting refiguration that the second one, which is the topic of this and the next chapter, can be set forth.

The question about historical knowledge "standing for" the "real" past is born from the simple question: what does the term "real" mean when it is applied to the historical past? What are we saying when we say that something "really" happened?

This question is the most troubling of all the questions that historiography raises for thought about history. Even if the answer is difficult to find, the question is an inevitable one. Indeed, it accounts for the second difference between history and fiction, whose intersections would pose no problem if they were not grafted to a basic dissymmetry.

A robust conviction animates historians. Whatever may be said about the selective aspect of the gathering, conserving, and consulting of documents, or about their relationship to the questions historians put to them, or even about the ideological implications of all these maneuvers, the recourse to documents does indicate a dividing line between history and fiction. Unlike novels, historians' constructions do aim at being *re*constructions of the past. Through documents and their critical examination of documents, historians are subject to what once was. They owe a debt to the past, a debt of recognition to the dead, that makes them insolvent debtors.

Our problem is to articulate conceptually what is as yet only a feeling expressed through this sense of a debt.

To do so, let us take as our starting point what was the ending point of our preceding analysis, the notion of a trace, and let us attempt to disengage what constitues its mimetic function, in other words, its function of refiguration, following the analysis of mimesis₃ proposed in volume 1.

I shall say, following Karl Heussi, that the past is the *Gegenüber* to which historical knowledge tries to "correspond in an appropriate manner."[1] And I will adopt his distinction between representing in the sense of "standing for" (*vertreten*) something and representing something to oneself in the sense of giving oneself a mental image of some absent external thing (*sich vorstellen*).[2] In effect, insofar as a trace is left by the past, it stands for it. In regard to the past, the trace exercises a function of "taking the place of" [*lieutenance*], of "standing-for" [*représentance*] or *Vertretung*.[3] This function characterizes the indirect reference proper to knowledge through traces, and distinguishes it from every other referential mode of history in relation to the past. Of course, it is only by means of an endless rectification of our configurations that we form the idea of the past as an inexhaustible resource.

This problematic of history taking the place of or standing for the past concerns thinking about history rather than historical knowledge. For historical knowledge, the notion of a trace constitutes a sort of terminus in the series of references that leads back from archives to documents to the trace. Ordinarily, such knowledge does not linger over the enigma of this historical reference with its essentially indirect character. For historical knowledge, the ontological question, implicitly contained in the notion of a trace, is immediately covered over by the epistemological question relating to the document, that is, to its value as a warrant, a basis, a proof in explaining the past.[4]

With the notions of a *Gegenüber,* taking the place of, and standing for, we have merely given a name, but not yet a solution, to the problem of the mimetic value of the trace and, beyond this, to the feeling of a debt to the past.

The intellectual articulation I am proposing for this enigma is transposed from the dialectic of "leading kinds" that Plato elaborates in his *Sophist* (254b–259d). For reasons that will become clearer as we proceed, I have chosen the ideas of the Same, the Other, and the Analogous. I am not claiming that the idea of the past is constructed through the interconnections of these three leading kinds. I only maintain that we can say something meaningful about the past in thinking about it successively in terms of the Same, the Other, and the Analogous. In order to reply to any objection that might be raised about this contrivance, I shall demonstrate that each of these moments is represented by one or more of the most respectable efforts in the philosophy of history. The passage from any one of these philosophical positions to another results from their inability to resolve the enigma of standing-for in a unilateral and exhaustive manner.

UNDER THE SIGN OF THE SAME
THE "RE-ENACTMENT" OF THE PAST IN THE PRESENT

The first way of thinking about the pastness of the past is to dull the sting of what is at issue, namely, temporal distance. The historical operation will then appear as a de-distanciation, an identification with what once was. This conception is not without a basis in historical practice. Is not the trace, as a trace, present? Is to follow it not to render contemporary with their trace the events that it leads back to? As readers of history are we not ourselves made contemporaries of past events by a vibrant reconstruction of their intertwining? In short, is the past intelligible any other way than as persisting in the present?

To raise this suggestion to the rank of theory and formulate a conception of the past that is based exclusively on identity, we have: (1) to submit the notion of an event to a radical revision, namely, to dissociate its "inner" face, which we can call thought, from its "outer" face, namely, the physical events affecting bodies; (2) next, we have to take into consideration the historian's thought, which reconstructs a chain of events, as a way of rethinking what once was thought; (3) finally, we have to conceive of this rethinking as numerically identical with the initial thought.

This conception based on identity is illustrated in striking fashion by the conception of history as a "reenactment" of the past, to use the expression of R. G. Collingwood in his *The Idea of History*.[5]

We may set the three phases that Collingwood's analysis of historical thought goes through in correspondence with the three components of a conception of the pastness of the past listed above, namely, the documentary aspect of historical thought, the work of the imagination in the interpretation of what is given through the documents, and, finally, the ambition that the constructions of the imagination bring about the reenactment of the past. The theme of reenactment has to be kept in third place in order to indicate that it does not designate a distinct method but the result aimed at through the interpretation of the documents and the constructions of the imagination.[6]

1. The notion of documentary proof, placed at the head of his investigation under the title "evidence," immediately indicates the radical difference between the history of human affairs and the study of natural changes, including those of evolution in biology.[7] Only a historical event lends itself to the dissociation of the "inside" face of the event, which has to be called "thought," and the "outside" face, which stems from natural changes.[8] To make this radical starting point plausible, Collingwood adds two clarifications. First, the

outside face is far from being inessential. Action, in fact, is the unity of the outside and the inside of an event. Furthermore, the term "thought" has to be taken as having a broader extension than just rational thought. It covers the whole field of intentions and motivations. For example, a desire is a thought, thanks to what E. Anscombe will later call its desirability characterization, which by hypothesis is sayable and allows the statement of a desire to figure in the major premise of a syllogism.[9]

2. The second component of a conception of the pastness of the past based on identity is not far off. From the notion of an inside of an event, conceived of as its "thought," we can pass directly to the notion of reenactment as the act of rethinking what was once thought for the first time. Indeed, it belongs to the historian alone, to the exclusion of the physicist and the biologist "to think himself into this action, to discern the thought of its agent" (p. 213).[10] All history, it is further stated, "is the reenactment of past thought in the historian's own mind" (p. 215). This abrupt access to reenactment has the drawback, however, of giving credit to the idea that reenactment is a form of intuition. But to reenact does not consist in reliving what happened. And rethinking already contains the critical moment that requires us to detour by way of the historical imagination.[11]

The document, in fact, is a good way of posing the question of the relation of historical thinking to the past as past. But it can only pose this question. The answer lies in the role of the historical imagination, which indicates the specificity of history in relation to all observation of something present and given, such as in perception.[12] Collingwood's section on the "historical imagination" is surprising for its audacity. Faced with the authority of written sources, "the historian is his own authority" (p. 236). His autonomy combines the selective aspect of the work of thinking, the audacity of "historical construction," and the suspicious tenacity of someone who, following Bacon's adage, "puts Nature to the question" (p. 237). Collingwood does not even hesitate to speak of an "*a priori* imagination" (p. 241) to indicate that the historian is the judge of his sources and not the reverse; the criterion for his judgment is the coherence of his construction.[13]

Every intuitionist interpretation that would situate the concept of reenactment on a methodological plane is excluded. The place supposedly assigned to intuition is occupied instead by the imagination.[14]

3. We have yet to take the decisive step, namely, to say that reenactment is numerically identical with the initial thought. Collingwood takes this audacious step at the moment when the historical construction, the work of the a priori imagination, makes its claim to truth. Detached from the context of reenactment, the historian's imagination could be confused with that of the novelist. Unlike the novelist, however, the historian has a double task: to construct a coherent image, one that makes sense, and "to construct a picture of things as they really were and of events as they really happened" (*The Idea of*

History, p. 246). This latter task is only partially fulfilled if we cling to the "rules of method" (ibid.) that distinguish the work of the historian from that of the novelist: localize every historical narrative in the same space and time; be able to attach every historical narrative to a unique historical world; and make the picture of the past agree with the documents in their known state or as historians have uncovered them.

If we stop here, however, the truth claim of these imaginary constructions would not be satisfied. The "imaginary picture of the past" (p. 248) would remain something other than the past. For it to be the same, it has to be numerically identical with the past. Rethinking has to be a way of annulling temporal distance. This annihilation constitutes the philosophical (hyper-epistemological) significance of reenactment.

This idea is initially formulated in general terms, but without equivocation, in the first section of the "Epilogomena" ("Human Nature and Human History"). Thoughts, we are told, are in one sense events that happen in time, but in another sense they are not at all in time (p. 217).[15] That this thesis should appear during a comparison of ideas of human nature and human history is readily comprehensible. It is in nature that the past is separate from the present. "The past, in a natural process, is a past superseded and dead" (p. 225). In nature, each moment dies and is replaced by another one. On the other hand, the same event, known historically, "survives in the present" (ibid.).[16]

But what does "survive" mean here? Nothing apart from the act of reenactment. The only meaningful thing, in the final analysis, is the current possession of past activity. Someone may say that the past survives by leaving a trace, and we become its heirs so that we can reenact past thoughts. But survival and a heritage are natural processes; historical knowledge begins with the way we come into possession of them. We might even go so far as to say, paradoxically, that a trace only becomes a trace of the past at the moment when its character of pastness is abolished by the atemporal act of rethinking the event in its internal thought. Reenactment, so understood, gives the paradox of the trace a solution based on identity, the phenomenon of the mark, the imprint, along with that of its perpetuation, being purely and simply referred to natural knowledge. The idealist thesis of the mind's producing itself, already visible in the concept of an a priori imagination, is thus crowned by the idea of reenactment.[17]

This maximal interpretation of the thesis of identity gives rise to objections that, step by step, call this very thesis into question.

At the end of this analysis, we have to say that historians do not know the past at all but only their own thought about the past. But history is not possible unless historians know that they reenact an act that is not their own. Collingwood may attempt to respond to this by introducing into thought a power whereby it distanciates itself from itself. But this self-distanciation will never be equivalent to the distanciation between one self and another. His whole enterprise breaks down over this impossibility of passing from thought about the past as my thought to thought about the past as other than my own. The identity of reflection cannot account for the otherness of repetition.

Returning from the third component of his thesis about identity to the second one, we may ask whether reenacting the past is to rethink it. Admitting that no consciousness is transparent to itself, can we conceive of reenactment as going so far as to include the opacity that is as much a portion of the original act in the past as it is of the present reflective act? What becomes of the notions of process, acquisition, incorporation, development, and even criticism if the event-like character of the act of reenactment is itself abolished? How can we call an act that abolishes its own difference in relation to some original act of creation, re-creation? In a multitude of ways, the "re" in the term reenactment resists the operation that seeks to wipe out temporal distance.

If we continue our path backwards even further, we have also to call into question the very decomposition of an action into an outside, which would be just physical movement, and an inside, which would be just thought. This split lies at the origin of the disarticulation of the very notion of historical time into two notions that both negate it: on the one side, change, where one occurrence comes to replace another; on the other side, the atemporality of the act of thinking. The very mediations that make historical time a mixed form of time are lost: the survival of the past that makes the trace possible, the tradition that we inherit, the preservation that makes new possession possible.

These mediations cannot be placed under the "leading kind" of the Same.

UNDER THE SIGN OF THE "OTHER"
A NEGATIVE ONTOLOGY OF THE PAST?

Let us now consider the dialectical reversal inherent in the following question. If the past cannot be thought in terms of the leading kind of the Same, might it not be better to do so in terms of the Other?

We can find in the work of some historians who remain open to philosophical questioning suggestions that, in spite of their diversity, point in the direction of what we may call a negative ontology of the past.

Taking a stand opposed to that of Collingwood, many contemporary historians see in history an affirmation of otherness, a restoration of temporal distance, even an apology for difference pushed to the point of becoming a sort of temporal exoticism. Few of them have taken the risk of theorizing about this preeminence of the Other in thought about history.

I have arranged the following short review of some efforts which share this tendency in an order of increasing degree of radicalness. The concern to restore the sense of temporal distance turns against the ideal of reenactment as soon as the principal accent, in the idea of historical inquiry, is put on taking a distance with regard to every temptation toward or every attempt at "empathy." Then received traditions are made problematic and the simple transcription of experience in terms of its own language gives way to problems of conceptualization. History then attempts generally to distance the past from the present. It may even aim frankly at producing an effect of something felt as alien over against every wish to become familiar again with the unfamiliar, to use the vocabulary of Hayden White, which we shall return to below. And why should this effect of something alien not go so far as a deracination? For this, it suffices that the historian become the ethnologist of past times. This strategy of taking one's distance is put in service of an attempt at mental "decentering" practiced by those historians most concerned to repudiate the Western ethnocentricism of traditional history.[18]

Under what category should we think about this taking of distance?

We may begin with a concept especially familiar to authors influenced by the German *Verstehen* tradition. For this tradition, understanding other people is the best analogue of historical understanding. Dilthey was the first to try to ground all the human sciences, the *Geisteswissenschaften*—including history—on the ability of one mind to transport itself into an alien psychic life on the basis of the signs that "express"—that is, make external—the intimate experience of the other person. Correlatively, the transcendence of the past has as its primary model alien psychic life made external by some "meaningful" behavior. In this way, two bridges are constructed toward each other. From the one side, expression crosses the gap between inside and outside; from the other side, the transfer in imagination to an alien life crosses the interval between the self and the nonself. This double externalization allows a private life to be open to an alien life before the most important form of objectification is grafted to this movement toward the outside, the one that results from the inscription of expression in enduring signs, especially those that come about through writing.[19]

A model based on others is certainly a strong one in that it brings into play not just otherness but also joins the Same to the Other. But its paradox is that in abolishing the difference between other people today and other people from earlier times, it obliterates the problematic of temporal distance and eludes the specific difficulty attached to the survival of the past in the present—the difficulty that brings about the difference between knowledge of others and knowledge of the past.[20]

Another logical equivalent to the otherness of the historical past in relation to the present has been sought on the side of the notion of "difference," which, in turn, lends itself to multiple interpretations. Here we pass from the pair same/other to the pair identical/different, with no variations in meaning other than contextual ones. Since the notion of difference does lend itself to quite different uses, I will consider two cases borrowed from professional historians concerned to reflect deeply on their work.

An initial way of making use of the notion of difference, in a historical context, is to couple it to the notion of individuality, or better, individualization, a notion that the historian necessarily encounters in correlation with that of historical "conceptualization," whose opposite pole it constitutes. Individualization, in effect, tends to lean on proper names (of persons, places, singular events), whereas conceptualization tends to emphasize ever broader abstractions (war, revolution, crisis, etc.).[21] It is this use of the term difference, correlated with individuality, that Paul Veyne stresses in his *L'Inventaire des différences*. For individuality to appear as difference, historical conceptualization itself has to be conceived of as the search for and the positing of invariants, where this latter term is understood to mean a stable correlation between a small number of variables capable of engendering their own modifications. The historical fact will then be circumscribed as one variant engendered by the individualization of these invariants.[22]

But is a logical difference a temporal one? Paul Veyne seems, at first, to admit it is not, in that he substitutes for the investigation of the distant, as temporal, an investigation of the event characterized in as atemporal a fashion as possible by its individuality.[23] So the epistemology of the individual seems to eclipse the ontology of the past. If explanation in terms of invariants is the contrary of narrating, it is because events have been detemporalized to the point of no longer being either near or far away.[24]

But, in fact, individualization through the variation of an invariant and individualization by time do not completely overlap. The former is relative to the scale specifying the chosen invariants. In this logical sense, it is true to say that in history the notion of individuality rarely is identified with an individual in the ultimate sense of this term. Marriage in the peasant class under Louis XIV is an individual topic relative to some chosen problematic without it being a question of narrating the lives of the peasants under Louis XIV one by one. Individuation in terms of time is another thing. It is what makes the inventory of differences not an atemporal classification but something presented in narratives.

So we are brought back again to the enigma of temporal distance, an overdetermined enigma owing to the axiological shift that has made us strangers to the customs of past times, to the point that the otherness of the past in relation to the present is more important than the survival of the past in the present. When curiosity gains the upper hand over sympathy, the stranger becomes alien. The difference that separates gets substituted for the difference that binds together. With this, the notion of difference loses its transcendental purity as a "leading kind," through being overdetermined. Along with its transcendental purity, it also loses its univocity, to the extent that temporal distance can be evaluated in opposite ways, depending upon whether the ethic of friendship (Marrou) or the poetry of distance (Veyne) predominates.

I will conclude this review of figures of otherness with the contribution of Michel de Certeau, who seems to me to have gone the furthest in the direction of a negative ontology of the past.[25] This is again an apology for difference, but in a context of thought that takes it in a direction almost diametrically opposed to that of Paul Veyne in *L'Inventaire des différences*. Here the context is that of a "sociology of history writing," in which it is not the object or the method of history that is made problematic, but historians themselves in terms of how they work. To do history is to make something. So the question of the social setting of the historical operation arises.[26]

This place or setting, according to de Certeau, is what, above all else, is not spoken of in historiography. Indeed, in its claim to be scientific, history believes—or claims to be—produced nowhere. Not that the argument holds as much for the critical school as for the positivist one. Where, indeed, does the tribunal of historical judgment hold court?

This is the context of questions in which a new interpretation of the event as a difference comes to light. Once the false claim of historians to produce history in a sort of state of sociocultural weightlessness is unmasked, the suspicion arises that all history with a scientific pretension is vitiated by a desire for mastery that sets up historians as the arbiter of meaning. This desire for mastery constitutes the implicit ideology of history.[27]

How does this type of ideological criticism lead to a theory of the event as a difference? If it is true that a dream of mastery inhabits scientific historiography, the construction of models and research into invariants—as well as, by implication, the conception of difference as the individualized variant of an invariant—falls under the same ideological criticism. So the question arises about the status of a history that would be less ideological. This would be a history that would not be confined to constructing models, but that would instead indicate the differences in the deviations that exist in relation to these models. A new version of difference is born here from its being identified with the idea of a deviation, which comes from structural linguistics and semiology (from Ferdinand de Saussure to Roland Barthes), assisted by some contemporary philosophers (from Deleuze to Derrida). However, for de Certeau, difference understood as a deviation preserves a solid anchorage point in the contemporary epistemology of history inasmuch as it is the very progress of model-building that calls for the spotting of deviations: deviations, like variants for Veyne, are "relative to models" (p. 25). But while differences conceived of as variants are homogeneous with invariants, differences as deviations are heterogeneous with them. Coherence comes first, "difference occurs at the limits" (p. 27).[28]

Does this version of the notion of difference as a deviation offer a better approximation of the event as "having been"? Yes, to a point. What de Certeau calls labor at the limit puts the event itself in the position of being a deviation in relation to historical discourse. It is in this sense that the difference/deviation contributes to a negative ontology of the past. For a philosophy of history faithful to the idea of difference as a deviation, the past is what is missing, a "pertinent absence."

Why then not stop with this characterization of the past event? For two reasons. First, the deviation is no less relative to an enterprise of systematization than is the modification of an invariant. The deviation, of course, is excluded from the model while the modification is inscribed on the periphery of the model. But the notion of a deviation remains just as atemporal as that of a modification insofar as it remains relative to some model. What is more, I do not see how difference as a deviation is more apt for signifying the "having been" of the past than is difference as variant. The real in the past remains the enigma for which the notion of the difference/deviation, as the fruit of labor at the limit, provides only a kind of negative image, one, moreover, divested of its properly temporal intention.

Of course, a critique of the totalizing intentions of history, joined to an exorcism of the substantial past and, even more, the abandonment of the idea of representation, in the sense of a mental reduplication of presence, do constitute cleansing operations that must be taken up again and again. And the notion of a difference/deviation is a good one to preside over them. But these are preliminary maneuvers. In the last analysis, the notion of difference does not do justice to what seems to be positive in the persistence of the past in the present. This is why, paradoxically, the enigma of temporal distance seems more opaque at the end of this cleansing labor. For how can a difference, always relative to some abstract system and itself as detemporalized as possible, take the place of what, although today absent and dead, was once real and alive?

UNDER THE SIGN OF THE ANALOGOUS
A TROPOLOGICAL APPROACH?

The two groups of attempts examined above are not for naught, even given their unilateral character.

One way of "saving" their respective contributions to the question of the ultimate referent of history is to conjoin their efforts in terms of the leading kind that itself associates the Same and the Other. The "similar" is one such form. Or to put it a better way: the Analogous, which is a resemblance between relations rather than between terms per se.

This is not the only dialectical or even didactic virtue of the series Same, Other, Similar that spurred me on in seeking a solution to the problem I have posed. What first alerted me to the possibilities of the Analogous were the hidden anticipations of this categorization of the relationship of "taking the place of" or "standing-for" in the preceding analyses, where expressions of the form "such that" (such that it was) continually reappeared. In this respect, Ranke's formula—*wie es eigentlich war*—immediately comes to mind.[29] When we want to indicate the difference between fiction and history, we inevitably refer to the idea of a certain correspondence between our narrative and what really happened. At the same time, we are well aware that this reconstruction is a different construction of the course of events narrated. This is why so many authors rightly reject the term "representation" which seems to them to be tainted by the myth of a term-by-term reduplication of reality in the image that we construct. However, the problem of correspondence to the past is not eliminated by this change in vocabulary. If history is a construction, historians, by instinct, would like this construction to be a reconstruction. Indeed, it seems as though this plan to reconstruct something in constructing it is a necessary part of the balance sheet of good historians. Whether they put their work under the sign of friendship or that of curiosity, they are all moved by the desire to do justice to the past. And their relationship to the past is first of all that of someone with an unpaid debt, in which they represent each of us who are the readers of their work. This idea of a debt, which may appear strange at first sight, seems to me to stand out against the background of an expression common both to painters and historians: They all seek to "render" something, a landscape or a course of events. In this term "to render," I see the desire to "render its due" to what is and to what once was.

It is this intention that gives soul to the sometimes abstract following reflections.

A second motif also oriented my thinking here. While it is true that the Analogous does not appear in any of Plato's lists of the "leading kinds," it does find a place in Aristotle's *Rhetoric* under the title of "proportional metaphor," which is in fact called *analogia*. Therefore the question comes to mind whether a theory of tropes, a tropology, might not serve as a relay station at this critical moment we have come to with our two preceding analyses. It was at this stage of my reflections that I encountered Hayden White's attempt, in his *Metahistory* and *Tropics of Discourse: Essays in Cultural Criticism,* to complete a theory of emplotment with a theory of tropes (metaphor, metonymy, synecdoche, irony).[30] This recourse to tropology is imposed by the unique structure of historical discourse, as contrasted with mere fiction. Indeed, this discourse seems to call for a double allegiance: on the one hand, to the constraints attached to the privileged plot type; on the other hand, to the past itself, by way of the documentary information available at a given moment. The work of the historian thus consists in making narrative structure into a "model," an "icon" of the past, capable of "representing" it.[31]

How does tropology respond to the second challenge? As follows: "before a given domain can be interpreted, it must first be construed as a ground inhabited by discernible figures" (*Metahistory*, p. 30). "In order to figure out 'what *really* happened' in the past, therefore, the historian must first *pre*figure as a possible object of knowledge the whole set of events reported in the documents" (ibid.; his emphasis). The function of this poetic operation is to outline possible itineraries within the "historical field" and thus to give an initial shape to possible objects of knowledge. The intention here is certainly directed toward what really happened in the past, but the paradox is that we can only designate what happened prior to any narrative by first prefiguring it.[32]

The prerogative of the four basic tropes of classical rhetoric is that they offer a variety of figures of discourse for this work of prefiguration and hence preserve the richness of the historical object both by the equivocity proper to each trope and by the multiplicity of figures available.[33]

In truth, however, of the four tropes considered—metaphor, metonymy, synecdoche, and irony—it is the first one that has an explicitly representative vocation. White, moreover, seems to want to say that all the other tropes, even though they are distinct from each other, are variants of metaphor[34] and that their function is to correct the naiveté of metaphor when it comes to hold the stated resemblance as adequate ("my love, a rose"). Thus metonomy, by reducing the part and the whole to one another, tends to make one historical factor the mere manifestation of another one. Synecdoche, by turning the extrinsic relation between two orders of phenomena into an intrinsic relation between shared qualities, presents the figure of an integration without reduction. It remains for irony to introduce a negative note in this work of prefiguration—almost as a second thought—as a suspension of belief. In contrast to metaphor, which inaugurates and in a sense pulls together the tropological domain, irony, White says, is "metatropological" (*Metahistory,* p. 37) insofar as it gives rise to an awareness of the possible misuse of figurative language and constantly recalls the problematic nature of language as a whole. None of these initiatives toward structuration expresses a logical constraint, and the figurative operation may stop at this first stage, the one of metaphorical characterization. However, only the complete course from the most naive apprehension (metaphor) to the most reflective one (irony) allows us to speak of a tropological structure of consciousness.[35] In sum, the theory of tropes, through its deliberately linguistic character, may be integrated into the table of modes of historical imagination without thereby being integrated into its properly explanatory modes. In this sense, it constitutes the deep structure of the historical imagination.[36]

The benefit expected of this tropological map of consciousness, with respect to history's representative intention, is enormous. Rhetoric governs the description of the historical field just as logic governs argument that has an explanatory value: "for it is by figuration that the historian virtually *constitutes* the subject of the discourse" (*Tropics,* p. 106; his emphasis). In this sense, identification of the plot type stems from logic, but the intending of the set of events that history, as a system of signs, undertakes to describe, stems from the tropology. So the tropic prefiguration turns out to be what is more specific, in that explanation by emplotment is taken as the more generic form.[37]

We must not therefore confuse the iconic value of a representation of the past with a model, in the sense of a scale model, such as a map, for there is no original with which to compare this model. It is precisely the strangeness of the original, as the documents make it appear to us, that gives rise to history's effort to prefigure it in terms of a style.[38] This is why, between a narrative and a course of events, there is not a relation of reproduction, reduplication, or equivalence but a metaphorical relation. The reader is pointed toward the sort of figure that likens the narrated events to a narrative form that our culture has made us familiar with.

I would like at this point to indicate in a few words where I situate myself in relation to White's subtle but often obscure analyses. I will not hesitate to say that, to my mind, they constitute a decisive contribution to the exploration of the third dialectical moment of the idea of "taking the place of" or "standing-for" by which I am trying to express the relationship of historical narrative to the "real" past. By giving support to the tropological resources for matching up this or that narrative and this or that course of events, these analyses give valuable credibility to our suggestion that our relation to the reality of the past has to pass successively through the filters of the Same, the Other, and the Analogous. White's tropological analysis is the sought-for explication of the category of the Analogous. It tells us but one thing: things must have happened *as* they are told in a narrative such as this one. Thanks to this tropological filter, the being-as of the past event is brought to language.

Having said this, I willingly grant that, when isolated from the context of the two other leading kinds—the Same and the Other—and when, above all, detached from the constraint that the *Gegenüber* exercises on discourse—wherein lies the past event's aspect of having-been—White's recourse to tropology runs the risk of wiping out the boundary between fiction and history.[39]

By putting the accent almost exclusively on rhetorical procedures, White risks covering over the intentionality that runs across the "tropics of discourse" in the direction of past events. If we cannot reestablish the primacy of this referential intention, we may not say, with White himself, that the competition between configurations is at the same time "a contest between contending poetic figurations of what the past *might* consist of" (p. 98; his emphasis). I do like his statement that "we only can know the *actual* by contrasting it with or likening it to the *imaginable*" (ibid.; his emphasis). If this saying is to keep its full weight, however, the concern for "returning history to its origins in the literary imagination" must not lead to giving more weight to the verbal force invested in our redescriptions than to the incitations to rediscription that arise from the past itself. In other words, a sort of tropological arbitrariness[40] must not make us forget the kind of constraint that the past event exercises on historical discourse by way of the known documents, by requiring of this discourse an endless rectification. The relation between fiction and history is assuredly more complex than we will ever be able to put into words. And, of course, we have to combat the prejudice that the historian's language can be made entirely transparent, to the point of allowing the things themselves to speak; as if it sufficed to eliminate the ornaments of prose to be done with the figures of poetry. But we cannot combat this initial prejudice without also struggling against a second one, which holds that the literature of imagination, because it always makes use of fiction, can have no hold on reality. These two prejudices both have to be fought against.[41]

To clarify this role assigned to tropology in the inmost articulation of the notion of "standing-for," it seems to me that we have to return to the "as" in Ranke's expression, which has continued to prod us on our way: the facts *as* they *really* happened. In the analogical interpretation of the relationship of "taking the place of" or "standing-for," the "really" is signified only through the "as." How is this possible? It seems to me that the key to the problem lies in the functioning, which is not merely rhetorical but also ontological, of the "as," as I analyzed it in the seventh and eighth studies of my *Rule of Metaphor.* What gives metaphor a referential import, I said, itself has an ontological claim, and this is the intending of a "being-as . . ." correlative to the "seeing-as . . ." in which the work of metaphor on the plane of language may be summed up. In other words, being itself has to be metaphorized in terms of the kinds of being-as, if we are to be able to attribute to metaphor an ontological function that does not contradict the vivid character of metaphor on the linguistic plane; that is, its power of augmenting the initial polysemy of our words. The correspondence between seeing-as and being-as satisfies this requirement.

Thanks to this power, which I spoke of as redescription, we may legitimately demand of tropology that it prolong the dialectic of the leading kinds through a rhetoric of the "major-tropes." In the same way, our concept of the refiguration of time by narrative—which is the heir of this metaphorical redescription—alludes to the notion of "figure," which is the core of any tropology.

But, to the extent that we have been able to accord to the rhetorical and ontological functioning of poetic language a complete autonomy, in order to account for poetic language, illustrated in the first place by lyrical poetry, to the same extent we have to reattach the analogous to the complex interplay of the Same and the Other, in order to account for the essentially temporalizing function of "standing-for." In the hunt for what has been, analogy does not operate alone but in connection with identity and otherness. The past is indeed what, in the first place, has to be reenacted in the mode of identity, but it is no less true, for all that, that it is also what is absent from all our constructions. The Analogous, precisely, is what retains in itself the force of reenactment and of taking a distance, to the extent that being-as is both to be and not to be.

It is not just with the Same and the Other that the Analogous has to be placed in relation, as it was in this chapter, but also with the problematic of the preceding chapter, as well as with that of those that follow.

Looking back, we have to make apparent the tight connection between the problematic of the trace and that of standing-for. It is by the twist of the "as" of analogy that the analysis of standing-for continues that of the trace. In the preceding chapter, the trace was interpreted from the point of view of the reinscription of phenomenological time on cosmic time. And we saw in it the conjunction of a causal relation, on the physical plane, and a relation of significance, on the semiological plane. Hence we could speak of it as a sign-effect. And in saying this, we may have believed for an instant that we had exhausted the phenomenon of the trace. Under the impetus of a text from Lévinas, we were able to conclude our meditation on a deliberately enigmatic note. The trace, we said, signifies without making anything appear. Here is where our analysis of standing-for takes over. The aporia of the trace as "counting-as" the past finds some outcome in "seeing-as." This assertion stems from what our analysis of standing-for, taken in the overall sense of its three moments—the Same, the Other, the Analogous—adds to the problematic of the reinscription of phenomenological time on cosmic time: the problematic of temporal distance. But it does not add this from the outside, for, in the final analysis, temporal distance is what the trace unfolds, runs along, and crosses. The relation of standing-for just makes explicit this crossing of time by the trace. More exactly, it makes explicit the dialectical structure of this crossing that converts this interval into a form of mediation.

If, to conclude, we turn our gaze ahead, toward the process of totalization to which the following analyses will be devoted, we may suspect why our exploration must remain incomplete—incomplete because abstract. As phenomenology, particularly Heidegger's, has taught us, the past separated from the dialectic of future, past, and present remains an abstraction. This is why this chapter at its end only constitutes an attempt to think somewhat better about what remains enigmatic in the pastness of the past as such. By placing it successively under the leading kinds of the same, the Other, and the Analogous, we have at least preserved the mysterious aspect of the debt that makes the master of the plot a servant of the memory of past human beings.[42]

7

The World of the Text and the World of the Reader

We shall take a new step in the direction of the intersection of the time of fiction and the time of history if we ask what, on the side of fiction, can be considered as the counterpoint to what, on the side of history, is given as the "real" past. The problem would be not merely insoluble but senseless, if we continued to pose it in the traditional terms of reference. Indeed, only historians can, absolutely speaking, be said to refer to something "real," in the sense that that about which they speak was observable to witnesses in the past. In comparison, the characters of the novelist are themselves quite simply "unreal"; "unreal," too, is the experience described by fiction. Between the "reality of the past" and the "unreality of fiction," the dissymmetry is total.

We have already made a first break with this manner of posing the problem by questioning the concept of "reality" that is applied to the past. To say that a given event reported by a historian was observable by witnesses in the past solves nothing. The enigma of pastness is simply shifted from the event reported to the testimony that reports it. Having-been poses a problem in the very fact that it is not observable, whether it be a question of the having-been of events or the having-been of testimony. The pastness of an observation in the past is not itself observable but it is memorable. To resolve this enigma, I elaborated the concept of standing-for or taking-the-place-of, signifying by this that the constructions of history are intended to be reconstructions answering to the need for a *Gegenüber*. What is more, I discerned between the function of standing-for and the *Gegenüber* that is its correlate a relation of indebtedness which assigns to the people of the present the task of repaying their due to people of the past—to the dead. The fact that this category of standing-for or of taking-the-place-of—reinforced by the feeling of a debt—is ultimately irreducible to the category of reference, as it functions in an observational language and in an extensional logic, is confirmed by the fundamentally dialectical structure of the category of standing-for. Standing-for, we said, means by turns the reduction to the Same, the recognition of Otherness, and the analogizing of apprehension.

This critique of the naive concept of "reality" applied to the pastness of the past calls for a systematic critique of the no less naive concept of "unreality" applied to the projections of fiction. The function of standing-for or of taking-the-place-of is paralleled in fiction by the function it possesses, with respect to everyday practice, of being undividedly revealing and transforming. Revealing, in the sense that it brings features to light that were concealed and yet already sketched out at the heart of our experience, our praxis. Transforming, in the sense that a life examined in this way is a changed life, another life. Here we reach the point where discovering and inventing are indistinguishable, the point, therefore, where the notion of reference no longer works, no more than does that of redescription. The point where, in order to signify something like a productive reference in the sense in which, following Kant, we speak of a productive imagination, the problematic of refiguration must free itself, once and for all, from the vocabulary of reference.

The parallel between the function of standing-for belonging to knowledge of the past and the corresponding function of fiction thus reveals its secret only at the price of a revision of the concept of unreality, a revision just as drastic as the one I made in the concept of the reality of the past.

In moving away from the vocabulary of reference, I am adopting instead that of "application," handed down by the hermeneutical tradition and awarded a new place of honor by Hans-Georg Gadamer in his *Truth and Method*.[1] From Gadamer we have learned that application is not a contingent appendix added onto understanding and explanation but an organic part of every hermeneutic project.[2] But the problem of application—to which elsewhere I have given the name "appropriation"[3]—is far from being a simple one. It can no more receive a direct solution than can the problem of standing for the past, whose counterpart it is in the realm of fiction. It has its own dialectic, which, without resembling in any exact way that of the *Gegenüber* characteristic of the relation of standing-for, does generate comparable difficulties. Indeed, it is only through the mediation of reading that the literary work attains complete significance, which would be to fiction what standing-for is to history.

Why is this mediation of reading required? Because, at the end of Part III, where the notion of the world of the text, implied in every fictive temporal experience, was introduced, we had covered only half of the distance along the road to application. To be sure, in adopting in this way, as I also did in *The Rule of Metaphor,* the thesis that the literary text transcends itself in the direction of a world, I removed the literary text from the closure imposed upon it— legitimately, moreover—by the analysis of its immanent structures. At that time I said that the world of the text marked the opening of the text to its "outside," to its "other," in that the world of the text constitutes an absolutely original intentional object in relation to its "internal" structure. It must be admitted, however, that considered apart from reading, the world of the text remains a transcendence in immanence. Its ontological status remains in suspension—an excess in relation to structure, an anticipation in relation to reading. It is only in reading that the dynamism of configuration completes its course. And it is beyond reading, in effective action, instructed by the works handed down, that the configuration of the text is transformed into refiguration.[4] In this way, we link up once again with the formulation whereby I defined mimesis$_3$ in volume 1. Mimesis$_3$, I said, marks the intersection between the world of the text and the world of the listener or the reader, the intersection, therefore, between the world configured by the poem and the world within which effective action is unfolded and itself unfolds its specific temporality.[5] The significance of the work of fiction stems from this intersection.

This recourse to the mediation of reading marks the most obvious difference between the present work and *The Rule of Metaphor.* In addition to the fact that, in the previous work, I thought I could retain the vocabulary of reference, characterized as the redescription of the poetic work at the heart of everyday experience, I also ascribed to the poem itself the power of transforming life by means of a kind of short-circuit operating between the "seeing-as," characteristic of the metaphorical utterance, and "being-as," as its ontological correlate. And, since fictional narrative can legitimately be held to be a special case of poetical discourse, we might be tempted to employ the same short-circuit between "seeing-as" and "being-as" on the level of narrativity. This simple solution to the old problem of reference on the plane of fiction would seem to be encouraged by the fact that action already possesses a first-order readability due to the symbolic mediations articulating it on the primary level of mimesis$_1$. We might believe that the only mediation required between the pre-signification of mimesis$_1$ and the over-signification of mimesis$_3$ is the one that is brought about by the narrative configuration itself through its internal dynamics. A more precise reflection on the notion of the world of the text and a more exact description of its status of transcendence within immanence have, however, convinced me that the passage from configuration to refiguration required the confrontation between two worlds, the fictive world of the text and the real world of the reader. With this, the phenomenon of reading became the necessary mediator of refiguration.

What is important now is to elucidate the dialectical structure—which replies, *mutatis mutandis,* to that of the function of standing-for exercised by a historical narrative with respect to the "real" past—of this phenomenon of reading, which plays, as we have just seen, a strategic role in the operation of refiguration.

To what discipline does a theory of reading belong? To poetics? Yes, insofar as the composition of the work governs its reading; no, insofar as other factors enter into play, factors that concern the sort of communication that finds its starting point in the author, crosses through the work, and finds its end-point in the reader. For it is, indeed, from the author that the strategy of persuasion that has the reader as its target starts out. And it is to this strategy of persuasion that the reader replies by accompanying the configuration and in appropriating the world proposed by the text.

Three moments need to be considered then, to which correspond three neighboring, yet distinct, disciplines: (1) the strategy as concocted by the author and directed toward the reader; (2) the inscription of this strategy within a literary configuration; and (3) the response of the reader considered either as a reading subject or as the receiving public.

This schema allows us to take a brief look at several theories of reading that I have expressly arranged starting from the pole of the author and moving toward that of the reader, who is the ultimate mediator between configuration and refiguration.

FROM POETICS TO RHETORIC

At the first stage of our itinerary, we are considering a strategy from the point of view of the author who carries it through. The theory of reading then falls within the field of rhetoric, inasmuch as rhetoric governs the art by means of which orators aim at persuading their listeners. More precisely, for us, and this has been recognized since Aristotle, it falls within the field of a rhetoric of fiction, in the sense that Wayne Booth has given to this phrase in his well-known work *The Rhetoric of Fiction*.[6] An objection, however, immediately comes to mind: in bringing the author back into the field of literary theory, are we not denying the thesis of the semantic autonomy of the text, and are we not slipping back into an outmoded psychological analysis of the written text? By no means. First, the thesis of the semantic autonomy of the text holds only for a structural analysis that brackets the strategy of persuasion running through the operations belonging to a poetics as such; removing these brackets necessarily involves taking into account the one who concocts the strategy of persuasion, namely, the author. Next, rhetoric can escape the objection of falling back into the "intentional fallacy" and, more generally, of being no more than a psychology of the author inasmuch as what it emphasizes is not the alleged creation process of the work but the techniques by means of which a work is made communicable. These techniques can be discerned in the work itself. The result is that the only type of author whose authority is in question here is not the real author, the object of biography, but the implied author. It is this implied author who takes the initiative in the show of strength underlying the relation between writing and reading.

Before entering this arena, I should like to recall the terminological convention I adopted in introducing the notions of point of view and narrative voice in the preceding volume, at the end of the analyses devoted to "Games with Time." There I considered these notions only to the extent that they contributed to the understanding of the narrative composition as such, apart from their effect on the communication of the work. But the notion of implied author belongs to this problematic of communication inasmuch as it is closely bound up with a rhetoric of persuasion. Conscious of the abstract character of this distinction, I stressed at that time the role of transition brought about by the notion of narrative voice. The narrative voice, I said, is what offers the text as something to be read. To whom does it make this offer if not to the virtual reader of the work? It was a deliberate choice on my part, therefore, not to consider the notion of implied author when we talked about point of view and narrative voice, but instead to emphasize at this time the ties between this implied author and the strategies of persuasion stemming from a rhetoric of fiction, without making any further allusions to the notions of narrative voice and point of view, from which this notion of implied author obviously cannot be dissociated.

Set back within the framework of communication to which it belongs, the category of implied author has the important advantage of sidestepping a number of futile disputes that conceal the primary meaning of a rhetoric of fiction. For example, we shall not attach an exaggerated originality to the efforts of modern novelists to make themselves invisible—unlike previous authors, inclined to intervene unscrupulously in their narratives—as if the novel were suddenly to have emerged authorless. Effacement of the author is one rhetorical technique among others; it belongs to the panoply of disguises and masks the real author uses to transform himself or herself into the implied author.[7] The same can be said of the author's right to describe minds from the inside, which in so-called real life is something that can only be inferred with great difficulty. This right is part of the pact of trust concluded with the reader, which we shall discuss below.[8] Also, whatever the angle of vision chosen by the author,[9] this is in every instance an artifice to be attributed to the exorbitant rights the reader grants the author. Nor does the author disappear simply because the novelist has attempted to "show" rather than to "inform and instruct." We discussed this in volume 2 in connection with the search for verisimilitude in the realistic novel, and even more so in the naturalistic novel.[10] Far from being abolished, the artifice proper to the narrative operation is augmented by the task of simulating real presence through writing. However much this simulation may be opposed to the omniscience of the narrator, it conveys no less a mastery of rhetorical techniques. The alleged faithfulness to life merely hides the subtlety of the maneuvers by which the work governs, on the side of the author, the "intensity of the illusion" desired by Henry James. The rhetoric of dissimulation, the summit of the rhetoric of fiction, must not fool the critic, even if it may fool the reader. The height of such dissimulation would be that the fiction appear never to have been written.[11] The rhetorical procedures by which the author sacrifices his presence dissimulate his artifice by means of the verisimilitude of a story that appears to narrate itself and to let life speak, whether this be called social reality, individual behavior, or the stream of consciousness.[12]

This brief discussion of the misunderstandings that the category of implied author is able to dissipate underscores the rightful place of this category in a comprehensive theory of reading. The reader has an intimation of the role it plays inasmuch as this reader intuitively apprehends the work as a unified totality.

Spontaneously, the reader does not ascribe this unification to the rules of composition alone but extends it to the choices and to the norms that make the text, precisely, the work of some speaker, hence a work produced by someone and not by nature.

I would readily compare this unifying role intuitively assigned by the reader to the implied author with the notion of style, proposed by G. Granger in his *Essai d'une philosophie du style*.[13] If a work is considered as the resolution of a problem, itself arising out of prior successes in the field of science as well as in the field of art, then style may be termed the adequation between the singularity of this solution, which the work constitutes by itself, and the singularity of the crisis situation as this was apprehended by the thinker or artist. This singularity of the solution, replying to the singularity of the problem, can take on a proper name, that of the author. Thus we speak of Boole's theorem just as we speak of a painting by Cézanne. Naming the work in terms of its author implies no conjecture about the psychology of invention or of discovery, therefore no assertion concerning the presumed intention of the inventor; it implies only the singularity of a solution to a problem. This comparison reinforces the right of the category of implied author to figure in a rhetoric of fiction.

The related notion of a reliable or unreliable narrator, to which we now turn, is far from constituting a marginal notion.[14] It introduces into the pact of reading a note of trust that counterbalances the violence concealed in the strategy of persuasion. The question of reliability is to the fictional narrative what documentary proof is to historiography. It is precisely because novelists have no material proof that they ask readers to grant them not only the right to know what they are recounting or showing but to allow them to suggest an assessment, an evaluation of the main characters. Was it not just such an evaluation that allowed Aristotle to classify tragedy and comedy in terms of characters who are "better" or "worse" than we are, and, in particular, to give the *hamartia*—the terrible flaw—of the hero its full emotional power, inasmuch as the tragic flaw must be that of a superior individual and not of an individual who is mediocre, evil, or perverse?

Why is this category not applied to the narrator rather than to the implied author? In the rich repertory of forms adopted by the author's voice, the narrator is distinguished from the implied author whenever the narrator is dramatized as narrator. In this way, it is the unknown wise man who says that Job is a "just" man; it is the tragic chorus that utters the sublime words of horror and pity; it is the fool who says aloud what the author thinks deep down; it is a character as a witness, possibly a scoundrel, a knave, who makes known the point of view of the narrator on his own narrative. There is always an implied author. The story is told by someone. There is not always a distinct narrator. But when there is one, the narrator shares the privilege of the implied author, who, without always being omniscient, does always have the power to reach knowledge of others from the inside. This privilege is one of the rhetorical powers invested in the implied author by reason of the tacit pact between the author and the reader. The degree to which the narrator is reliable is one of the clauses of this reading pact. As for the reader's responsibility, it is another clause of the same pact. Indeed, inasmuch as the creation of a dramatized narrator, whether reliable or unreliable, permits variation in the distance between the implied author and his characters, a degree of complexity is induced, at the same time, in the reader, a complexity that is the source of the reader's freedom in the face of the authority that the fiction receives from its author.

The case of the unreliable narrator is particularly interesting from the point of view of an appeal to the reader's freedom and responsibility. The narrator's role here may perhaps be less perverse than Wayne Booth depicts it.[15] Unlike the reliable narrator, who assures readers than in the journey they are embarking upon they need not bother about false hopes or groundless fears concerning either the facts reported or the implicit or explicit evaluations of the characters, the unreliable narrator foils these expectations by leaving readers uncertain about where this is all meant to lead. In this way, the modern novel will fulfill all the better its function of criticizing conventional morality, and possibly even its function of provocation and insult, as the narrator will be increasingly suspect and the author ever more invisible, the two resources of the rhetoric of concealment mutually reinforcing each other. In this regard, I do not share Wayne Booth's severity concerning the equivocal narrator cultivated by contemporary literature. Does not an entirely reliable narrator, such as the eighteenth-century novelist, so quick to intervene and lead the reader by the hand, thereby dispense the reader from taking any emotional distance from the characters and their adventures? And is not a disoriented reader, such as the reader of *The Magic Mountain*, led astray by an ironic narrator, summoned, on the contrary, to greater reflection? May we not make a plea on behalf of what Henry James, in *The Art of the Novel*, called the "troubled vision" of a character, "reflected in the equally troubled vision of an observer"?[16] Cannot the argument that impersonal narration is more clever than another type of narration lead to the conclusion that such narration calls for the active deciphering of "unreliability" itself?

There is no denying that modern literature is dangerous. The sole response worthy of the criticism it provokes, of which Wayne Booth is one of the most highly esteemed representatives, is that this poisonous literature requires a new type of reader: a reader who responds.[17]

It is at this point that a rhetoric of fiction centered on the author reveals its limits. It recognizes just a single initiative, that of an author eager to communicate his vision of things.[18] In this regard, the affirmation that the author creates his readers[19] appears to lack a dialectical counterpart. Yet it may be the function of the most corrosive literature to contribute to making a new kind of reader appear, a reader who is himself suspicious, because reading ceases to be a trusting voyage made in the company of a reliable narrator, becoming instead a struggle with the implied author, a struggle leading the reader back to himself.

The Rhetoric between the Text and Its Reader

The image of a combat between a reader and an unreliable narrator, with which we concluded the preceding discussion, might easily lead us to believe that reading is added onto the text as a complement it can do without. After all, libraries are full of unread books, whose configuration is, nonetheless, well laid out and yet they refigure nothing at all. Our earlier analyses should suffice to dispel this illusion. Without the reader who accompanies it, there is no configuring act at work in the text; and without a reader to appropriate it, there is no world unfolded before the text. Yet the illusion is endlessly reborn that the text is a structure in itself and for itself and that reading happens to the text as some extrinsic and contingent event. In order to defeat this tenacious suggestion, it may be a good stratagem to turn to a few exemplary texts that theorize about their being read. This is the path chosen by Michel Charles in his *Rhétorique de la lecture*.[20]

Charles's choice of this title is itself significant. It is no longer a question of a rhetoric of fiction, carried out by an implied author, but of a rhetoric of reading, oscillating between the text and its reader. This is still a rhetoric, inasmuch as its stratagems are inscribed within the text and inasmuch as even the reader is in a way constructed in and through the work.

It is not without import, however, that Charles's work begins with an interpretation of the first strophe of Lautréamont's *Les Chants de Maldoror*. The choices with which the reader is confronted by the author himself in this case—whether to turn back or to continue on through the book, whether or not to lose himself in reading, whether to be devoured by the text or to savor it—are themselves prescribed by the text. The reader is set free but what reading choices there are have already been encoded.[21] The violence of Lautréamont, we are told, consists in reading in place of the reader. Better, a particular reading situation is established in which the abolition of the distinction between reading and being read amounts to prescribing the "unreadable" (p. 13).

The second text selected, the Prologue to Rabelais' *Gargantua*, is in turn treated as a "mechanism for producing meanings" (p. 33).[22] By this, Michel

Charles means the sort of logic by which this text " 'constructs' the reader's freedom, but also limits it" (p. 33). The Prologue does possess the remarkable feature that the relation of the book to the reader is built upon the same metaphorical network as is the relation of the writer to his own work: "the drug contained within," "the outside form of Silenus," taken from the Socratic dialogues, "the bone and the marrow," which the book holds within itself and allows to be discovered and savored. The same "metaphorical rhapsody" (pp. 33f.) in which we can discern a recovery of the medieval theory of the multiple senses of Scripture and a recapitulation of Platonic imagery, Erasmian parable, and patristic metaphor, governs the text's reference to itself and the reader's relation to the text. In this way, the Rabelaisian text attempts to interpret its own references. Nevertheless, the hermeneutic woven in the Prologue is so rhapsodic that the author's designs become impenetrable and the reader's responsibility overwhelming.

We might say as regards the first two examples chosen by Michel Charles that the prescriptions for reading already inscribed in these texts are so ambiguous that, by disorienting the reader, they free him. Charles admits as much. The task of revealing the text's incompleteness falls to reading, through the interplay of transformations it involves.[23] The efficacy of the text is, as a consequence, no different from its fragility (p. 91). And there is no longer any incompatibility between a poetics that, in Jakobson's definition, places the accent on orienting the message back toward itself and a rhetoric of effective discourse, oriented toward a receiver, once "the message which is itself its own end, continues its *questioning*" (p. 78; his emphasis). As with the image of a poetics of an open work, the rhetoric of reading renounces setting itself up as a normative system, in order to become a "system of possible questions" (p. 118).[24]

The final texts chosen by Michel Charles open a new perspective. By seeing the "reading in the text" (the title of part three of *Rhétorique de la lecture*), what we find is a style of writing that allows itself to be interpreted only in terms of the interpretations it opens up. At the same time, the "reading-to-come" is the unknown that the writing puts into perspective.[25] Ultimately, the very structure of the text is but an effect of reading. After all, is not structural analysis itself the result of a work of reading? But then the initial formulation—"reading is part of the text, it is inscribed in it"—takes on a new meaning: reading is no longer that which the text prescribes; it is that which brings the structure of the text to light through interpretation.[26]

Charles's analysis of Benjamin Constant's *Adolphe* is particularly well-suited for demonstrating this, in that the author feigns to be merely the reader of a manuscript that has been found and in that, moreover, the interpretations internal to the work constitute so many virtual readings. Narrative, interpretation, and reading thus tend to overlap. Here Charles's thesis reaches its full strength, at the very moment when it is turned upside down. The reading is in the text, but the writing of the text anticipates the readings to come. With this, the text that is supposed to prescribe its reading is struck by the same indeterminacy and the same uncertainty as the readings to come.

A similar paradox results from the study of one of Baudelaire's *Petit Poèmes en prose:* "Le chien et le flacon." On the one hand, the text restrains its indirect receiver, the reader, by way of its direct receiver, the dog. The reader is really in the text and, to this extent, "this text has no response" (p. 251). But, just when the text seems to close itself up upon the reader in a terrorist act, by splitting its receivers in two it reopens a play space that rereading can turn into a space of freedom. This "reflexivity of reading"—in which I perceive an echo of what I shall below call, following Hans Robert Jauss, reflective reading—is what allows the act of reading to free itself from the reading inscribed within the text and to provide a response to the text.[27]

The final text chosen by Michel Charles—Rabelais' *Quart Livre*—reinforces this paradox. Once again, we see an author take a stand in relation to his text and, in doing this, set in place the variability of interpretations. "Everything happens as if the Rabelaisian text had *foreseen* the long parade of commentaries, glosses, and interpretations that have followed it" (p. 287; his emphasis). But, as a repercussion, this long parade makes the text a "machine for defying interpretations" (ibid.).

Rhétorique de la lecture appears to me to culminate in this paradox. On the one hand, the thesis of the "reading contained in the text," taken absolutely, as Charles asks us to do time and time again, gives the image not of manipulated readers, as the readers seduced and perverted by the unreliable narrator described by Wayne Booth appeared to be, but of readers terrorized by the decree of predestination striking their reading. On the other hand, the perspective of an infinite reading that, interminably, structures the very text prescribing it, restores to reading a disturbing indeterminacy. So we can understand, after the fact, why Michel Charles, from the opening pages of his work, gives equal measure to constraint and to freedom.

In the field of theories of reading, this paradox places *Rhétorique de la lecture* in a median position, halfway between an analysis that emphasizes the place of origin of the strategy of persuasion—the implied author—and an analysis that sets up the act of reading as the supreme authority. The theory of reading, at this point, ceases to belong to rhetoric and slips over into a phenomenology or a hermeneutics.[28]

A Phenomenology and an Aesthetic of Reading

From a purely rhetorical perspective, the reader is, finally, the prey and the victim of the strategy worked out by the implied author, and is so to the very extent this strategy is more deeply concealed. Another theory of reading is required, one that places an emphasis on the reader's response—the reader's response to the strategems of the implied author. A new element enriching poetics arises here out of an "aesthetic" rather than a "rhetoric," if we restore to the term "aesthetic" the full range of meaning of the Greek word *aisthēsis,* and if we grant to it the task of exploring the multiple ways in which a work, in acting on a reader, *affects* that reader. This being-affected has the note-worthy quality of combining in an experience of a particular type passivity and activity, which allows us to consider as the "reception" of a text the very "action" of reading it.

As I announced in Part I,[29] this aesthetic, as it complements poetics, en-compasses in turn two different forms, depending on whether the emphasis is placed on the effect produced on the individual reader and his response in the reading process, as in the work of Wolfgang Iser,[30] or on the response of the public on the level of its collective expectations, as in the work of Hans-Robert Jauss. These two aesthetics may appear to be opposed to each other, inasmuch as the one tends toward a phenomenological psychology while the other aims at reshaping literary history, but in fact they mutually presuppose each other. On the one hand, it is through the individual process of reading that the text reveals its "structure of appeal"; on the other hand, it is inasmuch as readers participate in the sedimented expectations of the general reading public that they are constituted as competent readers. The act of reading thus becomes one link in the chain of the history of the reception of a work by the public. Literary history, renovated by the aesthetic of reception, may thus claim to include the phenomenology of the act of reading.

It is, nevertheless, legitimate to begin with this phenomenology, for it is here that the rhetoric of persuasion encounters its first limit, by encountering its first reply. If the rhetoric of persuasion is supported by the coherence, not of the work to be sure, but of the strategy—evident or concealed—of the im-plied author, phenomenology has its starting point in the incomplete aspect of the literary text, which Roman Ingarden was the first to develop, in two im-portant works.[31]

For Ingarden, a text is incomplete, first, in the sense that it offers different "schematic views" that readers are asked to "concretize." They strive to pic-ture the characters and the events reported in the text. It is in relation to this image-building concretization that the work presents lacunae, "places of inde-terminacy." However well-articulated the "schematic views" proposed for our execution may be, the text resembles a musical score lending itself to different realizations.

A text is incomplete, second, in the sense that the world it proposes is de-fined as the intentional correlate of a sequence of sentences (*intentionale Satz-korrelate*), which remains to be made into a whole for such a world to be in-tended. Turning to advantage the Husserlian theory of time and applying it to the sequential chain of sentences in the text, Ingarden shows how each sentence points beyond itself, indicates something to be done, opens up a perspective. We recognize Husserlian protention in this anticipation of the sequence, as the sentences follow one another. This play of retentions and protentions functions in the text only if it is taken in hand by readers who welcome it into the play of their own expectations. Unlike the perceived object, however, the literary object does not intuitively "fulfill" these expectations; it can only modify them. This shifting process of the modification of expectations constitutes the image-building concretization mentioned above. It consists in traveling the length of the text, in allowing all the modifications performed to "sink" into memory, while compacting them, and in opening ourselves up to new expectations entailing new modifications. This process alone makes the text a work. So this work may be said to result from the interaction between the text and the reader.

Taken up again by Wolfgang Iser, these observations borrowed from Husserl by way of Ingarden undergo a remarkable development in the phenomenology of the act of reading.[32] The most original concept here is that of the "wandering viewpoint" (*The Act of Reading*, p. 108). It expresses the twofold fact that the whole of the text can never be perceived at once and that, placing ourselves within the literary text, we travel with it as our reading progresses. "This mode of grasping an object is unique to literature" (p. 109). This concept of a wandering viewpoint fits perfectly with the Husserlian description of the interplay of protentions and retentions. Throughout the reading process there is a continual interplay between modified expectations and transformed memories (p. 111). In addition, this concept incorporates into the phenomenology of reading the synthetic process by which a text constitutes itself sentence by sentence, through what might be called an interplay of sentential retentions and protentions. I am also retaining here the concept of the depragmatizing of objects, borrowed from the description of the empirical world. Literary texts "depragmatize [objects], for these objects are not to be denoted [*Bezeichnung*] but are to be transformed" (p. 109).

Leaving aside the other riches of this phenomenology of reading, I shall concentrate on those features that characterize the reader's response,[33] or even retort, to the rhetoric of persuasion. These features stress the dialectical character of the act of reading and lead us to speak of the work of reading in the same way we speak of the dream-work. Reading works on the text thanks to these dialectical features.

First, the act of reading tends to become, with the modern novel, a response to the strategy of deception so well illustrated by Joyce's *Ulysses*. This strategy consists in frustrating the expectation of an immediately intelligible configuration and in placing on the reader's shoulders the burden of configuring the work. The presupposition of this strategy, without which it would have no object, is that the reader expects a configuration, that reading is a search for coherence. In my own terms, I would say that reading itself becomes a drama of discordant concordance, inasmuch as the "places of indeterminacy" (*Unbestimmtheitstellen*)—to borrow Ingarden's expression—not only designate the lacunae of the text with respect to image-building concretization, but are themselves the result of the strategy of frustration incorporated in the text as such on its rhetorical level. What is at issue is therefore something quite different than providing ourself with a figure, an image, of the work; the work has also to be given a form. At quite the other extreme from readers on the edge of boredom from following a work that is too didactic, whose instructions leave no room for creative activity, modern readers risk buckling under the load of an impossible task when they are asked to make up for this lack of readability fabricated by the author. Reading then becomes a picnic where the author brings the words and the readers the meaning.

The first dialectic, by which reading comes close to being a battle, gives rise to a second one. What the work of reading reveals is not only a lack of determinacy but also an excess of meaning. Every text, even a systematically fragmentary one, is revealed to be inexhaustible in terms of reading, as though, through its unavoidably selective character, reading revealed an unwritten aspect in the text. It is the perogative of reading to strive to provide a figure for this unwritten side of the text. The text thus appears, by turns, both lacking and excessive in relation to reading.

A third dialectic takes shape on the horizon of this search for coherence. If it is too successful, the unfamiliar becomes familiar, and readers, feeling themselves to be on an equal footing with the work, come to believe in it so completely they lose themselves in it. Concretizing then becomes an illusion in the sense of believing that one actually sees something.[34] If the search for coherence fails, however, what is foreign remains foreign, and the reader remains on the doorstep of the work. The "right" reading is, therefore, the one that admits a certain degree of illusion—another name for the "willing suspension of disbelief" called for by Coleridge—and at the same time accepts the negation resulting from the work's surplus of meaning, its polysemanticism, which negates all the reader's attempts to adhere to the text and to its instructions. This process of "defamiliarizing" on the side of the reader corresponds to that of depragmatizing on the side of the text and its implied author. The "right" distance from the work is the one from which the illusion is, by turns, irresistible and untenable. As for a balance between these two impulses, it is never achieved.

Taken together, these three dialectics make reading a truly vital experience [*expérience vive*].

It is here that the "aesthetic" theory of reading authorizes a slightly different interpretation than that provided by the rhetoric of persuasion. The authors who most respect their readers are not the ones who gratify them in the cheapest way; they are the ones who leave a greater range to their readers to play out the contrast we have just discussed. On the one hand, they reach their readers only if, first, they share with them a repertoire of what is familiar with respect to literary genre, theme, and social—even historical—context, and if, on the other hand, they practice a strategy of defamiliarizing in relation to all the norms that any reading can easily recognize and adopt. In this regard, the unreliable narrator becomes the object of a more lenient judgment than that made by Wayne Booth. The unreliable narrator is one element in the strategy of illusion-breaking that illusion-making requires as its antidote. This strategy is one of those more apt to stimulate an active reading, a reading that permits us to say that something is happening in this game in which what is won is of the same magnitude as what is lost.[35] The balance of this gain and loss is unknown to readers; this is why they need to talk about it in order to formulate it. The critic is the one who can help to clarify the poorly elucidated potentialities hidden in this situation of disorientation.

In fact, it is what comes after reading that determines whether or not the stasis of disorientation has generated a dynamics of reorientation.

The advantage of this theory of response-effect is clear. A balance is sought between the signals provided by the text and the synthetic activity of reading. This balance is the unstable effect of the dynamism by which, I would say, the configuration of the text in terms of structure becomes equal to the reader's refiguration in terms of experience. This vital experience, in turn, is a genuine dialectic by virtue of the negativity it implies: depragmatization and defamiliarization, inversion of the given in image-building consciousness, illusion-breaking.[36]

Is the phenomenology of reading thereby entitled to make the category of "implied reader" the exact counterpart to that of the "implied author" introduced by the rhetoric of fiction?

At first sight, a symmetry does appear to be established between the implied author and the implied reader, each represented by its corresponding marks in the text. By implied reader we must then understand the role assigned to the real reader by the instructions in the text. The implied author and the implied reader thus become literary categories compatible with the semantic autonomy of the text. Inasmuch as they are constructed in the text, they are both fictional correlates of real beings. The implied author is identified with the unique style of the work, the implied reader with the receiver to whom the sender of the work addresses himself. This symmetry, however, proves finally misleading. On the one hand, the implied author is a disguise of the real author, who disappears by making himself the narrator immanent in the work—the narrative voice. On the other hand, the real reader is a concretization of the implied reader, intended by the narrator's strategy of persuasion. In relation to the narrator, the implied reader remains virtual as long as this role has not been actualized.[37] Thus, whereas the real author effaces himself in the implied author, the implied reader takes on substance in the real reader. This real reader is the pole opposite the text in the process of interaction giving rise to the meaning of the work. It is in fact this real reader who is in question in a phenomenology of the act of reading. This is why I would be more inclined to praise Iser for getting rid of the aporias arising out of the distinctions made at various points between intended reader, ideal reader, competent reader, reader contemporary with the work, today's reader, and so on. Not that these distinctions are groundless, but various figures of the reader do not take us even a single step outside the structure of the text, of which the implied reader continues to be a variable. To give full scope to the theme of interaction, the phenomenology of the act of reading requires a flesh-and-blood reader, who, in actualizing the role of the reader prestructured in and through the text, transforms it.[38]

The aesthetic of reception, as we stated above, can be taken in two senses: either in the sense of a phenomenology of the individual act of reading in the "theory of aesthetic response" of Wolfgang Iser, or in the sense of a hermeneutic of the public reception of a work as in Hans Robert Jauss's *Toward an Aesthetic of Reception*.[39] However, as we have already hinted, these two approaches intersect at some point—precisely, in *aisthēsis*.

Let us therefore follow the movement by which the aesthetic of reception leads back to this point of intersection.

In its initial formulation,[40] Jauss's aesthetic of reception was not intended to complete a phenomenological theory of the act of reading but rather to renew the history of literature, which is said at the start of this essay to have "fallen into disrepute, and not at all without reason" (p. 3).[41] Several major theses make up the program for this aesthetic of reception.

The basic thesis from which all the others are derived holds that the meaning of a literary work rests upon the dialogical (*dialogisch*)[42] relation established between the work and its public in each age. This thesis, similar to Collingwood's notion that history is but a reenactment of the past in the mind of the historian, amounts to including the effect produced (*Wirkung*) by a work—in other words, the meaning a public attributes to it—within the boundaries of the work itself. The challenge, as it is announced in the title of Jauss's essay consists in equating actual meaning with reception. It is not simply the actual effect but the "history of effects"—to use an expression from Gadamer's philosophical hermeneutics—that has to be taken into account, which requires restoring the horizon of expectation[43] of the literary work considered; that is, the system of references shaped by earlier traditions concerning the genre, the theme, and the degree of contrast for the first receivers between the poetic language and everyday practical language (we shall return to this important opposition).[44] In this way, we understand the sense of parody in *Don Quixote* only if we are capable of reconstructing its initial public's feeling of familiarity with chivalrous romances and, consequently, if we are capable of understanding the shock produced by a work that, after feigning to satisfy the public's expectation, runs directly counter to it. The case of new works is in this respect the most favorable for discerning the change of horizon that constitutes the major effect that occurs here. Hence the critical factor for establishing a literary history is the identification of successive aesthetic distances between the preexisting horizon of expectation and the new work, distances that mark out the work's reception. These distances constitute the moments of negativity in this reception. But what is it to reconstitute the horizon of expectation of a yet unknown experience, if not to discover the interplay of questions to which the work suggests an answer? To the ideas of effect, history of effects, and horizon of expectations must be added, following once again Collingwood and Gadamer, the logic of question and answer; a logic whereby we can understand a work only if we have understood that to which it responds.[45] This logic of question and answer, in turn, allows us to correct the idea that history would be no more than a history of gaps or deviations, hence a history of negativity. As a response, the reception of a work performs a certain mediation between the past and the present or, better, between the horizon of expectation coming from the past and the horizon of expectation belonging to the present. The thematic concern of literary history lies in this "historical mediation."

Having arrived at this point, we may ask whether the horizons stemming from this mediation can stabilize in any lasting way the meaning of a work, to the point of conferring a transhistorical authority on it. In opposition to Gadamer's thesis concerning "the classical,"[46] Jauss refuses to see in the enduring character of great works anything other than a temporary stabilization of the dynamic of reception; any Platonic hypostasizing of a prototype offered to our recognition would, according to him, violate the rule of questions and answers. For what, to us, is classical was not first perceived as something outside of time but rather as opening up a new horizon. If we admit that the cognitive value of a work lies in its power to prefigure an experience to come, then there must be no question of freezing the dialogical relation into an atemporal truth. This open character of the history of effects leads us to say that every work is not only an answer provided to an earlier question but a source of new questions, in turn. Jauss refers to Hans Blumenberg, for whom "each work of art poses and leaves behind, as a kind of including horizon, the 'solutions' which are possible after it."[47] These new questions are opened not only in front of the work but behind it as well. For example, it is after the fact, by a recoil-effect of Mallarmé's lyrical hermeticism, that we are able to release virtual meanings in baroque poetry that had hitherto remained unnoticed. But it is not only before and behind, in diachrony, that the work opens up distances, this also occurs in the present, as a synchronic cross-section of a phase of literary evolution will show. We may hesitate here between a conception that underscores the total heterogeneity of culture at any given moment, to the point of proclaiming the pure "coexistence of the simultaneous and the non-simultaneous,"[48] and a conception where the emphasis is placed on the effect of totalization resulting from the redistribution of horizons through the interplay of question and answer. We thus find on the synchronic plane a problem comparable to that posed by "the classical" on the diachronic plane; the history of literature must break a path through the same paradoxes and the same extremes.[49] Just as it is true that at any given moment, a particular work may have been perceived as out of step, not current, premature, or outmoded (Nietzsche would say "untimely"), so too it must also be admitted that, owing to the history of reception itself, the multiplicity of works tends to form one great tableau that the public perceives as the production of *its* time. Literary history would not be possible without a few great works serving as reference points, relatively enduring in the diachronic process, and acting as powerful forces of integration in the synchronic dimension.[50]

We can see the fruitfulness of these theses with respect to the old problem of the social influence of the work of art. We must challenge with equal force the thesis of a narrow structuralism which forbids "moving outside the text" and that of a dogmatic Marxism which merely shifts onto the social plane the worn-out topos of *imitatio naturae*. It is on the level of a public's horizon of expectations that a work exercises what Jauss terms the "creative function of the work of art."[51] The horizon of expectation peculiar to literature does not coincide with that of everyday life. If a new work is able to create an aesthetic distance, it is because a prior distance exists between the whole of literary life and everyday practice. It is a basic characteristic of the horizon of expectation against the background of which new reception stands out that it is itself the expression of an even more basic noncoincidence, namely, the opposition in a given culture "between poetic language and practical language, imaginary world and social reality" (p. 24).[52] What we have just indicated as literature's function of social creation arises quite precisely at this point of articulation between the expectations turned toward art and literature and the expectations constitutive of everyday experience.[53]

The moment when literature attains its highest degree of efficacity is perhaps the moment when it places its readers in the position of finding a solution for which they themselves must find the appropriate questions, those that constitute the aesthetic and moral problem posed by a work.

If *Toward an Aesthetic of Reception,* whose basic theses we have just summarized, could link up with and complete the phenomenology of the act of reading, this was through an expansion of its initial undertaking, which was to renew literary history, and from its insertion within a more ambitious project, that of constituting a literary hermeneutics.[54] This hermeneutics is assigned the task of equaling the other two regional hermeneutics, theological and juridical, under the auspices of a philosophical hermeneutics akin to that of Gadamer. Literary hermeneutics, as Jauss admits, continues to be the poor relation of hermeneutics. A literary hermeneutics worthy of the name must assume the threefold task, referred to above, of understanding (*subtilitas intelligendi*), explanation (*subtilitas interpretandi*), and application (*subtilitas applicandi*). In contrast to a superficial view, reading must not be confined to the field of application, even if this field does reveal the end of the hermeneutical process; instead, reading must pass through all three stages. A literary hermeneutics will, therefore, reply to these three questions: in what sense is the primary undertaking of understanding entitled to characterize the object of literary hermeneutics as an aesthetic one? What does reflective exegesis add to understanding? What equivalent to a sermon in biblical exegesis and to a verdict in juridical exegesis does literature offer on the level of application? In this triadic structure, application orients the entire process teleologically, but primary understanding guides the process from one stage to the next by virtue of the horizon of expectation it already contains. Literary hermeneutics is thus oriented both toward application and by understanding. And it is the logic of question and answer that ensures the transition to explanation.

The primacy accorded to understanding explains why literary hermeneutics, unlike Gadamer's philosophical hermeneutics, is not directly produced by the logic of question and answer. Finding the question to which a text offers a reply, reconstructing the expectations of a text's first receivers in order to restore to the text its original otherness—these are already steps in rereading, standing second in relation to a primary understanding that allows the text to develop its own expectations.

This primacy ascribed to understanding is explained by the wholly original relation between knowledge and enjoyment (*Genuss*) that ensures the aesthetic quality of literary hermeneutics. This relation parallels that between the call and promise, committing a whole life, characterizing theological understanding. If the specific nature of literary understanding in terms of enjoyment has been neglected, this is due to the curious convergence between the interdiction uttered by structural poetics, forbidding us to step outside the text or to move beyond the reading instructions it contains,[55] and the disfavor cast on enjoyment by Adorno's negative aesthetic, which sees in it merely a "bourgeois" compensation for the asceticism of labor.[56]

Contrary to the common idea that pleasure is ignorant and mute, Jauss asserts that it possesses the power to open a space of meaning in which the logic of question and answer will subsequently unfold. It gives rise to understanding—*il donne à comprendre*. Pleasure is a perceptive reception, attentive to the prescriptions of the musical score that the text is, one that opens up by virtue of the horizonal aspect that Husserl attributed to all perception. By all these features, aesthetic perception is distinguished from everyday perception and thus establishes a distance in relation to ordinary experience, as this was underscored above in Jauss's theses on the renewal of literary history. The text asks its readers, first of all, to entrust themselves to this perceptive understanding, to the suggestions of meaning that a second reading will thematize, suggestions of meaning that will provide a horizon for this reading.

The passage from the first reading, the innocent reading—if there is one— to the second reading, a reading at a distance, is governed, as we stated above, by the horizonal structure of immediate understanding. This structure is not simply staked out by the expectations stemming from the dominant tendencies in taste of the epoch when a text is read or from the reader's familiarity with earlier works. This horizonal structure gives rise, in turn, to expectations of meaning that are not satisfied, which reading reinscribes within the logic of question and answer. So reading and rereading have their respective advantages and weaknesses. Reading includes both richness and opacity; rereading clarifies but in so doing makes choices. It is based on the questions that remained open after the first passage through the text but offers only one interpretation among others. So a dialectic of expectations and of questions governs the relation between reading and rereading. Expectations are open but more undetermined; questions are determined but more closed-in upon themselves. Literary criticism must take its stand on the basis of this hermeneutical precondition of partiality.

The elucidation of this partiality gives rise to a third reading. This emerges from the question: what historical horizon has conditioned the genesis and the effect of the work and limits, in turn, the interpretation of the present reader? Literary hermeneutics delimits in this way the legitimate space for the historico-philological methods that predominated in the prestructuralist era and that were dethroned in the age of structuralism. Their proper place is defined by their function of verification which, in a certain sense, makes immediate reading, and even reflective reading, dependent on the reading based on historical reconstruction. By a recoil-effect the reading of verification helps to disentangle aesthetic pleasure from the mere satisfaction of contemporary prejudices and interests, by tying it to the perception of the difference between the past horizon of the work and the present horizon of reading. A strange feeling of distancing is thus inserted at the heart of present pleasure. The third reading brings about this effect by redoubling the logic of question and answer that governed the second reading. What, it asks, were the questions to which the work was the answer? Yet this third "historical" reading continues to be guided by the expectations of the first reading and by the questions of the second reading. The merely historicizing question—what did the text say?—remains under the control of the properly hermeneutical question—what does the text say to me and what do I say to the text?[57]

What becomes of application in this schema? At first sight, the application proper to this hermeneutics does not appear to produce any effect comparable to preaching in theological hermeneutics or to a verdict in juridical hermeneutics. The recognition of the text's otherness in scholarly reading seems to be the final word of literary aesthetics. This hesitation is understandable. If it is true that *aisthēsis* and enjoyment are not restricted to the level of immediate understanding but carry through all the levels of hermeneutical "subtility," we may be tempted to consider the aesthetic dimension that accompanies pleasure in its traversal of the three hermeneutical stages as the final criterion for literary hermeneutics. If so, then application does not constitute a genuinely distinct stage. *Aisthēsis* itself already reveals and transforms. Aesthetic experience draws this power from the contrast it establishes from the outset in relation to everyday experience. Because it is "refractory" to anything other than itself, it asserts its ability to transfigure the everyday and to transgress accepted standards. Before any reflective distanciation, aesthetic understanding as such appears to be application. Attesting to this is the range of effects it deploys: from the seduction and illusion so dear to popular literature, to the appeasement of suffering and the aestheticizing of the experience of the past, to the subversion and utopia characteristic of so many contemporary works. Through this variety of effects, aesthetic experience as it is invested in reading directly corroberates Erasmus's aphorism: *lectio transit in mores.*

It is possible, however, to discern a more distinct contour for application if it is set at the end of another triad, which Jauss interweaves with that of the three subtleties without establishing a term-by-term correspondence between the two series—the triad here is *poiēsis, aithēsis, catharsis.*[58] A complex set of effects is attached to catharsis. It designates first of all the effect of the work that is more moral than aesthetic: new evaluations, hitherto unheard of norms, are proposed by the work, confronting or shaking current customs.[59] This first effect is closely boound up with readers' tendency to identify with the hero, and to allow themselves to be guided by the reliable or unreliable narrator. Catharsis, however, has this moral effect only because, first of all, it displays the power of clarifying, examining, and instructing exerted by the work in virtue of the distanciation that takes place in relation to our own affects.[60] It is an easy passage from this sense to the one most strongly emphasized by Jauss, namely, the work's communicative efficacy. A clarification is, indeed, essentially communicative; through it, the work "teaches."[61] What we find here is not simply a notation from Aristotle but a major feature of Kantian aesthetics—the contention that the universal nature of the beautiful consists in nothing else than in its a priori communicability. Catharsis thus constitutes a distinct moment from *aisthēsis,* conceived of as pure receptivity; namely, the moment of communicability of perceptive understanding. *Aisthēsis* frees the reader from everyday concerns, catharsis sets the reader free for new evaluations of reality that will take shape in rereading. An even more subtle effect results from catharsis. Thanks to the clarification it brings about, catharsis sets in motion a process of transposition, one that is not only affective but cognitive as well, something like *allégorèse,* whose history can be traced back to Christian and pagan exegesis. Allegorization occurs whenever we attempt "to translate the meaning of a text in its first context into another context, which amounts to saying: to give it a new signification which goes beyond the horizon of meaning delimited by the intentionality of the text in its original context." [62] It is ultimately this allegorizing power, related to catharsis, that makes literary application the response most similar to the analogizing apprehension of the past in the dialectic of the *Gegenüber* and of indebtedness.

This is the distinct problematic arising from application, which, however, never entirely escapes the horizon of perceptive understanding and the attitude of enjoyment.

At the end of our perusal of several theories of reading, chosen in view of their contribution to our problem of refiguration, several major features stand out that underscore, each in its own way, the dialectical structure of the operation of refiguration.

The first dialectical tension arose from the comparison we could not help but make between the feeling of a debt, which appeared to us to accompany the relation of standing-for the past, and the freedom of the imaginative variations performed by fiction on the theme of the aporias of time, as we described them in the preceding section of this volume. The analyses we have just made of the phenomenon of reading lead us to nuance this overly simple opposition. It must be stated, first of all, that the projection of a fictive world consists in a complex creative process, which may be no less marked by an awareness of a debt than is the historian's work of reconstruction. The question of creative freedom is not a simple one. The liberation of fiction as regards the constraints of history—constraints summed up in documentary proof—does not constitute the final word concerning the freedom of fiction. It constitutes only the Cartesian moment: free choice in the realm of the imaginary. But its service to the worldview that the implied author strives to communicate to the reader is for fiction the source of more subtle constraints, which express the Spinozist moment of freedom: namely, internal necessity. Free from the external constraint of documentary proof, fiction is bound internally by the very thing that it projects outside itself. Free from . . . , artists must still make themselves free for. . . . If this were not the case, how could we explain the anguish and suffering of artistic creation as they are attested to by the correspondence and diaries of a van Gogh or a Cézanne? Thus, the stringent law of creation, which is to render as perfectly as possible the vision of the world that inspires the artist, corresponds feature by feature to the debt of the historian and of the reader of history with respect to the dead. [63] What the strategy of persuasion, wrought by the implied author, seeks to impose on the reader is, precisely, the force of conviction—the illocutionary force, we might say in the vocabulary of speech-act theory—that upholds the narrator's vision of the world. The paradox here is that the freedom of the imaginative variations is communicated only by being cloaked in the constraining power of a vision of the world. The dialectic between freedom and constraint, internal to the creative process, is thus transmitted throughout the hermeneutical process that

Jauss characterizes by means of the triad poiēsis, aisthēsis, catharsis. The final term of this triad is the very one in which this paradox of a constrained freedom, of a freedom released by constraint, culminates. In the moment of clarification and of purification, readers are rendered free in spite of themselves. It is this paradox that makes the confrontation between the world of the text and the world of the reader a struggle to which the fusion of horizons of expectation of the text with those of the reader brings only a precarious peace.

A second dialectical tension arises from the structure of the operation of reading itself. Indeed, it appeared impossible to give a simple description of this phenomenon. We had to start from the pole of the implied author and his strategy of persuasion, then to cross over the ambiguous zone of a prescription for reading, which at once constrains readers and sets them free, in order, finally, to reach an aesthetic of reception, which places the work and the reader in a synergetic relation. This dialectic should be compared with the one that appeared to us to mark the relation of standing-for resulting from the enigma of the pastness of the past. To be sure, it is not a matter of seeking a term-by-term resemblance between the moments of the theory of standing-for and those of the theory of reading. Nonetheless, the dialectical constitution of reading is not foreign to the dialectic of the Same, the Other, and the Analogous.[64] For example, the rhetoric of fiction brings on stage an implied author who, through the ploy of seduction, attempts to make the reader identical with himself. But, when readers, discovering the place prescribed for them in the text, no longer feel seduced but terrorized, their only recourse is to set themselves at a distance from the text and to become fully conscious of the distance between the expectations developed by the text and their own expectations, as individuals caught up in everyday concerns and as members of a cultured public formed by an entire tradition of readings. This oscillation between Same and Other is overcome only in the operation characterized by Gadamer and Jauss as the fusion of horizons and that may be held to be the ideal type of reading. Beyond the alternatives of confusion and alienation, the convergence of writing and reading tends to establish, between the expectations created by the text and those contributed by reading, an analogizing relation, not without resemblance to that in which the relation of standing-for the historical past culminates.

Another remarkable property of the phenomenon of reading, one which also generates a dialectic, has to do with the relation between communicability and referentiality (if it is still legitimate to employ this term, with the appropriate reservations) in the operation of refiguration. We can enter this problem from either end. We can say, as in our sketch of mimesis$_3$ in volume 1, that an aesthetics of reception cannot take up the problem of communication without taking up that of reference, inasmuch as what is communicated is, in the final analysis, beyond the sense of the work, the world the work projects, the world that constitutes the horizon of the work.[65] But, from the opposite direction, we must say that the reception of the work and the welcome given what Gadamer likes to call the "issue" of the text are extracted from the sheer subjectivity of the act of reading only on the condition of being inscribed within a chain of readings, which gives a historical dimension to this reception and to this welcome. The act of reading is thereby included within a reading community, which, under certain favorable conditions, develops the sort of normativity and canonical status that we acknowledge in great works, those that never cease decontextualizing and recontextualizing themselves in the most diverse cultural circumstances. From this angle we return to a central theme in Kantian aesthetics, namely, that communicability constitutes an intrinsic component of the judgment of taste. To be sure, it is not to reflective judgment that we ascribe this sort of universality which Kant held to be a priori but, quite the contrary, to the "thing itself" that summons us in the text. However, between this "appeal structure," to speak as Iser does, and the communicability characteristic of a reading-in-common, a reciprocal relation is established, intrinsically constitutive of the power of refiguration belonging to works of fiction.

A final dialectic brings us to the threshold of our next chapter. It concerns the two, if not antithetical at least divergent, roles assumed by reading. Reading appears by turns as an interruption in the course of action and as a new impetus to action. These two perspectives on reading result directly from its functions of confrontation and connection between the imaginary world of the text and the actual world of readers. To the extent that readers subordinate their expectations to those developed by the text, they themselves become unreal to a degree comparable to the unreality of the fictive world toward which they emigrate. Reading then becomes a place, itself unreal, where reflection takes a pause. On the other hand, inasmuch as readers incorporate—little matter whether consciously or unconsciously—into their vision of the world the lessons of their readings, in order to increase the prior readability of this vision, then reading is for them something other than a place where they come to rest; it is a medium they cross through.

This twofold status of reading makes the confrontation between the world of the text and the world of the reader at once a stasis and an impetus.[66] The ideal type of reading, figured by the fusion but not confusion of the horizons of expectation of the text and those of the reader, unites these two moments of refiguration in the fragile unity of stasis and impetus. This fragile union can be expressed in the following paradox: the more readers become unreal in their reading, the more profound and far-reaching will be the work's influence on social reality. Is it not the least figurative style of painting that has the greatest chance of changing our vision of the world?

From this final dialectic comes the result that, if the problem of the refiguration of time by narrative comes together in the narrative, it does not find its outcome there.

8

The Interweaving of History and Fiction

With this chapter we reach the goal that has never ceased to guide the progress of our investigation, namely, the actual refiguration of time, now become human time through the interweaving of history and fiction.[1] Whereas in the first stage the accent was on the heterogeneity of the replies brought by history and fiction to the aporias of phenomenological time, that is, on the opposition between the imaginative variations produced by fiction and the reinscription of phenomenological time onto cosmological time as stipulated by history; and whereas, in the second stage a certain parallel became apparent between standing for the historical past and the transfer from the fictive world of the text to the actual world of the reader—what will concern us now is the confluence of the two series of analyses devoted to history and to fiction, respectively, even the mutual encompassing of the two processes of refiguration.

This passage from a stage where the heterogeneity of intentional aims predominates to a stage where interaction holds sway has been carefully prepared by the preceding analyses.

First, between the time of fiction and historical time a certain commensurability was assured by phenomenology, which provided a thematics common to both narrative modes, however riddled with aporias this phenomenology may be. At the end of the first stage, there was at least the possibility of asserting that history and fiction came to grips with the same difficulties, difficulties that may, of course, be unresolved but that are recognized and brought to the level of language by phenomenology. Next, the theory of reading created a common space for exchanges between history and fiction. Here we acted as though reading concerned only the reception of literary texts. Yet we are readers of history just as much as we are readers of novels. All forms of writing, including historiography, take their place within an extended theory of reading. As a result, the operation of mutually encompassing one another, which I referred to above, is rooted in reading. In this sense, the analyses of the interweaving of history and fiction that will be sketched out here belong to an extended theory of reception, within which the act of reading is considered as the phenomenological moment. It is within such an extended theory of reading that the reversal from divergence to convergence occurs in the relation between historical narrative and fictional narrative.

What remains then is the step from convergence to interconnection or interweaving.

By the interweaving of history and fiction I mean the fundamental structure, ontological as well as epistemological, by virtue of which history and fiction each concretize their respective intentionalities only by borrowing from the intentionality of the other. In narrative theory, this concretization corresponds to the phenomenon of "seeing as . . ." by which I characterized metaphoric reference in my *Rule of Metaphor*. We have touched upon this problem of concretization at least twice: once when, following Hayden White, we attempted to elucidate the relation of historical consciousness standing for the past as such through the notion of an analogous apprehension; a second time, when in a perspective similar to that of Roman Ingarden, we described reading as an actualization of the text considered as a score to be performed. I am now going to show that this concretization is obtained only insofar as, on the one hand, history in some way makes use of fiction to refigure time and, on the other hand, fiction makes use of history for the same ends. This reciprocal concretization marks the triumph of the notion of figure in the form of "imagining that"; or more literally: "providing oneself a figure of . . ." [*se figurer que . . .*].

THE FICTIONALIZATION OF HISTORY

The first half of my thesis is easier to demonstrate. Nevertheless, we must not misconstrue its import. For one thing, it is not simply a matter of repeating what was stated in volume 1 about the role of the imagination in historical narrative on the level of configuration. Instead it is a question of the role of the imaginary in intending the past as it actually was. On the other hand, I am by no means denying the absence of symmetry between a "real" past and an "unreal" world, the object being instead to show in what unique way the imaginary is incorporated into the intended having-been, without weakening the "realist" aspect of this intention.

The empty place to be filled by the imaginary is indicated by the very nature, as nonobservable, of what has been. To be convinced of this we have only to retrace our series of three successive approximations to having-been as it once was. We then see that the role of the imaginary grows as the approximation becomes increasingly precise. Consider the most realist hypothesis about the historical past, the one I began with in order to situate the response of historical consciousness to the aporias of time. History, I said, reinscribes the time of narrative within the time of the universe. This is a "realist" thesis in the sense that history locates its chronology on the single scale of time common to what is called the "history" of the earth, the "history" of living species, the "history" of the solar system and the galaxies. This reinscription of the time of narrative within the time of the universe in accordance with a single time scale marks the specificity of the referential mode characteristic of historiography.

It is precisely in connection with this, the most "realist" thesis, that the imaginary enters for the first time into the intending of what has been.

We have not forgotten that the gap between the time of the world and lived time is bridged only by constructing some specific connectors that serve to make historical time conceivable and manipulable. The calendar, which I placed at the head of these connectors, stems from the same inventiveness that can be seen at work already in the construction of the *gnomon*. As J. T. Frazer notes at the beginning of his work on time, if the very name "gnomon" preserves something of its ancient meaning of counsellor, inspector, expert, this is because an activity of interpretation is at work in it, directing the very construction of this device, which in appearance is so simple.[2] Just as an interpreter does a continuous translation from one language to another, conjoining in this way two linguistic universes in accordance with a certain principle of transformation, so the gnomon conjoins two processes in accordance with certain hypotheses about the world. One process is the movement of the sun, the other the life of the person who consults the gnomon. This hypothesis includes the principle implicit in the construction and functioning of the sundial (p. 3). The double affiliation that seemed to me to characterize the calendar is already apparent here. On the one hand, the sundial belongs to the human universe. It is an artifact intended to regulate the life of its constructor. On the other hand, it also belongs to the astronomical universe: the movement of the shadow is independent of human will. But these two worlds would not stand in relation to each other unless people were convinced that it were possible to derive signals relating to time from the movement of the projected shadow. This belief allows them to organize their lives on the basis of the movements of the shadow, without expecting the shadow to comply with the rhythm of their own needs and desires (p. 4). This conviction would not arise, however, if it did not embody two kinds of information in the construction of the device: one concerning the hour, resulting from the orientation of the shadow on the sundial; the other concerning the season, resulting from the length of the shadow at noon. Without hourly divisions and concentric circles, we would be unable to read the gnomon. To place two heterogeneous courses side by side, to form a general hypothesis about nature as a whole, and to construct an appropriate device—these are the principal steps of invention that, incorporated in the reading of the sundial, make it a reading of signs, a translation and an interpretation, in J. T. Frazer's words. This reading of signs can, in turn, be considered a schematizing operation, wherein two perspectives on time are thought together.

All we have said about the calendar could be restated in similar terms. The intellectual operations are, certainly, much more complex, in particular the numerical calculations applied to the different periodicities involved with an eye to making them commensurable. In addition, the institutional, and ultimately political, aspect of establishing a calendar emphasizes the synthetic nature of the conjunction of the astronomical and the eminently social aspects of the calendar. Despite all the differences that can be found between the clock and the calendar, however, reading the calendar is also an interpretation of signs comparable to reading a sundial or a clock. On the basis of a periodic system of dates, a perpetual calendar allows us to allocate a particular date, that is, some particular place in the system of all possible dates, to an event that bears the mark of the present and by implication that of the past or the future. Dating an event thus displays a synthetic character by which an actual present is identified with some particular instant. What is more, if the principle of dating consists in allocating a lived-through present to some particular instant, in practice it consists in allocating a present as-if (to follow the Husserlian definition of recollection) to a particular instant. Dates are assigned to potential presents, to imagined presents. In this way, all the memories accumulated by a collective memory can become dated events, due to their reinscription in calendar time.

It would be an easy matter to apply the same argument to the other connectors between narrative time and universal time. The succession of generations is at once a biological datum and a prosthesis for recollection in the Husserlian sense. It is always possible to extend recollection through the chain of ancestral memories, to move back in time by extending this regressive movement through imagination, just as it is possible for every one of us to situate our own temporality in the series of generations, with the more or less necessary help of calendar time. In this sense, the network of contemporaries, predecessors, and successors schematizes—in the Kantian sense of the term— the relation between the more biological phenomenon of the succession of generations and the more intellectual phenomenon of the reconstruction of the realm of contemporaries, predecessors, and successors. The mixed character of this threefold realm underscores its imaginary aspect.

Obviously, it is in the phenomenon of the trace that we find the culmination of the imaginary character of the connectors that mark the founding of historical time. This imaginary mediation is presupposed by the mixed structure of the trace itself, considered as a sign-effect. This mixed structure expresses in shorthand a complex synthetic activity, involving causal types of inference applied to the trace as a mark left behind and activities of interpretation tied to the signifying character of the trace as something present standing for something past. This synthetic activity, which is well expressed by the verb "to retrace," sums up in turn operations as complex as those at the origin of the gnomon and the calendar. These are the activities of preserving, selecting, assembling, consulting, and finally, reading documents and archives, which mediate and, so to speak, schematize the trace, making it the ultimate presupposition of the reinscription of lived time (time with a present). If the trace is a more radical phenomenon than the document or the archive, it is, nevertheless, the use of documents and archives that makes the trace an actual operator of historical time. The imaginary character of the activities that mediate and schematize the trace is evident in the intellectual work that accompanies the interpretation of remains, fossils, ruins, museum pieces, or monuments. They are attributed the value of being a trace, that is a sign-effect, only when we provide ourselves with a figure of the context of life, of the social and cultural environment, in short—to use one of Heidegger's expressions referred to above—only when we provide ourselves with a figure of the world surrounding the relic that today is missing, so to speak. Here, with the expression "to provide ourselves with a figure of," we touch upon an activity of the imagination that is easier to grasp within the framework of the following analysis.

The mediating role of fiction, in fact, increases when we move from the theme of the reinscription of lived time within cosmic time to that of the pastness of the past. On the one hand, the historian's spontaneous "realism" found its critical expression in the difficult concept of standing-for, which we expressly distinguished from that of representation. By this we wished to convey the claim of a *Gegenüber* no longer in existence today on the historical discourse that intends it, its power of incitement and rectification in relation to all historical constructions, insofar as these are considered to be reconstructions. I myself have emphasized this right of the past as it once was, by placing in correspondence with it the idea of a debt we owe the dead. On the other hand, the elusive character of this *Gegenüber*, however imperative it may be, has led us into a logical game where the categories of the Same, the Other, and the Analogous give shape to the enigma without resolving it. At each stage of this logical game the imaginary imposes itself as the indispensable servant of standing-for, making us once again come face-to-face with the operation that consists in providing ourselves with a figure of what was. Nor have I forgotten what we found in Collingwood, taken as the spokesman for the Same, concerning the intimate union between the historical imagination and reenactment. Reenactment is the telos of the historical imagination, what it intends, and its crowning achievement. The historical imagination, in return, is the organon of reenactment. If we pass from the category of the Same to that of the Other in order to express the moment of what is no more in standing for the past, it is still the imaginary that keeps otherness from slipping into the unsayable. It is always through some transfer from Same to Other, in empathy and imagination, that the Other that is foreign to me is brought closer. In this respect, Husserl's analysis in his fifth *Cartesian Meditation*, dealing with the operation of pairing (*Paarung*) and the inference by analogy that is the basis for it, is here perfectly appropriate. In addition, the central theme of Dilthey's interpretive sociology is preserved here, namely, that all historical intelligence is rooted in the capacity of a subject to transport itself into an alien psychic life. As Gadamer notes in this regard, here mind comprehends mind. It is this transfer by analogy, to combine the themes of Husserl and Dilthey, that justifies our passage to the Analogous and our recourse, with Hayden White, to tropology in an effort to provide an acceptable sense for the expression handed down to us by Ranke, one that takes its distance from every form of positivism: knowing the past *wie es eigentlich gewesen* (the past as it actually happened). The *wie*—which, paradoxically, acts to balance the *eigentlich*—thus assumes the tropological value of "such as . . ." interpreted as metaphor, metonomy, synecdoche, and irony. What Hayden White terms the "representative" function of the historical imagination once again borders on the act of providing "ourselves a figure of . . ." by which the imagination manifests its ocular dimension. The past is what I would have seen, what I would have witnessed if I had been there, just as the other side of things is what I would see if I were looking at them from the side from which you are looking at them. In this way, tropology becomes the imaginary aspect of standing-for.

One more step is left to be taken; it consists in moving from the dated past and the reconstructed past to the refigured past, and in specifying the modality of the imaginary that corresponds to this requirement for figurativeness. In this respect, up to now we have merely indicated the empty place of the imaginary in the work of refiguration.

We must now say how it happens that just these features of the imaginary, made explicit by fictional narrative, come to enrich these imaginary mediations and how, by this very fact, the actual interweaving of fiction and history occurs in the refiguration of time.

I have alluded to these features by introducing the expression "to provide ourselves a figure of. . . ." They all share the property of conferring on the intending of the past a quasi-intuitive fulfillment. A key modality here is borrowed directly from the metaphorical function of "seeing as." We have long been prepared to welcome the help that the split reference of metaphor contributes to the refiguration of time by history. Once we have admitted that the writing of history is not something added from outside to historical knowledge but is one with it, nothing prevents us from admitting as well that history imitates in its own writing the types of emplotment handed down by our literary tradition. In this way, we saw Hayden White borrow from Northrop Frye the categories of tragedy, comedy, romance, irony, and so on, and pair up these literary genres with the tropes of our rhetorical tradition. But what history borrows from literature can by no means be limited to the level of composition, hence to the moment of configuration. What is borrowed also involves the representative function of the historical imagination. We learn to see a given series of events *as* tragic, *as* comic, and so on. What it is, precisely, that makes for the perenniality of certain great historical works, whose scientific reliability has been eroded by documentary progress, is the appropriateness of their poetic art and their rhetoric with respect to their way of "seeing" the past. One and the same work can thus be a great book of history and a fine novel. What is surprising is that this interlacing of fiction and history in no way undercuts the project of standing-for belonging to history, but instead helps to realize it.

This fiction-effect, if we may call it so, is also found to be augmented by the various rhetorical strategies that I mentioned in my review of theories of reading. A history book can be read as a novel. In doing this, we enter into an implicit pact of reading and share in the complicity it establishes between the narrative voice and the implied reader. By virtue of this pact, the reader's guard is lowered. Mistrust is willingly suspended. Confidence reigns. The reader is prepared to accord the historian the exorbitant right to know other minds. In the name of this right, ancient historians did not hesitate to place in the mouths of their heroes invented discourses, which the documents did not guarantee but only made plausible. Modern historians no longer permit themselves these fanciful incursions, fanciful in the strict sense of the term. They do, however, still appeal in more subtle ways to the novelistic genius when they strive to reenact, that is, to rethink, a certain weighing of means and ends. Historians, then, are not prohibited from "depicting" a situation, from "rendering" a train of thought, or from giving it the "vividness" of an internal discourse. Through this aspect we rediscover an effect of discourse stressed by Aristotle in his theory of *lexis*. "Locution"—or "diction"—according to his *Rhetoric,* has the virtue of "placing before our eyes" and so of "making visible."[3] An additional step is thus taken, over and beyond seeing-as, which does not prohibit the marriage of metaphor, which assimilates, and irony, which creates a distance. We have entered into the realm of illusion that confuses, in the precise sense of the term, "seeing-as" with "believing we are seeing." Here, "holding as true," which defines belief, succumbs to the hallucination of presence.

This most peculiar effect of fiction and diction assuredly enters into conflict with the critical vigilance that historians exercise in other respects for their own purposes and that they try to communicate to the reader. But a strange complicity is sometimes created between this vigilance and the willing suspension of disbelief, out of which illusion emerges in the aesthetic order. The phrase "controlled illusion" comes to mind to characterize this happy union, which makes Michelet's picture of the French Revolution, for example, a literary work comparable to Tolstoy's *War and Peace,* in which the movement occurs in the opposite direction, that is, from fiction to history and no longer from history to fiction.

I now want to suggest a final modality of the fictionalizing of history, which, instead of abolishing history's intention of standing-for, gives this intention the fulfilment it is lacking and which, in the circumstances I shall state, is truly expected of it. I have in mind those events that a historical community holds to be significant because it sees in them an origin, a return to its beginnings. These events, which are said to be "epoch-making," draw their specific meaning from their capacity to found or reinforce the community's consciousness of its identity, its narrative identity, as well as the identity of its members. These events generate feelings of considerable ethical intensity, whether this be fervent commemoration or some manifestation of loathing, or indignation, or of regret or compassion, or even the call for forgiveness. Historians, as such, are supposed to set aside their own feelings. In this respect, François Furet's critique of the commemoration and loathing that have created obstacles for a fruitful discussion of the explanations and interpretations of the French Revolution is still valid.[4] However, when it is a question of events closer to us, like Auschwitz, it seems that the sort of ethical neutralization that may perhaps be fitting in the case of the history of a past that must be set at a distance in order better to be understood and explained, is no longer possible or desirable. In this regard, we should recall the biblical watchword (from Deuteronomy) *Zakhor,* "Remember!" which is not necessarily the same thing as a call to historiography.[5]

I readily admit that the rule of abstinence applied to reverent commemoration should more properly be respected than its application to indignation or to grief, insofar as our taste for celebrating events turns more willingly toward the great deeds of those whom Hegel called history's great men, and arises out of the ideological function that legitimizes domination. What makes reverential commemoration suspect is its affinity with the history of conquerors, although I consider the elimination of admiration, veneration, and gratitude to be impossible, and not really desirable. If, as Rudolf Otto would have it, the *tremendum fascinosum* constitutes the emotional core of our experience of the Sacred, the meaning of the Sacred remains an inexpungible dimension of historical meaning.[6]

The *tremendum,* however, has another side to it, the *tremendum horrendum,* whose cause also deserves to be pleaded. And we shall see what beneficial aid fiction can bring to this plea. Horror is the negative form of admiration, as loathing is of veneration. Horror attaches to events that must never be forgotten. It constitutes the ultimate ethical motivation for the history of victims. (I prefer to say the history of victims rather than the history of the vanquished, for the vanquished are also, in part, candidates for domination who failed.) The victims of Auschwitz are, par excellence, the representatives in our memory of all history's victims. Victimization is the other side of history that no cunning of reason can ever justify and that, instead, reveals the scandal of every theodicy of history.

The role of fiction in this memory of the horrible is a corollary to the capacity of horror, and also of admiration, to address itself to events whose explicit uniqueness is of importance. By this I mean that horror, like admiration, exerts a specific function of individuation within our historical consciousness. An individuation that cannot be incorporated into a logic of specification or, even, into a logic of individuation like the one Paul Veyne shares with Pariente.[7] In relation to this logical individuation, and even in relation to the individuation by time that I spoke of above, I am prepared to use the phrase "uniquely unique events." Every other form of individuation is the counterpart to a work of explanation that connects things together. But horror isolates events by making them incomparable, incomparably unique, uniquely unique. If I persist in associating horror with admiration, it is because horror inverts the feeling with which we go forth to meet all that seems to us to be generative, creative. Horror is inverted veneration. It is in this sense that the Holocaust has been considered a negative revelation, an Anti-Sinai. The conflict between explanation that connects things together and horror that isolates is carried to its pinnacle here, and yet this latent conflict must not lead to a ruinous dichotomy between a history that would dissolve the event in explanation and a purely emotional retort that would dispense us from thinking the unthinkable. It is important instead to elevate, each by means of the other, historical explanation and individuation through horror. The more we explain in historical terms, the more indignant we become; the more we are struck by the horror of events, the more we seek to understand them. This dialectic rests in the final analysis on the very nature of historical explanation that makes retrodiction a singular causal implication. The conviction expressed here rests on the singularity of genuinely historical explanation, that is, on the fact that historical explanation and the individuation of events through horror, just as through admiration or veneration, cannot remain mutually antithetical.

In what way is fiction a corollary of this individuation by horror and by admiration?

Here we once again encounter fiction's capacity for provoking an illusion of presence, but one controlled by critical distance. Here again, part of the function of "standing for . . ." belonging to imaginary acts is to "depict" by "making visible." The new element here is that the controlled illusion is not intended to please or to divert. It is placed in the service of the individuation produced by the horrible as well as by admiration. Individuation by means of the horrible, to which we are particularly attentive, would be blind feeling, regardless of how elevated or how profound it might be, without the quasi-intuitiveness of fiction. Fiction gives eyes to the horrified narrator. Eyes to see and to weep. The present state of literature on the Holocaust provides ample proof of this. Either one counts the cadavers or one tells the story of the victims. Between these two options lies a historical explanation, one that is difficult (if not impossible) to write, conforming to the rules of singular causal imputation.

By fusing in this way with history, fiction carries history back to their common origin in the epic. More precisely, what the epic did in the sphere of the admirable, the story of victims does in the sphere of the horrible. This almost negative epic preserves the memory of suffering, on the scale of peoples, as epic and history in its beginnings transformed the ephemeral glory of heroes into a lasting fame. In both cases, fiction is placed in the service of the un-forgettable.[8] It permits historiography to live up to the task of memory. For historiography can exist without memory when it is driven by curiosity alone. It then tends toward exoticism, which is by no means reprehensible in itself, as Paul Veyne eloquently pleads with respect to the history of Rome as he teaches it. But there are perhaps crimes that must not be forgotten, victims whose suffering cries less for vengeance than for narration. The will not to forget alone can prevent these crimes from ever occurring again.

THE HISTORIZATION OF FICTION

Does fiction offer, on its side, features conducive to its historization, in the same way that history, in the manner we have just stated, calls for a certain fictionalization in the service of its own intention of standing for the past?

I shall now examine the hypothesis that fictional narrative in some way imitates historical narrative. Recounting something can then be said to be re-counting it *as if* it were past. To what degree is this "as if past" essential to narrative meaning?

The first indication that this "as if past" is part of the sense we ascribe to every narrative is of a strictly grammatical nature. Narratives are recounted in the past tense. In fairytales, the "once upon a time . . ." marks our entry into narrative. I am, of course, not unaware that this criterion is challenged by Harald Weinrich in his *Tempus*.[9] According to Weinrich, the organization of tenses can be understood only if they are dissociated from the determinations related to the partitioning of time into past, present, and future. *Tempus* owes nothing to *Zeit*. Tenses are no more than signals addressed by a speaker to a listener, inviting this listener to receive and decode a verbal message in a cer-tain way. In volume 2, I examined this interpretation of tenses in terms of communication.[10] It is the "speech situation" that presides over the first dis-tinction that is of interest to us here since it governs the opposition between narrating (*erzählen*) and commenting (*besprechen*). The tenses that govern narrating are held to have no properly temporal function; instead they act as a notice to the reader: this is a narrative. The attitude that corresponds to the narrative would then be relaxation, disengagement, in contrast to the tension and involvement of the entry into commentary. The historical past and the imperfect are, therefore, said to be the tenses of narrative, not because the narrative relates in one way or another to past events, whether real or fictive, but because these tenses orient us toward an attitude of relaxation. The same thing is true, we recall, with regard to the marks of retrospection and prospec-tion along the second axis of communication, the axis of locution, and with regard to "putting into relief" along the third axis of communication. I discussed in volume 2 what a theory of time in fiction owes to Weinrich's work. What *Tempus* demonstrates is that tenses form an infinitely more complex system than the linear representation of time, to which Weinrich is too quick to connect the lived temporal experience expressed in terms of present, past, and future. The phenomenology of temporal experience has acquainted us with many nonlinear aspects of time and with the significations of the notion of past that stem from these nonlinear aspects. So *Tempus* can be related to *Zeit* in accordance with modalities other than those of linearity. It is precisely one of the functions of fiction to detect and to explore some of these temporal significations that everyday experience levels off or obliterates. Moreover, to say that the preterite simply signals the entry into narrative without any temporal signification does not really seem plausible. The idea that narrative has to do with something like a fictive past seems more fruitful to me. If narrative calls for an attitude of detachment, is that not because the past tense of the narrative aims at a temporal quasi-past?

What can "quasi-past" mean? In Part III of this work, at the end of my analysis of "Games With Time," I ventured the hypothesis that seems to me to find its best justification in the present discussion. According to this hypothesis, the events recounted in a fictional narrative are past facts for the narrative voice, which we can consider here to be identical with the implied author; that is, with a fictive disguise of the real author. A voice speaks, recounting what for it has taken place. To enter into reading is to include in the pact between the reader and the author the belief that the events reported by the narrative voice belong to the past of that voice.[11]

If this hypothesis stands up, we can say that fiction is quasi-historical, just as much as history is quasi-fictive. History is quasi-fictive once the quasi-presence of events placed "before the eyes of" the reader by a lively narrative supplements through its intuitiveness, its vividness, the elusive character of the pastness of the past, which is illustrated by the paradoxes of standing-for. Fictional narrative is quasi-historical to the extent that the unreal events that it relates are past facts for the narrative voice that addresses itself to the reader. It is in this that they resemble past events and that fiction resembles history.

The relationship is, moreover, circular. It is, we might say, as quasi-historical that fiction gives the past the vivid evocation that makes a great book of history a literary masterpiece.

A second reason for holding the "as if past" to be essential to narrative fiction has to do with the golden rule of emplotment that we read in Aristotle, namely, that a good plot must be probable or necessary. Of course, Aristotle attaches no temporal or quasi-temporal significance to the probable. He even expressly opposes what might have happened to what actually did happen (*Poetics*, 1452b4–5). History takes care of the actual past, poetry takes charge of the possible. This objection, however, is no more constraining than that made by Weinrich. Aristotle, in fact, is not at all interested in the difference between past and present. He defines what occurred in terms of the particular and what might have occurred in terms of the universal: "The sort of thing that (in the circumstances) a certain person will say or do either probably or necessarily" (1451b9).[12]

It is the probability of the universal that poses a problem here. This probability is not unrelated, for Aristotle himself, to what we have just called the quasi-past. In the same page where history is opposed to poetry, the tragic poets are praised for having restricted themselves to "the use of historical names; and the reason is that what we are disposed to believe, we must think possible. Now, what has been is unquestionably so" (1451b15–18). Aristotle suggests here that, in order for us to be disposed to believe, the probable must have a relation of verisimilitude to what has been. He is not actually concerned with knowing whether Ulysses, Agamemnon, or Oedipus are real people of the past. Tragedy, however, must simulate a reference to a legend whose main function is to tie memory and history to the archaic levels of the reign of predecessors.

Unfortunately, this simulation of the past by fiction has subsequently been covered over by the aesthetic discussions provoked by the realistic novel. Verisimilitude is then confused with a mode of resemblance to the real that places fiction on the same plane as history. In this respect, it is certainly true that the great novelists of the nineteenth century can be read as auxiliary historians or, better, as sociologists before the fact, as if the novel occupied a still vacant place in the realm of the human sciences. This example, however, is finally misleading. It is not when the novel has a direct historical or sociological role, combined with its aesthetic role, that it poses the most interesting problem with respect to its verisimilitude. The true mimesis of action is to be found in the works of art least concerned with reflecting their epoch. Imitation, in the usual sense of the term, is here the unparalleled enemy of mimesis. It is precisely when a work of art breaks with this sort of verisimilitude that it displays its true mimetic function. The quasi-past of the narrative voice is then entirely different from the past of historical consciousness. It is, however, identified with the probable in the sense of what might have been. This is the "pastlike" note that resonates in every claim to verisimilitude, outside of any mirroring of the past.

The interpretation I am proposing here of the "quasi-historical" character of fiction quite clearly overlaps with the interpretation I also proposed of the "quasi-fictive" character of the historical past. If it is true that one of the functions of fiction bound up with history is to free, retrospectively, certain possibilities that were not actualized in the historical past, it is owing to its quasi-historical character that fiction itself is able, after the fact, to perform its liberating function. The quasi-past of fiction in this way becomes the detector of possibilities buried in the actual past. What "might have been"—the possible in Aristotle's terms—includes both the potentialities of the "real" past and the "unreal" possibilities of pure fiction.

This deep affinity between the verisimilitude of pure fiction and the unrealized possibilities of the historical past explains perhaps, in turn, why fiction's freedom in relation to the constraints of history—constraints epitomized by documentary proof—does not constitute, as was stated above, the final word about the freedom of fiction. Free from the external constraint of documentary proof, is not fiction internally bound by its obligation to its quasi-past, which is another name for the constraint of verisimilitude? Free *from* . . . , artists must still render themselves free *for*. . . . If this were not the case, how could we explain the anguish and the suffering of artistic creation? Does not the quasi-past of the narrative voice exercise an internal constraint on novelistic creation, which is all the more imperious in that it does not coincide with the external constraint of documentary facts? And does not the difficult law of creation, which is "to render" in the most perfect way the vision of the world that animates the narrative voice, simulate, to the point of being indistinguishable from it, history's debt to the people of the past, to the dead? Debt for debt, who, the historian or the novelist, is the most insolvent?

In conclusion, the interweaving of history and fiction in the refiguration of time rests, in the final analysis, upon this reciprocal overlapping, the quasi-historical moment of fiction changing places with the quasi-fictive moment of history. In this interweaving, this reciprocal overlapping, this exchange of places, originates what is commonly called human time, where the standing-for the past in history is united with the imaginative variations of fiction, against the background of the aporias of the phenomenology of time.[13]

To what kind of totalization does this time, issuing from the refiguration through narrative, lend itself, if this time has to be considered as the collective singular reality that groups together all the procedures of interweaving described above? This is what still remains to be examined.

9

Should We Renounce Hegel?

The confrontation with Hegel that I am about to undertake has been made necessary by the emergence of a problem resulting from the very conclusion to which the five preceding chapters have led. This problem, whose broad outlines I sketched in the introductory pages to this second section of this volume, stems from the presupposition, reiterated by every great philosophy of time, of the oneness of time. Time is always represented in these philosophies as a singular collective. This presupposition cannot be made by the phenomenologies of time, referred to above, except at the price of great difficulties, which I shall consider once more in my concluding chapter. The question for the moment is whether a unitary historical consciousness, capable of comparing itself to this postulated oneness of time, and of making its aporias fruitful, proceeds from the interweaving referential intentions of historical and fictional narrative.

As regards the legitimacy of this ultimate question, I will not turn to the argument drawn from the semantics of the word "history," at least in the modern period. That argument, however, will be taken up at the beginning of the next chapter. Here I prefer to seek a handhold for our question about the totalization of the historical consciousness in the difficulties encountered above in the course of our chapter devoted to the reality of the past as such. If, as we then admitted, the relative failure of all thought about the past as such stems from the abstraction of the past, from the breaking of its bonds with the present and the future, is not the true riposte to the aporias of time to be sought in a mode of thought that embraces past, present, and future as a whole? Ought we not to decipher from the disparity of the leading kinds, which articulate the representation of the past as such (reenactment, the positing of otherness and difference, metaphorical assimilation), the symptom of a kind of thinking that has not dared to elevate itself to grasping history as the totalization of time in the eternal present?

From this question comes the Hegelian temptation.

THE HEGELIAN TEMPTATION

The history that Hegelian philosophy takes as its theme is no longer a historian's history, it is a philosopher's history.[1] Hegel speaks of "world history," not "universal history." Why? Because the idea capable of conferring a unity on history—the idea of freedom—is only understood by someone who has traversed the whole philosophy of the Spirit presented in the *Encyclopedia of the Philosophical Sciences,* that is, by someone who has thought through the conditions that make fredom both rational and real in the spirit's process of self-realization. In this sense, only the philosopher can write this history.[2]

There is no real introduction to the "application of thought to history" (p. 25), therefore. It establishes itself without any transition or intermediary stage upon the philosophical act of faith that is consubstantial with the system: "the only thought which philosophy brings with it is the simple idea of *reason*—the idea that reason governs the world, and that world history is therefore a rational process" (p. 27).[3] For the historian, this conviction remains a hypothesis, a "presupposition," and therefore an idea imposed a priori on the facts. For the speculative philosopher, it has the authority of the "self-presentation" (the *Selbstdarstellung*) of the whole system. It is a truth—the truth that reason is not an impotent ideal but a force. It is not a mere abstraction, something that ought to be, but an infinite force that, unlike finite forces, produces the circumstances for its own realization. This philosophical credo sums up rather well the *Phenomenology of Spirit* as well as the *Encyclopedia* and takes up again their obstinate refutation of the split between a formal system based on the idea and an empirical system based on facts. What is, is rational—what is rational is real. This conviction, which governs the whole Hegelian philosophy of history, can only be introduced in an abrupt way inasmuch as it is the system as a whole that confirms it.[4]

The philosophy of history, however, is not confined to the simple tautology of the declaration I have cited. Or if, in the final analysis, it does reveal itself to be one giant tautology, this is at the end of a traversal that, as such, counts as a proof. It is upon the articulations of this traversal that I want now to concentrate for it is in them that the *Aufhebung* of narration is consummated. Hegel places these articulations under the sign of the "determination" (*Bestimmung*) of Reason. Being unable, in a relatively popular work, to reproduce the complex proof structure that the *Encyclopedia* borrows from philosophical logic, the *Lectures on the Philosophy of History* content themselves with a more exoteric form of argumentation, constructed on the familiar moments of the ordinary notion of teleology (without for all that returning to external finality): goal, means, material, actualization. And this progression in terms of four moments at least has the advantage of making clear the difficulty of equating the rational and the real, which a hastier form of reflection, limited to the relationship between means and end, would appear to be able to establish more easily. This retreat out of reach of the ultimate adequation is not without significance for our problem of a perfect mediation, as will become apparent shortly.

The initial moment of the process consists in positing an ultimate end to history: "To try to define reason in itself—if we consider reason in relation to the world—amounts to asking what the ultimate end [*Endzweck*] of the world is" (p. 44). This abrupt declaration is not surprising if we recall that the philosophy of history presupposes the whole system. It alone authorizes us to declare that this ultimate goal is the self-realization of freedom. This starting point, with one move, distinguishes philosophical world history, once again called a thoughtful consideration of history. As a result, a philosophical history will read history—principally political history—under the guidance of an idea that only philosophy can entirely legitimate. Philosophy, it must be said, introduces itself into the very posing of the question.

In any case, a meditation that does not take up the questions of means, material, and actualization will not be able to get beyond the level of "the abstract determination of spirit" (p. 47), separated from its historical "proof." In fact, the determination of the Spirit other than through its proofs can be designated only through its opposition to nature (ibid.). Freedom itself remains abstract so long as it remains opposed to external material determinations. The Spirit's power of remaining "within itself" (*bei sich*) then still finds its contrary "outside" itself in matter. Even the brief "presentation" (*Darstellung*) of the history of freedom, as the quantitative extension of freedom—in the Orient, just one person is free; with the Greeks, some are free; and with Germanic Christianity, humanity as such is free (p. 54)—remains abstract so long as we do not know its means. Certainly, we do have here the schematism of the development of the Spirit as well as that of the "phases" (*Einteilung*) of world history, but we lack the realization and the reality that goes with the ringing affirmation that the only goal of the Spirit is to make freedom real (pp. 55–67). The only " concrete" note given the affirmation that the Spirit produces itself as "its own product" (p. 48) is its identification with "the spirit of a nation" (*Volksgeist*) (p. 55). It is precisely this spirit of a nation, in its substance and its consciousness, that, in actual history, attains representation. In a general way, with this spirit of a nation, we have crossed the threshold of history and left behind the limited perspective of the individual. Nonetheless, this real advance toward what is concrete does not cross the frontiers of "abstract determination" insofar as, in the development of a national spirit, we are restricted to juxtaposing the multiple national spirits to the unique world spirit (*Weltgeist*), thereby leaving side by side the polytheism of such spirits and the monotheism of the Spirit. So long has we have not brought to light how such a national spirit is part of the world spirit, we have not overcome the abstractness of the affirmation that "world history belongs to the realm of spirit." How does the decline of the different national spirits, taken one at a time, and the rise of others, attest to the immortality of the world spirit, of the Spirit as such? That the Spirit is engaged successively in this or that historical configuration is just a corollary of the (still abstract) affirmation that the Spirit is one throughout its various particularizations. To attain the meaning of this passage of the Spirit from one people to another is the high point of the philosophical comprehension of history.

It is at this critical stage that the question arises of the means freedom gives itself in order to actualize itself in history. It is also at this point that the overly renowned thesis of the "cunning of reason" intervenes. But what is important at this point is to note that the cunning of reason constitutes just one step on the way to the full actualization of Reason in history. What is more, this argument itself includes several steps, all marked with warnings, as if to soften an expected blow (cf. pp. 68–93).

The first thing to see is that it is within the field of a theory of action that the solution is to be sought. This is where the very first realization takes place, where an intention gets expressed in a selfish interest, for the "infinite right of the subject is the second essential moment of freedom, in that the subject must itself be satisfied by whatever activity or task it performs" (p. 70). In this way, every moralizing denunciation of the alleged egoism of interests is set aside. And it is on this same level of a theory of action that it may also be affirmed that interest gets its energy from "passion." We recall another well-known saying of Hegel's: "nothing great has been accomplished in the world without passion" (p. 73). In other words, moral conviction is nothing without the total and unreserved motivation of an idea mobilized by passion. What is at stake in this saying is precisely what the judging consciousness in the *Phenomenology of Spirit* calls evil, that is, the focusing of all my forces on my own satisfaction.

How can the world spirit, born from the spirit of a nation, annex, as its "means" of realization, these convictions incarnated in interests and moved by passions that the moralist identifies as evil? Hegel's meditation calls for three new steps.

First, a decisive step is added to the analysis of passion. In the intention that goes with a passion are concealed two intentions, one that the individual is aware of and one that is unknown to him. On the first side, the individual directs himself toward determined and finite ends, on the other, he unknowingly serves interests that surpass him. Whoever does something, produces unintended effects that make his acts escape his intentions and that develop their own logic. As a rule, "an action may have implications which transcend the intention and consciousness of the agent" (p. 75).[5]

By making recourse to this second, hidden intention, Hegel believes he gets closer to his goal, which is to abolish the contingent (p. 28). For original history and reflective history, this "other than intended" would be the last word.[6]

The "cunning of reason" is precisely what is to take this "other than . . ." up again into the plans of the *Weltgeist*.

How? By a second step forward, we leave the sphere of selfish interests and begin to consider the unintended effects of the individual in the sphere of the interests of a people and of the state. Therefore we must include within the theory of "means" that of the "material" of rational history. The state is the place, the historical configuration where the idea and its satisfaction come together. Outside the state, there is no reconciliation between the Spirit, seeking to actualize freedom, and individuals, passionately seeking their own satisfaction within the horizon of their own interests. Between the in-itself of this will-toward-freedom and the for-itself of passion a gap remains. Hegel does not respond to this contradiction with an easy reconciliation. The contradiction remains pointed as long as the argument remains within the bounds of the antithesis of happiness and unhappiness. Indeed, we must admit that "history is not the soil in which happiness grows" (p. 79). Paradoxically, the periods of happiness of a people are the blank pages of history. *We must renounce consolation to attain reconciliation.* We may then link this second step to the first one. From the point of view of the individual, the disastrous fate of an Alexander, a Caesar (and maybe also a Napoleon) is the history of a failed project (and this history remains imprisoned within the same subjective circle of action that nevertheless betrays its intention). It is only from the point of view of the higher interests of freedom and its progress in the state that the failure of these individuals may appear as significant.

There remains one last step to dare, one that the preceding example anticipates. Beyond a "soil" (*Boden*)—that is, the State—where the higher interests of freedom, which are also the interests of the spirit, and the selfish interests of individuals can coincide, the argument also requires extraordinary agents, capable of carrying out destinies that are themselves out of the ordinary, where the unintended consequences of their actions add to the progress of institutions upholding freedom. These agents of history, in which passion and the Idea overlap, are the ones Hegel calls "the great men of history" (*die grossen Welthistorischen Individuen*) (p. 76). They appear on the scene when conflicts and oppositions bear witness to the vitality of the spirit of a nation and when a "productive Idea" (p. 82) seeks to open the way to further development. This productive idea is known to no one. It inhabits great men without their knowing it, and their passion is entirely guided by this idea that is seeking realization. We might say, in another vocabulary, that they incarnate the *kairos* of an age. Men of passion, they are also men of unhappiness. Their passion gives them life, their fate kills them. This evil and this unhappiness are "the realization of the Spirit." In this way, not only the dissenting tone of the moralists but also the envy of the mean-spirited is overthrown. There is no use in lingering over the saying taken from the *Phenomenology*, which had taken it from Goethe, that "no man is a hero to his *valet de chambre*" (p. 87). In contrast to these two types of ill-tempered individuals, who are often one and the same person, we must dare to affirm that "a mighty figure must trample many an innocent flower underfoot, and destroy much that lies in the path" (p. 89).

It is only now that Hegel speaks of the "cunning of reason" (*List der Vernunft*) (ibid.). He does so therefore in a context that has been made precise through the double stamp of evil and unhappiness—on the condition, first, that a particular interest animated by a great passion unknowingly serves freedom's self-production; on the condition, second, that the particular be destroyed in order that the universal may be saved. The "cunning" here consists simply in the fact that reason "sets the passions to work in its service [*für sich*]" (ibid.). Along with their apparently destructive appearance from an external perspective, and their apparently suicidal nature internally, they bear the destiny of higher ends. Hence the thesis of the cunning of reason comes to occupy exactly the place that theodicy assigns to evil when it protests that evil is not in vain. However, Hegel believes the philosophy of the Spirit succeeds where theodicy has hitherto failed, because it alone demonstrates how reason makes use of the passions, unfolds their concealed intentionality, incorporates their second intention into the political destiny of states, and finds in the great men of history the elect of this adventure of the Spirit. The ultimate end has finally found its "means," one which is not external to it, inasmuch as it is in satisfying their particular ends that these elect of the Spirit accomplish goals that transcend them, and inasmuch as the sacrifice of particularity, which is the price to be paid, is justified by the office of reason that this sacrifice fills.

The critical point is thereby indicated. In a reconciliation without consolation, the particularity that suffers, for a reason unknown to itself, receives no satisfaction. Schiller is left with his sadness: "reason . . . cannot concern itself with particular and finite ends, but only with the absolute" (p. 28).

However the Introduction to Hegel's lectures is not yet complete. There is still something lacking if the concrete reality of the Spirit, its *Wirklichkeit,* is to equal its final goal, the *Endzweck* of history.

There follows a long development devoted to the material (*das Material*) (pp. 93–115) of free Reason. This is nothing other than the state, whose role we anticipated in speaking of the soil in which the whole process of the actualization of freedom takes root. Around this pole gravitate all the powers that give flesh to the spirit of a nation (religion, science, art), which we shall not consider here.

What is more surprising is that the outcome of the course pursued, which goes beyond this section, seems to suggest that the project of realization, of actualization (*Verwirklichung*) of the Spirit is never finished. To the fourth stage, entitled actualization (pp. 44–124), marked by the establishing of the State founded on rights on the basis of the idea of a constitution, is added another supplementary one on the "course of world history" (pp. 124–51), where the "principle of development" must in turn be articulated in terms of a *Stufengang,* those "successive stages" (p. 129) which themselves call for an investigation directed not so much at the beginning as at the "course" (*Verlauf*) of this development (p. 138). It is only with this *Verlauf* that the concept of philosophical world history is complete—or rather, with it, we finally reach the basis of the work that is to follow. All that remains is to put together the philosophical history of the ancient world, "the real theatre of world history" (p. 190), where this "course" has to be organized in terms of an adequate principle of "phases" (*die Einteilung der Weltgeschichte*) (p. 197), for it is the carrying out of this task that constitutes the required proof.[7]

What becomes of historical time in this process of actualization? As a first approximation, the philosophy of history seems to consecrate the irreducibly temporal character of Reason itself, to the extent that Reason gets equated with its works. It is as a "development" (*Entwicklung*) that we may characterize this process. But this temporalization of history, to use an expression of Reinhart Koselleck's that I shall return to in the next chapter, does not exhaust itself in the historization of Reason which seems to be the result of this process. It is the very mode of this temporalization that raises a question.

For a narrower approximation, it seems as though the process of temporalization gets sublimated into the idea of a "return upon itself" (*Rückkehr in sich selber*) (p. 149) of the Spirit and its concept, by means of which its reality is identical to its presence. Philosophy, it must be said, "is concerned with what is present and real [*dem Gegenwärtigen, Wirklichen*]" (p. 151). This equating of reality and presence marks the abolition of narrativity in the thoughtful consideration of history. It is the final meaning of the passage from original and reflective history to philosophical history.[8]

The way in which this equation is obtained merits attention. It is, in fact, a matter of something quite different than any amelioration of the idea of progress, despite the initial assertion of "an impulse of perfectibility" (p. 125), of a *Treib der Perfektibilität* that sets the principle of development within the space of the philosophy of the Enlightenment. The harsh tone with which the conceptual negligence and the triviality of the *Aufklärar* are denounced leaves little doubt of this. The tragic version of development that is given, along with the effort to make the tragic and the logical correspond, leaves no doubt about Hegel's originality in treating the temporalization of history. The opposition between Spirit and nature is the didactic instrument of this conceptual breakthrough: "Development, therefore, is not just a harmless and peaceful process of growth [*Hervorgehen*] like that of organic life, but a hard and obstinate struggle with itself" (p. 127). This role for the negative, the work of the negative, will not surprise the reader familiar with the long Preface to the *Phenomenology of Spirit.* What is new is the correspondence between historical time and the work of the negative. "The concept of the spirit is such that his-torical development must take place in the temporal world. But time entails the property of negativity" (ibid.). Better: "this relation to non-existence is a function of time; it is a relation which exists not only for thought, but also for our immediate perception" (ibid.). How? And where? In and through "the successive stages in the development of that principle" (*Stufengang der Ent-wicklung des Prinzips*) (p. 129) that, in marking the break between biological time and historical time, indicates the "return" of the transitory to the eternal.

This concept of the *Stufengang der Entwicklung des Prinzips* is truly the tem-poral equivalent of the cunning of reason. It is the time of the cunning of rea-son. What is most noteworthy here is that the *Stufengang* repeats, at a higher altitude of the great spiral, one major feature of organic life, with which, however, it breaks. This is the feature of the permanence of species that as-sures the repetition of the same and that makes change a cyclic course. His-torical time breaks with organic time in that "in this case, change occurs not just on the surface but within the concept" (p. 128). "In the natural world, the species does not progress, but in the world of the spirit, each change is a form of progress" (ibid.), given the reservation of the change in meaning that henceforth affects the notion of progress. In the transformation from one spiritual configuration to another occurs the transfiguration (*Verklärung*) of the preceding one. This explains why "spiritual phenomena occur within the medium of time" (ibid.). And the history of the world, therefore, is in essence "the expression [*die Auslegung*] of spirit in time, just as nature is the expres-sion of the Idea in space" (ibid.). However, an analogy between Spirit and nature then turns this simple opposition into a dialectic. Spiritual configura-tions have a perenniality analogous to the permanence of the species. At first sight, this permanence seems to be impervious to the work of the negative. "If non-existence does not encroach upon something, we describe it as per-manent" (pp. 127–28). In fact, this perenniality integrates the work of the negative thanks to the cumulative character of historical change. The "stages" in world history in this sense are the analogue, on the plane of history, of the permanence of the natural species, but their temporal structure differs in that, while nations pass away, their creations "endure" (*fortbestehen*) (p. 129). This sequence of configurations can, in turn, elevate itself to eternity because the perenniality attained by each step, in spite of—and thanks to—the in-quietude of life, is taken up in a higher perenniality that is the present depth of the Spirit. We cannot overemphasize the qualitative aspect of this perenniality in opposition to the quantitative aspect of chronological time (ibid.). The lapidary formulation of the first version of the lectures—"The history of the world accordingly represents [*darstellt*] the successive stages [*Stufengang*] in the development of that principle whose substantial content is the conscious-ness of freedom" (pp. 129–30)—sums up well the differences and the analogies between the course of nature and the course of world history. The *Stufen-gang* is not a chronological sequence but a winding up that is at the same time an unfolding, a process of making explicit, and a return upon itself of the spirit. The identity between the becoming explicit (*Auslegung*) and the return is the eternal present. It is only for a purely quantitative interpretation of the sequence of historical stages that the process appears to be infinite and progress looks as though it will never rejoin its eternally postponed end. For the qualitative interpretation of the perenniality of the stages and their course, the return upon itself does not allow itself to become dissipated into the bad infinity of endless progress.

It is in this spirit that we should read the final paragraph of Hoffmeister's edition of *Reason in History:* "But what the spirit is now, it has always been. . . . The spirit has all the stages of the past still adhering to it, and the life of the spirit in history consists of a cycle of different states, of which some belong to the present and others have appeared in forms of the past. . . . Those moments which the spirit appears to have outgrown still belong to it in the depths of its present. Just as it has passed through all its moments in history, so also must it pass through them again in the present—in the concept it has formed of itself" (p. 151).

This is why the opposition between the past as no longer being and the future as open is inessential. The difference is between the dead past and the living past, this latter being related to what is essential. If our concern as historians carries us toward a past that is gone and a transitory present, our concern as philosophers turns us toward what is neither past nor future, toward what is, toward what has an eternal existence. Therefore, if Hegel limits himself to the past, like the nonphilosophical historian, and rejects all prediction and prophecy, it is because he abolishes the verbal tenses, just as Parmenides did in his poem and Plato did in his *Timaeus,* into the philosophical "is." It is true that freedom's realization of itself does require a "development" and cannot ignore the historian's "was" and "is," but only because we are to discern in them the signs of the philosophical "is." It is to this degree, and given this reservation, that philosophical history does bear the features of a form of retrodiction. It is true that in the philosophy of history, as in the philosophy of right, philosophy comes on the scene too late. But for the philosopher, what counts about the past are those signs of maturity from which shine a sufficient clarity concerning what is essential. Hegel's wager is that enough meaning has been accumulated for us to decipher in them the ultimate end of the world in its relation to the ends and the material that assure its realization.

Before submitting the Hegelian thesis about historical time to criticism, let us take stock of what is at stake in this discussion as regards our analyses in preceding chapters.

Hegelian philosophy seems at first able to do justice to the significance of the trace. Is not the *Stufengang* the trace of Reason in history? In the end, this is not the case. The assumption of historical time into the eternal present abolishes rather than challenges the unsurpassable character of the significance of the trace. This significance, it will be recalled, lay in the fact that the trace signified without making something appear. With Hegel, this restriction is abolished. To persist in the present, for the past, is to remain. And to remain is to have repose in the eternal present of speculative thought.

The same may be said of the problem posed by the pastness of the past. Hegelian philosophy is no doubt fully justified in denouncing the abstraction of the notion of the past as such. But it dissolves rather than resolves the problem of the relation of the historical past to the present. After all, is it not a question, even while conserving as much as possible of the Other, of affirming the final victory of the Same? As a result, any reason for having recourse of the leading kind of the analogous disappears, for it is the very relation of "standing-for" that has lost all its raison d'être, just as did the notion of the trace that is linked to it.

THE IMPOSSIBLE TOTAL MEDIATION

We must admit that a critique of Hegel is impossible that would not include the simple expression of our incredulity as regards his major proposition, to wit, that "the only thought which philosophy brings with it is the simple idea of reason—the idea that reason governs the world, and that world history is therefore a rational process." This is his philosophical credo, for which the cunning of reason is an apologetic doublet, and the *Stufengang* the temporal projection. Yes, intellectual honesty demands the confession that, for us, the loss of credibility the Hegelian philosophy of history has undergone has the significance of an event in thinking, concerning which we may say neither that we brought it about nor that it simply happened, and concerning which we do not know if it is indicative of a catastrophe that still is crippling us or a deliverance whose glory we dare not celebrate. The leaving behind of Hegelianism, whether from the point of view of Kierkegaard, or Feuerbach, or Marx, or the German school of history—to say nothing of Nietzsche, whom I shall refer to in the next chapter—appears to us, after the fact, as a kind of beginning, or even as an origin. I mean, this exodus is so intimately linked to our way of asking questions that we can no longer warrant it by some form of reason higher than that referred to in Hegel's title: *Reason in History*—no more than we can jump over our own shadow.

For the history of ideas, the incredibly rapid collapse of Hegelianism, as the dominant mode of thought, is a fact that stands out like an earthquake. But that it happened and happened so quickly is clearly not a proof of anything. This is all the more true in that the reasons for this downfall alleged by Hegel's adversaries, those who in fact replaced his philosophy, appear today as a monumental case of misunderstanding and malevolence, given a more careful reading of the Hegelian texts. Thus the paradox is that we should become aware of the unique character of this event in thinking only when we come to denounce the distortions of meaning that facilitated the elimination of Hegel's philosophy.[9]

A critique worthy of Hegel must measure itself against his central affirmation that philosophy can attain not only the present, by summing up the known past, taken as the seed of the anticipated future, but also the eternal present, which assures the underlying unity of the surpassed past and the coming manifestations of life that already announce themselves by means of what we understand, because what we understand has already grown old.

It is this passage, this step by which the surpassed past is retained in the present of each age, and equated with the eternal present of the Spirit, that seemed impossible to carry out to those successors of Hegel who had already taken their distance with regard to his work. What, in fact, is the Spirit that holds together the spirits of nations and the spirit of the world? Is it the same Spirit as the one that, in the philosophy of religion, both required and refused the narratives and the symbols of figurative thought?[10] Once transposed into the field of history, could the Spirit of cunning Reason appear otherwise than as the spirit of a shameful theology, even though Hegel no doubt did try to make philosophy a secularized form of theology? The fact is that the spirit of the century, at least from the end of the first third of the nineteenth century on, everywhere substituted the word "man"—or humanity, or the human spirit, or human culture—for Hegel's Spirit, concerning which we do not really know whether it is man or God.

Perhaps the Hegelian equivocation can only be denounced at the price of another equivocation of equal scale. Must not the human spirit avail itself of all the attributes of the Hegelian Spirit if it is to claim to have drawn the gods from the crucible of its own imagination? Is not theology all the more rampant and all the more shameful in Feuerbach's humanism with its "species being" (*Gattungswesen*)? These questions attest to why we are not capable of recognizing our reasons for not being Hegelian in the reasons given by those who carried the day against him.

What, too, are we to say of the transformation that has occurred in historical consciousness itself when it brings about an encounter with the grandeur of humanity, for its own reasons, by way of the humanistic conversion of the Hegelian Spirit? It is a fact that the emancipation of German historiography, stemming from even further afield than Ranke, and which Hegel battled in vain, could only reject all the directive concepts of Hegel's philosophy of history, from the idea of freedom to that of the *Stufengang* of development, as an arbitrary intrusion of the a priori into the field of historical inquiry. Hegel's argument that what is a presupposition for the historian is a truth for the philosopher was no longer understood or even paid any attention. The more history became empirical, the less credibility speculative history retained. But, in fact, who today does not see how laden with "ideas" this empirical historiography was that believed itself innocent of speculation? And in how many of these "ideas" do we recognize today unacknowledged doublets of some Hegelian ghost, beginning with the concepts of the spirit of a nation, of a culture, of an age?[11]

If these anti-Hegelian arguments no longer speak to us today, what then has that event in thought that is the loss of credibility of the Hegelian philosophical credo become? We must risk posing this issue for ourselves in a second reading of Hegel's text in which all the transitions appear to us to be errors and all the overlappings dissimulations.

Starting from the end and returning toward the beginning, in a backward reading, our suspicion finds an initial handhold in the final equating of the *Stufengang der Entwicklung* and the eternal present. The step we can no longer take is this one that equates with the eternal present the capacity of the actual present to retain the known past and anticipate the future indicated in the tendencies of this past. The very notion of history is abolished by philosophy as soon as the present, equated with what is real, abolishes its difference from the past. The self-understanding that goes with historical awareness is born precisely from the unescapable fact of this difference.[12] What stands out, for us, is the mutual overlapping of the three terms, Spirit in itself, development, and difference, that, taken together, make up the concept of the *Stufengang der Entwicklung*.

However, if this equating of development and present no longer holds, all the other equations also fall apart in a chain reaction. How can we bring together—totalize—all the national spirits in a single world spirit?[13] In fact, the more we think in terms of a *Volksgeist* the less we think of a *Weltgeist*. This is a gap that Romanticism continued to widen, drawing from the Hegelian concept of a *Volksgeist* a powerful plea for differences.

And how could the suture hold against the analyses devoted to the "material" of the realization of the Spirit, especially the State, whose absence on a worldwide level motivated the passage from the philosophy of right to the philosophy of history? Indeed, contemporary history, far from filling this lack in the philosophy of right, has accentuated it. In the twentieth century, we have seen Europe's claim to totalize the history of the world come undone. We have even seen the heritages it tried to integrate in terms of one guiding idea come undone. Eurocentrism died with the political suicide of Europe in the First World War, with the ideological rending produced by the October Revolution, and with the withdrawal of Europe from the world scene, along with the fact of decolonization and the unequal—and probably antagonistic—development that opposes the industrialized nations to the rest of the world. It now seems to us as though Hegel, seizing a favorable moment, a *kairos,* which has been revealed for what it was to our perspective and our experience, only totalized a few leading aspects of the spiritual history of Europe and of its geographical and historical environment, ones that, since that time, have come undone. What has come undone is the very substance of what Hegel sought to make into a concept. Difference has turned against development, conceived of as a *Stufengang*.

The victim of this chain reaction is the conceptual conglomeration Hegel gave the title "realization of the Spirit." Here too, what was made has become undone. On the one hand, the interest of individuals no longer seems to us to be satisfied, if this satisfaction does not take into account the conscious intentions of their action, but only retains a second intention that goes unknown to them. Before so many victims and so much suffering that we have seen, the dissociation Hegel introduces between consolation and reconciliation has become intolerable. On the other hand, the passion of the great men of history no longer seems capable to us of carrying, by itself, the whole weight of meaning, like Atlas. As the emphasis on political history wanes, it is the great anonymous forces of history that hold our attention, fascinate us, and make us uneasy, more than do the disastrous fates of Alexander, Caesar, and Napoleon, and the involuntary sacrifice of their passions on the altar of history. So at the same time, all the components that come together in the concept of the cunning of reason—particular interests, the passions of great historical men, the higher interests of the state, the spirit of a nation, and the world spirit—come apart and appear to us today like the *membra disjecta* of an impossible totalization. Even the expression "cunning of reason" no longer intrigues us. Instead we find it repugnant, almost like a magician's trick that does not work.

Moving even further backward in Hegel's text, what seems to us highly problematic is the very project of composing a philosophical history of the world that would be defined in terms of the "realization of the Spirit in history." However much we may misunderstand the term "Spirit"—in itself, as the spirit of a nation, or as the world spirit; however much we may fail to recognize the self-realizing intention already contained in the "abstract determination" of reason in history; however unjust most of our criticisms may be, what we have abandoned is Hegel's very work site. We no longer seek the basis upon which the history of the world may be thought of as a completed whole, even if this realization is taken as inchoative or only present as a seed. We are no longer even sure whether the idea of freedom is or should be the focal point of this realization, especially if we put the accent on the political realization of freedom. Even if we do take it as our guideline, we are not certain that its historical incarnations form a *Stufenfolge* rather than just a branching development where difference constantly wins out over identity. Perhaps among all the aspirations of people for freedom there is just a family resemblance such as the one with which Wittgenstein wanted to credit the least discredited philosophical concepts. In fact, it is the very project of totalization that indicates the break between Hegel's philosophy of history and every model of understanding, however distantly akin, to the idea of narration and emplotment. Despite the seduction of the idea, the cunning of reason is not the peripeteia that can encompass all the reversals of history, because the realization of freedom cannot be taken as the plot behind every plot. In other words, the leaving behind of Hegelianism signifies renouncing the attempt to decipher the supreme plot.

We now understand better the sense in which the exodus from Hegelianism may be called an event in thinking. This event does not affect history in the sense of historiography but rather historical consciousness's understanding of itself, its self-understanding. In this sense, it is inscribed in the hermeneutics of historical consciousness. This event is even in its way a hermeneutical phenomenon. To admit that the self-understanding of the historical consciousness can be so affected by events that, to repeat, we cannot say whether we produced them or they simply happened, is to admit the finitude of the philosophical act that makes up the self-understanding of the historical consciousness. This finitude in interpretation signifies that all thought about thought has presuppositions that it can never master, which in their turn become the situations beginning from which we think, without our being able to think them through in themselves. Consequently, in quitting Hegelianism, we have to dare to say that the thoughtful consideration of history attempted by Hegel was itself a hermeneutical phenomenon, even an interpretive one, submitted to the same condition of finitude.

Yet to characterize Hegelianism as a event of thought arising from the finite condition of the self-understanding of the historical consciousness does not constitute an argument against Hegel. It simply testifies to the fact that we no longer think in the same way Hegel did, but after Hegel. For what readers of Hegel, once they have been seduced by the power of Hegel's thought as I have, do not feel the abandoning of this philosophy as a wound, a wound that, unlike those that affect the absolute Spirit, will not be healed? For such readers, if they are not to give into the weaknesses of nostalgia, we must wish the courage of the work of mourning.[14]

10

Towards a Hermeneutics of Historical Consciousness

Having left Hegel behind, can we still claim to think about history and the time of history? The answer would be negative if the idea of a "total mediation" were to exhaust the field of thought. But another way remains, that of an open-ended, incomplete, imperfect mediation, namely, the network of interweaving perspectives of the expectation of the future, the reception of the past, and the experience of the present, with no *Aufhebung* into a totality where reason in history and its reality would coincide.

The following pages are devoted to the exploration of this way. They begin from one particular strategic decision.

Having renounced attacking head-on the question of the vanishing reality of the past as it really was, we have to reverse the order of problems and begin from the project of history, from history as what has to be made, in order to rediscover in it the dialectic of the past and the future and their exchanges in the present. As regards the reality of the past, no one can, I think, really go beyond, by way of any direct approach, the preceding interplay of broken-off perspectives arising from the reactualization of the Same, the recognition of Otherness, and the assumption of the analogous. To go any further, we have to take up the problem from the other end and to explore the idea that these broken-off perspectives come together in a sort of pluralistic unity if we bring them together under the idea of a reception of the past, pushed to the point of becoming a "being-affected" by the past. And this idea takes on meaning and strength only if it is opposed to the idea of "making" history. Even the idea of tradition—which already includes a genuine tension between the perspective of the past and that of the present, and thereby increases temporal distance at the same time that it crosses it—does not give rise to thought, either by itself or as coming first, in spite of its undeniable mediating virtues, unless it is by way of the intentionality of a history to be made that refers back to it. In the end, the idea of the historical present, which, for a first approximation at least, seems to be dethroned from the inaugurating function it had for Augustine and Husserl, will receive a new luster from its terminal position in the interplay of interweaving perspectives. Nothing says that the present reduces to presence. Why, in the transition from future to past, should the present not be the *time of initiative*—that is, the time when the weight of history that has already been made is deposited, suspended, and interrupted, and when the dream of history yet to be made is transposed into a responsible decision?

Therefore it is within the dimension of acting (and suffering, which is its corollary) that thought about history will bring together its perspectives, within the horizon of the idea of an imperfect mediation.

THE FUTURE AND ITS PAST

The immediate benefit of this reversal of strategy is that it gets rid of the most tenacious abstraction that our attempts to circumscribe the reality of the past suffered from, the abstraction of the past as past. This abstraction is a result of forgetting the complex interplay of significations that takes place between our expectations directed toward the future and our interpretations oriented toward the past.

To combat this forgetfulness I propose to adopt as a guideline for the following analyses the polarity Reinhart Koselleck has introduced between the two categories of "space of experience" and "horizon of expectation."[1]

The choice of these terms seems to me a judicious and particularly illuminating one, especially as regards a hermeneutics of historical time. But why speak of a space of experience rather than of the persistence of the past in the present, even if these notions are related?[2] For one thing, the German word *Erfahrung* has a noteworthy scope. Whether it be a question of private experience or of experience transmitted by prior generations or current institutions, it is always a question of something foreign being overcome, of some acquisition that has become a *habitus*.[3] For another thing, the term "space" evokes the idea of different possible traversals following a multitude of itineraries, and above all the idea of a stratified structure assembled like a pile of sheets of paper, an idea that gets away from the idea of the past so assembled as a simple chronology.

As for the expression "horizon of expectation," it could not have been better chosen. For one thing, the term "expectation" is broad enough to include hope and fear, what is wished for and what is chosen, rational calculations, curiosity—in short, every private or public manifestation aimed at the future. As with experience in relation to the present, expectation relative to the future is inscribed in the present. It is the future-become-present (*ver-gegenwärtige Zukunft*), turned toward the not-yet. If, for another thing, we speak here of a horizon rather than of space, this is to indicate the power of unfolding as much as of surpassing that is attached to expectation. In this way, the lack of symmetry between the space of experience and the horizon of expectation is underscored. This opposition between gathering together and unfolding implies that experience tends toward integration, expectation tends toward the breaking open of perspectives: "*Gehegte Erwartungen sind überholbar, gemachte Erfahrungen werden gesammelt,*" "cultivated expectations can be revised; experiences one has had are collected" (*Futures Past*, p. 273). In this sense, expectation cannot be derived from experience. "Put another way, the previously existing space of experience is not sufficient for the determination of the horizon of expectation" (p. 275). Conversely, there is no surprise for which the baggage of experience is too light, it could not be otherwise. Hence the space of experience and the horizon of expectation do more than stand in a polar opposition, they mutually condition each other: "This is the temporal structure of experience and without retroactive expectation it cannot be accumulated" (ibid.).

Before thematizing each of these expressions in turn, it is important first to recall, under Koselleck's guidance, some of the major changes that affected the vocabulary of history during the second half of the eighteenth century in Germany. New meanings, often attributed to old words, will later serve to identify the in-depth articulation of the new historical experience indicated by a new relation between the space of experience and the horizon of expectation.

The word *Geschichte* stands at the center of the conceptual network then in movement. For example, in German, we see the term *Historie* give way to the term *Geschichte*, with the double connotation of a sequence of events taking place and the relating of events done or undergone; in other words, in the twofold sense of actual history and told history. *Geschichte* signifies precisely the relationship between the series of events and the series of narratives. In history as narrative, history as event comes to know itself, in Droysen's formula.[4] Yet for this convergence in meaning to be realized, it was necessary that both senses come together in the unity of a whole. It is a single course of events, in its universal interconnections, that is spoken of in a history that is itself elevated to the rank of a collective singular. Beyond histories, says Droysen, there is history. The word history could henceforth be used without a genitive complement. "Histories of . . ." became history *tout court*. On the level of narrative, this history presents the epic unity that corresponds to the one "epic" that human beings write.[5] For the sum of individual histories to become "history," however, it was necessary that history itself should become *Weltgeschichte*, hence that it become a system instead of an aggregation. In return, the epic unity of narrative could bring to language an assembling of the events themselves, an interconnection between them, which conferred their own epic upon them. What the historians contemporary with philosophical Romanticism discovered was more than an internal form of coherence, it was a force—a *Macht*—that propelled history according to a more or less secret plan, all the while that it left human beings responsible for its emergence. This is why other collective singular terms flocked to history's side: freedom, justice, progress, revolution. In this sense, "revolution" served as the revealer of an earlier process which at the same time it accelerated.

There is little doubt that it was the idea of progress that served as the tie between these two connotations of history. If actual history follows a intelligible course, then the narrative we make of it may claim to equate itself with this meaning, which is the meaning of history itself. This is why the emergence of the concept of history as a collective singular is one of the conditions for the constitution of the notion of universal history, which we have already considered in the preceding chapter. I shall not take up again the problematic of totalization or of a total mediation that was grafted to the knowledge of history as a unique whole. Instead I shall turn toward two features of this collective singular that give rise to a significant variation in the relation of the future to the past.

Three themes stand out among Koselleck's careful semantic analyses. First, the belief that the present age has a new perspective on the future that is without precedent. Second, the belief that changes for the better are accelerating. Third, the belief that human beings are more and more capable of making their own history. A new time, an acceleration of progress, and the availability of history—these three themes contributed to the unfolding of a new horizon of expectation that by a kind of recoil effect transformed the space of experience within which the acquisitions of the past are deposited.

1. The idea of a new time is inscribed in the German expression *neue Zeit*, which precedes by a century the term *Neuzeit*, the term that since about 1870 has been used to designate modern times. This latter expression, when isolated from the context of its semantic formation, seems to stem merely from the vocabulary of periodization, which itself goes back to the old classifying of "ages" in terms of metals, or law and grace, or the apocalyptic vision of the succession of empires, which is given such a striking image in the book of Daniel. We can also discern in this idea of a new time one effect of the recasting of the term "Middle Ages" that, since the Renaissance and the Reformation, no longer applies to the whole of time between the epiphany and the parousia but comes to designate one limited and already past period. It is precisely conceptual history that provides the key to why the Middle Ages were rejected and cast into a shadowy past. It is not just in the trivial sense—that is, that each moment is a new one—that the expression *Neuzeit* imposes itself, but in the sense of a new quality of time that has come to light, stemming from a new relationship to the future. It is especially noteworthy that it should be time itself that is declared to be new. Time is no longer just a neutral form of history but its force as well.[6] The "centuries" themselves no longer designate just chronological units but "epochs." The idea of a *Zeitgeist* is not far away, the unity of each such age and the irreversibility of their succeeding one another along the trajectory of "progress." The present, henceforth, will be

perceived as a time of transition between the shadows of the past and the light of the future. Only a change in the relationship between the horizon of expectation and the space of experience can account for this semantic change. Outside of this relation the present is indecipherable. Its sense of newness stems from how it reflects the light of the expected future. The present is only new, in the strong sense of the word, insofar as we believe that it "opens" new times.[7]

2. New times, and therefore also accelerated times. This theme of acceleration appears to be strongly connected to the idea of progress. Because progress is accelerating, we recognize the amelioration of the human condition. Correlatively, our space of experience noticeably contracts, burdened as it is by the acquisitions of tradition, and the authority of these acquisitions withers.[8] It is by way of contrast with this presumed acceleration that reactions, delays, and survivals of the past can be denounced. These are all expressions that still have a place in contemporary language and they give a dramatic accent to the belief in the acceleration of time inasmuch as it is still threatened by the semipeternal rebirth of the hydra of reaction, something that gives the expected future state of paradise the aspect of a "futureless future" (p. 18), equivalent to the Hegelian bad infinity. It is undoubtedly this conjunction between the sense of the newness of modern times and the acceleration of progress that has allowed the word "revolution"—previously reserved for the circulation of the stars, as we see in the title of Copernicus's famous work of 1543, *De Revolutionibus oribium caelestium*—to signify something other than the disorderly reversals that afflict human affairs, whether this refers to those occasional exemplary turns of fortune or the dreary alternation of reversals and restorations. We now call revolutions those uprisings that we can no longer catalogue as civil wars, but which testify, through the way they suddenly break out, to the general revolution that the civilized world has entered into. This is what has to be accelerated and whose course has to be regulated. In other words, the word "revolution" now bears witness to the opening of a new horizon of expectation.

3. That history is something to be made, and that it can be made, constitutes the third component of what Koselleck calls the "temporalization of history." It is already apparent in the theme of acceleration and in its corollary, revolution. We recall Kant's remark in the "Conflict of the Faculties" about the prophet who proclaims himself such and who brings about the events he predicted. In this sense, if a new future is opened by our new times, we can bend it to our plans, we can make history. And if progress can be accelerated, it is because we can speed up its course and struggle against what delays it, reaction and harmful survivals.[9]

The idea that history is submitted to human action is the newest and—as I shall say below—the most fragile of the three ideas that indicate the new way of perceiving the horizon of expectation. From being an imperative, the availability of history has become a optative, even a future indicative. This shift in meaning has been facilitated by the insistence of thinkers related to Kant, as well as by Kant himself, on discerning the "signs" that, already, authenticate the appeal of the task before us and encourage our efforts in the present. This way of justifying a duty by demonstrating the beginning of its execution is wholly characteristic of the rhetoric of progress, for which the expression "to make history" is the high point. Humanity becomes its own subject in talking about itself. Narrative and what is narrated can again coincide, and the two expressions "making history" and "doing history" overlap. Making and narrating have become the two sides of one process.[10]

We have been interpreting the dialectic between horizon of expectation and space of experience by following the guideline of three topoi—new times, the acceleration of history, and the mastery of history—that broadly characterize the philosophy of the Enlightenment. But it seems difficult to separate the discussion about the constituents of historical thinking from a properly historical consideration about the rise and fall of particular topoi. So the question arises of how much the main categories of a horizon of expectation and a space of experience are dependent upon these topoi, put forth by Enlightenment thinkers, that have served to illustrate them. We cannot avoid this difficulty. Let us speak, first, of their decline at the end of our twentieth century.

The idea of a new time appears suspect to us in many ways. First of all, it seems to us to be linked to the illusion of an origin.[11] But the discordances between the temporal rhythms of the various components of the overall social phenomenon make it difficult to characterize a whole epoch as both a break and an origin. Galileo, for Husserl in the *Krisis,* was such an origin, one beyond comparison with the French Revolution, because Husserl was considering only a battle between giants, that between transcendentalism and objectivism. Even more seriously, ever since the reinterpretation of the Enlightenment by Adorno and Horkheimer, we may doubt whether this epoch was always the dawn of progress it has been so celebrated for being. The beginning of the rule of instrumental reason, the power given to rationalizing hegemonies in the name of universalism, the repression of differences in the name of these Promethean claims are all stigmata, visible to all, of those times so conducive to liberation in many ways.

As for the acceleration in the march of progress, we hardly believe in it any longer, even if we do rightly speak of an acceleration in historical mutations. What we really doubt, however, is that the time separating us from better days is diminishing. Too many recent disasters and disorders speak against this. Koselleck himself emphasizes that the modern age is not only characterized by a contracting of the space of experience, which makes the past seem ever more distant in that it seems ever more passed, but also by an increasing gap between our space of experience and our horizon of expectation. Do we not see our dream of a reconciled humanity withdrawing into an ever more distant future and one ever more uncertain of realization? The task that, for our pred-ecessors, prescribed the journey by pointing the way has turned into a utopia or, better, a uchronia, where our horizon of expectation withdraws from us faster than we can advance toward it. And when our expectation can no longer fix itself on a determined future, outlined in terms of distinct, discernible steps, our present finds itself torn between two fleeing horizons, that of the surpassed past and that of an ultimate end that gives rise to no penultimate term. So torn within itself, our present sees itself in "crisis," and this is, as I shall say below, perhaps one of the major meanings of our present.

Of the three topoi of modernity, it is undoubtedly the third one that seems the most vulnerable to us and, in many ways, also the most dangerous. First, because as I have already said a number of times, the theory of history and the theory of action never coincide, due to the perverse effects issuing from our best conceived projects, the ones most worthy of our efforts. What happens is always something other than what we expected. Even our expectations change in largely unforeseeable ways. For example, it is no longer certain that free-dom, in the sense of the establishment of a civil society and a state of law, is the only hope or the major expectation of a great part of humanity. Above all, the vulnerability of the theme of mastering history is revealed even on the level where it is called for, the level of humanity taken as the sole agent of its own history. In conferring on humanity the power to produce itself, the au-thors of this claim forget one constraint that affects the destiny of great his-torical bodies as much as it affects individuals—in addition to the unintended results that action brings about, such action only takes place in circumstances that it has not produced. Marx, who was in fact one of the heralds of this topos, knew this when he wrote in his work on the eighteenth Brumaire of Louis-Napoleon that "men make their own history, but not as they please. They do not choose for themselves, but have to work upon circumstances as they find them, have to fashion the material handed down by the past." [12]

The theme of mastering history thus rests on a basic misunderstanding of the other side of thinking about history, which we shall consider below, namely, the fact that we are affected by history and that we affect ourselves by the history we make. It is precisely this tie between historical action and a re-ceived past, which we did not make, that preserves the dialectical relation be-tween our horizon of expectation and our space of experience. [13]

It remains true that these criticisms have to do with our three topoi, and that the categories of a horizon of expectation and a space of experience are more basic than the topoi in which they were instanciated by the philosophy of the Enlightenment, even if we must acknowledge that it is this philosophy that allows us to become aware of them because we live in the moment when their difference from it has itself become a major historical event.

Three arguments seem to me to speak in favor of a certain universality for these categories.

First, by appealing to the definitions I proposed when I introduced them, I will say that these categories stand on a higher categorial level than any of the envisaged topoi, whether it be a question of the ones the Enlightenment dethroned (the last judgment, *historia magistra vitae*), or the ones it set up. Koselleck is perfectly justified in taking them as metahistorical categories, applicable at the level of a philosophical anthropology. In this sense, they govern all the ways in which human beings in every age have thought about their existence in terms of history—whether it be made history or spoken history or written history.[14]

A second reason for taking these categories of the horizon of expectation and the space of experience as genuine transcendentals in the service of thought about history lies in the variability of instanciations they authorize at different times. Their metahistorical status implies that they serve as indicators regarding the variations affecting the temporalization of history. In this respect, the relationship between horizon of expectation and space of experience is itself a varying one. And it is because these categories are transcendentals that they make possible a conceptual history of the variations in their content. In this respect, the difference between them is not noticeable unless they change. If, therefore, the thought of the Enlightenment has such a privileged place in our discussion, it is because the variation in the relationship between the horizon of expectation and the space of experience it brought about was so apparent that it could serve as revelatory of the categories in terms of which we can think about this variation. There is an important corollary to this. by characterizing the topoi of modernity as a variation in the relationship between the horizon of expectation and the space of experience, conceptual history contributes to the relativizing of these topoi. We are now able to situate them in terms of the same kind of thinking that we apply to the political eschatology that reigned until the seventeenth century, whether in terms of its political vision governed by the relationship between *virtù* and Fortune, or in terms of the topos of the lessons of history. In this sense, formulating the concepts of a horizon of expectation and a space of experience gives us the means to understand the dissolution of the topos of progress as one plausible variation of the relationship between these concepts.

To finish, and this will be my third argument, I want to say that the universal ambition of these metahistorical categories is assured only by the permanent ethical and political implications of these categories of thought. In saying this, we do not slip from the problematic of the transcendental categories of historical thought to that of politics. With Karl-Otto Apel and Jürgen Habermas, I affirm the underlying unity of these two thematic issues. For one thing, modernity itself may be taken, despite the decline of its particular expressions, for an "incomplete project." [15] For another thing, this very project requires a legitimating argumentation that stems from the kind of truth claimed by practice in general and politics in particular.[16] The unity of these two problematics defines practical reason as such.[17] It is only under the aegis of such practical reason that the universal ambition of the metahistorical categories of historical thought can be affirmed. Their description is always inseparable from a prescription. If, therefore, we admit that there is no history that is not constituted through the experiences and the expectations of active and suffering human beings, or that our two categories taken together thematize historical time, we then imply that the tension between the horizon of expectation and the space of experience has to be preserved if there is to be any history at all.

The transformations in their relations that Koselleck describes confirm this. If it is true that the belief in a new time contributed to narrowing our space of experience, even to rejecting the past as forgotten shadows—the obscurantism of the Middle Ages!—while our horizon of expectation tended to withdraw into an ever more distant and indistinct future, we may ask whether this tension between expectation and experience did not begin to be threatened from the very day when it was first recognized. This paradox is easily explained. If the newness of the *Neuzeit* was only perceived thanks to the growing difference between experience and expectations—in other words, if the belief in new times rests on expectations that distance themselves from all prior experience—then the tension between experience and expectation could only be recognized at the moment when its breaking point was already in sight. The idea of progress which still bound the past to a better future, one brought closer by the acceleration of history, tends to give way to the idea of utopia as soon as the hopes of humanity lose their anchorage in acquired experience and are projected into an unprecedented future. With such utopias, the tension becomes a schism.[18]

The permanent ethical and political implication of these metahistorical categories of expectation and experience is thus clear. The task is to prevent the tension between these two poles of thinking about history from becoming a schism. This is not the place to spell out this task in more detail, so I will confine myself to two imperatives.

On the one hand, we must resist the seduction of purely utopian expectations. They can only make us despair of all action, for, lacking an anchorage in experience, they are incapable of formulating a practical path directed to the ideals that they situate "elsewhere."[19] Our expectations must be determined, hence finite and relatively modest, if they are to be able to give rise to responsible commitments. We have to keep our horizon of expectation from running away from us. We have to connect it to the present by means of a series of intermediary projects that we may act upon. This first imperative leads us back, in fact, from Hegel to Kant, in that post-Hegelian Kantian style I favor. Like Kant, I hold that every expectation must be a hope for humanity as a whole, that humanity is not one species except insofar as it has one history, and, reciprocally, that for there to be such a history, humanity as a whole must be its subject as a collective singular. Of course, it is not certain that we can today purely and simply identify this task with the building of "a universal civil society administered in accord with the right." More and more social rights have appeared in the world and continue to do so. In particular, the right to be different ceaselessly counterbalances the threats of oppression linked to the very idea of a universal history, if the realization of this history is confused with the hegemony of one society or of a small number of dominant societies. Yet, in return, the modern history of torture, of tyranny, and of oppression in all its forms has taught us that neither social rights nor the right to be different now recognized would merit the name "right" without the simultaneous realization of a rule of law where individuals and collectivities other than the state remain the ultimate subjects of these rights. In this sense, the task defined above, the one that according to Kant "men's unsocial sociability" requires us to resolve, has not been surpassed today. For it has not been attained, even when it has not been lost sight of, gone astray, or been cynically scoffed at.

On the other hand, we must also resist any narrowing of the space of experience. To do this, we must struggle against the tendency to consider the past only from the angle of what is done, unchangeable, and past. We have to reopen the past, to revivify its unaccomplished, cut-off—even slaughtered—possibilities. In short, when confronted with the adage that the future is open and contingent in every respect but that the past is unequivocally closed and necessary, we have to make our expectations more determinate and our experience less so. For these are two faces of one and the same task, for only determinate expectations can have the retroactive effect on the past of revealing it as a living tradition. It is in this way that our critical meditation on the future calls for the complement of a similar meditation on the past.

BEING-AFFECTED BY THE PAST

It is the very proposal of "making history" that calls for the step backward from the future toward the past. Humanity, we have said with Marx, only makes its history in circumstances it has not made. The notion of circumstances thus becomes an indicator of an inverted relation to history. We are only the agents of history inasmuch as we also suffer it. The victims of history and the innumerable masses who, still today, undergo history more than they make it are the witnesses par excellence to this major structure of our historical condition. And those who are—or who believe themselves to be—the most active agents of history suffer it no less than do its—or their—victims, even if this only be in terms of the unintended effects of their most calculated enterprises.

However, I do not want to deal with this theme in a way that deplores or execrates it. The sobriety that goes with thinking about history requires that we extract from the experience of submitting and suffering, in its most emotion-laden aspects, the most primitive structure of being-affected by the past, and that we reattach this to what I have called, following Reinhart Koselleck, the space of experience correlative to our horizon of expectation.

In order to derive this being-affected by the past from the notion of a space of experience, I shall take as my guide the theme introduced by Gadamer, in his *Truth and Method,* of the consciousness of being exposed to the efficacity of history, of our *Wirkungsgeschichtliches Bewusstsein.*[20] This concept has the advantage of forcing us to apprehend our "being-affected by . . ." as the correlative of the action (*Wirken*) of history upon us or, as one commentator has aptly translated it, as the "work of history."[21] We must be careful not to allow this theme, with its great heuristic power, to collapse into an apology for tradition, as is the tendency of the regrettable polemic that opposed Habermas's critique of ideology to Gadamer's so-called hermeneutic of traditions.[22] I shall refer to this debate only in closing.

The first way to attest to the fruitfulness of the theme of being-affected-by-history is to test it through a discussion we began above but interrupted at the moment when it turned from epistemology to ontology.[23] What is ultimately at stake in this discussion is the apparent antinomy between discontinuity and continuity in history. We can speak of an antinomy here inasmuch as, on the one hand, it is the very reception of the historical past by present consciousness that seems to require the continuity of a common memory, and because, on the other hand, the documentary revolution brought about by the new history seems to make breaks, ruptures, crises, and the irruption of changes in thinking—in short, discontinuity—prevail.

It is in Michel Foucault's *The Archeology of Knowledge* that this antinomy receives its most rigorous formulation, while at the same time it is resolved in terms of the second alternative.[24] On the one side, the asserted privilege of discontinuity is associated with a new discipline, the archeology of knowledge, which does not coincide with the history of ideas, in the sense that historians usually understand this. On the other side, the contested privilege of continuity is associated with the ambition of a constituting consciousness and the mastery of meaning.

Confronted with this apparent antinomy, I need to add that I have no strictly epistemological objection to raise against the first part of the argument. It is just the second part that I have to dissociate myself from entirely, in the name precisely of our theme of consciousness as affected by the efficacity of history.

The thesis that the archeology of knowledge does justice to the epistemological breaks that the classical history of ideas overlooks is legitimated by the very practice of this new discipline. In the first place, it starts from a stance whose originality becomes evident if we oppose it to the model of the history of ideas I borrowed from Maurice Mandelbaum at the end of the first volume of *Time and Narrative.*[25] There the history of ideas found a place among the special histories, artificially set off by historians against the background of general history, which is the history of first-order entities (actual communities, nations, civilizations, etc.), which are defined by their historical persistence, hence by the continuity of their existence. These special histories are those of art, science, and so forth. They gather together works that are by nature discontinuous, which are only connected with one other by some thematic unity that is not given by life in society but rather is authoritatively defined by historians, who decide, following their own conceptions, what is to be taken as art, science, etc.

Unlike Mandelbaum's special histories, which are abstracted from general history, Foucault's archeology of knowledge has no allegiance whatsoever to the history of actual first-order entities. This is the initial stance assumed by the archeology of knowledge. Next, this methodological choice is confirmed and legitimated by the nature of the discursive fields considered. The forms of knowledge at issue for this archeology are not "ideas" measured by their influence on the course of general history and the first-order entities that figure in it. The archeology of knowledge prefers to deal with anonymous structures within which individual works are inscribed. It is at the level of these structures that the events in thinking that mark the shift from one episteme to another are located. Whether it be a matter of the clinic, of madness, of taxonomies in natural history, economics, grammar, or linguistics, it is the forms of discourse closest to anonymity that best express the synchronic consistency of the dominant epistemes and their diachronic ruptures. This is why the leading categories of the archeology of knowledge—"discursive formations," "modes of assertion," "the historical a priori," "archives"—do not have to be brought to a level of utterance that brings into play individual speakers responsible for what they say. It is also, and particularly, why the notion of an "archive" can appear, more than any other, as diametrically opposed to that of traditionality.[26] Now no serious epistemological objection prevents treating discontinuity as "both an instrument and an object of research," thereby effecting the passage from "the obstacle to the work itself" (p. 9). A hermeneutics more attentive to the reception of ideas will limit itself here to recalling that the archeology of knowledge cannot completely break away from the general context wherein temporal continuity finds its legitimacy, and therefore must be articulated in terms of a history of ideas in the sense of Mandelbaum's special histories. Similarly, epistemological breaks do not prevent societies from existing in a continuous manner in other registers—whether institutional or not—than those of knowledge. This is even what allows different epistemological breaks not to coincide in every case. One branch of knowledge may continue, while another undergoes the effects of a break.[27] In this respect, a legitimate transition between the archeology of knowledge and the history of ideas is provided by the category of a "transformation rule," which seems to me the one most favorable to continuity of all those categories brought into play by Foucault's archeology.

For a history of ideas that refers to the enduring entities of general history, the notion of a transformation rule draws upon some discursive apparatus characterized not just by its structural coherence but also by unexploited potentialities that a new event in thinking will bring to light, at the price of a reorganization of the whole apparatus. Understood in this way, the passage from one episteme to another comes close to the dialectic of innovation and sedimentation by which we have more than once characterized traditionality—discontinuity corresponding to the moment of innovation, continuity to that of sedimentation. Apart from this dialectic, the concept of transformation, wholly thought of in terms of breaks, risks leading us back to the Eleatic conception of time which, according to Zeno, comes down to making time something composed of indivisible *minima*.[28] And we must say that the *Archeology of Knowledge* runs this risk with its methodological stance.

As for the other branch of the antinomy, nothing obliges us to tie the fate of the point of view emphasizing the continuity of memory to the pretensions of a constituting consciousness.[29] In any case, this argument holds only for thought about the Same, which we examined above.[30] It seems to me perfectly admissible to refer to a "continuous chronology of reason," that is, "the general model of a consciousness that acquires, progresses, and remembers" (p. 8), without thereby eluding the decentering of the thinking subject brought about by Marx, Freud, and Nietzsche. Nothing requires that history should become "a safer, less exposed shelter" (p. 14) for consciousness, an ideological expedient destined to "restore to man everything that has unceasingly eluded him for over a hundred years" (ibid.). On the contrary, the notion of a historical memory prey to the work of history seems to me to require the same decentering as the one Foucault refers to. What is more, "the theme of a living, continuous, open history" (ibid.) seems to me to be the only one capable of joining together vigorous political action and the "memory" of snuffed out or repressed possibilities from the past. In short, if it is a question of legitimating the assumption of a continuity to history, the notion of consciousness as exposed to the efficacity of history, which I shall now directly address, offers a viable alternative to that of the sovereign consciousness, transparent to itself and the master of meaning.

To make explicit the notion of receptivity to the efficacity of history is fundamentally to clarify the notion of tradition that is too rapidly identified with it. Instead of speaking indiscriminately of tradition, we need to distinguish several different problems that I will set under three headings: traditionality, traditions, tradition. Only the third of these lends itself to the polemic that Habermas undertook against Gadamer in the name of the critique of ideology.

The term "traditionality" is already familiar to us.[31] It designates a style of interconnecting historical succession, or, to speak as Koselleck does, a feature of the "temporalization of history." It is a transcendental for thinking about history just as are the notions of a horizon of expectation and a space of experience. Just as horizon of expectation and space of experience form a contrasting pair, traditionality stems from a subordinate dialectic, internal to the space of experience itself. This second dialectic proceeds from the tension, at the very heart of what we call experience, between the efficacity of the past that we undergo and the reception of the past that we bring about. The term "trans-mission" (which translates the German *Uberlieferung*) is a good way of expressing this dialectic internal to experience. The temporal style that it designates is that of time traversed (an expression we also encountered in Proust).[32] If there is one theme in *Truth and Method* that corresponds to this primordial signification of transmitted tradition, it is that of temporal distance (*Abstand*).[33] This is not just a separating interval, but a process of mediation, staked out, as I shall say below, by the chain of interpretations and reinterpretations. From the formal point of view we are still occupying, the notion of a traversed distance is opposed both to the notion of the past taken as simply passed and gone, abolished, and the notion of complete contemporaneity, which was the ideal of Romantic philosophy. Uncrossable distance or annulled distance, this seems to be the dilemma. But traditionality designates the dialectic between remoteness and distanciation, and makes time, in Gadamer's words, "the supportive ground of the process [*Geschehen*] in which the present is rooted" (p. 264).

To think through this dialectical relation, phenomenology offers the help of two well-known and complementary notions, that of a situation and that of a horizon. We find ourselves in a situation, and from this point of view every perspective opens on a vast, but limited, horizon. However, if the situation limits us, the horizon presents itself as something to be surpassed, without ever being fully reached.[34] To speak of a moving horizon is to conceive of a unique horizon constituted, for each historical consciousness, by the alien worlds not related to our own, into which we put ourselves by turns.[35] This idea of a unique horizon does not lead us back to Hegel. It is only intended to set aside Nietzsche's idea of a hiatus between changing horizons that must itself continually be replaced. Between the absolute knowledge that would abolish every horizon and the idea of a multitude of incommensurable horizons we have to put the idea of a "fusion of horizons," which occurs every time we test our prejudgments in setting out to conquer some historical horizon, imposing upon ourselves the task of overcoming our tendency to assimilate the past too quickly to our own expected meanings.

This notion of a fusion of horizons leads to the theme that finally what is at stake in the hermeneutics of historical consciousness is the tension between the horizon of the past and that of the present.[36] In this way, the problem of the relation between past and present is set in a new light. The past is revealed to us through the projection of a historical horizon that is both detached from the horizon of the present and taken up into and fused with it. This idea of a temporal horizon as something that is both projected and separate, distinguished and included, brings about the dialectizing of the idea of traditionality. At the same time, the concept of a fusion of horizons corrects what remains unilateral in the idea of being-affected by the past. It is in projecting a historical horizon that we experience, through its tension with the horizon of the present, the efficacity of the past, for which our being-affected by it is the correlate. Effective-history, we might say, is what takes place without us. The fusion of horizons is what we attempt to bring about. Here the work of history and the work of the historian mutually assist each other.

In this first respect, tradition, formally conceived of as traditionality, already constitutes a broadly significant phenomenon. It signifies that the temporal distance separating us from the past is not a dead interval but a transmission that is generative of meaning. Before being an inert deposit, tradition is an operation that can only make sense dialectically through the exchange between the interpreted past and the interpreting present.

In saying this, we already cross the threshold leading to the second sense of the term "tradition," that is, from the formal concept of traditionality to the material concept of the contents of a tradition. From here on, by "tradition" we shall mean "traditions." The passage from one connotation to the other is contained in the recourse we made to the notions of meaning and interpretation that appeared at the end of our analysis of traditionality. To give a positive evaluation to traditions is not yet, however, to make tradition a hermeneutical criterion of truth. To give the notions of meaning and interpretation their full scope, we must provisionally place between parentheses the question of truth. The notion of tradition, taken in the sense of traditions, signifies that we are never in a position of being absolute innovators, but rather are always first of all in the situation of being heirs. This condition essentially stems from the language-like [*langagière*] structure of communication in general and of the transmission of past contents in particular. For language is the great institution, the institution of institutions, that has preceded each and every one of us. And by language we must here understand not just the system of *langue* in each natural language, but the things already said, understood, and received. Through tradition, therefore, we understand the things already said, insofar as they are transmitted along the chains of interpretation and reinterpretation.

This recourse to the language-like structure of tradition-transmission is not extrinsic in any way to the thesis of *Time and Narrative*. In the first place, we have known since the beginning of our inquiry that the symbolic function itself is not foreign to the domain of acting and suffering. This is why the initial mimetic relation borne by narrative could be defined by its reference to the primordial aspect of action as being symbolically mediated. Next, the second mimetic relation of narrative to action, identified with the structuring operation of emplotment, taught us to treat imitated action as a text. Without thereby neglecting the oral tradition, the effectivity of the historical past can be said to coincide in large part with that of texts from the past. Finally, the partial equivalence between a hermeneutic of texts and a hermeneutic of the historical past finds reinforcement in the fact that historiography, as a knowledge by traces, largely depends on texts that give the past a documentary status. It is in this way that the understanding of texts inherited from the past can be set up, with all the necessary reservations, as a kind of exemplary experience as regards every relation to the past. The literary aspect of our heritage is, Eugen Fink would have put it, equivalent to cutting out a "window," one that opens on the vast landscape of what is past per se.[37]

This partial identification between consciousness exposed to the efficacity of history and the reception of past texts transmitted to us allowed Gadamer to move from the Heideggerian theme of understanding historicality, which we considered in the first section of this volume, to the opposite problem of the historicality of understanding itself.[38] In this respect, the reading he gives of this theory shows the reception that replies to and corresponds with being-affected-by-the-past in its language-like and textual dimension.

The dialectical character of our second concept of tradition—still internal to the space of experience—cannot be ignored. It redoubles the formal dialectic of temporal distance stemming from the tension between remoteness and distanciation. As soon as, by traditions, we mean the things said in the past and transmitted to us by a chain of interpretations and reinterpretations, we have to add a material dialectic of the contents to the formal dialectic of temporal distance. The past questions us and calls us into question before we question it or call it into question. In this struggle for a recognition of meaning, text and reader are in turn made familiar and unfamiliar. So this second dialectic has to do with the logic of question and answer, taken up by both Collingwood and Gadamer in succession.[39] The past questions us to the extent that we question it. It answers us to the extent we answer it. This dialectic finds its material handhold in the theory of reading elaborated above.

We come at last to the third sense of the term "tradition," which we deliberately put off examining until this point. This is the sense that has provided an opportunity for the confrontation between the so-called hermeneutic of traditions and the critique of ideologies. This confrontation results from a shift from the consideration of traditions to an apology for tradition.

Two preliminary remarks are called for before we take up this confrontation.

Let us first note that the slide from the question of traditions to the question of tradition per se is not entirely out of place. There is, in fact, a problematic worthy of being placed under the heading "tradition." This is the case because the question of meaning, posed by every transmitted content, cannot be separated from that of truth except in abstraction. Every proposal of a meaning is at the same time a claim to truth. What we receive from the past are, in effect, beliefs, persuasions, convictions; that is, ways of "holding for true," to use the insight of the German word *Für-wahr-halten,* which signifies belief. In my opinion, it is this tie between the language-like realm of traditions and the truth claim bound to the order of meaning that confers a certain plausibility on the threefold plea for prejudice, authority, and, finally, tradition through which Gadamer introduces us to his major problematic of consciousness exposed to the efficacity of history—in a quite openly polemic spirit.[40] Indeed, it is in relation to the claim of traditions to truth, a claim included in the holding-for-true of every proposal of meaning, that these three controversial notions are to be understood. In Gadamer's vocabulary, this truth claim, insofar as it does not proceed from us, but rather rejoins us as a voice coming from the past, gets enunciated as the self-presentation of the "things themselves."[41] The prejudged is thus a structure of the preunderstanding outside of which the "thing itself" cannot make itself heard. It is in this sense that his rehabilitation of prejudice takes on the Enlightenment's prejudice against prejudice. As for authority, it signifies in the first place the augmentation—*auctoritas* comes from *augere*—the increase that the claim to truth adds to mere meaning, in the context of "holding for true." On the side of reception, its *Gegenüber* is not blind obedience but the recognition of superiority. Tradition, in the end, receives a status close to that which Hegel assigned to customs—*Sittlichkeit.* We are carried along by it before we are in a position of judging it, or of condemning it. It "preserves" (*bewahrt*) the possibility of our hearing the extinguished voices of the past.[42]

My second preliminary remark is that the major participant in the argument is not critical thinking, in the sense inherited from Kant, by way of Horkheimer and Adorno, but what Gadamer calls "methodologism." With this title, he is aiming not so much at the concept of "methodic" research as at the pretensions of a judging consciousness, set up as the tribunal of history and itself unencumbered with any prejudices. This judging consciousness is, at bottom, akin to the constituting consciousness, the master of meaning, denounced by Foucault, from which we dissociated ourselves earlier. This critique of methodologism has no other ambition than to recall to judging consciousness the fact that tradition binds us to things already said and to their truth claim before we submit them to research. Taking a distance, or freedom as regards transmitted contents, cannot be our initial attitude. Through tradition, we find ourselves already situated in an order of meaning and therefore also of possible truth. Gadamer's critique of methodologism is meant to emphasize the fundamentally antisubjectivist accent of his notion of effective history.[43] Research, then, is the obligatory partner of tradition inasmuch as the latter presents truth claims. "At the beginning of all historical hermeneutics," writes Gadamer, "the abstract antithesis between tradition and historical research, between history and knowledge, must be discarded" (p. 251). With the idea of research, a critical moment is affirmed, one that comes second, it is true, but is unavoidable; this is what I call the relationship of distanciation, and from here on it will designate the opening for the critique of ideologies. It is essentially the vicissitudes of tradition, or, to put it a better way, rival traditions to which we belong in a pluralistic society and culture—their internal crises, their interruptions, their dramatic reinterpretations, their schisms that introduce, into our tradition, as one instance of truth, a "polarity of familiarity and strangeness on which hermeneutic work is based" (*Truth and Method,* p. 262).[44] After all, how could hermeneutics carry out its task if it did not make use of historiographical objectivity as a means for sifting through dead traditions or what we take as deviations from those traditions in which we no longer recognize ourselves?[45] It is in fact this passage through objectification that distinguishes post–Heideggerian hermeneutics from Romanticist hermeneutics where understanding was conceived of "as the reproduction of an original production" (*Truth and Method,* p. 263). It cannot be, of course, a question of understanding better. "It is enough to say that we understand in a different way, if we understand at all" (p. 264). As soon as hermeneutics distances itself from its Romantic origins, it is obliged to include within itself what was good in the attitude it reproves. To do so, it has to distinguish the honest methodology of the professional historian from the alienating (*Verfremdung*) distanciation that turns criticism into a more basic philosophical gesture than is the humble acknowledgment of "the supportive ground of the process [*Geschehen*] in which the present is rooted." Hermeneutics can indeed reject the ideology of methodology as a philosophical position that is unaware of itself as philosophical, but it has to integrate "method" into itself. What is more, it is hermeneutics that, on the epistemological level, demands "a sharpening of the methodological self-consciousness of science" (p. 265). For how can interpreters allow themselves to be called by the things themselves if they do not make use of, if only negatively, the filtering action of temporal distance? We must not forget that it is the fact of understanding that gave birth to hermeneutics. The properly critical question of "distinguishing the true prejudices, by which we understand, from the false ones by which we misunderstand" (p. 266) thus becomes an internal question of hermeneutics itself. Gadamer himself willingly grants this. "Hence the hermeneutically trained mind will also include historical [*historisch*] consciousness" (ibid.).

Having made these two remarks, we can at last turn to the debate between the critique of ideologies and the hermeneutic of tradition, with the single purpose in mind of better circumscribing the notion of effective history, along with its correlate, our being-affected-by this effectiveness.[46]

There is something to argue about to the extent that passing from "traditions" to "tradition" is, essentially, to introduce a question of legitimacy. The notion of authority, linked in this context with that of tradition, cannot fail to set itself up as a legitimating instance. It is what transforms the Gadamerian prejudice in favor of prejudice into a position of being based on right. However, what legitimacy can stem from what seems to be only an empirical condition, namely, the unavoidable finitude of all understanding? How can a necessity—*müssen*—convert itself into a right—*sollen*? The hermeneutic of tradition, it seems, cannot escape this question, which is posed by the very notion of "prejudice." As the term indicates, prejudice places itself within the orbit of judgment. Hence it makes its plea before the tribunal of reason. And, before this tribunal, it has no other resource than to submit to the law of the better argument. It cannot, therefore, set itself up as an authority without behaving like someone accused who refuses to accept the judge without becoming its own tribunal.

Does this mean that the hermeneutic of tradition has no answer here? I do not think so. Let us inquire what kind of arms are available to reason in this competition that opposes it to the authority of tradition.

They are, first of all, the weapons of a critique of ideologies. These begin by setting language, which hermeneutics seems to enclose itself within, into a much broader constellation, which also includes labor and domination. Under the gaze of the materialist critique that follows from doing this, the practice of language is revealed to be the place of those systematic distortions that resist the corrective action that a generalized philology (which is what hermeneutics seems to be in the last analysis) applies to the simple misunderstandings inherent in the use of language, once separated arbitrarily from the conditions for its social use. In this way, a presumption of ideology applies to every claim to truth.

However, such a critique, under the threat of undermining itself by self-reference to its own statements, has to limit itself. It does so by relating the set of all possible utterances to distinct interests. An interest in instrumental control characterizes the empirical sciences and their technological prolongations, so here we have to do with the domain of labor. The hermeneutical sciences correspond to an interest in communication, so here we have the tradition of language. Finally, we find an interest in emancipation with the critical social sciences, among which the critique of ideologies is, along with psychoanalysis and based upon its model, the most accomplished expression. Hermeneutics must therefore renounce its universalist claim if it is to preserve a regional legitimacy. On the other hand, the coupling of the critique of ideologies to an interest in emancipation raises a new claim to universality. Emancipation holds for everyone and always. But what is it that legitimates this new claim? This question is unavoidable. If we take seriously the idea of systematic distortions of language, connected with the dissimulated effects of domination, the question arises: before what nonideological tribunal might such perverted communication appear? This tribunal has to consist in the self-positing of an ahistorical transcendental, whose schematism, in the Kantian sense of the term, would be the representation of an unfettered and unlimited communication, hence of a speech situation characterized by a consensus arising out of the very process of argumentation.

Can we conceive of the conditions that determine such a speech situation?[47] The critique based on reason has to be able to escape a still more radical critique of reason itself. Indeed, critique is itself carried along by a historical tradition, that of the Enlightenment, some of the illusions of which we referred to in passing above. The violence characteristic of the Enlightenment, resulting from the instrumental conversion of modern reason, has been unmasked by the acerbic criticism of Horkheimer and Adorno. An excess of surpassings—and of surpassings of surpassings—is thus unleashed. Having lost itself in a "negative dialectic," which knows perfectly well how to recognize evil, as in Horkheimer and Adorno, the critique of critique projects the "principle of hope" into a utopia with no historical handhold, as in Ernst Bloch. All that remains, then, is the solution consisting of grounding the transcendental of the ideal speech situation in a new version, drawn from Kant and Fichte, of *Selbstreflexion,* the seat of every right and all validity. But, in order not to return to a principle of radically monological truth, as in the Kantian transcendental deduction, it is necessary to posit the original identity of the reflective principle together with an eminently dialogical one, as with Fichte. Otherwise, *Selbstreflexion* will not be able to ground the utopia of an unfettered and unlimited communication. This can be the case if the principle of truth is articulated on the basis of thinking about history, such as we have presented it in this chapter, which brings into relation a determined horizon of expectation and a specified space of experience.

It is along the path that leads back from the question of a ground to that of effective history that the hermeneutic of tradition makes itself more understandable. To escape the continual withdrawal of perfect ahistorical truth, we must attempt to discern the signs of truth in the anticipations of understanding at work in every successful communication where we have the experience of a type of reciprocity of intention and recognition of this intention. In other words, the transcendence of the idea of truth, inasmuch as it is immediately a dialogical idea, has to be seen as already at work in the practice of communication. When so reinstalled in the horizon of expectation, this dialogical idea cannot fail to rejoin those anticipations buried in tradition per se. Taken as such, the pure transcendental quite legitimately assumes the negative status of a limit-idea as regards many of our determined expectations as well as our hypostatized traditions. However, at the risk of remaining alien to effective-history, this limit-idea has to become a regulative one, orienting the concrete dialectic between our horizon of expectation and our space of experience.

The by turns negative and positive positing of this idea therefore affects our horizon of expectation as much as it does our space of experience. Or rather, it only affects our horizon of expectation insofar as it also affects our space of experience. This is the hermeneutical moment of criticism.

So we may trace out the path followed by the notion of tradition as follows. 1. Traditionality designates a formal style of interconnectedness that assures the continuity of the reception of the past. In this respect, it designates the reciprocity between effective-history and our being-affected-by-the-past. 2. Traditions consist of transmitted contents insofar as they are bearers of meaning; they set every received heritage within the order of the symbolic and, virtually, within a language-like and textual tradition; in this regard, traditions are proposals of meaning. 3. Tradition, as an instance of legitimacy, designates the claim to truth (the taking-for-true) offered argumentation within the public space of discussion. In the face of criticism that devours itself, the truth claim of the contents of traditions merits being taken as a presumption of truth, so long as a stronger reason, that is, a better argument, has not been established. By a "presumption of truth," I mean that credit, that confident reception by which we respond, in an initial move preceding all criticism, to any proposition of meaning, any claim to truth, because we are never at the beginning of the process of truth and because we belong, before any critical gesture, to a domain of presumed truth.[48] With this notion of a presumption of truth, a bridge is thrown over the abyss that, at the beginning of this argument, separated the unavoidable finitude of all understanding and the absolute validity of the idea of communicative truth. If a transition is possible between necessity and right, it is the notion of a presumption of truth that assures it. In it, the inevitable and the valuable asymptotically rejoin each other.

Two groups of conclusions may be drawn from this meditation on the condition of being-affected-by-the-past.
    First, we must recall that this condition forms a pair with the intending of a horizon of expectation. In this regard, a hermeneutic of effective-history only illumines the dialectic internal to the space of experience, abstraction being made of the exchanges between the two great modes of thinking about history. The restoration of this enveloping dialectic has its consequences for the meaning of our relation to the past. For one thing, the repercussion of our expectations relative to the future on the reinterpretation of the past may have as one of its major effects opening up forgotten possibilities, aborted potentialities, repressed endeavors in the supposedly closed past. (One of the functions of history in this respect is to lead us back to those moments of the past where the future was not yet decided, where the past was itself a space of experience open to a horizon of expectation.) For another thing, the potential of meaning thereby freed from the solid mass of traditions may contribute to determining the regulative but empty idea of an unhindered and unlimited communication, in the sense of a history yet to be made. It is through this interplay of expecta-

tion and memory that the utopia of a reconciled humanity can come to be invested in effective-history.

Next we have to reaffirm the preeminence of the notion of effective history and its correlate, our being-affected-by-the-past, over the constellation of significations gravitating around the term "tradition." I will not go over again here the importance of the distinctions introduced between traditionality, understood as a formal style for the transmission of received heritages, traditions, as contents endowed with meaning, and tradition, as a legitimation of the claim to truth raised by every heritage that bears a meaning. Instead I would like to show in what way this preeminence of the theme of the efficacity of the past over that of tradition allows the former to enter into relation with various notions relative to the past that were examined in preceding chapters of this volume.

If we move back step-by-step through the series of previous analyses, it is first of all the problematic of the *Gegenüber* from chapter 6 that takes on a new coloration. The dialectic of the Same, the Other, and the Analogous receives a new hermeneutical significance from being submitted to thought about the efficacity of the past. Taken in isolation, this dialectic runs the risk at each of its stages of turning into a dream of power exercised by the knowing subject. Whether it be a question of reenacting past thoughts, of difference in relation to the invariants posited by historical inquiry, or of the metaphorization of the historical field prior to any emplotment, in each case we perceive in the background the effort of a constituting consciousness to master the relation of the known past to the actual past. It is precisely this search for mastery, even when it is made dialectical in the manner we have spoken of, that the past as it was constantly escapes. The hermeneutical approach, on the contrary, begins by acknowledging this exteriority of the past in relation to every attempt centered upon a constituting consciousness, whether it be admitted, concealed, or simply not recognized as such. The hermeneutical approach shifts the problematic from the sphere of knowledge into that of being-affected-by, that is, into the sphere of what we have not made.

In return, the idea of a debt in regard to the past, which seemed to me to govern the dialectic of the Same, the Other, and the Analogous, adds a considerable enrichment to the idea of a tradition. The idea of a "heritage," which is one of the more appropriate expressions for the efficacity of the past, can be interpreted as the fusion of the ideas of a debt and a tradition. Without the dialectic of the Same, the Other, and the Analogous, which develops the seed of dialectization contained in the idea of a mediating transmission, the heart of the idea of tradition, this fusion does not come about. This seed grows when we submit the idea of tradition itself to the triple filter of reenactment, differentiation, and metaphorization. The various dialectics of the near and the far, the familiar and the alien, of temporal distance and the fusion of the horizons of the past and the present without confusing them bear witness to this. Finally, this inclusion of the dialectic of the Same, the Other, and the Analogous in the hermeneutics of history is what preserves the notion of tradition from succumbing again to the charms of Romanticism.

When we move back one more step in our analyses, the idea of tradition has to be brought together with that of a trace, where our fourth chapter ended. Between a trace left behind and followed, and transmitted and received tradition, there is a deep-lying affinity. As left behind, through the materiality of the mark, the trace designates the exteriority of the past, that is, its inscription in the time of the universe. Tradition puts the accent on another kind of exteriority, that of our being-affected-by a past that we did not make. However, there is also a correlation between the significance of the followed trace and the efficacity of transmitted tradition. These are two comparable mediations between the past and us.

By means of this connection between trace and tradition, all the analyses of chapter 4 can be taken up by what we are calling thought about history. As we move back again from our analyses of the trace toward those that preceded it, it is first the function of the document in the constitution of a large-scale memory that is clarified. The trace, we said, is left behind, the document collected and preserved. In this sense, it links together trace and tradition. Through the document, the trace is already part of a tradition. Correlatively, the criticism of documents is inseparable from the critique of traditions. But as such, this criticism is just one variant in the style of traditionality.

At another remove, tradition has to be brought together with the succession of generations. It underscores the hyper-biological aspect of the network of contemporaries, predecessors, and successors, namely, that this network belongs to the symbolic order. Reciprocally, the succession of generations provides the chain of interpretations and reinterpretations with a basis in life, as well as in the continuity of the living.

Finally, insofar as the trace, the document, and the succession of generations express the reinsertion of lived time in the time of the world, calendar time, too, comes into the range of the phenomenon of tradition. This articulation is visible on the level of the axis that defines the zero moment for computing time and that confers its bidimensionality on the system of dates. For one thing, this axial moment allows the inscription of our traditions in the time of the universe, and thanks to this inscription, effective-history, marked out by the calendar, is grasped as encompassing our own lives and the series of its vicissitudes. In return, if a founding event is to be judged worthy of constituting the axis of calendar time, we must be linked to it by way of a tradition that is a transmission. Hence it stems from the efficacity of a past that surpasses all individual memory. Calendar time thus provides our traditions with the framework of an institution based on astronomy, while the efficacity of the past provides calendar time with the continuity of a temporal distance that is traversed.

THE HISTORICAL PRESENT

Is there a place for a distinct meditation on the historical present in an analysis that has taken as its guide the opposition between a space of experience and a horizon of expectation? I think so. If traditionality constitutes the past dimension of the space of experience, it is in the present that this space comes together, it is there that this space can, as suggested above, expand or contract.

I would like to place the following philosophical meditation under the aegis of the concept of "initiative." I shall outline its contours by tracing out two concentric circles. The first circumscribes the phenomenon of initiative without regard to its insertion in thinking about history, which is the issue for us. The second makes more precise the relationship of initiative to a we-relation that brings initiative to the level of the historical present.

To tie the fate of the present to that of initiative is to subtract the present from the prestige of presence, in the quasi-optical sense of the term. Perhaps it is because looking back toward the past tends to make retrospection prevail—therefore a view or vision, rather than our being affected by our consideration of the past—that we tend also to think of the present in terms of vision, of *spectio.* Thus Augustine defined the present by *attentio,* which he also calls *contuitus.* Heidegger, on the other hand, rightly characterizes circumspection as an inauthentic form of Care, as a kind of fascination for looking at the things we are preoccupied with. "Making-present" thus turns into a kind of Medusa's gaze. To restore to making-present an authenticity equal to that of anticipatory resoluteness, I propose to connect the two ideas of making-present and initiative. The present is then no longer a category of seeing but one of acting and suffering. One verb expresses this better than all the substantive forms, including that of presence: "to begin." To begin is to give a new course to things, starting from an initiative that announces a continuation and hence opens something ongoing. To begin is to begin to continue—a work has to follow.[49]

But under what conditions does initiative give rise to thought about itself? The most radical position in this respect is that by which Merleau-Ponty characterized the insertion of the acting subject in the world, namely, the experience of the "I can," the root of the "I am." This experience has the major advantage of designating the lived body as the most original mediator between the course of lived experience and the order of the world. For the mediation of the lived body precedes all the connectors on the historical level that we have considered in the first chapter of the preceding section, and to which, below, we shall link the historical present. The lived body—or better, the flesh—has to do with what Descartes, in the Sixth meditation, called the "third substance," bridging the break between space and thought. In a more appropriate vocabulary, that of Merleau-Ponty himself, we should say that the flesh defies the dichotomy of the physical and the psychical, of cosmic exteriority and reflective interiority.[50] It is on the ground of such a philosophy of the flesh that the "I can" can be thought. The flesh, in this sense, is the coherent ensemble of my powers and nonpowers. Around this system of carnal possibilities the world unfolds itself as a set of rebellious or docile potential utensils, a set of permissions and obstacles. The notion of circumstances, referred to above, is articulated in terms in my nonpowers, insofar as it designates what "circumscribes"—what limits and situates—my power to act.

This description of the "I can," coming from a phenomenology of existence, provides an appropriate framework for taking up again those analyses that have been done regarding the field of the theory of action, which we have referred to regarding the initial mimetic relation of narrative to the practical sphere. Recall that, following Arthur Danto, I distinguished between basic actions, which we know how to do on the basis of mere familiarity with our powers, and derived actions, which require that we do something so that we bring about some event, which is not the result of our basic actions but the consequence of a strategy of action including calculations and practical syllogisms.[51] This adding of strategic actions to basic actions is of the greatest importance for a theory of initiative. Indeed, it extends our being-able-to-do-something well beyond the immediate sphere of the "I can." In return, it places the distant consequences of our action within the sphere of human action, removing them from the status of being mere objects of observation. So, as agents, we produce something, which, properly speaking, we do not see. This assertion is of the greatest importance for the quarrel about determinism, and it allows us to reformulate the Kantian antinomy of the free act, considered as the beginning of a causal chain. Indeed, it is not from the same attitude that we observe something that happens or that we make something happen. We cannot be observers and agents at the same time. One result is that we can only think about closed systems, partial determinisms, without being able to move on to extrapolations extending to the whole universe, except at the price of excluding ourselves as agents capable of producing events. In other words, if the world is the totality of what is the case, doing cannot be included in this totality. Better, doing means [*fait*] that reality is not totalizable.

A third determination of initiative will bring us closer to our meditation on the historical present. It brings us from the theory of action to that of systems. It is anticipated in an implicit way in the preceding determination. Models of states of systems and of the transformation of systems, including tree-like structures, with branches and alternatives, have been constructed. Thus, in volume 1, with von Wright, we defined interference—a notion equivalent to that of initiative within the framework of systems theory—by the capacity agents have of conjoining the being-able-to-do-something of which they have an immediate comprehension—Danto's basic actions—with the internal relations that condition a system.[52] Interference is what assures the closure of the system, by setting it into motion starting from an initial state determined by this very interference. By doing something, we said, agents learn to isolate a closed system from their environment and discover the possibilities of development inherent in this system. Interference is thus situated at the intersection of one of an agent's powers and the resources of the system. With the idea of putting a system in motion, the notions of action and causality overlap. The argument about determinism, just mentioned, can be taken up again here with a much stronger conceptual insight. If, in effect, we doubt our free ability to do something, it is because we extrapolate to the totality of the world the regular sequences we have observed. But we forget that causal relations are relative to segments of the history of the world that have the aspect of closed systems, and that the capacity for setting a system in motion by producing its initial state is a condition for its closure. Action thus finds itself implied in the very discovery of causal relations.

Transposed from the physical plane to the historical, interference constitutes the nodal point of a model of explanation said to be quasi-causal. This model, it will be recalled, is articulated in terms of teleological segments, corresponding to the intentional phases of action, and law-like segments, corresponding to its physical phases. It is within this model that our reflection on the historical present finds its most appropriate epistemological basis.

I do not want to end this initial cycle of considerations bearing on the concept of initiative without emphasizing how language is incorporated into the mediations internal to action, and more precisely those interventions by means of which agents take the initiative for the beginnings that they insert into the course of things. We recall that Emile Benveniste defined the present as the moment when speakers make their act of utterance contemporary with the statements they make.[53] In this way, the self-referentiality of the present was underscored. Of all the developments of this property of self-referentiality that Austin and Searle have added, I want to retain just those that contribute to indicating the ethical aspect of initiative.[54] This is not some artificial detour insofar as, on the one hand, speech acts or acts of discourse bring language into the dimension of action (it is significant that Austin entitled his work *How to Do Things with Words*), and, on the other hand, human acting is intimately articulated by signs, norms, rules, and evaluations that situate it in the region of meaning, or, if you will, within the symbolic dimension. Therefore it is legitimate to take into consideration linguistic mediations that make initiative into a meaningful action.

In a broad sense, every speech act (or every act of discourse) commits the speaker and does so in the present. I cannot assert something without introducing a tacit clause of sincerity into my saying it, in virtue of which I effectively signify what I am saying, any more than I can do so without holding as true what I affirm. It is in this way that every speech initiative—Benveniste would say, every instance of discourse—makes me responsible for what is said in my saying it. However, if every speech act implicitly commits its speaker, some types do so explicitly. This is the case with "commissives," for which the promise is the model. By promising, I intentionally place myself under the obligation to do what I say I will do. Here, commitment has the strong sense of speech that binds me. This constraint that I impose upon myself is noteworthy in that the obligation posited in the present engages the future. One remarkable feature of initiative is thereby underlined, which is well expressed by the adverbial phrase "from now on" (in French, by the adverb *désormais*). Indeed, to promise is not just to promise that I will do something, but also that I shall keep my promise. So to speak up is to make my initiative have a continuation, to make this initiative truly inaugurate a new course of things; in short, to make the present not just be an incident but the beginning of a continuation.

These are the phases traversed by a general analysis of initiative. Through the "I can," initiative indicates my power; through the "I do," it becomes my act; through interference or intervention, it inscribes my act in the course of things, thereby making the lived present coincide with the particular instant; through the kept promise, it gives the present the force of persevering, in short, of enduring. By this last trait, initiative is clothed with an ethical signification that announces the more specifically political and cosmopolitan characterization of the historical present.

The wider contour of the idea of initiative having been traced out, it remains to indicate the place of initiative between the horizon of expectation and the space of experience, thanks to which initiative can be equated with the historical present.

To make this equivalence appear, we must show how consideration of the historical present brings to its ultimate stage the reply of thought about history to the aporias of speculation about time, nourished by phenomenology. This speculation, it will be recalled, deepened the abyss between the notion of an instant without thickness, reduced to just the mere break between two temporal extensions, and the notion of a present, thick with the imminence of the near future and the record of a just passed past. The point-like instant imposed the paradox of the nonexistence of the "now," reduced to the break between a past that is no longer and a future that is not yet. The lived-through present, on the other hand, presents itself as the incidence of a "now" solidary with the imminence of the near future and the record of the just-passed past. The first connection brought about by thought about history was, we also recall, the time of the calendar. Our meditation on the historical present finds an initial handhold in the constituting of calendar time insofar as it rests, among other things, on the choice of an axial moment in terms of which events can be dated. Our own lives as well as those of the communities to which we belong are part of those events that calendar time allows us to situate at a variable distance in relation to this axial moment. This moment can be taken as the first foundation of the historical present, and it communicates to this present the virtue of calendar time, where it constitutes a third time between physical time and phenomenological time. The historical present thus participates in the mixed character of calendar time that joins the point-like instant to the lived-through present. It builds upon this foundation of calendar time. What is more, as linked to a founding event, held to open a new era, the axial moment constitutes the model of every beginning, if not of time, at least in time; that is, of every event capable of inaugurating a new course of events.[55]

The historical present is also based, as are the past and the historical future with which it is in solidarity, on the phenomenon, both biological and symbolic, of the succession of generations. Here the basis of the historical present is provided by the notion of the realm of contemporaries, which we have learned, following Alfred Schutz, to intercalate between that of predecessors and that of successors. Mere physical simultaneity, with all the difficulties that its purely scientific determination gives rise to, is thus carried on by the notion of contemporaneity, which immediately confers on the historical present the dimension of a we-relation, in virtue of which several flows of consciousness are coordinated in terms of "growing old together," to use Schutz's magnificent expression. The notion of a realm of contemporaries—wherein *Mitsein* is directly implied—thus constitutes the second foundation of the historical present. The historical present is therefore immediately apprehended as a common space of experience.[56]

We have still to give this historical present all the features of an initiative that will allow it to bring about the mediation we are seeking between the reception of a past transmitted by tradition and the projection of a horizon of expectation.

What was said about promises can serve as an introduction to the development that will follow. The promise, we said, formally engages the promiser because it puts the speaker under the obligation of doing something. An ethical dimension is thereby conferred on our consideration of the present. A comparable feature of the notion of the historical present is born from the transposition of our analysis of promises on the ethical plane to the political one. This transposition takes place through consideration of the public space into which the promise is inscribed, where the transposition from one plane to another is facilitated by consideration of the dialogical character of promises, which we did not emphasize above. Indeed, there is nothing solipsistic about promises. I do not confine myself to binding just myself in making a promise. I always promise something to someone. If this someone is not the beneficiary of my promise, at least he or she is its witness. Even before the act by which I commit myself, therefore, there is a pact that binds me to other people. The rule of fidelity in virtue of which one ought to keep one's promises thus precedes any individual promise made in the ethical order. In turn, the act of one person toward another that presides over this rule of fidelity stands out against the background of a public space governed by the social contract, in virtue of which discussion is preferred over violence and the claim to truth inherent in all taking-for-true submits to the rule of the better argument. The epistemology of true discourse is thus subordinated to a political—or better, cosmological—rule about truthful discourse. So there is a circular relation between the personal responsibility of the speakers who commit themselves through promises, the dialogical dimension of the pact of fidelity in virtue of which one ought to keep one's promises, and the cosmo-political dimension of the public space engendered by the tacit or virtual social contract.

The responsibility thereby unfolded in a public space differs radically from Heideggerian resoluteness in the face of death, which we know at some point is not transferable from one Dasein to another.

It is not the task of this work to outline even the lineaments of an ethical and political philosophy in light of which individual initiative could be inserted into a project of reasonable collective action. We can, however, at least situate the present of this indivisibly historical and political action at the point of articulation between the horizon of expectation and the space of experience. We then rediscover the assertion made earlier where, with Reinhart Koselleck, we said that our age is characterized both by the withdrawal of the horizon of expectation and a narrowing of the space of experience. If submitted to passively, this rending makes the present a time of crisis, in the double sense of a time of judgment and a time of decision.[57] In this idea of crisis is expressed the distention of our historical condition homologous with the Augustinian *distentio animi*. The present is wholly a crisis when expectation takes refuge in utopia and when tradition becomes only a dead deposit of the past. Faced with this threat of the historical present exploding, we have the task anticipated above: to prevent the tension between the two poles of thinking about history from turning into a schism. Therefore, on the one hand, to bring purely utopian expectations into connection with the present by strategic action concerned to take the first steps in the direction of the desirable and the reasonable; on the other hand, to resist the narrowing of our space of experience by liberating the unused potentialities of the past. Initiative, on the historical plane, consists in nothing other than the incessant transaction between these two tasks. However if this transaction is not to express just a reactive will, but instead to confront this crisis, it has to express the "force of the present."

One philosopher has had the strength to think through this "force of the present"—Nietzsche, in the second of his "untimely" meditations, entitled "On the Advantage and the Disadvantage of History for Life."[58] What Nietzsche dared to conceive of was the interruption the lived-through present brings about in regard to, if not the influence of the past, at least its influence over us—even by means of historiography insofar as it carries out and calls for the abstraction of the past as the past for itself.

Why is such a reflection untimely? For two related reasons. First, because it breaks immediately with the problem of knowledge (*Wissen*) in favor of that of life (*Leben*), and thereby puts the question of truth beneath that of utility (*Nutzen*) and the inconvenient (*Nachteil*). What is untimely is the unmotivated leap into a criteriology, which we know from the remainder of this book stems from Nietzsche's genealogical method, whose legitimacy is only guaranteed by the life it itself engenders. Equally untimely is the mutation the word "history"—Nietzsche writes *Historie*—undergoes. It no longer designates either of the two terms we have attempted to reconnect after having severed them from each other, neither the *res gestae* nor narrative, but rather "historical culture" or "historical meaning." In Nietzsche's philosophy, these two untimely phenomena are inseparable. A genetic evaluation of anything is at the same time an evaluation of culture. This shift in meaning has as its major effect that it substitutes for every epistemological consideration on the conditions of history, in the sense of historiography, and even more so for every speculative attempt to write world history, the question of what it means to live historically. To struggle with this question is for Nietzsche the gigantic struggle with modernity that runs through all his work.[59] Modern historical culture has transformed our ability to remember, which distinguishes us from other animals, into a burden, the burden of the past, which makes our existence (*Dasein*) into "a never to be completed imperfect tense" (p. 9). Here is where we find the most untimely point of his pamphlet. To escape from this perverse relationship to the past, we must become capable again of forgetting "or, to express it in a more learned fashion, [we must have] the capacity to live *unhistorically*" (ibid.; his emphasis). Forgetting is a force, a force inherent in the "plastic power of a man, a people or a culture. . . . I mean the power distinctively to grow out of itself, transforming and assimilating everything past and alien, to heal wounds, replace what is lost and reshape broken forms out of itself" (p. 10). Forgetting is the work of this force, and inasmuch as it is itself willed, it delimits the "closed and whole" horizon within which alone a living being may remain healthy, strong, and fruitful.[60]

The displacement from the question of history (as historiography or world history) to that of the historical is thus brought about in Nietzsche's text by the opposition between the historical and the unhistorical, the fruit of the untimely irruption of forgetfulness within the philosophy of culture. "The unhistorical and the historical are equally necessary for the health of an individual, a people and a culture" (p. 10). This "proposition" (*Satz*) is itself untimely insofar as it turns the unhistorical state (*Zustand*) into an instance of judgment concerning the abuse, the excess, constitutive of the historical culture of modern people. Then the man of life judges the man of knowledge, for whom history is one manner of closing off the life of humanity.[61] To denounce an excess (*Übermass*) (p. 14) is to assume that there is a good use for it. Here is where the arbitration of "life" begins. But we must not misunderstand what is going on here. The sort of typology that has made this essay by Nietzsche famous—its distinctions between monumental history, antiquarian history, and critical history—is not a neutral epistemological one. Still less does it represent an ordered progression as a function of some pure form, as does Hegel's philosophy of history (just as Nietzsche's third term occupies Hegel's second place, which it is important to note; perhaps there is an ironical relation to Hegel in Nietzsche's threefold division). In each instance it is a question of a cultural figure, not of an epistemological mode of thought.

They provide in turn an occasion for discerning the sort of wrong that written history does to actual history in a particular cultural constellation. And in each instance it is the service of life that is the criterion.

Monumental history stems from learned culture. Even if it is written by enlightened minds, it is addressed to men of action and strength, to combatants, in search of models, teachers, and comforters that they cannot find among their associates or their contemporaries (p. 14).[62] As the way it is named suggests, it both teaches and gives warning by its insistence on an obstinately retrospective perspective that interrupts all action with the held breath of reflection. Nietzsche speaks of it without sarcasm. Without a view of the whole chain of events, one cannot form an idea of man. Grandeur is only revealed in the monumental. Such history builds the famous man a mausoleum, which is nothing other than "the belief in the affinity and continuity of the great of all ages, it is a protest against the change of generations and transitoriness" (p. 16). Nowhere else does Nietzsche come so close to seconding Gadamer's plea in favor of the "classical." From its commerce with the classical, the monumental consideration of history draws the conviction that "the great which once existed was at least *possible* once and may well again be possible sometime" (ibid.). "And yet . . . !" (*Und doch*). The secret vice of monumental history is that it misleads through the force of analogy, by the very fact that it equalizes differences and disperses disparities, leaving only the "effect in itself" (p. 17), which is never imitable, ones such as are celebrated by our great holidays. In this effacing of singularity, "the past itself suffers damage [*so leidet die Vergangenheit selbst Schaden*]" (ibid.). And if this is so for the greatest of the men of action and power, what is there to say of the mediocre who hide behind the authority of the monumental in order to thereby disguise their hatred for all grandeur?[63]

If monumental history may assist the strong in mastering the past in order to create grandeur, antiquarian history helps ordinary people to persist in what a well-established tradition rooted in familiar soil offers as habitual and worthy of reverence. Preserve and revere—this motto is instinctually understood by a household, a generation, a city. It justifies an enduring neighborliness and sets us on guard against the seductions of cosmopolitan life, which is always seeking novelty. For this kind of history, to have roots is not some arbitrary accident, but to grow out of the soil of the past, to become the heir of its flowering and its fruits. But danger is not far off. If everything that is old and past is equally venerable, history is again injured not only by the shortsightedness of reverence but by the mummification of a past no longer animated by the present nor inspired by it. Life does not want to preserve itself but simply to go on.

This is why there is need of a third kind of history to serve life, critical history. Its tribunal is not that of critical reason but the strong life. For this type of history, "every past . . . is worth condemning" (p. 22). For to live is to be unjust and, even more so, unmerciful. If there is a time for forgetting, it is surely the one that condemns the aberrations, the passions, the errors, and the crimes of which we are the descendants. This cruelty is the time of forgetfulness, not through negligence but through deliberate misunderstanding. This is the time of a present that is as active as is the time of promise-making.

It is clear that the reader of these awesome pages by Nietzsche has to know that all these sayings must be set within the framework of Nietzsche's great metaphorical stance that joins philology and physiology within a genealogy of morals, in what is also a theory of culture.

This, in fact, is why the remainder of this essay breaks away from the taxonomic appearances of this typology to take up a more accusatory tone—against the science of history! Against the cult of interiority, stemming from the distinction between "inside" and "outside" (p. 24), in short, against modernity![64] This invective is not off-target. Look at us, library rats turned into walking encyclopedias; individuals, void of any creative instinct, reduced to wearing masks, born with gray hairs. Historians, charged to guard history, have become eunuchs and history a harem which they oversee (p. 31). It is no longer the eternal feminine that draws us upward—as in the closing verses of Goethe's *Faust*—but the eternal objective, celebrated by our historical education and culture.

Let us set aside this tone of invective, retaining from it only the important opposition it establishes between objectivity and the virtue of justice, which is rarer even than "generosity" (*Grossmut*) (p. 34). Unlike the icy demon of objectivity, justice—which a few pages before had been called injustice!—dares to take up the scales, to judge and condemn, to set itself up as the Last Judgment. In this sense, truth itself is nothing without "that striving . . . which has its root in justice" (p. 33). For mere justice, without the "power of judgment" (ibid.), has inflicted the most horrible sufferings on human beings. Only "superior power can judge . . . , weakness must tolerate" (p. 34). Even the art of composing a whole cloth from the course of events, like a drama-tist—or by what I have called emplotment—still stems, due to its cult of being intelligible, from the illusions of objective thought. Objectivity and jus-tice have nothing to do with each other. It is true that it is not so much the art of composition that Nietzsche is against as the aesthetic attitude of detach-ment that once again aligns art on the side of monumental and antiquarian history. Here, too, as in those cases, the force of justice is missing.[65]

If this "untimely" plea for a just history has a place in my own inquiry it is because it grapples with and depends upon the crest of the present, between the projection of the future and the grasp of the past. "Only from the stand-point of the highest strength [*Kraft*] of the present may you interpret [*deuten*] the past" (p. 37). Only today's grandeur can recognize the grandeur of the past, as one equal to another. In the last analysis, it is from the strength of the present that proceeds the strength to refigure time: "the genuine historian must have the strength to recast the well known into something never heard before and to proclaim the general so simply and profoundly that one over-looks its simplicity because of its profundity and its profundity because of its simplicity" (p. 37). It is this strength that makes all the difference between a master and a slave.

Even less is the present, in the suspension of the unhistorical, the eternal present of the Hegelian philosophy of history. Earlier, I referred to some of the serious misunderstandings inflicted on Hegel's philosophy of history. Nietzsche contributed much to this process.[66] But if Nietzsche could have helped to spread the misinterpretation of the Hegelian theme of the end of history, it was because he saw in the culture he was denouncing the exact culmination of this misinterpretation.[67] For the epigones, what could their age mean other than the "musical coda of the world-historical rondo" (p. 47), or, in short, a super-fluous existence? In the end, the Hegelian theme of the "power [*Macht*] of history" can only serve as a warning against making an idol of success, of fact (p. 48). Nietzsche takes these "apologists of the factual" as proclaiming, "we are the goal, we are the completion of nature" (p. 50).

In doing this, has Nietzsche accomplished anything more than the castiga-tion of the arrogance of nineteenth-century Europe? If this were all, his pam-phlet would not remain "untimely" for us as well. If it does remain so, it is because it contains within itself an enduring significance that a hermeneutic of historical time has the task of reactualizing in ever new contexts. For my own inquiry concerning the interconnections among the three ecstases of time, brought about poetically by historical thought, this enduring significance con-cerns the status of the present in regard to history. On the one hand, the his-torical present is, in each era, the final term of a completed history, which itself completes and ends history. On the other hand, the present is, again in every era, or at least it may become, the inaugural force of a history that is yet to be made.[68] The present, in the first sense, speaks of the aging of the youth of history and establishes us as "firstcomers."[69]

In this way, Nietzsche makes the notion of the historical present shift from the negative to the positive, by proceeding from the mere suspension of the historical—through forgetfulness and the claims of the unhistorical—to the affirmation of the "strength of the present." At the same time, he inscribes this force of the present in the "inspiring consolation of hope" (*das hoffendes Streben*) (p. 63), which allows him to set aside the vituperation of the disadvantages of history in favor of what remains as "the advantage of history for life."[70]

So a certain iconoclasm directed against history, as sealed up in what is past and gone, is a necessary condition for its ability to refigure time. No doubt a time in suspension is required if our intentions directed at the future are to have the force to reactivate the unaccomplished possibilities of the past, and if effective-history is to be carried by still living traditions.

Conclusions

The conclusions I propose to draw at the end of our long journey will not be limited to summing up the results attained. They have the further aim of exploring the limits our enterprise runs into, just as I did previously in the concluding chapter of *The Rule of Metaphor*.[1]

What I should like to explore both in shape and limits is the hypothesis that has oriented this work from its very beginning, namely, that temporality cannot be spoken of in the direct discourse of phenomenology, but rather requires the mediation of the indirect discourse of narration. The negative half of this demonstration lies in our assertion that the most exemplary attempts to express the lived experience of time in its immediacy result in the multiplication of aporias, as the instrument of analysis becomes ever more precise. It is these aporias that the poetics of narrative deals with as so many knots to be untied. In its schematic form, our working hypothesis thus amounts to taking narrative as a guardian of time, insofar as there can be no thought about time without narrated time. Whence the general title of this third volume: *Narrated Time*. We apprehended this correspondence between narrative and time for the first time in our confrontation between the Augustinian theory of time and the Aristotelian theory of the plot, which began volume 1. The whole continuation of our analyses has been one vast extrapolation from this initial correlation. The question that I now pose, upon rereading all this material, is whether this amplification is equivalent to a mere multiplication of mediations between time and narrative, or whether the initial correspondence changed its nature over the course of our developments.

This question first arose on the epistemological level, under the title "the configuration of time by narrative"; next within the framework of historiography (Part II of volume 1); then within that of fictional narrative (volume 2). We were able to measure the enrichments that the central notion of emplotment received in these two cases, when historical explanation or narratological rationality were superimposed on underlying basic narrative configurations. Conversely, thanks to the Husserlian method of "questioning back"

(*Rückfrage*), we showed that such rationalizations of narrative lead back, through appropriate intermediary terms, to the formal principle of configuration described in the first part of volume 1. The notions of quasi-plot, quasi-character, and quasi-event elaborated at the end of Part II, bear witness, on the side of historiography, to this always possible derivation, as does, on the side of narratology, the persistence of the same formal principle of configuration even in those forms of composition of the novel apparently most inclined toward schism, as shown in our analyses in volume 2. Hence I believe that we can affirm that on the epistemological plane of configuration, the multiplication of intermediary links merely extends the mediations without ever breaking the chain, despite the epistemological breaks legitimately made in our day by historiography and narratology in their respective domains.

Does the same thing apply on the ontic plane of the refiguration of time by narrative, the plane upon which the analyses in this third volume have unfolded? There are two reasons for posing this question. For one thing, the aporetics of time, which occupied section 1 in this volume, was considerably enriched by our adding to the Augustinian core of our initial analyses the important developments made by phenomenology, so that we may rightly question whether our expansion of this aporetics has been homogeneous. Secondly, it is not clear that the structure of the seven chapters in section 2 of this volume, which give the reply of the poetics of narrative to the aporetics of time, obeys the same law of derivation from the simple to the complex, illustrated by the epistemology of historiography and of narratology.

It is to answer this double interrogation that I propose here a rereading of the aporetics of time, one that will follow another order of composition than the one imposed by the history of the doctrines involved.

It seems to me that three problematics have remained entangled in our analyses from author to author, even from work to work, in the first section.

1. We concentrated on the aporia resulting from the mutual occultation of the phenomenological and the cosmological perspectives. This difficulty seemed so serious to me that it governed the construction, in the form of a polemic, of section 1: Aristotle against Augustine, Kant against Husserl, the upholders of so-called "ordinary" time against Heidegger. What is more, it took no less than five chapters to elaborate the response of the narrative function to this most visible of the aporias of temporality. The first question we must pose, therefore, is to verify at what point the interweaving of the referential intentions of history and fiction constitutes an adequate response to this initial great aporia, the aporia of a double perspective in speculation on time.

2. Our mostly positive response to this first question must not, in turn, conceal a difficulty that is rebellious in another way, one that has remained bound up with the preceding one in the aporetics of time. It is the question of what meaning to give to the process of totalization of the ecstases of time, in virtue of which time is always spoken of in the singular. This second aporia is not

just irreducible to the first one, it dominates it. The representation of time as a collective singular surpasses the split into phenomenological and cosmological approaches. So it will be necessary to undertake a review of the aporias bound to this representation and lost sight of in our historical inquiry, so as to give them the preeminence due them that the privilege accorded the first cycle of aporias may have covered over. Having done this, we shall be in a position to pose the question whether our two final chapters bring as adequate a response to the aporia of the totality of time as the five preceding ones bring to the aporia of the double perspective on time. A less adequate reply to the question on the level of this second great aporia of temporality will give us a premonition of the limits ultimately encountered by our ambition of saturating the aporetics of time with the poetics of narrative.

3. Is the aporia of totalization the last word in the aporetics of time? Upon reflection, I do not think so. An even more intractable aporia is concealed behind the two preceding ones. It has to do with the ultimate unrepresentability of time, which makes even phenomenology continually turn to metaphors and to the language of myth, in order to talk about the upsurge of the present or the flowing of the unitary flux of time. No particular chapter was devoted to this aporia, which in a way circulates among the interstices of our aporetics. The corresponding question is thus whether narrativity is capable of giving an adequate reply to this failure to represent time, a reply drawn from its own resources. The response to this embarrassing question was not the object of a separate examination in the second section of this volume, any more than the question itself was. Therefore we shall have to gather up the *membra disjecta* of the broken discourse supposed to respond to this powerful aporia. For the moment, let us be content to formulate the problem in the briefest possible manner: can we still give a narrative equivalent to the strange temporal situation that makes us say that everything—ourselves included—is *in* time, not in the sense given this "in" by some "ordinary" acceptation as Heidegger would have it in *Being and Time,* but in the sense that myths say that time encompasses us with its vastness? To answer this question constitutes the supreme test of our ambition to reply adequately to the aporetics of time with a poetics of narrative.

The new hierarchy between the aporias of temporality that we are proposing here thus runs the risk of making apparent an increasing inadequacy in our response to the question, and hence in the response of the poetics of narrative to the aporetics of time. The virtue of this test of adequation will be at least to have revealed both the scope of the domain where the reply of the poetics of narrative to the aporetics of time is pertinent—and the limit beyond which temporality, escaping from the grid-work of narrativity, moves once again from being a problem to being a mystery.

THE FIRST APORIA OF TEMPORALITY
NARRATIVE IDENTITY

Most certainly it is to the first aporia that the poetics of narrative provides the least sketchy response. Narrated time is like a bridge set over the breach speculation constantly opens between phenomenological time and cosmological time.

A rereading of what has been said about this aporetics confirms to what point the progression of our analyses has accentuated the seriousness of this aporia.

Augustine has no other resource when it comes to the cosmological doctrines than to oppose to them the time of a mind that distends itself. This mind has to be that of an individual soul but by no means that of a world soul. Yet his meditation on the beginning of Creation leads Augustine to confess that time itself had a beginning along with created things. This time must be that of every creature, therefore, in a sense that cannot be explicated within the framework of the doctrine in Book XI of the *Confessions,* a cosmological time. On the other hand, Aristotle is quite sure that time is not movement, and that it requires a soul to distinguish instants and count intervals. But this implication of a soul cannot figure in the pure definition of time as "the number of movement in respect of the 'before' and 'after,'" out of fear that time will be elevated to the rank of the ultimate principles of the *Physics,* which only allows this role to movement, with its enigmatic definition as "the fulfilment of what is potentially, as such." In short, the physical definition of time by itself is incapable of accounting for the psychological conditions for the apprehension of this time.

As for Husserl, he may try to set objective time with its already constituted determinations in parentheses, since the actual constitution of phenomenological time has to take place on the level of a pure hyletics of consciousness. But a discourse about the hyletic can occur only thanks to the borrowings it makes from the determinations of constituted time. So constituting time cannot be elevated to the rank of pure appearing without some shift in meaning from the constituting to the constituted. Yet if this has to occur, it is difficult to see how we can draw from phenomenological time, which must be the time of an individual consciousness, the objective time that, by hypothesis, is the time of the whole of reality. Conversely, time according to Kant immediately has all the features of a cosmological time, inasmuch as it is the presupposition of every empirical change. Hence it is a structure of nature, which includes the empirical egos of each and every one of us. Yet I cannot see how such time can "reside" in the *Gemüt,* since we cannot articulate any phenomenology of this *Gemüt* without bringing back to life that rational psychology that the paralogisms had condemned once and for all.

It is with Heidegger that this aporia stemming from the mutual occultation of phenomenological time and cosmological time seems to me to have reached its highest degree of virulence, despite the fact that the hierarchy of levels of temporalization brought to light by the hermeneutic phenomenology of Dasein does assign a place to within-time-ness, that is, to Being-within-time. When taken in this derived, yet original, sense time does appear to be coextensive with Being-in-the-world, as is attested to by the very expression "world time." However even world time remains the time of some Dasein, individual in every case, in virtue of the intimate tie between Care and Being-towards-death, that untransferable feature that characterizes every Dasein as "existing." This is why the derivation of ordinary time through a leveling off of the aspects of the worldliness of authentic temporality seemed to me to lack credibility. On the contrary, it seemed more enriching to the discussion to situate the dividing line between the two perspectives on time at the very point where Heidegger sees an operation of leveling off, which must appear to him as an error in thinking, a betrayal of authentic phenomenology. The fracture here seems all the deeper because it is so narrow.

It is to this aporia of the mutual occultation of these two perspectives on time that our poetics of narrative seeks to offer its answer.

The mimetic activity of narrative may be schematically characterized as the invention of a third-time constructed over the very fracture whose trace our aporetics has brought to sight. This expression—"third-time"—appeared in our analysis as a way of characterizing the construction by historical thinking of connectors as determinate as calendar time. Yet this expression merits being extended to all of our analyses, or at least up to the threshold of our last two chapters. The question, in any case, which has not been answered, which we are posing here, is how to evaluate the degree of adequacy of this reply. In other words, to what point does the interweaving of the respective ontological intentions of history and fiction constitute an appropriate response to the mutual occultation of the phenomenological and cosmological perspectives on time?

In order to set the stage for our response, let us sum up the strategy we have been following. We started from the idea that this third-time had its own dialectic, its production not being able to be assigned in any exhaustive way to either history or fictional narrative, but rather to their interweaving. This idea of an interweaving of the respective referential intentions of history and fictional narrative governed the strategy we followed in the first five chapters of the second section of this volume. In order to make sense of the criss-crossing reference of history and fiction, we in effect interwove our own chapters about them. We began with the contrast between a historical time reinscribed on cosmic time and a time handed over to the imaginative variations of fiction. Next we paused at the stage of the correspondence between the function of "standing-for" the historical past and the meaning effects produced by the confrontation between the world of the text and the world of the reader. Finally, we moved to the level of an interpenetration of history and fiction, stemming from the criss-crossing processes of a fictionalization of history and a historization of fiction. This dialectic of interweaving might in itself be one sign of the inadequacy of our poetics to our aporetics, if there were not born from this mutual fruitfulness an "offshoot," whose concept I will introduce here, one that testifies to a certain unification of the various meaning effects of narrative.

The fragile offshoot issuing from the union of history and fiction is the assignment to an individual or a community of a specific identity that we can call their narrative identity. Here "identity" is taken in the sense of a practical category. To state the identity of an individual or a community is to answer the question, "Who did this?" "Who is the agent, the author?" [2] We first answer this question by naming someone, that is, by designating them with a proper name. But what is the basis for the permanence of this proper name? What justifies our taking the subject of an action, so designated by his, her, or its proper name, as the same throughout a life that stretches from birth to death? The answer has to be narrative. To answer the question "Who?" as Hannah Arendt has so forcefully put it, is to tell the story of a life. The story told tells about the action of the "who." And the identity of this "who" therefore itself must be a narrative identity. Without the recourse to narration, the problem of personal identity would in fact be condemned to an antinomy with no solution. Either we must posit a subject identical with itself through the diversity of its different states, or, following Hume and Nietzsche, we must hold that this identical subject is nothing more than a substantialist illusion, whose elimination merely brings to light a pure manifold of cognitions, emotions, and volitions. This dilemma disappears if we substitute for identity understood in the sense of being the same (*idem*), identity understood in the sense of oneself as self-same [*soi-même*] (*ipse*). The difference between *idem* and *ipse* is nothing more than the difference between a substantial or formal identity and a narrative identity. Self-sameness, "self-constancy," can escape the dilemma of the Same and the Other to the extent that its identity rests on a temporal structure that conforms to the model of dynamic identity arising from the poetic composition of a narrative text. The self characterized by self-sameness may then be said to be refigured by the reflective application of such narrative configurations. Unlike the abstract identity of the Same, this narrative identity, constitutive of self-constancy, can include change, mutability, within the cohesion of one lifetime.[3] The subject then appears both as a reader and the writer of its own life, as Proust would have it.[4] As the literary analysis of autobiography confirms, the story of a life continues to be refigured by all the truthful or fictive stories a subject tells about himself or herself. This refiguration makes this life itself a cloth woven of stories told.

This connection between self-constancy and narrative identity confirms one of my oldest convictions, namely, that the self of self-knowledge is not the egotistical and narcissistic ego whose hypocrisy and naiveté the hermeneutics of suspicion have denounced, along with its aspects of an ideological super-structure and infantile and neurotic archaism. The self of self-knowledge is the fruit of an examined life, to recall Socrates' phrase in the *Apology*. And an examined life is, in large part, one purged, one clarified by the cathartic effects of the narratives, be they historical or fictional, conveyed by our culture. So self-constancy refers to a self instructed by the works of a culture that it has applied to itself.

The notion of narrative identity also indicates its fruitfulness in that it can be applied to a community as well as to an individual. We can speak of the self-constancy of a community, just as we spoke of it as applied to an individual subject. Individual and community are constituted in their identity by taking up narratives that become for them their actual history.

Here two examples may be set parallel to each other. The one is drawn from the sphere of the most thoroughgoing individual subjectivity, the other is drawn from the history of cultures and of *mentalités*. On the one side, psycho-analytic experience throws into relief the role of the narrative component in what are usually called "case histories." It is in the work of the analysand, which by the way Freud called "working-through" (*Durcharbeitung*), that this role can be grasped. It is further justified by the very goal of the whole process of the cure, which is to substitute for the bits and pieces of stories that are unintelligible as well as unbearable, a coherent and acceptable story, in which the analysand can recognize his or her self-constancy. In this regard, psychoanalysis constitutes a particularly instructive laboratory for a properly philosophical inquiry into the notion of narrative identity. In it, we can see how the story of a life comes to be constituted through a series of rectifica-tions applied to previous narratives, just as the history of a people, or a collec-tivity, or an institution proceeds from the series of corrections that new histo-rians bring to their predecessors' descriptions and explanations, and, step by step, to the legends that preceded this genuinely historiographical work. As has been said, history always proceeds from history.[5] The same thing applies to the work of correction and rectification constitutive of analytic working-through. Subjects recognize themselves in the stories they tell about themselves.

Our comparison between analytic working-through and the work of the his-torian facilitates the transition from our first to our second example. This is borrowed from the history of a particular community, biblical Israel. This example is especially applicable because no other people has been so over-whelmingly impassioned by the narratives it has told about itself. On the one hand, the delimitation of narratives subsequently taken as canonical expresses, even reflects, the character of this people who gave themselves, among other writings, the patriarchal narratives, those of the Exodus, those of the settlement in Caanan, then those of the Davidic monarchy, then those of the exile and return. But we may also say, with just as much pertinence, that it was in telling these narratives taken to be testimony about the founding events of its history that biblical Israel became the historical community that bears this name. The relation is circular—the historical community called the Jewish people has drawn its identity from the reception of those texts that it had produced.

This circular relation between what we may call a "character"—which may be that of an individual as well as that of a people—and the narratives that both express and shape this character, illustrates in a marvelous way the circle referred to at the beginning of our description of threefold mimesis.[6] The third mimetic relation of narrative to practice, we said, leads back to the first relation by way of the second relation. At that time, this circle disturbed us in that it might be objected that the first mimetic relation already bears the mark of previous narratives, in virtue of the symbolic structure of action. Is there, we asked, any experience that is not already the fruit of narrative activity? At the end of our inquiry into the refiguration of time by narrative we can affirm without hesitation that this circle is a wholesome one. The first mimetic relation refers, in the case of an individual, to the semantics of desire, which only includes those prenarrative features attached to the demand constitutive of human desire. The third mimetic relation is defined by the narrative identity of an individual or a people, stemming from the endless rectification of a previous narrative by a subsequent one, and from the chain of refigurations that results from this. In a word, narrative identity is the poetic resolution of the hermeneutic circle.

At the end of this first set of conclusions, I would like to indicate the limits of the solution that the notion of narrative identity brings to the initial aporia of temporality. Certainly, the constitution of narrative identity does illustrate in a useful way the interplay of history and narrative in the refiguration of a time that is itself indivisibly phenomenological time and cosmological time. But it also includes, in turn, an internal limitation that bears witness to the first inadequacy of the answer narration brings to the question posed by the aporetics of temporality.

In the first place, narrative identity is not a stable and seamless identity. Just as it is possible to compose several plots on the subject of the same incidents (which, thus, should not really be called the same events), so it is always possible to weave different, even opposed, plots about our lives. In this regard, we might say that, in the exchange of roles between history and fiction, the historical component of a narrative about oneself draws this narrative toward the side of a chronicle submitted to the same documentary verifications as any other historical narration, while the fictional component draws it toward those imaginative variations that destabilize narrative identity. In this sense, narrative identity continues to make and unmake itself, and the question of trust that Jesus posed to his disciples—Who do you say that I am?—is one that each of us can pose concerning ourself, with the same perplexity that the disciples questioned by Jesus felt. Narrative identity thus becomes the name of a problem at least as much as it is that of a solution. A systematic investigation of autobiography and self-portraiture would no doubt verify this instability in principle of narrative identity.

Next, narrative identity does not exhaust the question of the self-constancy of a subject, whether this be a particular individual or a community of individuals. Our analysis of the act of reading leads us to say rather that the practice of narrative lies in a thought experiment by means of which we try to inhabit worlds foreign to us. In this sense, narrative exercises the imagination more than the will, even though it remains a category of action. It is true that this opposition between imagination and will applies most aptly to that moment of reading we called the moment of stasis. But we added that reading also includes a moment of impetus. This is when reading becomes a provocation to be and to act differently. However this impetus is transformed into action only through a decision whereby a person says: Here I stand! So narrative identity is not equivalent to true self-constancy except through this decisive moment, which makes ethical responsibility the highest factor in self-constancy. Lévinas's well-known analysis of promise-keeping and, in a way, his whole work bear witness to this. The plea that the theory of narrative can always oppose to ethics' claim to be the sole judge of the constitution of subjectivity would be to recall that narrativity is not denuded of every normative, evaluative, or prescriptive dimension. The theory of reading has warned us that the strategy of persuasion undertaken by the narrator is aimed at imposing on the reader a vision of the world that is never ethically neutral, but that rather implicitly or explicitly induces a new evaluation of the world and of the reader as well. In this sense, narrative already belongs to the ethical field in virtue of its claim—inseparable from its narration—to ethical justice. Still it belongs to the reader, now an agent, an initiator of action, to choose among the multiple proposals of ethical justice brought forth by reading. It is at this point that the notion of narrative identity encounters its limit and has to link up with the nonnarrative components in the formation of an acting subject.

The Second Aporia of Temporality
Totality and Totalization

This is an aporia distinct from that of totality per se. The preceding aporia stemmed from the noncongruence between two perspectives on time, that of phenomenology and that of cosmology. This second aporia is born from the dissociation among the three ecstases of time—the future, the past, and the present—despite the unavoidable notion of time conceived of as a collective singular. We always speak of "time." If phenomenology does not provide a theoretical response to this aporia, does thought about history, which we have said transcends the duality of historical and fictional narrative, provide a practical one? The answer to this question constituted what was at stake in our final two chapters. In what way does this response have to do with practice? In two ways. First, renouncing the speculative solution proposed by Hegel forced us to substitute the notion of totalization for that of totality. Next, this totalization appeared to us to be the fruit of an imperfect mediation between a horizon of expectation, the retrieval of past heritages, and the occurrence of the untimely present. In this double sense, the process of totalization places thinking about history in the practical dimension.

In order to measure the degree of adequation between this practical process of totalization and the theoretical aporia of totality, it will be necessary to undertake another reading of our aporetics inasmuch as the historical approach of our first section emphasized our initial aporia while leaving the various expressions of this second one scattered here and there.

That there is just one time is what the *Timaeus* presupposes as soon as it defines time as "a moving image of eternity" (37d). Furthermore, this time is coextensive with the single world soul, and is born along with the heavens. Yet this world soul stems from multiple divisions and admixtures, all governed by the dialectic of the Same and the Other.

The discussion that Aristotle devotes to the relations between time and movement also presupposes the oneness of time. The question that presides over his preliminary examination of the tradition and its aporias is "what time is and what is its nature" (*Physics*, IV, 218a32). The oneness of time is explicitly the aim of the argument that distinguishes time from movement, namely, that there are many movements but just one time. (This argument preserved its force as long as movement itself had not been unified into one thing, which could not occur before the formulation of the principle of inertia.) In return, Aristotle, by preventing himself from elevating time to the rank of a principle of nature, could not say how a soul, in distinguishing instants and counting intervals, could conceive of the unity of time.

As for Augustine, it will be recalled with what force he poses the troublesome question, "What, then, is time?" Nor have we forgotten the confession that follows, which gives his inquiry the tonality of interrogative thinking. The conflict between *intentio* and *distentio* may thus be reinterpreted in terms of a dilemma between the assembled unity of time and its bursting apart as a function of memory, anticipation, and attention. Our whole aporia lies in this structure of the threefold present.

It is with Kant, Husserl, and Heidegger that the oneness of time as such is made problematic.

Kant seems to echo Augustine when in turn he comes to pose the question, "What, then, are space and time?" (A23, B37). But he does so in order to introduce, with a confident tone, the table of possible answers from which he makes one unequivocal choice, namely, "that they belong only to the form of intuition, and therefore to the subjective constitution of our mind [*Gemüt*]" (A23, B37–38). So the ideal nature of time assures its oneness. And this oneness of time is that of a form in our capacity to take up a manifold of impressions. This oneness serves in turn the argument in the "metaphysical," then in the "transcendental exposition" of the concept of time. It is because time is a collective singular that it cannot be a discursive concept—that is, a genus divisible into species; instead it is an a priori intuition. Whence the axiomatic form of the argument: "Different times are but parts of one and the same time" (A31, B47). And again, "The infinitude of time signifies nothing more than that every determinate magnitude of time is possible only through limitations of one single time that underlies it" (A32, B48). In the same argument, he speaks of "the whole representation" of time which is nothing other than "the original representation" of time (ibid.). So it is as a priori that the intuition of time is posited as the intuition of one unique time.

Yet this unity becomes problematic in the "Transcendental Analytic." In the first place, the doctrine of the schematism introduces the distinction between the "series of time," the "content of time," the "order of time," and the "scope of time in respect of all possible objects." Yet this plurality of "determinations of time" (A145, B184), linked to the plurality of schemata, does not really threaten the unity established on the level of the "Aesthetic."[7] But it is not clear that the same thing may be said about the distinction between the "three modes of time" that the successive examination of the "Analogies of Experience" imposes; namely, permanence, succession, simultaneity. It is the permanence of time that poses the most serious problem. It is partially bound up with the schema of substance, and through this with the principle that bears the same name, permanence. And it is on the occasion of the first of these connections that Kant declares, in parentheses it is true, that "The existence of what is transitory passes away in time but not time itself. To time, itself non-transitory and abiding, there corresponds in the [field of] appearance what is non-transitory in existence, that is, substance. Only in [relation to] substance can the succession and coexistence of appearances be determined in time" (A143, B183). This statement has the ring of a paradox. Permanence somehow includes succession and simultaneity. The "aesthetic," not yet having to deal with specific objects, or objective phenomena, recognizes only the oneness and infinity of time. But now it happens that phenomenal objectivity gives rise to this unexpected feature, permanence, which participates in the same a priori character of all the aspects of time acknowledged by the "Aesthetic."

For the moment we shall confine this paradox to the limits of our second aporia as it confronts a transcendental reflection that is still the master of its thematic subject. But we shall also return to its examination again within the framework of our third aporia, because here reflection seems to run up against something inscrutable and resistant to any clarification. Nothing, however, allows us to think that Kant was surprised by this immutable and fixed time that does not flow.

This assertion of the unique and unitary character of the form of time, the least discussed assertion of any in Kant, becomes a problem for Husserl. We might think that this aspect belongs to objective time, which he begins by bracketing out. But such is not the case. Even the title of his lectures indicates this. The compound expression that is possible in German—*Zeitbewusst-sein*—suggests the idea of two things that are one: one consciousness, one time.[8] Indeed, what is ultimately at stake is the self-constitution of time as a single flux. But, within a hyletics—since the constitution of immanent time ultimately depends on this—how is it possible to constitute the unitary form of time without recourse to a principle extrinsic to the manifold of impressions, such as we find in Kant and Brentano? The major discovery with which we have credited Husserl, the constitution of an extended present by the continuous addition of retentions and protentions to the source-point of the living present, only partially answers this question. Only partial totalities—the well-known tempo-objects of the type of the sound that continues to resonate—are constituted in this way. So how are we to pass from such "fragments" of duration to "temporal duration itself"? (p. 45). The direction in which we have to look for a solution is of course well known: the totality of time has to be the corollary of its continuity. But can we draw this corollary from the simple iteration of the phenomenon of retention (and protention)? I do not see how retentions of retentions can make up a single flux. This cannot happen directly inasmuch as we must bring together, in this one flow, memories that are continually issuing from the living present, quasi-presents freely imagined along with their own sets of retentions and protentions, and recollections that do not stand in a direct connection with the living present, yet which are endowed with a positional character not found in merely imagined quasi-presents. Does the phenomenon of "coincidence" that is supposed to transpose, on a wider scale, the phenomenon of the continuation of the present into the recent past really account for what Husserl himself calls the "linking of time"? The insufficiency of this explanation is attested to by the necessity to pursue the constitution of immanent time on a more radical level, reached only in the Third Section of the *Phenomenology of Internal Time-Consciousness*. The difficulty that it is supposed to respond to results from the need to acknowledge that every kind of memory has a fixed place in the unitary flow of time, along with the increasing fading away of these contents resulting from their falling back into an ever more distant and hazy past. In order to confront this difficulty, Husserl splits up the intentionality that slides back and forth along the length of this flux, distinguishing from the primary intentionality that is directed toward the modifications in how a particular object is presented a second form of intentionality that aims at the temporal position of this experienced object independently of its degree of distance from the living present. But the place of a phenomenon in time refers to the totality of the flux of time considered as a form.[9] So we rediscover once again Kant's paradox that time itself does not flow. And it is this constitution that gives meaning to the expression "to happen *in* time." What the preposition "in" designates is precisely the fixity of the temporal position, distinct from the degree of distanciation of the lived contents.

The difficulty for Husserl is finally to draw, from a phenomenology applied in the first place to the continuous expansions of a point source, a phenomenology of the whole of time. But neither the constitution of tempo-objects that still have, if we may put it this way, one foot in the living present, nor the phenomenon of coincidence stemming from the mutual overlapping of the stages of retention and protention of every quasi-present can perfectly account for the self-constitution of immanent time as a total flux. Husserl's difficulty here is expressed in several ways. Sometimes he invokes "some a priori temporal laws" (the title of §33); sometimes he admits that it is "startling (if not at first sight even contradictory) to assert that the flux of consciousness constitutes its own unity" (p. 106); sometimes he simply confesses, "For all this, names are lacking" (p. 100).

We may ask therefore whether Husserl's obstinacy in looking for an answer appropriate to the question of the unity of this flux does not have to do with the most fundamental presupposition of all, that of the unity of consciousness itself, which the unity of time redoubles. Even assuming that such a unity can be spared the criticisms of a Hume or a Nietzsche, the monadic character of its constitution would still be a problem. And the constitution of a common time will then depend on the constitution of an intersubjectivity. We can doubt whether the "communalization" of individual experiences proposed in the fifth *Cartesian Meditation* succeeds any better in engendering a unique time than does the experience of the coincidence of what is experienced within a single consciousness.[10]

Finally, with Heidegger, the question of temporal totality reaches the highest point of critical reflection and, in this, of perplexity. By stressing, as we have done in our discussion, the aporia of "ordinary time," we have pushed into the background the theme that in fact opens the second section of *Being and Time,* the possibility of Dasein's Being-a-whole. Nowhere is it said why this question is the principal one that a hermeneutic phenomenology of time has to pose. It is just the answer brought by the analysis of Being-towards-death that reveals, after the fact, the urgency of the question of the "potentiality" of Being-a-whole. But whatever may be said about the priority of the question over the answer, an unexpected turn is given to the question of totality through this relation to mortality. In the first place, time will not be an infinite given, as in Kant, but rather an aspect of finitude. Mortality—not the event of death in public time, but the fact that each of us is destined for our own death—indicates the internal closure of primordial temporality. Next, time will not be a form, in either the Kantian or the Husserlian sense, but a process inherent in the most intimate structure of Dasein, namely, Care. There is no need, therefore, to assume a double intentionality, one part adhering to the contents and their interplay of retentions and protentions, the other designating the immutable place of a lived experience in a time that is itself fixed. The question of place is relegated, through the byways of within-time-ness and its leveling off, to the false pretensions of ordinary time.

The perplexity resulting from this response to the question of Being-a-whole arises for several reasons. First, the connection between Being-a-whole and Being-towards-death has to be attested to by the testimony of conscience, whose most authentic expression, according to Heidegger, lies in resolute anticipation. It follows that the meaning of the process of totalization is not accessible to the kind of impersonal reflection that governs Kant's "transcendental aesthetic," nor to as disinterested a subject as Husserl's transcendental ego. At the same time, it becomes difficult to distinguish, within this resolute anticipation, what is existential, hence communicable in principle, and what is existentiell, that is, a personal option for Heidegger the human being. I already indicated above that other existentiell conceptions, those of Augustine, Pascal, Kierkegaard, Sartre, are set aside here in the name of a kind of stoicism that makes resolution in the face of death the supreme test of authenticity. Heidegger's choice is certainly acceptable on the level of a personal ethics, but it sets his whole analysis of Being-a-whole in a conceptual fog that is difficult to pierce. Indeed, this analysis seems to be moved by two contrary impulses. According to the first of these, the hermeneutic phenomenology of Care tends to close in on itself in terms of an inner phenomenon, which is not transferable from one Dasein to another, that we can call one's own lived death, just as we speak of one's own lived body.[11] For the second impulse, the temporal structure of Care, restored to the opening of *Sich-vorweg*, Being-ahead-of-itself, opens on the immense dialectic of coming-towards, having-been, and making present. I will not deny that this second impulse given to the question of Being-a-whole takes precedence over the first one only if the existential analysis is borne by an existentiell attitude that places unconcern about one's own death above anticipatory resoluteness, and is thereby inclined to take philosophy as a celebration of life rather than as a preparation for death. The reasons for this other existentiell choice would have to be demonstrated elsewhere than within the framework of a simple analytic of Dasein, still too caught up in a philosophical anthropology.

If we assume that we can abstract the question of Being-a-whole from the kind of stranglehold inflicted upon it by the equating of Being-a-whole and Being-towards-death, an even more serious aporia concerning Being-a-whole is brought to light.

Recall how Heidegger moves from the notion of temporality to that of temporalization, in parallel with his replacement of possibility, in the Kantian sense, with "making-possible." What temporalization makes possible is precisely the unity of coming towards, having-been, and making-present. This unity is said to be undermined from within by the dehiscence of what Heidegger henceforth calls the ecstases of time, referring to the Greek *ekstatikon,* to which the German *Ausser-sich* corresponds. Whence the surprising assertion: "temporality is the primordial 'outside-of-itself' [*Ausser-sich*] in and for itself" (p. 377). In this way, we are returned in one step to the very beginning of our investigation, to the Augustinian *distentio animi;* in short, to the discordant concordance that launched all our analyses.[12]

This "outside-of-itself," by means of which time is externalized in relation to itself, constitutes such a powerful structure, at the heart of the basic experience of temporality, that it governs every process of differentiation that, on the two other levels of temporalization, breaks apart its unity. Whether it be a question of the stretching-along of time on the level of historicality, or of the extension of the lapse of time on the level of within-time-ness, the primordial "outside-of-itself" pursues its subversive career right up to its triumph in the ordinary concept of time, said to proceed from within-time-ness by means of a process of leveling off. This ultimate transition, which is also a fall, is made possible by extrapolating the temporal features of Care to the whole ensemble of Being-in-the-world, thanks to which we can speak of the "world-historical" character of beings other than Dasein. The mutual exteriority of the "nows" of chronological time is just a degraded representation. At least it does have the virtue of making explicit, at the price of a belated objectification, that aspect of primordial temporality that means that it gathers things together only by dispersing them.

But how do we know that temporality gathers things together, despite the power of dispersion that undermines it? Is it because, without ever having posed the question, Care is itself taken to be a collective singular—as was the Husserlian consciousness, which is originarily one with itself?

How has the poetics of narrative responded to this many-sided aporia concerning totality? It first opposed a firm but costly refusal to the ambition of thought to bring about a totalization of history entirely permeable to the light of concepts, and recapitulated in the eternal present of absolute knowledge.

To this unacceptable solution, the poetics of narrative next opposed an imperfect mediation between the three dimensions of expectation, tradition, and the force of the present.

Is this totalization through an imperfect mediation an adequate reply to the aporia of the totality of time? We may, in my opinion, recognize a good correlation between the imperfect mediation that governs thinking about history and the multiform unity of temporality, on the condition of stressing both the multiform character of the unity assigned to time taken as a collective singular and the imperfect character of said mediation between the horizon of expectation, traditionality, and the historical present.

It is noteworthy, in this respect, that historical thinking transposes, in a resolutely practical way and on the dialogical plane of a common history, the phenomenological analyses we have seen carried out in a speculative manner and on a monological plane. To see this, let us retrace again the principal steps of our ternary analysis of historical consciousness.

By deliberately beginning with the notion of a horizon of expectation, we in a way legitimated the reversal of priorities brought about by Heidegger within the framework of a hermeneutic phenomenology of Care. Horizon of expectation and Being-ahead-of-itself correspond term-by-term to each other in this sense. But, owing to the double transposition just spoken of, expectation is immediately conceived of as a structure of practice. It is acting beings who try to make their history and who undergo the evils engendered by this very effort. What is more, this projection is open to the future of the historical communities we belong to and, beyond these, to the undetermined future of humanity as a whole. The notion of expectation therefore differs from Heidegger's Being-ahead-of-itself, which runs up against the internal closure that Being-towards-death imposes on all anticipation.

The same kinship and the same contrast can be discerned between Heidegger's having-been and our concept of traditionality. The monological theme of fallenness is transposed into the dialogical theme par excellence of being affected by history. What is more, the pathetic aspect of fallenness is transposed into the practical category of the consciousness of the efficacity of history. Finally, it is the same concepts of trace, heritage, and debt that govern both analyses. But, whereas Heidegger only conceives, at least on the most primordial plane, of a transmission of a heritage from oneself to oneself, traditionality includes the confession of a debt that is fundamentally contracted on behalf of another. Heritages are transmitted principally through language and most often on the basis of symbolic systems implying a minimum of shared beliefs and understandings about the rules permitting the deciphering of signs, symbols, and norms current in a group.

A third set of correspondences, finally, may be discerned on the level of making-present, to which corresponds, on the side of historical consciousness, the force of the present. A kinship can be recognized between the circumspection accorded the presence of things present-at-hand and ready-to-hand and the historical present, concerning which, following Nietzsche, we have underscored its rootedness in "life," at least so long as history can be evaluated in terms of its "advantages" and "disadvantages." However it is here that the reply of historical consciousness to the aporetics of time indicates the greatest gap in the transposition from one plane to another. On the one hand, the frankly practical character of any initiative gives the notion of a historical present its primary force. Initiative is, above all else, what actualizes the competence of an acting subject. Therefore what comes under any "untimely consideration" are the untimely aspects of all initiative per se. So the present is most clearly grasped in terms of its occurrence in time. On the other hand, the dialogical character of the historical present immediately places it under the category of living-together. Initiatives are inscribed on the common world of contemporaries, to take up again the vocabulary of Alfred Schutz. We showed this with the example of promises, which commit the monadic subject only on the condition of a reciprocity governing mutual expectations and, in the end, a social pact dependent upon the idea of justice.

In many ways, therefore, the imperfect mediation of historical consciousness responds to the multiform unity of temporality.

We have yet to say what corresponds, on the side of historical consciousness, to the very idea of a unity of the three ecstases of time, beyond their differentiation. One important theme from *Being and Time* can perhaps point the way to an answer. This is the theme of repetition or, better, recapitulation (*Wiederholung*), whose analysis takes place precisely on the plane of historicality. Repetition, we said, is the name by which the anticipation of the future, the taking up of fallenness, and the *Augenblick* adjusted to "its time" reconstitute their fragile unity.[13] Repetition, says Heidegger, "is handing down explicitly—that is to say, going back into the possibilities of the Dasein that has-been-there" (p. 437). In this way, the primacy of anticipatory resoluteness over the passed past is affirmed. But it is not certain that repetition satisfies the prerequisites of time considered as a collective singular. In the first place, it is striking that this theme is not proposed in the chapter devoted to primordial temporality, at the same level as the ecstatic "Being-outside-itself" of time. In the second place, this theme does not really add much to the theme of anticipatory resoluteness, so strongly stamped by Being-towards-death. Finally, it seems to play no role when making-present, the third ecstasis of time, is taken up for its own sake. This is why the Kantian axiom that different times are just parts of the same time receives no satisfactory interpretation in the hermeneutic phenomenology of temporality.

What is especially remarkable about the reply of historical consciousness is that it proposes an original status for the practical and dialogical category that stands over against the axiom of the oneness of time. This status is that of a limit-idea that is at the same time a regulative one. This idea is, in fact, that of history itself considered as a collective singular. Ought we to speak of a return to Kant then? But it is not the Kant of the first *Critique,* instead it is the Kant of the second *Critique,* the *Critique of Practical Reason.* What is more, such a return to Kant can be made only after a necessary detour through Hegel. It is from the Hegel of the *Phenomenology of Spirit* and the *Philosophy of Right* that we have learned how a concept is patiently formed in traversing the great historical mediations that occur on the levels of the economy, law, ethics, religion, and culture in general. Yet, if we no longer believe that these great mediations can culminate in a form of absolute knowledge, set within the eternal present of contemplation, it is nevertheless our mourning for such absolute knowledge that brings us back to the Kantian idea, henceforth intended on the horizon of such historical mediations.

What did we do in our long chapter devoted to historical consciousness but articulate such practical and dialogical mediations? And how may we speak of mediations, even imperfect ones, unless it is within the horizon of a limit-idea that is also a regulative one? This intending of a guiding idea was expressed in a number of different ways in our analyses. The first one was the emergence of the very word "history" in the sense of a collective singular. An epic conception of humanity is presupposed here. Without it, there would be only different human species, and finally different races. To think of history as one is to posit the equivalence between three ideas: one time, one humanity, and one history. This, when we come down to it, is the presupposition behind the cosmopolitan point of view introduced by Kant in his essays on the philosophy of history. But Kant did not have the conceptual instruments, which were only available after Hegel, for integrating the concept of history considered from a cosmopolitan point of view into the edifice of his three *Critiques,* possibly as the third part of the *Critique of Judgment.*

That this idea of a single history and a single humanity is not an empty and lifeless transcendental is something we showed by basing the metahistorical categories of horizon of expectation and space of experience on the affirmation of political and ethical duty, so as to insure that the tension between this horizon of expectation and space of experience be preserved without giving way to schism. For this to happen, we made two propositions: that the utopian imagination always be converted into specific expectations, and that received heritages be freed of their scleroses. This second requirement dominated our whole analysis of traditionality. If we refused to be caught up in the disjunction of either a hermeneutic of traditions or a critique of ideologies, it was precisely in order to give the critical point of view a handhold. Without memory, we said again and again, there is no principle of hope. If we cease to believe that heritages from the past can yet be reinterpreted in a postcritical age, defined by Max Weber as a "disenchanted world," [14] critical thought would be returned to its pre–Hegelian stage, all historical mediation having become empty. The interest in anticipation, which in a way schematizes—in exactly the Kantian sense of the word—the idea of a single humanity and a single history, has to be seen as already at work in the prior and contemporary practice of communication, hence in continuity with anticipations buried in tradition itself.

Finally, I will recall the blossoming in our text of the thesis that this directive idea becomes meaningful only as the horizon of the imperfect mediation between future, past, and present, and thus has to do with our treatment of the present as initiative. This cannot be summed up, however, in just the untimely occurrence of a present experienced as an interruption; it also includes all the forms of transactions between expectation and memory. These transactions constitute the most appropriate reply, on the plane of collective practice, to Heideggerian repetition. This power of recapitulation of the present seemed to us to find its best illustration in the act of making a promise, in which are fused personal commitment, interpersonal trust, and the tacit or virtual social pact that confers on the dialogical relation itself the cosmopolitan dimension of a public space.

Such are the many ways in which the imperfect mediation between expectation, traditionality, and initiative require the horizon of a single history, which, in turn, responds to and corresponds to the axiom of a single time.

Does this mean that this good correlation between the multiform unity of the ecstases of time and the imperfect mediation of the historical consciousness can still be attributed to narrative? We may doubt so for two reasons.

First, narrative taken in the strict sense of a discursive "genre" offers only an inadequate medium for thinking about general history, inasmuch as there are multiple plots for the same course of events and they always get articulated in terms of fragmentary temporalities. Even if the disparity between historical and fictional narrative is surpassed by their interweaving, this never produces more than what above we called a narrative identity. And narrative identity remains that of a person or a character, including those particular collective entities that merit being raised to the rank of quasi-characters. So the notion of plot gives preference to the plural at the expense of the collective singular in the refiguration of time. There is no plot of all plots capable of equaling the idea of one humanity and one history.[15]

A second type of inadequation between narrative *stricto sensu* and the multiform unity of time results from the fact that the literary category of narrative is itself inadequate to thought about history. It is a fact that we did not openly make use of narrative categories, in the strict sense of the narrative genre, whether oral or written, to characterize the horizon of expectation, the transmission of past traditions, and the force of the present. We may therefore legitimately wonder whether historical thinking does not take us beyond the limits of narrative.

Two responses are possible. We may first observe that historical thinking, without being, as such, narrative, does have a particular affinity for the discursive genre of narrative, which will serve as its privileged medium. This mediating role of narrative is evident in the transmission of traditions. Traditions are essentially narratives.[16] In return, the connection between a horizon of expectation and narrative is less direct. However it does exist. Indeed, we can consider anticipations about the future as anticipated retrospections, thanks to that remarkable property of narrative voice—one of the categories of literary theory that we dealt with in volume 2—that it can place itself at any point of time, which becomes for it a quasi-present, and, from this observation point, it can apprehend as a quasi-past the future of our present.[17] In this way, a narrative past, which is the past of the narrative voice, is assigned to this quasi-present. Prophecy confirms this structure. The prophet sees the imminent future and its menace threatening the present, and recounts the precipitation of the present toward its future ruin as something that has already happened. We might then move from prophecy to utopia, which joins to its description of the perfect city an anticipatory narration of the steps that lead to it. What is more, this narration is often made from things borrowed from traditional narratives, repainted in new colors.[18] So the future seems to be representable only given the assistance of anticipatory narratives that transform a living present into a future perfect mode—this present will have been the beginning of a history that will one day be told.

We must not abuse this extension of the category of narrative, taken as a narrative genre, lest we do violence to the very notion of projecting a horizon, concerning which narrative cannot be more than a subordinate mediation.

A second more pertinent response can be made to the objection given above. The notion of narrativity can be taken in a broader sense than the discursive genre that codifies it. We can speak of a narrative program to designate a course of action arising out of an interconnected series of performances. This is the meaning adopted in narrative semiotics and in the psychosociology of speech acts, which speak of narrative programs, narrative series, and narrative schemas.[19] We may take such narrative schemas as underlying the narrative genres properly speaking, which confer upon them an appropriate discursive equivalent. It is the potentiality of narrative that the strategic articulation of action holds in reserve that links the narrative schema to the narrative genre. We may express the proximity between these two senses of narrative by distinguishing the recountable from the recounted. It is the recountable rather than narrative in the sense of a discursive genre that can be taken as coextensive with the mediation brought about by thinking about history between the horizon of expectation, the transmission of traditions, and the force of the present.

To conclude, we can say that narrativity does not offer the second aporia of temporality as adequate a response as it offered to the first aporial. This inadequacy will not be seen as a failure if we do not lose sight of the following two maxims. First, the reply of narrativity to the aporias of time consists less in resolving these aporias than in putting them to work, in making them productive. This is how thinking about history contributes to the refiguration of time. Second, any theory reaches its highest expression only when the exploration of the domain where its validity is verified is completed with a recognition of the limits that circumscribe this domain of validity. This is the great lesson we have learned from Kant.

However it is only with the third antinomy of temporality that our second maxim will take on its full meaning.

THE APORIA OF THE INSCRUTABILITY OF TIME AND THE LIMITS OF NARRATIVE

Here my rereading reaches the point where our meditation on time not only suffers from its inability to go beyond the bifurcation into phenomenology and cosmology, or even its difficulty in giving a meaning to the totality that is made and unmade across the exchanges between coming-towards, having-been, and being present—but suffers, quite simply, from not really being able to think time. This aporia remained so dissimulated in our analyses that no separate study was devoted to it. It only emerges here and there when the very work of thinking seems to succumb to the weight of its theme. This aporia springs forth at the moment when time, escaping any attempt to constitute it, reveals itself as belonging to a constituted order always already presupposed by the work of constitution. This is what is expressed by the word "inscrutability," which is the one Kant uses when he runs up against the question of the origin of evil that resists any explanation. Here is where the danger of misinterpretation is greatest. What fails is not thinking, in any acceptation of this term, but the impulse—or to put it a better way, the *hubris*—that impels our thinking to posit itself as the master of meaning. Thinking encounters this failure not only on the occasion of the enigma of evil but also when time, escaping our will to mastery, surges forth on the side of what, in one way or another, is the true master of meaning.

To this aporia, so diffuse in all our reflections on time, will respond, on the side of poetics, the confession of the limits narrativity encounters outside itself and inside itself. These limits will attest that not even narrative exhausts the power of the speaking that refigures time.

Among the conceptions of time that guided our reflection, some bore the mark of archaisms that cannot entirely be mastered by a concept, while others turned in a prospective manner toward hermeticisms that they refused to accept as such into their thinking, but which imposed on it the reversal that puts time in the position of an always already presupposed ground.

To the first group belong the two thinkers who guided our first steps in volume 1, and again at the beginning of our discussion of the aporetics of time in this volume. What is surprising, here, is that Augustine and Aristotle appear not only as the first phenomenologist and the first cosmologist but as borne along by two archaic currents, stemming from different sources—one Greek and one biblical—whose waters subsequently intermingled in Western thought.

The tinge of archaism in Aristotle seems to me easiest to discern in his interpretation of the expression "being in time." This expression, which traverses the whole history of thought about time, allows for two interpretations. According to the first one, the "in" expresses a certain fall of thinking, leading to a representation of time as a series of "nows," that is, point-like instants. According to the second one, which is what concerns me here, the "in" expresses the precedence of time as regards any thinking that wants to circumscribe its meaning, hence to envelop it. These two lines of interpretation of the "in" get confused in Aristotle's enigmatic affirmation that things in time are "contained by time." Of course, as Victor Goldschmidt emphasizes, the interpretation that Aristotle gives to the expression "to be in time" "continues to clarify the meaning of the 'number of movement.'"[20] Indeed, says Aristotle, "things are in time as they are in number. If this is so, they are contained by time as things in number are contained by number and things in place by place." The oddness of this expression cannot help but strike us: "to be contained by number." In fact, Aristotle returns to this issue a few lines later. "So it is necessary that all things in time should be contained in time. . . . a thing, then, will be affected by time." The addition of this last remark tilts the interpretation toward the side of an ancient saying about time, itself expressed in a popular saying that "time wastes things away, and that all things grow old through [hupo] time, and that people forget owing to the lapse of time, but we do not say the same of getting to know or of becoming young or fair." The richness of meaning of such expressions does not pass completely over into the explication Aristotle gives of them. "For time is by its nature the cause rather of decay, since it is the number of change, and change removes what is." I ended my commentary with an assertion that was left hanging. Ancient wisdom, I said, seems to see a hidden collusion between change that destroys things—forgetting, aging, death—and time that simply passes.[21]

If we journey back in the direction of the archaism that Aristotle's text points to, we encounter the "philosophical story" of the *Timaeus,* to which, unfortunately, we could devote only one lengthy note. In the expression, "a moving image of eternity," it is not just the aspect of time's being a collective singular that sets thinking to questioning, but precisely this theme's belonging to a philosophical "story." It is only within a philosophical retrieval of a myth that the genesis of time can be brought to language. Being "born along with the heavens" can be spoken of only figuratively. Such a form of philosophical thinking can be said, in turn, to "contain" the highly dialectical operations that preside over the divisions and the intermixings, the entanglements of the circle of the Same and the Other. Above all, only a philosophical story can situate the genesis of time beyond the distinction between psycho-logy and cosmo-logy, by forging the representation of a world soul that both moves and thinks itself. Time is related to this hyper-psychological, hyper-cosmological "reflection."[22]

How, then, can we avoid being pulled backwards toward the archaism that, without being the oldest either chronologically or culturally, is the archaic element inherent in philosophy—that of the three great pre–Socratics: Parmenides, Heraclitus, and Anaximander? It is not a question here of undertaking a study of time in the pre–Socratics at this late stage in our investigation.[23] Let us just say that this archaic form of thinking, which no doubt cannot be repeated today in its original and originary voice, points toward a region where the claim of a transcendental subject (in whatever form) to constitute meaning no longer holds sway. This kind of thinking is archaic because it dwells alongside an *arkhe* that is the condition of possibility for all the presuppositions we can posit. Only a form of thinking that renders itself archaic can understand Anaximander's saying, whose voice can still be heard—in our reading of Aristotle—as the isolated witness to this time that remains inscrutable as much for phenomenology as for its other, cosmology: "the source from which existing things derive their existence is also that to which they return as their destruction, according to necessity; for they give justice and make reparation to one another for their injustice, according to the arrangement of Time [kata tou khronou taxin]."[24]

This archaism of the pre–Socratics is still part of philosophy in the sense that it is its own *arkhe* that philosophy repeats when it returns to those who first separated their notion of *arkhe* from that of a mythical beginning, as found in theogonies and divine genealogies. This break that was brought about within the very idea of an *arkhe* did not prevent Greek philosophy from inheriting, in a transposed fashion, as a second archaism, the one that it had broken away from, the mythical archaism. We continue to try to avoid getting caught up in it.[25] We cannot completely overlook it, however, for it is from this ground that certain, apparently unavoidable, figures of inscrutable time arise. Of all these figures, I will retain only the one that seems to have provided the symbolic schematism to which is grafted the theme referred to above, that everything is contained in time. Jean-Pierre Vernant, in his *Myth and Thinking among the Greeks,* has traced out in Hesiod, Homer, and Aeschylus, therefore in terms of the three great genres of Greek poetry—theogony, epic, and tragedy—the comparison of *Khronos* to *Okēanos,* which encloses the universe in its untiring course.[26] As for those neighboring mythical figures that assimilate time to a circle, the ambivalence of the significations attached to them is for me of the highest importance. Sometimes the unity and perenniality attributed to this fundamental time radically negate human time, experienced as a factor of instability, destruction, and death; sometimes this great time expresses the cyclic organization of the cosmos, which harmoniously includes the passing of the seasons, the succession of generations, and the periodic return of festivals; sometimes the divine *aion* gets detached from this image of a circle, which is then connected with the unending round of births and rebirths, as can be seen in much Indian thinking and in Buddhism. The permanence of the *aion* becomes that of an eternally immobile identity. Here we rejoin Plato's *Timaeus,* by way of Parmenides and Heraclitus.

Two things stand out in this rapid survey of the double archaic ground which Aristotle takes his distance from, yet is secretly near to at the same time: on the one hand, the mark of the inscrutable that this double archaism stamps on the very work of the concept; on the other hand, the polymorphism of figurations and, across them, of the evaluations of human time, bound to the representation of something beyond time. The latter aspect is undoubtedly a corollary of the first one, for the unrepresentable can only be projected, it seems, in terms of fragmentary representations that prevail now and then, in relation to the variations of temporal experience itself in its psychological and sociological aspects.[27]

Therefore if an unordinary signification may be given to the expression "being in time," the thought of a Plato or an Aristotle owes such expression to the resurgences of this double archaism.

Western thought has two archaic inspirations: the Greek and the Hebraic. It is in the background of Augustine's phenomenology that we can hear the voice of the second one, just as we heard the voice of the first one in the background of Aristotle's *Physics*. The inscrutability of time, but also the diversity of figures of what is beyond time, give rise to thought for a second time.

As regards Book XI of the *Confessions,* we cannot speak of archaism insofar as it expresses a theological thinking strongly influenced by Neoplatonic philosophy. What, nevertheless, points to the archaic is the contrast between time and eternity that literally envelops the examination of the notion of time.[28] We saw in this contrast three themes that, each in its own way, bore time beyond itself. It is first in a spirit of praise that Augustine celebrates the eternity of the Word that remains when our words pass away. So immutability plays the role of a limit-idea with regard to temporal experience marked by the sign of the transitory. Eternity is "always stable"; created things never are.[29] To think of a present without a future or a past is, by way of contrast, to think of time itself as lacking something in relation to this plenitude; in short, as surrounded by nothingness. Next it is in the mode of lamentation, within the horizon of stable eternity, that the Augustinian soul finds itself exiled to the "region of dissimilarity." The moanings of the lacerated soul are indivisibly those of the creature as such and the sinner. In this way, Christian consciousness takes into account the great elegy that crosses cultural frontiers and sings in a minor key about the sorrow of the finite. And, finally, it is with a note of hope that the Augustinian soul traverses levels of temporalization that are always less "distended" and more "firmly held," bearing witness that eternity can affect the interior of temporal experience, hierarchizing it into levels, and thereby deepening it rather than abolishing it.

Just as in the background of the thought of a Plato and an Aristotle we caught sight of the depths of a double archaism, that of the pre–Socratics retained "in" and "through" classical philosophy, and that of mythical thinking "negated" but in no way abolished by philosophical thinking, so too must we hear behind the praise, the lamentation, and the hope that accompany Augustinian speculation on eternity and time, a specifically Hebraic form of speaking. Exegesis of this form of speaking reveals a multiplicity of significations that prevent eternity from being reduced to the immutability of a stable present. The difference in levels between Augustine's thought and the Hebraic thinking, which constitutes his archaism, is concealed by the Greek, and then by the Latin, translation of the well-known *ehyeh asher ehyeh* in Exodus 3:14a. The Revised Standard Version of the Bible has "I am who I am," as do current French translations. But thanks to this ontologizing of the Hebraic message, we occlude all the senses of eternity that rebel against Hellenization. For example, we thereby lose the most precious sense, whose best equivalent in modern language is expressed by the idea of fidelity. The eternity of Jahweh is above all else the fidelity of the God of the Covenant, accompanying the history of his people.[30]

As for the "beginning" as reported in Genesis 1:1, Hellenizing speculation must not seek to fix its meaning, first of all, outside of the history of "six days," a "history" marked by an articulated series of speech acts that by degrees inaugurate the rule-governed order of creatures, the seventh "day" being reserved for the joint celebration of creator and creature, in a primordial Sabbath, continually reactualized in worship and praise. Nor may the "beginning" of Genesis 1:1 be separated from that other beginning constituted by the election of Abraham in Genesis 12:1. In this sense, Genesis 1-11 unfolds like a long preface, with its own time, to the history of election. And in turn, the legends of the patriarchs serve as a long preface to the story of the exodus from Egypt, the giving of the law, the wandering in the wilderness, and the entry into Canaan. In this regard, the Exodus constitutes an event that generates history, thus as a beginning, but in another sense than Genesis 1:1 and 12:1. All these beginnings speak of eternity inasmuch as a certain fidelity is found rooted in them. Of course, there are also texts where God is said to live "forever," "throughout all ages." In Psalm 90:2 we read: "from everlasting to everlasting thou art God." But these texts, borrowed for the most part from hymns and wisdom literature, create a kind of space of dispersion, at least as vast as the one we referred to above in discussing the Greek domain, be it archaic or mythic. Such texts, culminating in lamentation and praise, soberly oppose the eternity of God to the transitory character of human life. "For a thousand years in thy sight are but as yesterday when it is past or as a watch in the night" (Psalm 90:4). Others tend more clearly toward the side of lamentation. "My days are like an evening shadow. . . . But thou, O Lord, art enthroned for ever" (Psalm 102:11–12). A slight difference in accent suffices to turn lamentation into praise. "A voice says, 'cry!' And I said, 'What shall I cry?'" "All flesh is grass / and all its beauty is like the flower of the field. / The grass withers, the flower fades, / when the breath of the Lord blows upon it; / The grass withers, the flower fades; / but the word of our God will stand for ever" (Isaiah 40:7–8). (This proclamation opens the book of consolation to Israel attributed to the second Isaiah.) A wholly different mood rules over the sayings of Qoheleth, who sees human life as dominated by ineluctable times (a time to be born, a time to die, etc.) and by an unending return of the same events ("What has been is what will be, and what has been done is what will be done" [Ecclesiastes 1:9]). This variety of tonalities agrees with an essentially nonspeculative, nonphilosophical mode of thinking, for which eternity transcends history from within history.[31]

This brief tour must suffice to let us sense the richness of meaning concealed as much as revealed in the *nunc stans* of Augustine's eternal present.

Situated, so to speak, halfway between thinkers who bear their own archaism and those who skirt hermeticism, Kant, at first sight, represents a totally neutral figure. The idea that time must be finally inscrutable seems totally foreign to the *Critique of Pure Reason*. The anchoring of the concept of time in the transcendental, taken at its lowest level, that of the "transcendental aesthetic," seems to place this concept outside any ontological speculation, as well as outside any fanatical enthusiasm. The status of being a presupposition that is a corollary to that of being transcendental keeps it under the surveillance of a thinking careful to hold in check every impulse of the understanding to cross the limits of its legitimate employment. Essentially, the transcendental stands on guard against all the seductions of the transcendent. And yet. . . . And yet we were surprised by the assertion that changes occur in time, but time does not flow. We were not entirely persuaded by the argument that the third "mode" of time, permanence, also called "time in general," is rendered completely intelligible by its correlation with the schematism of substance and the principle of permanence. The idea of the permanence of time seems richer in meaning than the permanence of something in time. In fact, it seems to be the ultimate condition of possibility for all such things. This suspicion finds reinforcement if we return to what we may well call the riddles of the "transcendental aesthetic." What can be meant by an a priori intuition for which there is no intuition since time is invisible? What meaning are we to give to the idea of a "formal a priori condition of all appearances whatsoever"? Is thinking still the master of meaning when it comes to this being-affected, more fundamental than the being-affected by history referred to in our earlier analyses?[32] What is that *Gemüt* concerning which it is said that it is affected by objects (A19, B33) and that it is that within which resides the form of receptivity (A20, B34)? This puzzle becomes all the more pressing when being-affected becomes self-affection. Time is implicated here in a much more radical way, emphasized in the second edition of the *Critique* (B66–69). Time is still where "we locate [*setzen*] our representations" and remains the "formal condition for the way we arrange [the representations] in our *Gemüt*." In this sense, it can be nothing else than the way in which our mind is affected by its own activity, that is, by this positing (*Setzung*); hence, by itself; that is, as an inner sense considered just in terms of its form. The conclusion Kant draws, that the mind does not intuit itself as it is but as it represents itself under the condition of this self-affection, cannot be allowed to cover up the specific difficulty attached to this self-affection, which being-affected culminates in. If there is a point where time is revealed to be inscrutable, at least to the gaze of a transcendental deduction in charge of itself, it most certainly has to do with this notion of the permanence of time, along with the implications for time of self-affection.

It would be useless to seek in Husserl for traces of an archaism or echoes of a hermeticism that would point toward a time more fundamental than any constitution. The goal of the lectures on internal time-consciousness is, as is well known, to constitute in a single stroke both consciousness and the time immanent to it. In this regard, Husserl's transcendentalism is no less vigilant than that of Kant. Nevertheless, beyond the difficulty referred to above about deriving the totality of time from the continuity of the process of the coincidence of longitudinal intentionalities, I would like to refer one last time to the paradox of attempting a discourse on the hyletic once intentionality *ad extra* has been suspended. All the difficulties, in Kant, tied to self-affection return with a vengeance to threaten the self-constitution of consciousness. These underlying difficulties find their translation on the level of the language in which we attempt to speak of this constitution. What is striking in the first place is the thoroughly metaphorical character of this transcendental hyletics: surging forth, source, falling-back, sinking, expire, etc. And at the center of this metaphorical constellation stands the key metaphor of flowing. What the lectures, in their third section, attempt to bring to language is "the absolute flux of consciousness, constitutive of time." These metaphors in no way constitute a figurative language that we might translate into a literal language. They constitute the only language available to the work of returning toward the origin. The use of metaphor is thus the first sign of the nonmastery of constituting consciousness over consciousness constituted in this way. What is more, a question of priority arises about this flux and this consciousness. Is it consciousness that constitutes the flux or the flux that constitutes consciousness? Given the first hypothesis, we return to a Fichtean kind of idealism. Given the second one, we are caught up in a phenomenology of a quite different kind, where the mastery of consciousness over its production is surpassed by the production that constitutes it. A hesitation between these two interpretations is permitted. Does not Husserl pose the question, "How [is it] possible to have knowledge [*wissen*] of a unity of the ultimate constitutive flux of consciousness?" The answer he gives to this question, namely, the splitting into two longitudinal intentionalities, draws the following declaration from Husserl. "As startling (if not at first sight even contradictory) as it may appear to assert that the flux of consciousness constitutes its own unity, it is still true, nevertheless." And another time, he frankly says that "for all this, names are lacking." From metaphors to a lack of words, it is this failure of language that points toward the ultimate "impressional" consciousness, concerning which we may say it is the flux that constitutes it, in constituting itself—and not the reverse.

The philosopher who, to my mind, comes closest to hermeticism is of course Heidegger. There is nothing denigrating about speaking this way. For a type of discourse that still claims to be phenomenological, like that of *Being and Time* and *The Basic Problems in Phenomenology,* the breakthrough brought about by an analytic of Dasein as concerns the understanding of Being itself may be said to verge on hermeticism insofar as it is true that this breakthrough brings hermeneutic phenomenology to the limits of its ownmost possibilities. In fact, Heidegger attempts this breakthrough without conceding anything to the modern equivalents of the *Schwärmerei*—that kind of delirious exaltation denounced by Kant—that were for Heidegger as for Husserl the philosophies of life, of existence, of dialogue.

The relation of the analytic of Dasein to the understanding of Being cannot be revealed, outside of the still programmatic declarations of the long Introduction to *Being and Time,* except in the signs of the incompleteness of the analytic, the only thing carried to its end in *Being and Time* as published—signs that also testify that this analytic is not meant to confine itself to a philosophical anthropology. The danger of misunderstanding Heidegger's philosophical project in the period of *Being and Time* is not only not set aside, it is even made stronger by the assimilation of the problematic of time to that of Being-a-whole, and of this latter to Being-towards-death. It is difficult to see at the end of the second section of *Being and Time* in what way its analyses satisfy the title given the first part: "The Interpretation of Dasein in Terms of Temporality, and the Explication of Time as the Transcendental Horizon for the Question of Being" (p. 67). It is the second half of this title that seems to lack a corresponding part in the analysis that, at best, proposes an interpretation of the ecstatic character of time, but says nothing about how it opens the way to the question of Being. The question of Being-a-whole as explicated by that of Being-towards-death seems instead to close off this horizon.

However, *The Basic Problems in Phenomenology* goes further in this regard than does *Being and Time,* by proposing to distinguish between temporal-being (*Temporalität*)—or "Temporality" in the English translation—and "temporality" (*Zeitlichkeit*) in the sense given by *Being and Time.*[33] It is precisely the constantly interrogatory aspect of the thinking that sustains this distinction that, after the fact, makes apparent the inscrutable character of temporality in *Being and Time.*

This distinction between temporal-being and temporality in fact finds its completion in a movement that remained unperceived in *Being and Time,* namely, a reversal in Heidegger's use of the notion of a condition of possibility. It is repeated that "the constitution of Dasein's being is grounded in temporality" (*Basic Problems,* p. 228). But Heidegger now adds that the meaning of temporality is the "ontological condition of the possibility of the understanding of being" (ibid.). This new use of the notion of possibility is governed by the description of temporality as the horizon in terms of which we understand Being. The conjunction of two words, ecstatic and horizonal (in the sense of having to do with a horizon), indicates the opening of the new problematic placed under the title temporal-being (pp. 265–68).

In this new problematic the horizonal aspect of time is directly linked to the intentionality constitutive of each of the ecstases of time, particularly to that of the future, understood in the sense of Being-ahead-of-itself and of coming-towards-itself. The role of Being-towards-death in relation to the totalization of ecstatic time is passed over in silence, while ecstatic transport towards . . . , in the direction of . . . , which indicates the inflection of the problematic, is accentuated. From here on, Heidegger speaks of ecstatic horizonal temporality, where it is understood that horizonal signifies "characterized by a horizon given with the ecstasis itself" (p. 267). To Heidegger, this deploying of a horizon on the basis of the ecstatic bears witness to the rule of the phenomenon of intentionality over any phenomenological approach. However, in contrast to Husserl, it is the ecstatic horizonal aspect of temporality that conditions intentionality, not the reverse. So intentionality is rethought in a deliberately ontological sense as the projection toward . . . implied in the understanding of Being. By discerning in this something like a "projection of being upon time" (p. 280), Heidegger thinks he also can discern the orientation of temporality toward its horizon, temporal-being or Temporality.

We must confess that, given the framework of a kind of thinking that still means to be phenomenological—that is, governed by the idea of intentionality—all Heidegger's assertions about this "projection of being upon time" are still cryptic. What help he proposes to making sense of them threatens to overturn them, for example, in the comparison of this new proposal to Plato's well-known "beyond being" (*epekeina tēs ousias*) in Book VI of the *Republic.* His proposal is certainly meant to inquire "even beyond being as to that upon which being itself, as being, is projected" (p. 282), but when separated from the idea of the Good, there is not much help to be found in the *epekeina tēs ousias.* All that remains is the element of directedness, the passage beyond. "We call this whither of the ecstasis the horizon or, more precisely, the horizonal schema of the ecstasis" (p. 302). But then what do we in fact understand when we say that the "most original temporalizing of temporality as such is Temporality"? (ibid.). In truth, nothing, if we are not in a position to be able to link the distinction between temporal and temporalizing to the ontological difference; that is, to the difference between Being and beings, which is set forth publicly for the first time in *The Basic Problems of Phenomenology.* The distinction between temporal and temporalizing thus has just a single function—to point toward the ontological difference. Apart from this role, it only succeeds in indicating the inscrutable character of temporality understood as the wholeness of Dasein. For, taken by itself, the distinction between temporal-being and temporality no longer designates a phenomenon accessible to hermeneutic phenomenology as such.[34]

The most cumbersome question our whole enterprise runs into may be summed up in the question of whether the unrepresentability of time still has a parallel on the side of narrativity. At first sight, this question seems incongruous. What sense is there in refiguring the inscrutable? However the poetics of narrative does have some resources when faced with this question. It is in the way that narrativity is carried toward its limits that the secret of its reply to the inscrutability of time lies.

Several times we have broached the question of the limits of narrativity, but never in relation to the unrepresentability of time. For example, we asked whether the Aristotelian model of emplotment could still account for the more complex forms of composition used in contemporary historiography and the modern novel. On the side of historiography, this question led us to elaborate the notions of a quasi-plot, a quasi-character, and a quasi-event, which indicate that the initial model of emplotment is pushed by historiography close to the breaking-point beyond which we may no longer say that history is an extension of narrative.[35] We had to say something similar regarding the novel, and to admit that, in this period that some call postmodern, it may be that we no longer know what narrating means. With Walter Benjamin, we deplored the fatal mutation that would result from the passage of humanity to a stage where no one any longer had any experience to communicate to someone else. And with Frank Kermode, we even declared our faith in narrative's capacity for metamorphoses that will allow it for a long time yet to resist such a schism.

But the limits that are at issue here are of another order. The earlier ones had to do with the capacity of narrative to refigure time on the basis of its own internal configuration. Now it is a question of the very limits of such a refiguration of time by narrative.

The term "limit" can be taken in two senses. By an internal limit, we mean that the art of narration exceeds itself to the point of exhaustion, in attempting to draw near the inscrutable. By an external limit, we mean that the narrative genre itself overflows into other genres of discourse that, in their own ways, undertake to speak of time.

Let us first consider the limits narrative itself explores inside its own domain. The fictional narrative is assuredly the form best equipped for this borderline work. And we already know its preferred method, that of imaginary variations. In the chapter devoted to them above, we were not able to remain within the boundaries we assigned ourselves, namely, examining solutions other than those of history that fiction brings to the problem of the duality of the phenomenological and the cosmological interpretations of time. Moving beyond this framework, we ventured to evaluate the contributions of our tales about time to the explorations of the relations between time and its other. The reader will undoubtedly recall our references to the high points of our three tales about time, moments when the extreme concentration on temporality leads to a variety of limit-experiences worthy of being placed under the sign of eternity. Unforgettable are the tragic choice Septimus makes in *Mrs. Dalloway,* the three figures of eternity in *The Magic Mountain—Ewigkeitssuppe, Walpurgisnacht,* and the *Schnee* episode—the double eternity of *Time Regained,* one form of which overcomes lost time and one form of which engenders the work that will attempt to redeem time itself. Fiction multiplies our experiences of eternity in these kinds of ways, thereby bringing narrative in different ways to its own limits. This multiplication of limit-experiences should not surprise us, if we keep in mind the fact that each work of fiction unfolds its own world. In each instance, it is in a different possible world that time allows itself to be surpassed by eternity. This is how tales about time become tales about time and its other. Nowhere is this function of fiction, which is to serve as a laboratory for an unlimited number of thought experiments, better verified. In other spheres of life—in religion, ethics and politics—a choice must be made; the imaginary does not tolerate censorship.

Nor can we forget the second transgression made by fiction in relation to the order of everyday time. By staking out the borderlines of eternity, the limit-experiences depicted by fiction also explore another boundary, that of the borderline between story and myth. Only fiction, we said, because it is fiction, can allow itself a certain degree of intoxication. We now understand better the meaning of this exaltation. It has as its vis-à-vis the sobriety of phenomenology when this phenomenology moderates the impulse it draws from the archaisms it distances itself from and in the hermeticisms it wishes not to draw too near to. Narrative is not afraid to appropriate the substance of these archaisms and hermeticisms by conferring a narrative transcription on them. Septimus, we said, knows how to listen to the "immortal ode to Time" beyond the noise of life. And, in dying, he takes with him "his odes to Time." As for the *Magic Mountain,* this work evokes an inverted double kind of magic. On the one hand, the enchantment of a time that has become unmeasurable through loss of its handholds and measures; on the other hand, the "elevation" (*Steigerung*) of a modest hero, confronted with the trials of sickness and death, an elevation that sometimes moves through the phases of a clearly acknowledged hermeticism, and that, as a whole, presents the features of an initiation with a cabalistic resonance. Irony is the only thing that stands between this fiction and the naive repetition of a myth. Proust, finally, it will be recalled, narrativizes a metaphysical experience of lost identity, stemming from German Idealism, to the point where we may just as well speak of the supratemporal experience of Beauty as an initiation, whence comes the impulse of creation as it moves toward the work wherein it must be incarnated. It is not by accident, therefore, that in *Remembrance of Things Past* time seems almost to be remythicized. Destructive time, on the one hand, "Time, the artist," on the other.[36] Nor is it an accident that *Remembrance of Things Past* ends with the words "in the dimension of Time." "In" is no longer taken here in the ordinary sense of a location in some vast container, but in the sense, close both to the archaic and the hermetic, where time contains all things— including the narrative that tries to make sense of this.

There is another way for time to envelop narrative. This is by giving rise to the formation of discursive modes other than the narrative one, which will speak, in another way, of the profound enigma. There comes a moment, in a work devoted to the power of narrative to elevate time to language, where we must admit that narrative is not the whole story and that time can be spoken of in other ways, because, even for narrative, it remains inscrutable.

I myself was made attentive to these external limits of narrative by biblical exegesis. Indeed, the Hebrew Bible can be read as the testament about time in its relations to divine eternity (given all the reservations mentioned above concerning the equivocity of the word "eternity"). And in this text, narrative is not the only way of speaking about time's relation to its other. Whatever the scope of narrative contained therein, it is always in conjunction with other genres that narrative functions in the Hebrew Bible.[37]

This conjunction, in the Bible, between the narrative and the nonnarrative invites us to inquire whether in other forms of literature as well, narrative does not join its meaning effects to those of other genres, to speak of what in time is most rebellious when it comes to representation. I shall limit myself here to referring briefly to the trilogy, well known even today to German poetics: epic, drama, lyric.[38] As regards the first two genres, we have allowed, ever since our analysis of Aristotle's *Poetics,* that they can be enrolled, without excessive violence, under the banner of narrative, taken in a broad sense, inasmuch as emplotment is common to all of them. But does the argument that holds for the point of view about the configuration of time still hold for the point of view about its refiguration? It is noteworthy that monologues and dialogues open, within the purely narrative framework of feigned action, breaches that allow for the embedding of short meditations, even ample speculations about the misery of humanity handed over to the erosion of time. These thoughts, placed in the mouth of Prometheus, Agamemnon, Oedipus, or the tragic chorus—and closer to us, Hamlet—are inscribed in the long tradition of a wisdom, unmarked by national boundaries, that, beyond the episodic, touches the fundamental. Lyric poetry gives a voice, which is also a song, to this fundamental element. It is not for the narrative art to deplore the brevity of life, the conflict between love and death, the vastness of a universe that pays no attention to our lament. The reader will have recognized, dissimulated at several places in our text, under the modesty and sobriety of prose, the echoes of the sempiternal elegy, the lyrical figure of the lament. For example, we allowed ourselves briefly, at the beginning of our aporetics, on the occasion of a short note on time in the *Timaeus,* a bittersweet reflection about the consolation a disconsolate soul may find in the contemplation of the order of the celestial movements, however inhuman they may be. The same tone imposed itself anew, at the end of our aporetics this time, on the occasion of a reflection provoked by Heidegger about the mutual overlapping of withintime-ness and so-called ordinary time. At that point, we noted the oscillations that our meditation imposed on our feelings. Sometimes the impression prevailed of a complicity between the nonmastery inherent in our thrownness and fallenness, and that other nonmastery recalled to us by the contemplation of the sovereign movement of the stars; sometimes, on the contrary, the feeling prevailed of the incommensurability between the time allotted mortals and the vastness of cosmic time. In this we found ourselves buffeted back and forth between the resignation engendered by the collusion between these two forms of nonmastery and the grief that is ceaselessly reborn from the contrast between the fragility of life and the power of time that destroys. In this, and other ways, the lyricism of meditative thinking goes right to the fundamental without passing through the art of narrating.

This final conjunction of the epic, the dramatic, and the lyric was announced in the Preface to volume 1 of *Time and Narrative.* Lyric poetry, we said, borders on dramatic poetry. The redescription referred to in *The Rule of Metaphor* and the refiguration of *Time and Narrative* thus change their roles, when, under the aegis of "Time, the artist," are conjoined the power of redescription unfolded by lyrical discourse and the mimetic power imparted by narrative discourse.

Let us cast one final glance over the path we have covered. In these concluding pages we have distinguished three levels in the aporetics of time that we first articulated in terms of particular authors and their works. The passage from one level to another indicates a certain progression without for all that turning into a system, under the threat of dismantling the systematic argumentation contained in each aporia and in the last one more than any other. The same thing must be said of the replies that the poetics of narrative opposes to the aporias of time. They constitute a meaningful constellation, without for all that forming a binding chain. Indeed, nothing obliges us to pass from the notion of narrative identity to that of the idea of the unity of history, then to the confession of the limits of narrative in the face of the mystery of time that envelops us. In one sense, the pertinence of the reply of narrative to the aporias of time diminishes as we move from one stage to the next, to the point where time seems to emerge victorious from the struggle, after having been held captive in the lines of the plot. It is good that it should be so. It ought not to be said that our eulogy to narrative unthinkingly has given life again to the claims of the constituting subject to master all meaning. On the contrary, it is fitting that every mode of thought should verify the validity of its employment in the domain assigned to it, by taking an exact measure of the limits to its employment.

Yet, if, from one aporia to another and from one poetic reply to another, the progression is a free one, the reverse order, in return, is binding. It is not true that the confession of the limits of narrative abolishes the positing of the idea of the unity of history, with its ethical and political implications. Rather it calls for this idea. Nor should it be said that the confession of the limits of narrative, correlative to the confession of the mystery of time, makes room for obscurantism. The mystery of time is not equivalent to a prohibition directed against language. Rather it gives rise to the exigence to think more and to speak differently. If such be the case, we must pursue to its end the return movement, and hold that the reaffirmation of the historical consciousness within the limits of its validity requires in turn the search, by individuals and by the communities to which they belong, for their respective narrative identities. Here is the core of our whole investigation, for it is only within this search that the aporetics of time and the poetics of narrative correspond to each other in a sufficient way.

Notes

INTRODUCTION

1. See Paul Ricoeur, *Time and Narrative,* vol. 1, trans. Kathleen McLaughlin and David Pellauer (Chicago, University of Chicago Press, 1984), pp. 52–87.

2. Here the classic works are: Pierre Janet, *Le Développement de la mémoire et de la notion de temps* (Paris: A. Chahine, 1928); Jean Piaget, *The Child's Conception of Time,* trans. A. J. Pomerans (New York: Basic Books, 1970); Paul Fraisse, *The Psychology of Time* (New York: Harper and Row, 1963) and *Psychologie du rythme* (Paris: Presses Universitaires de France, 1974). For a discussion of the current status of the problem, see Klaus F. Riegel, ed., *The Psychology of Development and History* (New York: Plenum Press, 1976); Bernard S. Gorman and Alden Wessman, eds., *The Personal Experience of Time* (New York: Plenum Press, 1977), especially Wessman and Gorman, "The Emergence of Human Awareness and Concepts of Time," pp. 3–57, and Klaus F. Riegel, "Towards a Dialectical Interpretation of Time and Change," pp. 58–108. The difference in approach between the psychologist's and the philosopher's point of view lies in the psychologist asking how certain concepts of time appear in personal and social development, whereas the philosopher poses the more radical question of the overall meaning of the concepts that serve as a teleological guide for the psychology of development.

3. Emile Durkheim, *The Elementary Forms of Religious Life,* trans. Joseph Ward Swain (New York: The Free Press, 1965); Maurice Halbwachs, *Les Cadres sociaux de la mémoire* (Paris: Alcan, 1925) and the posthumous work, *The Collective Memory,* trans. Francis J. Ditter, Jr. and Vida Uzadi Ditter (New York: Harper and Row, 1980); George Gurvitch, *The Spectrum of Social Time,* trans. and ed. Myrtle Korenbaum assisted by Phillip Bosserman (Dordrecht: D. Reidel, 1964).

4. André Jacob, *Temps et langage. Essai sur les structures du sujet parlant* (Paris: Armand Colin, 1967).

5. Paul Ricoeur, *The Rule of Metaphor: Multidisciplinary Studies of the Creation of Meaning in Language,* trans. Robert Czerny with Kathleen McLaughlin and John Costello, S.J. (Toronto: University of Toronto Press, 1977), pp. 216–56.

6. See *Time and Narrative,* 1:76–77.

7. See ibid., pp. 175–225.

SECTION ONE

1. See *Time and Narrative,* 1:70–87. Need we recall what was said above about the relation between the aporetics of time and the poetics of narrative? If the latter

belongs in principle to the cycle of mimesis, the former stems from a reflective, autonomous mode of thought. However, to the extent that this mode of thought formulates the question to which poetics offers a reply, a privileged relation is established between the aporetics of time and the mimetics of narrative by the logic of questions and answers.

CHAPTER ONE

1. The progress of the phenomenology of time in Husserl and Heidegger will reveal in retrospect other, more deeply hidden, defects in the Augustinian analysis. Their resolution of these difficulties will result in even more serious aporias.

2. Henri Bergson, *Time and Free Will: An Essay on the Immediate Data of Consciousness,* trans. F. L. Pogson (New York: Macmillan, 1912).

3. Below, we shall see that a theory of time enlightened by narrative understanding cannot do without measurable time, even if it cannot rest content with this time alone.

4. Saint Augustine, *Confessions,* trans. R. S. Pine-Coffin (New York: Penguin Books, 1961), XI, 23:29. Concerning the various identifications of this "learned man," see E. P. Meijering, *Augustin über Schöpfung, Ewigkeit und Zeit. Das elfte Buch der Bekenntnisse* (Leiden: E. J. Brill, 1979). See also J. C. Callahan, "Basil of Caesarea: A New Source for Augustine's Theory of Time," *Harvard Studies in Classical Philology* 63 (1958) 437–54; cf. A. Solignac, note complémentaire 18, to the French translation of the *Confessions* by E. Tréhorel and G. Bouissou (Paris: Desclée de Brouwer, 1962), p. 586.

5. Aristotle, *Physics,* Book IV, 219a4. I shall cite the translation of the *Physics* by R. P. Hardie and R. K. Gaye in *The Complete Works of Aristotle,* ed. Jonathan Barnes (Princeton: Princeton University Press, 1984), 1:315–446.

6. Augustine gives a single reply to both questions: when I compare long and short syllables, "it cannot be the syllables themselves that I measure since they no longer exist. I must be measuring something which remains fixed in my memory [quod infixum manet]" (*Confessions,* XI, 27:35). The notion of a fixed unit is thereby posed. "For everything which happens leaves an impression [affectionem] on it [my mind], and this impression remains [manet] after the thing itself has ceased to be. It is the impression that I measure, since it is still present, not the thing itself, which makes the impression as it passes" (ibid., 27:36).

7. I am adopting the interpretation of Paul F. Conen, *Die Zeittheorie des Aristoteles* (Munich: C. H. Beck, 1964), that the treatise on time (*Physics,* IV, 10–14) has as its core a short treatise (218b9–219b2) carefully constructed in three sections, to which are appended a series of smaller treatises, loosely connected to the central argument and replying to questions discussed in Aristotle's school or by his contemporaries. The question of the relation between the soul and time, along with that of the instant, are part of these important appendices. Victor Goldschmidt, in a study that is as meticulous and illuminating as his work always is, entitled *Temps physique et Temps tragique chez Aristote* (Paris: Vrin, 1982), attempts to connect the analyses that follow the definition of time more solidly to the core of this definition. The instant, however, has to be considered separately (ibid., pp. 147–89). When the time comes we shall carefully consider the suggestions contained in these insightful pages.

8. Aristotle, *Physics,* III, 1–3.

9. This negative thesis is treated under the heading "preliminary precisions" by Goldschmidt (pp. 22–29), who, unlike Paul Conen, makes the definition begin only at 219a11. As regards this minor problem of how to divide up the text, Goldschmidt himself advises us "not to insist on being more precise than the author, under pain of giving in, more than need be, to pedantry" (ibid., p. 22).

10. On magnitude, cf. Aristotle, *Metaphysics,* Δ 13 *(poson ti métrèton)* and *Categories,* 6.

11. On the phrase "goes with," cf. Goldschmidt, p. 32: "The verb *akolouthein* . . . does not always indicate a one-way relation of dependence: it may designate concomitance as well as consecutiveness." Thus it is stated further on in the *Physics* that movement and time "define each other" (220b16). "Therefore, it is not a question of ontological dependence but of determinations that mutually accompany each other" (Goldschmidt, p. 33).

12. *Physics,* IV, 2, 232b24–25; *Metaphysics,* Δ, 13.

13. This reference to the soul's activity, once again, must not lead us astray. It is certainly true that we could not discern the before and after, whether in time or in movement, without an activity of discrimination belonging to the soul. "But we apprehend time only when we have marked motion, marking it by before and after; and it is only when we have perceived before and after in motion that we can say that time has elapsed" (*Physics,* 219a22–24). The argument is not intended to stress the verbs "apprehend," "mark," and "perceive," but rather the priority of the before and after belonging to movement in relation to the before and after belonging to time. The order of priority, first noted on the level of apprehension, attests to the same order on the level of things themselves: first magnitude, then movement, and then time (through the mediation of place). "The distinction of before and after holds primarily, then, in place" (ibid., 219a14).

14. This aspect is emphasized by Joseph Moreau, *L'Espace et le Temps selon Aristote* (Paris: Editions Antenore, 1965).

15. J. C. Callahan notes that in the definition of time number is added to movement as form is to matter. The inclusion of number in the definition of time is essential, in the precise sense of this term (*Four Views of Time in Ancient Philosophy* [Cambridge: Harvard University Press, 1948], pp. 77–82).

16. Concerning the distinction between the counted and the countable, cf. Conen, pp. 53–58, and Goldschmidt, pp. 39–40

17. Aristotle admits this. But, scarcely having granted this concession, he returns to his task. Although there would not be time unless there were soul, there would exist "that of which time is an attribute, i.e. if *movement* can exist without the soul" (*Physics,* 223a27–28). He can then conclude, as he did above, that the "before and after are attributes of movement, and time is these *qua* countable" (ibid., 223a28). In other words, if a soul is required, in order actually to count, movement alone suffices to define the countable, which "has something to do with movement" and which we call time. Noetic activity may therefore be implied in the argumentation without being included in the definition of time, properly speaking.

18. The *Timaeus* deserves to be mentioned at this point in our investigation, for there time finds its original place not in the human soul but in the world soul, and has as its ultimate end the task of making the world "still more like the original" (37c). To what, then, is time added by this act of the Demiurge in this "likely story"? What added touch of perfection is given to the world order as its crowning achievement? The first noteworthy feature of the world soul is that its structure links together, before any phenomenology of time, the cosmological and the psychological; self-motion (as in the *Phaedo,* the *Phaedrus,* and the *Laws*) and knowledge (*logos, epistémè,* and even "solid and true" *doxai* and *pisteis*). A second, even more important feature is that what time completes is a highly dialectical, ontological constitution, depicted by a series of minglings, the terms of which are indivisible existence and divisible existence, then indivisible sameness and divisible sameness, and finally indivisible difference and divisible difference. In Francis M. Cornford's *Plato's Cosmology: The Timaeus of Plato translated with a running commentary* (New York: The Liberal Arts Press, 1957), pp. 59–67, we find a diagrammed discussion of this extremely complex ontological constitution. It is taken up again by Luc Brisson, *Le Même et l'Autre dans la structure ontologique du Timée de Platon: un commentaire systématique du Timée de*

Platon (Paris: Klincksieck, 1974), p. 275, where he offers a translation of this difficult passage that is quite enlightening. Brisson reconstructs the entire structure of the *Timaeus* around the polarity of sameness and difference, situating the bases of the philosophy of time on the same level as the dialectic of the "leading kinds" in the *Sophist*. Let us mention a final feature that distinguishes the ontology of time even further from any human psychology. I am referring to the harmonic relations (divisions, intervals, medians, proportional relations) that preside over the construction of the armillary sphere, with its circle of sameness and its circle of difference, and its inner circles. What does time add to this complex dialectical mathematical structure? First, it seals the unity of the movements of the great celestial clock. In this, it is singular, one ("a moving image of eternity" [37d]). Next, owing to the setting of the planets into their appropriate places—Cornford aptly translates *agalma* (37d) not as "image" but as "a shrine brought into being for the everlasting gods," that is, the planets (cf. pp. 97–101)—this unique time is divided up into days, months, years; hence it permits measurement. From this follows the second definition of time: an "eternal image, but moving according to number" (37d). When all the celestial revolutions, having harmonized their speeds, have returned to the starting point, then we may say that "the perfect number of time fulfills the perfect year" (39d). This perpetual return constitutes the nearest approximation that the world can provide to the perpetual duration of the immutable world. Therefore, beneath the distention of the soul, there is a time—the very one we call Time—that cannot exist without these celestial measures, because it "came into being at the same instant" with the heavens (38b). It is an aspect of the world order. Regardless of what we may think, do, or feel, it partakes of the regularity of circular locomotion. In saying this, however, we touch on the point where the marvelous borders on the enigmatic. In the universe of symbols, the circle signifies much more than the circle of geometers and astronomers. Under the cosmo-psychology of the world soul is concealed the ancient wisdom that has always known that time encircles us, surrounds us like an ocean. This is why no project of constituting time can ever abolish the certainty that, like all other beings, we, too, are in Time. This is the paradox that a phenomenology of consciousness cannot ignore. When our time is undone under the pressures of the spiritual forces of distraction, what is laid bare is the river of time, the bedrock of celestial time. There are perhaps moments when as discord wins out over concord, our despair finds, if not consolation, at least a recourse and a rest in Plato's marvelous certainty that time is the apex of the inhuman order of the celestial bodies.

19. Quoted by Goldschmidt, p. 85, notes 5 and 6.

20. Paul Conen does not really seem surprised here. The expression "being contained by time," refers, he thinks, to a figurative representation of time, on the basis of which time is put in an analogous relation to place. Through this representation, time is somewhat reified, "as if it had an independent existence itself and unfolded above the things that are contained by it" (p. 145). Can we be content with just observing "the overtly metaphorical character of the expression 'being contained by time'"? (ibid.). Is this not rather the ancient mythopoetical ground that resists philosophical exegesis? Conen, it is true, does not fail to mention in this connection the prephilosophical intuitions that underlie these common expressions (ibid., pp. 146f.). In *The Basic Problems of Phenomenology,* trans. Albert Hofstadter (Bloomington: Indiana University Press, 1982), Martin Heidegger comes upon this expression in his presentation of the plan of the Aristotelian treatise, which he simply identifies with his own concept of intratemporality (*Innerzeitigkeit*), "something is in time" (ibid., p. 236). We, too, have opened the door to this expression "being in time" by incorporating it into the temporal character of action of the level of mimesis$_1$ and hence into the narrative prefiguration of action.

21. Conen, pp. 72–73, readily grants this twofold incommensurability of the relation of time to movement itself.

22. A reader instructed by Augustine might solve the aporia in the following terms. The instant is always other, inasmuch as the undifferentiated points of time are always different; whereas what is always the same is the present, even though it is in each case designated by the instance of discourse that contains it. If we do not distinguish between the instant and the present, then we must say, along with W. D. Ross, that "every now is a now," and, in this sense, the same. The "now" is other simply "by being an earlier or a later cross-section of a movement" (*Aristotle's Physics, A Revised Text with Introduction and Commentary* [Oxford: Oxford University Press, 1936], pp. 86–87). The identity of the instant is therefore reduced to a tautology. Among the commentators who have sought to go beyond Aristotle's text in order to find a less tautological answer to the aporia, Conen (p. 81) quotes Bröcker, for whom the instant is considered to be the same as a substratum in the sense that "das was jeweilig jetzt ist, ist dasselbe, sofern es Gegenwart ist, jeder Zeitpunkt ist, wenn er ist und nicht war order sein wird, Gegenwart." The instant will always be different insofar as "jeder Zeitpunkt was erst Zukunft, kommt in die Gegenwart und geht in die Vergangenheit" (ibid.). In other words, the instant is held to be in one sense the present, in another sense a point of time, the present that is always the same passing through points in time that are unceasingly different. This solution is philosophically satisfying to the extent that it reconciles the present and the instant. But, we must say, it is not Aristotle's solution, for it breaks with his habitual use of the expression *ho potè*, in the sense of substratum, and does not take into account the reference of the instant as such to the identity of the body that is carried, which is supposed to be "followed" by the identity of the instant. Conen (ibid., p. 91) offers an interpretation which, like that of Ross, is intended to remain faithful to Aristotle and does not resort to the distinction between the present and the instant. The identity of the instant is held to be the simultaneity that is shared by different movements. However, this interpretation, which avoids Augustine only to call upon Kant, parts ways with Aristotle's argument, in which the entire weight of the identity of the instant rests on the relation of before and after, which, for another point of view, constitutes an alternative that is the source of difference. Goldschmidt dismisses this recourse to simultaneity to interpret the identity of the instant. "To be in one and the same 'now'" (*Physics*, 218a26) cannot mean to be simultaneous but must mean to have the same substratum. "The subject communicates its identity to the movement, with respect to which the before and after can then be said to be identical in two ways: inasmuch as one and the same movement is the substratum, and with regard to its essence, distinct from the movement, inasmuch as each instant makes the potentiality of the moving body pass into act" (p. 50). This actuality belonging to the instant, which is heavily emphasized throughout Goldschmidt's commentary, is finally what constitutes the dynamism of the instant, beyond the analogy between the instant and the point.

23. Ibid., p. 46.

24. This shift from one vocabulary to the other can be observed in this comment, made as if in passing: "Further, there is the same time everywhere at once, but not the same time before and after, for while the present [parousa] change is one, the change which has happened [gégénèménè] and that which will happen [mellousa] are different" (*Physics*, 220b5–8). In this way, Aristotle passes without difficulty from the ideas of the instant and the before and after to those of present, past, and future, inasmuch as the only thing that is relevant for the discussion of the aporias is the opposition between identity and difference.

25. It is in the context of analyses of the expressions occurring in ordinary language ("sometimes," "one day," "before," "suddenly") that Aristotle makes recourse to the

vocabulary of present, past, and future. "The 'now' is the link of time, as has been said (for it connects past and future time), and it is a limit [peras] of time (for it is the beginning of the one and the end of the other)" (*Physics*, 222a10–12). Once again, he admits the imperfect nature of the analogy with the point. "But this is not obvious as it is with the point, which is fixed" (ibid., 222a13–14). Conen, who did not follow Bröcker in his interpretation of the first aporia of the instant (as different and as same), comes closer to him in his interpretation of the second aporia (the instant as connecting and dividing). According to Conen, Aristotle had two notions of the instant. As long as he considered it as one *qua* substratum and as different *qua* essence, he conceived of it in relation to a multitude of points belonging to a single line. On the other hand, when he considered the "now" as the unity of a moving body, he conceived of the instant as producing time, even though it follows the fate of the body in the production of its movement. "According to the first conception, a number of 'nows' corresponds to the body in motion" (Conen, p. 115). Conen believes, however, that it is possible to reconcile these two notions *in extremis* (ibid., pp. 115–16). Here again, Goldschmidt's use of the notion of the dynamic instant, the true expression of potentiality in act, confirms and clarifies Conen's interpretation.

26. Without following in this direction, Goldschmidt observes in relation to the analyses of chapter 13, "Here it is no longer a question of time in its becoming, as undifferentiated, but of a structured time, one structured on the basis of the present instant. The latter determines not only the before and after (220a9) but, more precisely, the past and the future" (Goldschmidt, p. 98). It is then necessary to distinguish a narrow sense and a broad or derived sense of the instant. "The present instant is then no longer considered 'in itself' but related to 'something else,' to a future ('it will happen') or to a past ('it happened') that is still near, the whole being encompassed by the term 'today.' . . . We observe, then, starting with the point-like instant, a movement of expansion toward the past and the future, whether near or far, in the course of which 'other' events related to the present form with it in each case a determined and quantifiable lapse of time (227a27)" (ibid., p. 29). A certain polysemy of the instant thus seems unavoidable ("in how many ways we speak of the 'now,'" [*Physics*, 222b28]), as is suggested by the ordinary language expressions examined in chapter 14 (all of which, to different degrees, refer to the present instant). Goldschmidt comments, "The instant itself, which had served to determine time by before and after and which, in this function, was always 'other' (219a25), is now situated and understood as a present instant, starting from which, in both directions—although with opposite senses—the before and after are organized" (p. 110).

27. If a transition from Aristotle toward Augustine could be found in the Aristotelian doctrine, would this not be in the theory of time in the *Ethics* or the *Poetics*, rather than in the aporias of the instant in the *Physics?* This is the path that Goldschmidt explores (pp. 159–74). Indeed, pleasure, escaping all movement and all genesis, constitutes a complete whole that can only be an instantaneous production; sensation, too, is produced all at once; all the more so, the happy life that wrests us away from the vicissitudes of fortune. If this is the case, it is so insofar as the instant is that of an act, which is also an operation of consciousness, in which "the act transcends the genetic process of which it is, nevertheless, the term" (ibid., p. 181). This is no longer the time of movement, subjected to the order of the imperfect act of potentiality. It is rather the time of the completed act. In this respect, if tragic time never coincides with physical time, it does concur with the time of ethics. The time that "accompanies" the unfolding of the plot is not that of a genesis but that of a dramatic action considered as a whole; it is the time of an act and not that of a genesis (ibid., pp. 407–8). My own analyses of Aristotle's *Poetics* in volume 1 of this work agree with this conclusion. This development of the Aristotelian theory of time is impressive, but it does not lead from

Aristotle to Augustine. The instant-as-totality of the *Ethics* is distinguished from the instant-as-limit of the *Physics* only by being taken out of time. We can no longer say that it is "in time." Consequently, according to Victor Goldschmidt's analysis, it is less in the direction of Augustine than in that of Plotinus and Hegel that the instant-as-totality in the *Ethics* and—possibly—in the *Poetics* actually points.

CHAPTER TWO

1. Edmund Husserl, *Zur Phänomenologie des inneren Zeitbewusstseins (1893– 1917),* ed. Rudolf Boehm, *Husserliana,* vol. 10 (The Hague: M. Nijhoff, 1966). According to Boehm's important preface, these lectures were the result of Edith Stein's reworking (*Ausarbeitung*) of Husserl's manuscripts in her role as his assistant from 1916 to 1918. It was this manuscript, in Stein's handwriting, that Husserl entrusted to Heidegger in 1926, and which was then published by the latter in 1928, hence after *Being and Time* (1927), in volume 9 of the *Jahrbuch für Philosophie und phänomenologische Forschung,* under the title "Edmund Husserls Vorlesungen zur Phänomenologie des inneren Zeitbewusstseins." I shall cite the English translation by James S. Churchill, with an Introduction by Calvin O. Schrag, *The Phenomenology of Internal Time-Consciousness* (Bloomington: Indiana University Press, 1964). While it is incumbent on a historical reconstruction of the genuine thought of Husserl not to ascribe to him in its every detail a text that was prepared and written by Edith Stein, and to submit the main text to a critical examination in the light of the *Beilagen* and the *ergänzende Texte* published by Boehm in *Husserliana,* vol. 10, and finally to compare these lectures with the Bernau Manuscript soon to be published by the Husserl Archives of Louvain—a philosophical investigation like ours can be based on the text of the lectures as it appeared under Husserl's signature in 1928, and as it was edited by Boehm in 1966. It is, therefore, this text—and this text alone—that we will interpret and discuss under the title of the Husserlian theory of time.

2. "From an Objective point of view every lived experience, like every real being [*Sein*] and moment of being, may have its place in the one unique Objective time— consequently, also the lived experience of the perception and representation [*Vorstellung*] of time itself" (ibid., p. 22).

3. "What we accept, however, is not the existence of a world-time, the existence of a concrete duration, and the like, but time and duration appearing as such. These, however, are absolute data which it would be senseless to call into question" (ibid., p. 23.) There follows an enigmatic statement: "To be sure, we also assume an existing time; this, however, is not the time of the world of experience but the immanent time of the flow of consciousness" (ibid.).

4. By hyletics, Husserl means the analysis of the matter (*hylê*)—or raw impression—of an intentional act, such as perception, abstracting from the form (*morphê*) that animates it and confers a meaning on it.

5. These two functions of apprehensions—ensuring the expressibility of sensed time and making the constitution of objective time possible—are closely connected to each other in the following text. " 'Sensed' temporal data are not merely sensed; they are also charged [*behaftet*] with characters of apprehension, and to these again belong certain requirements and qualifications whose function on the basis of the sensed data is to measure appearing times and time-relations against one another and to bring this or that into an Objective order of one sort or another and seemingly to separate this or that into real orders. Finally, what is constituted here as valid, Objective being [*Sein*] is the one infinite Objective time in which all things and events—material things with their physical properties, minds with their mental states—have their definite temporal positions which can be measured by chronometers" (ibid., p. 26). And further on:

"Phenomenologically speaking, Objectivity is not even constituted through 'primary' content but through characters of apprehension and the regularities [*Gesetzmässigkeiten*] which pertain to the essence of these characters" (ibid., p. 27).

6. The comparison of the pair objective time/internal time with the pair perceived red/sensed red reinforces this suspicion. "Sensed red is a phenomenological datum which exhibits an Objective quality animated by a certain function of apprehension. This datum is not itself a quality. Not the sensed, but the perceived red is a quality in the true sense, i. e., a characteristic of an appearing thing. Sensed red is red only in an equivocal sense, for red is the name of a real quality" (ibid., p. 25). The phenomenology of time brings about the same sort of pairing and superimposition. "If we call a phenomenological datum 'sensed' which through apprehension as corporeally given makes us aware of something Objective, which means, then, that it is Objectively perceived, in the same sense we must also distinguish between a 'sensed' temporal datum and a perceived temporal datum" (ibid.).

7. In this respect, Gérard Granel, *Le Sens du temps et de la perception chez E. Husserl* (Paris: Gallimard, 1958), is not wrong in seeing the *Phenomenology of Internal Time-Consciousness* as an enterprise that runs counter to all of Husserlian phenomenology, inasmuch as this phenomenology is first and foremost a phenomenology of perception. For this phenomenology, a hyletics of the sensed must be subordinated to a noetics of the perceived. The *Empfindung* (sensation, impression) is always superseded in the intention of the thing. What appears is always, par excellence, the perceived, not the sensed. It is always traversed by the intending of the object. It is therefore only as a result of an inversion of the movement of intentional consciousness directed toward the object that the sensed can be established as a distinct appearing, in a hylectics that is itself autonomous. So we have to say that the phenomenology that is directed toward the object only temporarily subordinates the hyletic to the noetic, in anticipation of the elaboration of a phenomenology in which the subordinate layer would become the deepest one. The *Phenomenology of Internal Time-Consciousness* is held, by anticipation, to belong to this phenomenology that is deeper than any phenomenology of perception. The question thus arises whether a hyletics of time can free itself from the noetics required by a phenomenology directed toward objects, whether it can keep the promise made in §85 of *Ideas*, Book I, namely, "descending into the obscure depths of the ultimate consciousness which constitutes all such temporality as belongs to mental processes" (Edmund Husserl, *Ideas Pertaining to a Pure Phenomenology and to a Phenomenological Philosophy. First Book: General Introduction to a Pure Phenomenology*, trans. F. Kersten [The Hague: Martinus Nijhoff, 1982], p. 203). It is in *Ideas*, I, §81, that the suggestion is made that perception may perhaps constitute just the most superficial level of phenomenology and that the work as a whole is not placed on the level of the definitive and genuine absolute. And §81 refers precisely to the 1905 lectures on internal time-consciousness (ibid., p. 194, n. 26). At least we know what price is to be paid here—nothing less than the bracketing of perception itself.

8. The term *Erscheinung* (appearing) can thus be preserved, but its sense is restricted. The same thing is true of perceiving. "We speak here with reference to the perception of the duration of the sound" (*Phenomenology of Internal Time-Consciousness*, p. 46).

9. As early as the Introduction, Husserl had granted himself the following license. "The evidence that consciousness of a tonal process, a melody, exhibits a succession even as I hear it is such as to make every doubt or denial appear senseless" (ibid., p. 23). In speaking of "a sound" does Husserl not provide himself with the unity of a duration as required by intentionality itself? This would seem to be the case, insofar as

the capacity of an object to be apprehended as the same rests upon the unity of meaning of a concordant intention. Cf. Denise Souche-Dagues, *Le Développement de l'intentionalité dans la phénoménologie husserlienne* (The Hague: Martinus Nijhoff, 1972).

10. Granel aptly characterizes the *Phenomenology of Internal Time-Consciousness* as "a phenomenology without phenomena" (*Le Sens du temps*, p. 47), in which Husserl strives to describe "perception with or without the perceived" (ibid., p. 52). I part ways with Granel, however, when he compares the Husserlian present to the Hegelian absolute ("the proximity in question here is that of the Absolute, that is to say, of the Hegelian problem that necessarily emerges after the results of the truths on the Kantian level" [ibid., p. 46]). The interpretation I am proposing of the third section of the Lectures excludes this comparison inasmuch as it is the entire flow of time, as well as the living present, that would be carried to the level of the absolute.

11. "By *Zeitobjekte* [Churchill translates this as 'temporal Objects'], in this particular sense, we mean Objects which are not only unities in time but also . . . include temporal extension in themselves [*Zeitextension*]" (*Phenomenology of Internal Time-Consciousness*, p. 43).

12. Jacques Derrida, in *Speech and Phenomena*, trans. David B. Allison (Evanston: Northwestern University Press, 1973), pp. 60–69, stresses the subversive aspect of this solidarity between the living present and retention as regards the primacy of the *Augenblick*, hence the point-like present, identical to itself, required by the intuitionist conception of the sixth Logical Investigation. "Despite this motif of the punctual now as 'primal form' (*Urform*) of consciousness (*Ideas I*), the body of the description in *The Phenomenology of Internal Time-Consciousness* and elsewhere prohibits our speaking of a simple self-identity of the present. In this way not only is what could be called the metaphysical assurance par excellence shaken, but, closer to our concerns, the '*im selben Augenblick*' argument in the *Investigations* is undermined" (ibid., pp. 63–64). Irrespective of the alleged dependence of the Husserlian theory of intuition on pure self-presence in the point-like now, it is precisely to the Husserl of the *Phenomenology of Internal Time-Consciousness* that we must credit the discovery that "the presence of the perceived present can appear as such only inasmuch as it is *continuously compounded* with a nonpresence and nonperception, with primary memory and expectation (retention and protention)" (ibid., p. 64; his emphasis). And in so doing, Husserl gives a strong sense to the distinction between the present and the instant, which is the decisive moment of our entire analysis. To preserve his discovery, we must not place on the same side, under the common heading "otherness," the nonperception characteristic of recollection and the nonperception ascribed to retention, under the threat of cancelling out the essential phenomenological difference between retention, which is constituted in continuity with perception, and recollection, which alone is, in the strong sense of the word, a nonperception. In this sense, Husserl paves the way for a philosophy of presence that would include the sui generis otherness of retention. Derrida is not mistaken in seeing in the trace, as early as the writing of *Speech and Phenomena*, "a possibility which not only must inhabit the pure actuality of the now but must constitute it through the very movement of difference it introduces" (ibid., p. 67). And he goes on to add, "Such a trace is—if we can employ this language without immediately contradicting it or crossing it out as we proceed—more 'primordial' than what is phenomenologically primordial" (ibid.). Below, we shall subscribe to a similar conception of the trace. But it can only counter a phenomenology that confuses the living present with the point-like instant. By contributing to the defeat of this confusion, Husserl sharpens the Augustinian notion of the threefold present and, more precisely, of the "present of the past."

13.

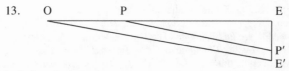

OE: Series of now-points
OE': Sinking-Down (*Herabsinken*)
EE': Continuum of Phases (Now-Point with Horizon of the Past)
(*The Phenomenology of Internal Time-Consciousness*, p. 49.)

14. Maurice Merleau-Ponty, *Phenomenology of Perception*, trans. Colin Smith (New York: Humanities Press, 1962), pp. 410–33, gives a different interpretation. Cf. my essay "Jenseits von Husserl und Heidegger," in Bernard Waldenfels, ed., *Leibhaftige Vernunft. Spüren von Merleau-Pontys Denken* (Munich: Fink, 1986), pp. 56–63.

15. Therefore "the continuity of running-off of an enduring Object is a continuum whose phases are the continua of the modes of running-off of the different temporal points of the duration of the Object" (*Phenomenology of Internal Time-Consciousness*, pp. 49–50). This continuity between the original impression and the retentional modification is stressed by R. Bernet, "Die ungegenwärtige Gegenwart. Anwesenheit und Abwesenheit in Husserls Analyse des Zeitbewusstseins," in Ernst Wolfgang Orth, ed., *Zeit und Zeitlichkeit bei Husserl und Heidegger* (Freiburg/Munich: Karl Alber, 1983), pp. 16–57; see also idem, "La présence du passé dans l'analyse husserlienne de la conscience du temps," *Revue de métaphysique et de morale* 88 (1983): 178–98. According to Bernet, what is in question is not the combining together of presence and nonpresence. "The crucial question becomes that of the phenomenalization of absence. . . . The subject can apprehend itself as a constituting subject only if its presence goes beyond the present and spills over onto the past present and the present to come" (ibid., p. 179). This "extended present" (ibid., p. 183) is indivisibly now (*Jetzpunkt*) and the present of the past.

16. "The parts [*Stüke*] which by a process of abstraction we can throw into relief can be only in the entire running-off. This is also true of the phases and points of the continuity of running-off" (*Phenomenology of Internal Time-Consciousness*, p. 48). A parallel with Aristotle might be sought in taking up the paradox that the instant both divides and connects. Under the first aspect, it proceeds from the continuity it interrupts; under the second aspect, it produces the continuity.

17. The German *sich abschatten* is difficult to translate. "Moreover, every earlier point of this series shades off [*sich abschattet*] again [*wiederum*] as a now in the sense of retention. Thus, in each of these retentions is included a continuity of retentional modifications, and this continuity is itself again a point of actuality which retentionally shades off" (ibid., p. 51).

18. It is interesting to note that Husserl introduces here the comparison to a heritage (*Erbe*) that will play a major role in Heidegger. He introduces this image at the moment he dismisses the hypothesis of an infinite regress in the retention process (ibid., p. 51). He thus seems to relate the idea of a heritage to that of a limitation of the temporal field, a theme that he returns to in the second part of §11, which, according to Rudolf Boehm, goes back to the manuscript of the lectures dating from 1905. According to Bernet, "the iterative structure of retentional modifications accounts both for the consciousness of the duration of the act and the consciousness of 'duration' as such, or rather the flow of absolute consciousness" ("La présence du passé," p. 189); by "iterative structure" we are to understand the modification of retentional modifications of an original impression due to which a "now" becomes not only a having-been-now but a having-been-a-having-been. It is in this way that each new retention modifies prior

retentions; because of the structure of this modification of modifications, each retention is said to carry within itself the "heritage" of the entire preceding process. This expression signifies that "the past is continually remodified on the basis of the present of retention and [that] it is only this present modification of the past that permits the experience of temporal duration" (ibid., p. 190). I would add that this iteration contains the seed of the apprehension of the duration as a form.

19. It is with the same intention that the source-point is said to begin the " 'generation' [*Erzeugung*] of the enduring Object," at the beginning of §11. The notions of "generation" and "source-point" are to be understood as making sense in terms of each other.

20. In the same sense, "Just as in perception, I see what has being now, and in extended perceptions, no matter how constituted, what has enduring being, so in primary resemblance I see what is past. What is past is given therein, and givenness of the past is memory" (ibid., p. 56).

21. The theory of retention represents a real advance in relation to the Augustinian analysis of the image of the past, held to be an "impression fixed in the mind." The intentionality of the present replies directly to the enigma of a vestige that would be at once something present and the sign of something absent.

22. These two terms are to be found side by side (ibid., p. 57).

23. "Everything thus resembles perception and primary remembrance and yet is not itself perception and primary remembrance" (ibid., p. 58).

24. Note the insistence on characterizing "the past itself as perceived" (ibid., p. 61), and on the "just past" in its "self-givenness" (*Selbstgegebenheit*) (ibid.).

25. In this, respect, the most forceful passage in the *Phenomenology of Internal Time-Consciousness* is the following. "Heretofore, consciousness of the past, i.e., the primary one, was not perception because perception was designated as the act originally constituting the now. Consciousness of the past, however, does not constitute a now but rather a 'just-having-been' [*ein soeben gewesen*] that intuitively precedes the now. However, if we call perception *the act in which all 'origination' lies, which constitutes originarily,* then *primary remembrance is perception.* For only in *primary remembrance do we see what is past;* only in it is the past constituted, i.e., *not in a representative but in a presentative way*" (ibid., p. 64; his emphases).

26. We therefore find in §20 a phenomenological elucidation of the phenomena classed by literary criticism under the headings of narrated time and the time of narration, or of acceleration and slowing down, of abbreviation, even of inserting one narrative inside another. For example, "And in the same temporal interval in which the presentification really takes place, we can 'in freedom' accommodate larger and smaller parts of the presentified event with its modes of running-off and consequently run through it more quickly or slowly" (ibid., p. 71). However, we must admit that Husserl hardly deviates from the identical reproduction of a past that is presented and then represented, and this considerably limits the foundational power of this analysis with respect to literary criticism.

27. Bernet uses the following terms to emphasize the significance of the theory of reproduction through recollection in ascertaining the status of truth in a metaphysics of the extended present. "The concept of truth inherent in the Husserlian analysis of recollection stems from the wish to neutralize the temporal difference in the split presence of intentional consciousness to itself. This analysis is marked by an epistemological preoccupation that entails an examination of the truth of memory as a correspondence, the being of consciousness as representation or reproduction, and the temporal absence of the past as a masked presence of consciousness to itself" ("La présence du passé," p. 197). Bernet is not wrong in opposing to this epistemological preoccupation at-

tempts such as Danto's and my own to connect historical truth to narrativity, rather than to a split presence of consciousness to itself (ibid., p. 198). I would say that narrativity constitutes this split presence and not the opposite.

28. Husserl no longer italicizes the "re-" of *Repräsentation* and he writes *repräsentieren* without a hyphen.

29. The assertion that "notwithstanding these differences, expectational intuition is something primordial and unique exactly as is intuition of the past" (ibid., p. 81) will find its full justification only in a philosophy that will put care in the place occupied by perception in Husserl's phenomenology of perception.

30. We may wonder, nevertheless, whether the appearance of a vocabulary relating to "form," to which is connected that of "place" or temporal position, is not an indication of the guiding role played secretly by the representation of objective time in the development of the pure description. Everything occurs as if the idea of unique linear succession served as a teleological guide for seeking and finding, in the relation between the secondary intentionality of representation and the primary intentionality of retention, an approximation that is as close as possible to the idea of linear succession. This presupposition is concealed under the a priori laws that Husserl deciphers in the constitution of the flux. This recurrent objection must be kept constantly in mind in order to understand the strategic role of the third section of the work. This is where we discover the true ambition of the Husserlian undertaking.

31. "We must distinguish at all times: consciousness (flux), appearance (immanent Object), and transcendent object (if it is not the primary content of an immanent Object)" (ibid., p. 101).

32. "Because it is individually preserved, the primordial now-intention appears in the ever new simultaneous consciousness, posited in one with intentions which, the further they stand temporally from the now-intention, the more they throw into relief an ever increasing difference or disparity. What is at first coincident and then nearly coincident becomes ever more widely separated: the old and the new no longer appear to be in essence completely the same but as ever different and strange, despite similarity as to kind. In this way arises the consciousness of the 'gradually changed,' of the growing disparity in the flux of continuous identification" (ibid., pp. 113–14).

33. §§42–45 are loosely connected to what precedes. Boehm considers them to have been written after 1911. The fact that they were added at a relatively late date confirms the hypothesis that this final touch added to the manuscripts also stands as the final word.

34. We cannot help but recall the Augustinian thesis that memory is a presence of things past, due to the impressional character of an image impressed upon the mind.

35. As early as the first edition of the *Critique of Pure Reason* (trans. Norman Kemp Smith [New York: St. Martin's Press, 1965]), this warning is clearly stated: "Inner sense, by means of which the mind [*das Gemüt*] intuits itself or its inner state, yields no intuition of the soul itself as an object" (A22, B37). The basis of the critique of the paralogisms afflicting rational psychology ("Transcendental Dialectic," A341–405, B399–432) is contained here.

36. The text quoted in the preceding note continues: "but there is nevertheless a determinate form [namely, time] in which alone the intuition of an inner state is possible, and everything which belongs to inner determinations is therefore represented in relations of time" (ibid.).

37. Gottfried Martin, *Kant's Metaphysics and Theory of Science*, trans P. G. Lucas (Manchester: Manchester University Press, 1955), pp. 11–16, has perfectly characterized the ontological form of the problem and stressed the role of Leibniz's refutation of Newton in eliminating the third solution. It remained for Kant to substitute for the

Leibnizian solution, which made time and space *phaenomena Dei,* one that would make them representations of the human mind.

38. On this interpretation of the "Transcendental Aesthetic" in terms of the axiomatization of mathematical science and the ability to construct mathematical entities in a Euclidian space, cf. Martin, pp. 29–36. This excellent interpreter of Kant refers the reader to the transcendental doctrine of "Method," chapter 1, section 1, A713, B741: "*Philosophical* knowledge is the *knowledge gained by reason from concepts,* mathematical knowledge is the knowledge gained by reason from the *construction* of concepts," where constructing a concept is representing (*darstellen*) a priori the intuition corresponding to it. In the second of his "General Observations on the Transcendental Aesthetic," Kant connects the intuitive character of space and time and the relational and constructivist character of the sciences made possible by the former as follows: "everything in our knowledge which belongs to intuition . . . contains nothing but mere relations" (B67). We shall return below to what follows in this text (B67–68), where time is considered as that in which we "place" our representations and where time is connected to *Selbstaffektion* through our action. It is noteworthy that it is still with respect to the *Gemüt* that this can be said "phenomenologically."

39. If "the subject, or even only the subjective constitution of the senses in general, be removed, the whole constitution and all the relations of objects in space and time, nay space and time themselves, would vanish. As appearances, they cannot exist in themselves, but only in us" (A42). At first sight, the "only in us" seems to align Kant with Augustine and Husserl. In fact, it separates him from them as well. The "only" marks the scar of his polemical argument. As for the "in us," it designates no one in particular, but the *humana conditio,* according to the words of the 1770 *Inaugural Dissertation.* See "On the Form and Principles of the Sensible and Intelligible World," in *Kant: Selected Precritical Writings and Correspondence with Beck,* trans. G. B. Kerferd and D. E. Walford (New York: Barnes & Noble, 1968), pp. 45–92.

40. J. N. Findlay, *Kant and the Transcendental Object: A Hermeneutic Study* (Oxford: Clarendon Press, 1981), pp. 82–83. According to Findlay, the Kantian conception of pure intuition "does not exclude many obscure and dispositional elements" (ibid, p. 90). Findlay finds in the handling of the schematism "the same sort of 'ontologization' of the dispositional" (ibid.).

41. The very definition of sensibility in terms of receptivity, which is maintained in the "Transcendental Aesthetic," opens the way for this consideration. "*Sensibility* is the *receptivity* of a subject by which it is possible for the subject's representative state to be affected in a definite way by the presence of some object" (*Inaugural Dissertation,* p. 54; his emphasis). The condition of our being-affected is not visibly identified with the conditions for the constitution of mathematical entities. Following the lines of the *Dissertation,* a phenomenology of configuration might be sketched out that would link together the condition of being-affected and the capacity for empirical structuring. The final lines of Section III give some credence to the idea of an implicit phenomenology that would be blind to—or rather, blinded by—the reasoning through presupposition. Concerning space and time, it is said, "But truly *each of the concepts* without any doubt *has been acquired,* not by abstraction from the sensing of objects indeed (for sensation gives the matter and not the form of human cognition), but from the very action of the mind, an action co-ordinating the mind's sensa according to perpetual laws, and each of the concepts is like an immutable diagram and so [ideoque] is to be cognized intuitively" (ibid., p. 74; his emphasis).

42. Kant sees in the sensible form "a law of coordination" (*lex quaedam . . . coordinandi*), by means of which the objects affecting our senses "coalesce into some representational whole" (*in totum aliquod repraesentationis coalescant*). For this to oc-

cur, there is a need for "an internal principle in the mind by which these various things may be clothed with a certain *specificity* [speciem quandam] in accordance with stable and innate laws" (ibid., p. 55; his emphasis). In §12, however, the epistemological import of the distinction between external sense and internal sense is asserted. Thus pure mathematics considers space in terms of geometry and time in terms of pure mechanics.

43. Findlay attaches great importance to the first three arguments of §14. Time, he says, is "given to us in a single overview, as a single, individual whole in which all limited time-lapses must find their places" (*Kant and the Transcendental Object,* p. 89). By virtue of this "primordial And So On," belonging to all empirical succession, "we can be taught to extend the map of the past and future indefinitely" (ibid.) Findlay emphasizes this dispositional aspect by reason of which, lacking the power to think of an absolutely empty time, we are able to continue indefinitely beyond any particular given.

44. Kant, it is true, observes, "the proposition that different times cannot be simultaneous is not to be derived from a general concept. The proposition is synthetic, and cannot have its origin in concepts alone" (A32, B47). He immediately adds, however, "It is immediately contained in the intuition and representation of time" (ibid.).

45. "Consequently there must be found in the objects of perception, that is, in the appearances, the substratum which represents time in general" (B225).

46. The kinship between the second analogy and the Leibnizian principle of sufficient reason does deserve special mention. "The principle of sufficient reason is thus the ground of possible experience, that is, of objective knowledge of appearances in respect of their relation in the order of time" (A210, B246). Martin has paid particular attention to this connection between the principle of sufficient reason and the synthetic a priori judgment.

47. "Now since absolute time is not an object of perception, this determination of position cannot be derived from the relation of appearances to it. On the contrary, the appearances must determine for one another their position in time, and make their time-order a necessary order. In other words, that which follows or happens must follow in conformity with a universal rule upon that which was contained in the preceding state" (B245).

48. "The three dynamical relations from which all others spring, are therefore inherence, consequence, and composition" (A215). These three dynamical relations are what imply the three "modes" in accordance with which the order of time is determined.

49. Thus we find three senses of "I" in Kant: the "I think" of transcendental apperception; the absolute self, in itself, that acts and suffers; and the represented self, represented as is every other object through self-affection. The error of rational psychology, which is laid bare by the paralogisms of Pure Reason, in the transcendental dialectic, amounts to confusing the self in itself, the soul, with the "I think," which is not an object, and in this way producing a philosophical monster: a subject that is its own object.

50. "Thus the understanding under the title of a *transcendental synthesis of imagination,* performs this act upon the *passive* subject, whose faculty [*Wirkung*] it is, and we are therefore justified in saying that inner sense is affected thereby" (B153–54). Herman de Vleeschauwer, *La Déduction transcendentale dans l'oeuvre de Kant* (Paris: Leroux, 1934–37), says regarding this passage, "Ultimately it is the understanding that, by restricting the form of time to the synthesis of this pure manifold, determines the internal sense of which time is the form and which is nothing other than the self considered in its passivity" (2:208).

51. Kant calls this activity a "movement." But this is not the same movement as that

to which Aristotle grafted his analysis of time. Empirical movement cannot have a place among the categories. Rather it is the movement implied in the description or construction of a space. "Movement consists in the succession of determinations of inner sense produced by the act of synthesis implied in the construction of a determined space" (de Vleeschauwer, 2:216).

52. Concerning the fate of inner sense, gradually dethroned from the role of the intuition of the soul and reduced to being a mere medium of self-affection, cf. de Vleeschauwer, 2:552–94; 3:85–140. See also Jean Nabert's admirable article, "L'expérience interne chez Kant," *Revue de métaphysique et de morale* 31 (1924): 205–68. Nabert places great emphasis on the mediation of space in determining temporal experience. Question: "If it could not find outside itself the regular movement of a body in space, in order to ground its own mobility, would our internal life still be able to discern its own flowing"? (ibid., p. 226). Answer: "the inner sense draws the material for its knowledge from external intuitions" (ibid., p. 231). "The deep-lying interconnection that binds the consciousness of succession to the determination of space" (ibid., p. 241) depends on the impossibility of finding any figure at all in internal intuition. The line, as a result, is more than simply an analogy that is added on; it is constitutive of the consciousness of succession, this consciousness being "the internal aspect of an operation that includes a determination in space" (ibid., p. 242). Nabert does concede, it is true, "But, on the other hand, there is no intuition of space that has not first been determined in its unity by the schematism of understanding. In this respect, time wins back its full rights; it provides thought with the means for its unfolding and for transferring the order of time to phenomena and to their existence. This is what the schematism will demonstrate in the pages that follow." Let us conclude with Nabert, "If, after this, things help us in determining our own existence in time, they are returning to us what we have lent them" (ibid., p. 254). Cf. also ibid., pp. 267–68.

53. Cf. de Vleeschauwer, 2:579–94.

54. In Note I we read the following astonishing assertion: "in the above proof it has been shown that outer experience is really immediate, and that only by means of it is inner experience—not indeed the consciousness of my own existence, but the determination of it in time—possible" (B276–77). Kant thought it useful to underscore this statement with the following addition. "The *immediate* consciousness of the existence of outer things is, in the preceding thesis, not presuppposed, but proved, be the possibility of this consciousness understood by us or not" (B278).

55. When Gottfried Martin places the conceptual network of the *Critique* under the title "The Being of Nature" (*Kant's Metaphysics and Theory of Science*, pp. 70–105), and within the context of the Leibnizian principle of sufficient reason, this is free of paradox for him since it is simply the axiomatic form of a Newtonian nature. It is this network, constituted jointly by the four tables—judgments, categories, schemata, and principles—that articulates the ontology of nature.

CHAPTER THREE

1. Martin Heidegger, *Being and Time*, trans. John Macquarrie and Edward Robinson (New York: Harper and Row, 1962). The first edition appeared in 1927 as a special issue of the *Jahrbuch für phänomenologische Forschung*, vol. 3 (Halle: Niemeyer Verlag), edited by Edmund Husserl. It included the subtitle "Part One," which was to disappear with the 5th edition. *Sein und Zeit* now forms volume 2 of Part I of the *Gesamtausgabe* (Frankfurt: Klostermann, 1975–) of Heidegger's writings. Today any reading of *Being and Time* must be completed by a reading of the lectures from the course Heidegger gave at the University of Marburg in the summer session of 1927 (hence shortly after the publication of *Being and Time*), now published as Volume 24

of the *Gesamtausgabe* under the title *Die Grundprobleme der Phänomenologie* (Frankfurt: Klostermann, 1975), *The Basic Problems of Phenomenology*, trans. Albert Hofstadter (Bloomington: Indiana University Press, 1982). I shall make frequent reference to this work, in part to make up for the absence of a French translation of the second division of *Being and Time*, because there are numerous parallels between these two works. My second reason for doing so has to do with the difference in strategy in each of them. Unlike *Being and Time*, the 1927 course proceeds from ordinary time back toward primordial time, moving in this way from misunderstanding to authentic understanding. Because of this regressive approach, we find a long discussion devoted to the Aristotelian treatise on time, held to be the authoritative document for all of Western philosophy, which is supposed to be conjoined with an interpretation of Augustine that is announced without being elaborated any further (See *Basic Problems*, p. 231). Unless otherwise noted all italics in the passages cited from *Being and Time* are from the English translation.

2. Question: "What is it that by its very essence is *necessarily* the theme whenever we exhibit something *explicitly?*" Answer: "Manifestly, it is something that proximally and for the most part does *not* show itself at all: it is something that lies *hidden*, in contrast to that which proximally and for the most part does show itself; but at the same time it is something that belongs to what thus shows itself and it belongs to it so essentially as to constitute its meaning and its ground" (*Being and Time*, p. 59).

3. The status of these existentials is a great source of misunderstanding. To bring them to language we must either create new words, at the risk of not being understood by anyone, or take advantage of long-forgotten semantic resonances in ordinary language still preserved in the treasury of the German language, or revive the ancient meanings of these words, or even apply an etymological method to them that, in practice, generates neologisms—the risk now being that they become untranslatable into other languages and even into ordinary German. The vocabulary of temporality will give us a broad idea of this almost desperate struggle to make up for the words that are lacking. The simplest words, such as "future," "past," and "present," will be the site of this extenuating labor of language.

4. According to its title, the first part of *Being and Time* (and the only one published) was intended to be "The Interpretation of Dasein in Terms of Temporality, and the Explication of Time as the Transcendental Horizon for the Question of Being" (ibid., p. 65).

5. This ambition of grasping time as a whole is the existential recovery of the well-known problem of the oneness of time, which Kant holds to be one of the major presuppositions of his "Aesthetic." There is but one time and all times are parts of it. However, according to Heidegger, this singular unity is taken at the level of serial time, which, as we shall see, results from the leveling off of within-time-ness, that is, from the least primordial and least authentic configuration. The question of totality must therefore be taken up again on another, more radical level.

6. I shall not repeat here the extraordinarily painstaking analyses by which Heidegger distinguishes Being-towards-the-end from all the ends that, in ordinary language, we assign to events, to biological or historical processes, and in general to all the ways in which things ready-to-hand and present-at-hand end. Nor shall I pursue the analyses that determine the untransferable character of someone else's death to my own death, and thus the untransferable character of my own death ("death is essentially always mine"). Nor shall I retrace the analyses that distinguish the possibility characteristic of Being-towards-death from all the forms of possibility in use in everyday language, in logic, and in epistemology. We cannot overemphasize the number of precautions taken against misunderstanding by these analyses, which, starting from apophantic propositions (§§46–49, death is not this, death is not that . . .), then move to a "preliminary

sketch" (*Vorzeichnung*), §50), which, only at the end of the chapter, becomes the "existential projection [*Entwurf*] of an authentic Being-towards-death" (the title of §53). In accordance with this projection, Being-towards-death constitutes a possibility of Dasein—an unparalleled one, to be sure—toward which we are pulled by an expectation that is itself unique—the possibility that is "not to be outstripped" (*aüsserste*) (ibid., p. 296), the "ownmost" (*eigenste*) possibility (ibid., p. 307) of our potentiality-for-Being.

7. The second division of *Being and Time,* entitled "Dasein and Temporality," begins with the expression of a doubt concerning the primordial character of the interpretation of Care as the totalizing structure of existence. "Are we entitled to claim that in characterizing Dasein ontologically *qua* Care we have given a *primordial* Interpretation of this entity? By what criterion is the existential analytic of Dasein to be assessed as regards its primordiality, or lack of it? What, indeed, do we mean by the '*primordiality*' of an ontological Interpretation?" (ibid., pp. 274–75). This question is, at first sight, surprising at this advanced stage in the investigation. Yet it is now stated that we do not possess at this stage the assurance (*Sicherung*) that the fore-sight (*Vorsicht*) that guides our interpretation has indeed brought the whole of the entity which it has taken as its theme into our fore-having (*Vorhabe*). So Heidegger's hesitation has to do with the quality of the seeing that is to grasp the unity of the structural moments of Care. "Only then can the question of the meaning of the unity which belongs to the whole entity's totality of Being [*Seinsgansheit*], be formulated and answered with any phenomenal assurance" (ibid., p. 275). But how can this primordial character be "guaranteed" (*gewährleistet*)? It is here that the question of the authenticity appears to parallel the question of primordiality. "As long as the existential structure of an authentic potentiality-for-Being has not been brought into the idea of existence, the fore-sight by which an *existential* Interpretation is guided will lack primordiality" (ibid., p. 276).

8. Being-towards-the-end is the existential with respect to which Being-towards-death is in each case and for each individual the existentiell. "But as something of the character of Dasein, death *is* only in an existentiell *Being towards death*" (ibid., p. 277).

9. "But can Dasein also exist *authentically* as a whole? How is the authenticity of existence to be determined at all, if not with regard to authentic existing? Where do we get our criterion for this? . . . But an authentic potentiality-for-Being is attested [*Bezeugung*] by the conscience [*Gewissen*]" (ibid.).

10. At the end of the analysis of Being-towards-death, we read this strange avowal: "The question of Dasein's authentic Being-a-whole and of its existential constitution still hangs in mid-air [*schwebende*]. It can be put on a phenomenal basis which will stand the test [*probhaftig*] only if it can cling [*sich . . . halten*] to a possible authenticity of its Being which is attested [*bezeugte*] by Dasein itself. If we succeed in uncovering that attestation [*Bezeugung*] phenomenologically, together with what it attests, then the problem will arise anew as to *whether the anticipation of [zum] death, which we have hitherto projected only in its* ontological *possibility, has an essential connection with that authentic potentiality-for-Being which has been attested [bezeugten]*" (ibid., p. 331).

11. Chapter 6 in the next section of this volume wil be devoted entirely to the search for a mode of totalizing the three orientations of historical time that, without ever returning to Hegel, will do justice to this need for a totalization amidst dispersion.

12. We shall see the place to be accorded to the idea of our debt to the past, to the dead, and to the forgotten victims in my attempt below to give a meaning to the notion of the past as it once was (see below, chap. 6).

13. In the following passage Heidegger seems to allow for the freedom of espousing his formula on the basis of different personal experiences: "Temporality has different

possibilities and different ways of *temporalizing* itself. The basic possibilities of existence, the authenticity and inauthenticity of Dasein, are grounded ontologically on possible temporalizations of temporality" (*Being and Time,* pp. 351–52). I believe that he was thinking here of differences related, not to the past, present, and future, but to the various ways of connecting the existential to the existentiell.

14. The initial program of *Being and Time,* as explicitly stated in the Introduction, was to bring us back to "the question of the meaning of Being" at the end of the analytic of Dasein. If the published work does not fulfill this vast program, the hermeneutics of Care does at least preserve this intention by closely binding the projection inherent in Care to "the primary projection of the understanding of Being" (ibid., p. 372). Human projections, in fact, are so only by reason of this ultimate grounding. "But in these projections there lies hidden the 'upon-which' [*ein Voraufhin*] of the projection; and on this, as it were, the understanding of Being nourishes itself" (ibid., p. 371).

15. The prefix *vor-* has the same expressive force as the *zu* of *Zukunft.* We find it in the expression *Sich vorweg,* ahead-of-itself, which defines Care in its widest scope, on the same level as coming-towards-itself.

16. This distinction between having-been, intrinsically implied in coming-towards, and the past, extrinsically distinct from the future, will be of the greatest importance when we discuss the status of the historical past in chapter 6.

17. The term "presentify" has already been used, in a Husserlian context, to translate *Vergegenwärtigen,* which has a sense closer to "representation" than to "presentation." "Enpresent," "enpresenting" are Albert Hofstadter's translation of *Gegenwärtigen* in the *Basic Problems of Phenomenology.*

18. If temporality can be thought of as temporalizing, nevertheless the ultimate relation between *Zeit* and *Sein* remains suspended in midair as long as the idea of Being has not been clarified. This lacuna will not be filled in *Being and Time.* Despite this incompletion, Heideger can be credited with the solution to one of the major aporias of time—its invisibility as a unique totality.

19. The essence of temporality "is a process of temporalizing in the unity of the ecstases" (ibid., p. 377).

20. An "equiprimordiality" (*Gleichursprünglichkeit*) (ibid., p. 378) of the three ecstases results from the difference among the modes of temporalizing. "But within this equiprimordiality, the modes of temporalizing are different. The difference lies in the fact that the nature of the temporalizing can be determined primarily in terms of the different ecstases" (ibid.).

21. We state above what Heidegger expects from these final analyses concerning the attestation of the primordial by the authentic. Chapter 3, devoted to fundamental temporality, ends with these words: "In working out [*Ausarbeitung*] the temporality of Dasein as everydayness, historicality, and within-time-ness, we shall be getting for the first time a relentless insight into the *complications* of a primordial ontology of Dasein" (ibid., p. 382). These complications are unavoidable inasmuch as factical (*faktisch*) Dasein exists in the world alongside and amidst the entities it encounters in the world. It is, therefore, the structure of Being-in-the-world, described in the first division, that must be "worked out" in this way, along with the complex concretizing of temporality, until it rejoins, by way of the structure of within-time-ness, its starting point in everydayness (as is made clear in Chapter IV, "Temporality and Everydayness"). But, for a hermeneutic phenomenology, what is closest is, in truth, what is farthest away.

22. "The specific movement [*Bewegtheit*] in which Dasein *is stretched along and stretches itself along,* we call its 'historizing'. The question of Dasein's 'connectedness' is the ontological problem of Dasein's historizing. To lay bare the *structure of historizing,* and the existential-temporal conditions of its possibility, signifies that one has achieved an *ontological* understanding of *historicality*" (ibid., p. 427).

23. Here the German language can play with the roots of words and divide the compound term *Selbstständigkeit* (translated as "self-constancy") into *Ständigkeit des Selbst,* which would be something like "keeping the self" in the sense in which one keeps a promise. Heidegger expressly connects the question "Who?" to that of the self: "the question of the constancy of the Self, which we defined as the 'who' of Dasein" (ibid., p. 427); cf. the note attached to this statement, which refers the reader to §64: *Sorge und Selbstheit).*

24. "The existential Interpretation of historiology as a science aims solely at demonstrating its ontological derivation from Dasein's historicality. . . . *In analyzing the historicality of Dasein we shall try to show that this entity is not 'temporal' because it 'stands in history', but that, on the contrary, it exists historically and can so exist only because it is temporal in the very basis of its Being"* (ibid., p. 428).

25. This initial reply does not facilitate the task of grounding historiography in historicality. How, indeed, can we ever move from the history of each person to the history of all? Is not the ontology of Dasein radically monadic in this respect? Below, we shall see to what extent a new transition, that from individual fate *(Schicksal)* to common destiny *(Geschick),* answers this major difficulty.

26. The German here plays on the prefixes *zurück* (back-) and *über* (over-) tacked to the verbs *kommen* (to come), *nehmen* (to take), and *liefern* (to hand over). English is better suited to render these expressions than is French: to come back, to take over a heritage, to hand down possibilities that have come down to one.

27. I do not deny that the deliberate choice of expressions such as these (in a text that was published, we must remember, in 1927) supplied ammunition for Nazi propaganda and that it contributed to blinding Heidegger to the political events of those dark years. However, it must also be said that he was not the only one to speak of community *(Gemeinschaft)* instead of society *(Gesellschaft),* of struggle *(Kampf),* of combative obedience *(kämpfende Nachfolge),* and of faithfulness *(Treue).* For my part, I would incriminate instead the unconditional transfer to the communal sphere of the most fundamental theme of all, Being-towards-death, despite the continually repeated affirmation that Being-towards-death is untransferable. This transfer is responsible for the sketch of a heroic and tragic political philosophy open to misapplication. It looks as though Heidegger did see the resources that might be offered by the concept of a "generation," introduced by Dilthey in an essay of 1875 to fill the gap between individual fate and collective destiny. "Dasein's fateful destiny in and with its 'generation' goes to make up the full authentic historizing of Dasein" (ibid., p. 436). I shall return to this concept of a generation in chapter 4.

28. By means of this roundabout expression, Heidegger succeeds in placing Being itself in the past *(dagewesen)* by a striking shortcut, but one that is exasperating for translators.

29. "The repeating of that which is possible does not bring again [*Weiderbringen*] something that is 'past,' nor does it bind the 'present' back to that which has already been 'outstripped'" (ibid., p. 437). Repetition, in this sense, confirms the gap in meaning separating having-been, which is intrinsically tied to coming-towards, and the past, which, stripped down to the level of things present-at-hand and ready-to-hand, is only extrinsically opposed to the future, as is attested to by common sense when it opposes, in a nondialectical manner, the determined, completed, necessary character of the past to the undetermined, open, possible nature of the future.

30. Heidegger is playing here on the quasi-homophony between the *wieder* of *Wiederholung* and the *wider* of *erwidern* and of *Widerruf.*

31. "*Authentic Being-towards-death—that is to say, the finitude of temporality—is the hidden basis of Dasein's historicality.* Dasein does not first become historical in repetition; but because it is historical as temporal, it can take itself over in its history by repeating. For this no historiology is as yet needed" (ibid., p. 438). *The Basic*

Problems of Phenomenology explicitly compares repetition to resoluteness. Resoluteness is, in effect, already Dasein's repetitive coming back to itself (see *Basic Problems,* p. 287). Finally, both phenomena can be considered as authentic modalities of the present, distinct from the simple "now."

32. §73 is boldly titled "The Ordinary Understanding of History, and Dasein's Historizing"—*Das vulgäre Verständnis der Geschichte und das Geschehen des Daseins (Being and Time,* p. 429).

33. The "*locus* of the problem of history. . . . is not to be sought in historiology as the science of history" (ibid., p. 427). "The existential Interpretation of historiology as a science aims solely at demonstrating [*Nachweis*] its ontological derivation from Dasein's historicality" (ibid., p. 428). It is noteworthy that, even in his preparatory statements, Heidegger anticipates the need to join within-time-ness to historicality in order, precisely, to account for the role of the calendar and the clock in establishing history as a human science. "Even without a developed historiology, factical Dasein needs and uses a calendar and a clock" (ibid., p. 429). This indicates that we have moved from historicality to within-time-ness. Both, however, proceed from the temporality of Dasein: "historicality and within-time-ness turn out to be equiprimordial. Thus, within its limits, the ordinary interpretation of the temporal character of history is justified" (ibid.).

34. "We contend that what is *primarily* historical is Dasein. That which is *secondarily* historical, however, is what we encounter within-the-world—not only equipment ready-to-hand, in the widest sense, but also the environing *Nature* as 'the very soil of history'" (ibid., p. 433).

35. The concept of a trace will play an eminent role in my own attempt to rebuild the bridges burned by Heidegger between the phenomenological concept of time and what he calls the "ordinary" concept of time.

36. Contrary to the reader's expectation, the final paragraph of the section on "Historicality" (§77) adds nothing to the thesis of the subordination of historiology to historizing, even though Heidegger directly takes on Dilthey, with the assistance of Count Yorck, Dilthey's friend and correspondent. What is at issue is the alternative that a philosophy of "life" and a "psychology" might offer to hermeneutic phenomenology that puts historizing at the basis of the human sciences. In the correspondence of Count Yorck, Heidegger finds reinforcement for his thesis that what governs the methodology of the human sciences is not a special type of object but an ontological feature of human beings, which Yorck called *das Ontische* to distinguish it from *das Historische.*

37. At the end of §75 we read, "Nevertheless, we may venture a projection of the ontological genesis of historiology as a science in terms of Dasein's historicality. This projection will serve to prepare us for the clarification of the task of destroying the history of philosophy historiologically—a clarification which is to be accomplished in what follows" (ibid., p. 444). By referring in this way to §6 of *Being and Time,* Heidegger confirms that these pages mark the dismissal of the human sciences on behalf of the true task, left unfinished in *Being and Time:* "the task of destroying the history of ontology" (ibid., p. 41).

38. Heidegger had intimated at the outset of his study on historicality that within-time-ness was, in a sense yet to be determined, anticipated by historicality. In the final lines of §72 that open this study, we read, "Nevertheless [*gleichwohl*], Dasein must also [*auch*] be called 'temporal' in the sense of Being 'in time'" (ibid., p. 429). We have to admit that, "since . . . time as within-time-ness also 'stems' [*aus . . . stammt*] from the temporality of Dasein, historicality and within-time-ness turn out to be equiprimordial. Thus [*daher*], within its limits, the ordinary interpretation of the temporal character of history is justified" (ibid., p. 429). This turn of events in the analysis is, moreover, anticipated at the very heart of the study of historicality. The interpretation

of Dasein's stretching along in terms of the "connectedness of life" had already intimated that the analysis of historicality could not be brought to its conclusion without
including what everydayness teaches. But everydayness is not confined to producing
figures of fallenness; it functions as a reminder of the horizon against which all these
analyses are conducted, namely, the horizon of the world, which the subjectivism of
the philosophies of life—and also, we might add, the intimist tendency in Heidegger
himself, seen in all his analyses centered around Being-towards-death—threatens to
conceal from our sight. Contrary to all subjectivism, we must say, "*The historizing of
history is the historizing of Being-in-the-world*" (ibid., p. 440). Moreover, we must
speak of "the history of the world" (*Geschichte der Welt*) in an entirely different sense
than Hegel did, for whom world-history (*Weltgeschichte*) is made up of the succession
of spiritual configurations: "*With the existence of historical Being-in-the-world, what
is ready-to-hand and what is present-at-hand have already, in every case, been incorporated into the history of the world*" (ibid.). There is no doubt that Heidegger wanted
to shatter the dualism of Mind and Nature. "And even Nature is historical," not in the
sense of natural history but in the sense in which the world is hospitable or inhospitable.
Whether it signifies a countryside, a place to live, a resource to exploit, a battlefield,
or a cultic site, nature makes Dasein a being within-the-world that, as such, is historical, beyond any false opposition between an "external" history and an "inner" one,
which would be that of the soul. "We call such entities the '*world-historical*' [*Welt-
Geschichtliche*]" (ibid.). Heidegger readily admits that, here, he is about to exceed the
limits of his theme but claims that it does lead to the threshold of "the ontological
enigma of the movement of historizing in general" (ibid., p. 441).

39. The analysis of within-time-ness begins with the admission that the analysis of
historicality was made "without regard for the 'fact' (*Tatsache*) that all historizing runs
its course 'in time'" (ibid., p. 456). This analysis cannot help but be incomplete if it
must include the everyday understanding of Dasein—in which "factically (*faktisch*)
. . . all history is known merely as that which happens 'within-time'" (ibid.). The
term that poses a problem here is not so much "everyday" (the first part of *Being and
Time* begins all of its analyses on this level) as "factically" and "facticity" (*Fäktizität*),
which indicate the link between an analysis that remains within the sphere of phenomenology and the one that already belongs to the natural sciences and to history. "If
the existential analytic is to make Dasein ontologically transparent in its very facticity,
then the factical 'onto-temporal' interpretation of history must also be *explicitly* given
its due" (ibid.). The transition made through everyday time along the path from ordinary time to primordial time in the *Basic Problems of Phenomenology* confirms that
within-time-ness (intratemporality), the final stage of the process of derivation in
Being and Time, also stems from primordial time.

40. "Factical Dasein takes time into its reckoning, without any existential understanding of temporality. Reckoning with time is an elemental kind of behavior which
must be clarified before we turn to the question of what it means to say that entities are
'in time'. All Dasein's behaviour is to be Interpreted in terms of its being—that is, in
terms of temporality. We must show how Dasein *as* temporality temporalizes a kind of
behaviour which relates itself to time by taking it into its reckoning. Thus our previous
characterization of temporality is not only quite incomplete in that we have not paid
attention to all the dimensions of this phenomenon; it is also defective in principle
because something like world-time, in the rigorous sense of the existential-temporal
conception of the world, belongs to temporality itself. We must come to understand
how this is possible and why it is necessary. Thus the 'time' which is familiar to us in
the ordinary way—the time 'in which' entities occur—will be illuminated, and so will
the within-time-ness of these entities" (ibid., pp. 456–57).

41. "The making-present which awaits and retains, interprets *itself*. . . . The

making-present which interprets itself—in other words, that which has been interpreted and is addressed in the 'now'—is what we call 'time'" (ibid., p. 460).

42. "*The 'there' is disclosed in a way which is grounded in Dasein's own temporality as ecstatically stretched along, and with this disclosure a 'time' is allotted to Dasein; only because of this can Dasein, as factically thrown, 'take' its time and lose it*" (ibid., p. 463).

43. In *The Basic Problems of Phenomenology*, it is ordinary time that refers back to primordial time, by means of the authentic pre-understanding of time contained in the "now," which, in the ordinary conception, adds onto itself to constitute the whole of time. The use of the clock assures the transition between the operation of counting "nows" and the intervals between them and that of counting with . . . or reckoning with time (ibid., pp. 257f.). In this way, the self-explicitation of what is pre-understood in the common conception gives rise to the understanding of original time that *Being and Time* ascribes to the level of within-time-ness. It is noteworthy that phenomena ascribed to different moments in *Being and Time*—significance (tied to the usefulness of clocks), datability, the spanneddess (*Gespanntheit*) resulting from being stretched along (*Erstreckung*), publicness—are all grouped together in *The Basic Problems of Phenomenology* (pp. 261–64). World-time (*Weltzeit*), for example, is articulated in terms of the *Bedeutsamkeit* in virtue of which an instrument refers to every other instrument on the level of everyday understanding.

44. "Such reckoning does not occur by accident, but has its existential-ontological necessity in the basic state of Dasein as Care. Because it is essential to Dasein that it exists fallingly as something thrown, it interprets its time concernfully by way of time-reckoning. *In this,* the 'real' *making-public* of time gets temporalized, so that we must say that *Dasein's thrownness is the reason why 'there is' time publicly*" (*Being and Time*, p. 464).

45. "In its thrownness Dasein has been surrendered to the changes of day and night. Day with its brightness gives it the possibility of sight; night takes this away" (ibid., p. 465). But what is day if not what the sun dispenses? "The sun dates the time which is interpreted in concern. In terms of this dating arises the 'most natural' measure of time—the day. . . . Dasein historicizes *from day to day* by reason of its way of interpreting time by dating it—a way which is adumbrated in its thrownness into the 'there'" (ibid., pp. 465–66).

46. "Thus when *time* is *measured,* it is *made public* in such a way that it is encountered on each occasion and at any time for everyone as 'now and now and now.' This time which is 'universally' accessible in clocks is something that we come across as a *present-at-hand multiplicity of 'nows',* so to speak, though the measuring of time is not directed thematically towards time as such" (ibid., p. 470). The consequences for historiography are considerable to the extent that the latter depends on the calendar and on clocks. "Provisionally it was enough for us to point out the general 'connection' of the use of clocks with that temporality which takes its time. Just as the concrete analysis of astronomical time-reckoning in its full development belongs to the existential-ontological Interpretation of how Nature is discovered, the foundations of historiological and calendrical 'chronology' can be laid bare only within the orbit of the tasks of analyzing historiological cognition existentially" (ibid., p. 471).

47. "With the disclosedness of the world, world-time has been made public, so that every temporally concernful Being alongside entities *within-the-world* understands these entities circumspectively as encountered 'in time'" (ibid.).

48. "This entity does not have an end at which it just stops, but is *exists finitely*" (ibid., p. 378). Infinity is the product of both deviation and leveling-off. How does "inauthentic temporality, as inauthentic," temporalize "an in-finite time out of the finite"? "Only because primordial time is *finite* can the 'derived' time temporalize it-

self as *infinite*. In the order in which we get things into our grasp through the understanding, the finitude of time does not become fully visible [*sichtbar*] until we have exhibited [*heraugestellt*] 'endless time' so that these may be contrasted" (ibid., p. 379). The premise of the infinity of time, which *Being and Time* derives from the failure to recognize the finitude of Being-towards-death, will in *The Basic Problems of Phenomenology* be directly related to the "endlessness" characterizing the series of "nows" in the ordinary conception of time. To be sure, the 1927 course also mentions Dasein's forgetfulness of its own essential finitude; but it does so only to add that it "is not possible to go into further detail here on the finitude of time, because it is connected with the difficult problem of death, and this is not the place to analyze death in that connection" (*Basic Problems*, p. 273). Does this mean that the sense of *Ganzsein* is less an integral part of Being-towards-death in this course than in *Being and Time?* This suspicion receives support in the addition—to which we shall return in our concluding pages—of the problematic of *Temporalität* to that of *Zeitlichkeit*. This problematic, which is new in relation to *Being and Time*, indicates the primacy of the question of an ontological horizon that is now grafted to the ecstatic character of time, which stems solely from an analytic of Dasein.

49. "In the everyday way in which we are with one another, the levelled-off sequence of 'nows' remains completely unrecognizable as regards its origin in the temporality of the individual [*einzelner*] Dasein" (*Being and Time*, p. 477).

50. This remark has all the more importance for us in that history's equal legitimacy is recalled here as it is "understood *publicly* as happening *within-time*" (p. 478). This sort of oblique recognition of history plays an important role in subsequent discussions of the status of history in relation to a hermeneutic phenomenology.

51. Heidegger translates this passage as follows. *"Das nämlich ist die Zeit: das Gezählte an der im Horizont des Früher und Später begegnenden Bewegung."* In the English translation of *Being and Time* we read: "For this is time: that which is counted in the movement which we encounter within the horizon of earlier and after" (p. 473). This translation suggests the ambiguity of a definition in which leveling-off has already taken place but remains indiscernible as such, even while admitting the possibility of an existential interpretation. I shall refrain from making any definitive judgment concerning the interpretation of the Aristotelian conception of time in Heidegger. He himself promised to return to it in the second part of *Being and Time* after a discussion of the *Seinsfrage* of ancient ontology. *The Basic Problems of Phenomenology* will fill this lacuna (pp. 232–56). The discussion of Aristotle's treatise on time is so important in the strategy developed in the 1927 course that it determines the starting point for the return path from the ordinary concept of time toward the understanding of primordial time. Everything turns around the interpretation of the Aristotelian "now" (*to nun*). We also have important texts by Heidegger on Aristotle's *Physics* that restore the context of the Greek *physis*, the underlying meaning of which, Heidegger claims, has been radically misconstrued by philosophers and by historians of Greek thought. Cf. "Ce qu'est et comment se détermine la *Physis*: Aristotle, *Physics* B, 1," seminar given during 1940, in Martin Heidegger, *Questions II*, trans. F. Fédier (Paris: Gallimard, 1968), pp. 165–276. The German original was published with a facing Italian translation by G. Guzzoli in *Il Pensiero* nos. 2 and 3 (1958).

52. "Ever since Aristotle all discussions [*Erörterung*] of the concept of time have clung *in principle* to the Aristotelian definitions; that is, in taking time as their theme, they have taken it as it shows itself in circumspective concern" (*Being and Time,*) p. 473). I shall not discuss here the famous note in *Being and Time* where it is stated that the "priority which Hegel has given to the 'now' which as been levelled-off, makes it plain that in defining the concept of time he is under the sway of the manner in which time is *ordinarily* understood; and this means that he is likewise under the sway

of the *traditional* conception of it" (ibid., p. 484, n. xxx). Jacques Derrida provides a translation and interpretation of this note in "*Ousia* and *Gramme:* Note on a Note from *Being and Time,"* in his *Margins of Philosophy,* trans. Alan Bass (Chicago: University of Chicago Press, 1982), pp. 29–67. We should also mention, in this regard, Denise Souche-Dagues's refutation of Heidegger's argumentation in §82 directed against "Hegel's way of taking the relation between time and spirit": "Une exégèse heideggerienne: le temps chez Hegel d'après le §82 de *Sein und Zeit," Revue de métaphysique et de morale* 84 (1979): 101–20. Finally, the Heideggerian interpretation of Aristotle is taken up again by Emmanuel Martineau, "Conception vulgaire et conception aristotélicienne du temps. Notes sur *Grundprobleme der Phänomenologie* de Heidegger," *Archives de philosophie* 43 (1980): 99–120.

53. For example, Hans Reichenbach, *The Philosophy of Space and Time,* trans. John Freund (New York: Dover Books, 1957); Adolf Grünbaum, *Philosophical Problems of Space and Time* (Dordrecht and Boston: D. Reidel, 1973,[2] 1974); Olivier Costa de Beauregard, *La Notion de temps, Equivalence avec l'espace* (Paris: Hermann, 1963); idem, "Two Lectures on the Direction of Time," *Synthèse* 35 (1977): 129–54.

54. I am adopting here the distinction made by Hervé Barreau in *La Construction de la notion de temps* (Strasbourg: Atelier d'impression du Département de Physique, 1985).

55. Stephen Toulmin and June Goodfield, *The Discovery of Time* (Chicago: University of Chicago Press, 1972).

56. Toulmin and Goodfield cite a poem by John Donne deploring "the world's proportion disfigured" (ibid., p. 77).

57. Ibid., pp. 141–70.

58. Ibid., pp. 197–229.

59. Ibid., p. 251.

60. The full significance of this paradox is revealed only when narrative, understood as a mimesis of action, is taken as the criterion for this meaning.

61. R. G. Collingwood, *The Idea of History,* ed. T. M. Knox (Oxford: Oxford University Press, 1946), pp. 17–23. See my discussion of Collingwood, below, chap. 6.

62. The discontinuity between a time without a present and a time with a present does not seem to me to be incompatible with C. F. von Weizsäcker's hypothesis concerning the irreversibility of physical processes and the termporal logic of probability. According to von Weizsäcker, quantum physics forces us to reinterpret the second law of thermodynamics, which links the direction of time to the entropy of a closed system, in terms of probabilities. The entropy of a given state must henceforth be conceived of as the measure of the probability of the occurrence of this state—more improbable earlier states being transformed into more probable later ones. If we ask what is meant by the terms "earlier" and "later" implied by the metaphors of the direction of time or the arrow of time, the renowned physicist replies that everyone in our culture, hence every physicist, implicitly understands the difference between past and future. The past is more like the order of facts; it is unalterable. The future is the possible. Probability, then, is a quantitative, mathematizable grasp of possibility. As for the probability of becoming, in the direct sense in which it is taken by physics here, it will always be in the future. It follows that the quantitative difference between past and future is not a consequence of the second law of thermodynamics. Instead it constitutes its phenomenological premise. It is only because we first have an understanding of this difference that we are able to do physics. Generalizing this thesis, we can say that this distinction is constitutive for the fundamental concept of experience. Experience draws a lesson from the past for the future. Time, in the sense of this qualitative difference between fact and possibility, is a condition for the possibility of experience. So, if experience presupposes time, the logic in which we describe the propositions express-

ing experience must be a logic of temporal statements, more precisely, a logic of future modalities—cf. "Zeit, Physick, Metaphysik," in *Die Erfahrung der Zeit. Gedenkenschrift für Georg Picht,* ed. Christian Link (Stuttgart: Klett-Cotta, 1984), pp. 22–24. Nothing in this argument challenges the distinction between instants as indistinguishable and the present as distinguishable. The qualitative difference between the past and the future is actually a phenomenological difference in the sense of Husserl and Heidegger. However, the proposition "the past is factual, the future possible," says more than this. It connects together lived-through experience, in which the distinction between past and future takes on meaning, and the notion of a course of events including the notions of an earlier state and a later one. The problem that remains has to do with the congruence of two irreversibilities: that of the relation past/future on the phenomenological plane, and that of the relation before/after on the plane of physical states, in which former states are considered to be more improbable and later ones more probable.

63. We shall return at length to the problem of dating within the framework of a study of connectors set in place by historical thought between cosmic time and phenomenological time.

64. This is perhaps the sense we should give to the bothersome expression *faktisch* in Heidegger. While adding a foreign accent to worldhood—an existential term—it clings to worldhood thanks to the phenomenon of contamination between the two orders of the discourse on time.

65. The objection of circularity that could easily be directed at the reversibility of all these analyses is no more threatening here than it was when I turned this argument against my own analyses in Part I in volume 1, when I introduced the stage of mimesis$_3$. Circularity is a healthy sign in any hermeneutical analysis. This suspicion of circularity can, in any event, be attributed to the basic aporetical character of the question of time.

SECTION TWO

1. *Time and Narrative,* 1:70–71.
2. Ibid., pp. 172–225.
3. Ibid., 2:100–152.
4. Ibid., 1:76–77.
5. Ibid., pp. 77–82.

CHAPTER FOUR

1. See above, p. 17.
2. *Physics,* IV, 12, 220b1–222a9.
3. We may characterize the following analysis as a transcendental one inasmuch as it is the universal aspect of the institution of the calendar that is addressed. Thus it is to be distinguished from, without rejecting, the genetic approach practiced by French sociology at the beginning of this century. There the problem of the calendar was treated within the framework of the social origin of reigning notions, including that of time. The danger for this school of thought was its making a collective consciousness the source of all these notions, somewhat like a Plotinian *Nous.* This danger was greatest in Durkheim, in his *The Elementary Forms of Religious Life,* for whom social origin and religious origin tended to become confused. It was less present in the work of Maurice Halbwachs cited above, p. 275, n. 3. There the project of a total genesis of concepts was reduced to more modest proportions, the collective memory being attributed to some specific group rather than to society in general. However, on oc-

casion, the problems of origins were well posed in terms of problems of structures. The differentiation of different moments, inherent in the conception of time, wrote Durkheim, "does not consist merely in a commemoration, either partial or integral, of our past life. It is an abstract and impersonal frame which surrounds, not only our individual existence, but that of humanity. It is like an unlimited chart, where all duration is spread out before the mind, and upon which all possible events can be located in relation to fixed and determinate guidelines. . . . This alone is enough to give us a hint that such an arrangement ought to be collective" (*Elementary Forms,* p. 23). The calendar is an appropriate instrument for this collective memory. "A calendar expresses the rhythm of the collective activities, while at the same time its function is to assure their regularity" (ibid.). Here is where a genetic sociology contributes in a decisive way to the description of the connectors used in history, whose significance rather than origin we are attempting to disentangle. The same thing may be said concerning inquiries into the history of calendars still in use today, such as the Julian-Gregorian calendar (cf. P. Couderc, *Le Calendrier* [Paris: Presses Universitaires de France, 1961]).

4. René Hubert, in "Etude sommaire de la représentation du temps dans la religion et la magie," in his *Mélanges d'histoire des religions* (Paris: Alcan, 1909), attaches great importance to the notion of a festival. On this ground, he proposes the idea of "critical dates" tied to the necessity of giving order to the periodicity of festivals. No less important is the fact that the intervals between such critical dates are qualified by the aftereffects of the festivals and made equivalent to one another by their return, given the reservation that, for magic and religion, the function of the calendar is not so much to measure time as to give it a rhythm, to assure the succession of lucky and unlucky days, of favorable and unfavorable times.

5. In a noteworthy text, "Temps et Mythe," *Recherches Philosophiques* 5 (1935–36): 235–51, Georges Dumézil strongly emphasizes the "amplitude" of mythical time, whatever differences there may be between myth and ritual. In the case where a myth is the narrative of events that are themselves periodic, the ritual assures the correspondence between mythical and ritual periodicity. In the case where a myth relates unique events, the efficacity of these founding events spreads over a broader stretch of time than that of the action recounted. Here again, ritual assures the correspondence between this longer stretch of time and the founding mythical event by commemoration and imitation, when it is a question of past events, or by prefiguration and preparation, when it is a question of future events. In a hermeneutics of historical consciousness, to commemorate, to actualize, and to prefigure are three functions that underline the scansion of the past as tradition, the present as actual, and the future as the horizon of expectation and as eschatological. On this point, see below, chap. 10.

6. Emile Benveniste, "Le langage et l'expérience humaine," *Diogène* no. 51 (1965): 3–13; reprinted in idem, *Problèmes de linguistique générale* (Paris: Gallimard, 1974) 2:67–78. I shall refer to this latter source.

7. I borrow this concept of *étayage* from Jean Granier, *Le Discours du monde* (Paris: Seuil, 1977), pp. 218ff.

8. The basic text here is chapter 4 of Schutz's *The Phenomenology of the Social World,* trans. George Walsh and Frederick Lehnert (Evanston: Northwestern University Press, 1967), pp. 139–214: "The Structure of the Social World: The Realm of Directly Experienced Social Reality, the Realm of Contemporaries, and the Realm of Predecessors."

9. Recall our earlier discussion of the problem, in *Being and Time,* posed by the passage from mortal temporality to public historicality (cf. above, pp. 67–68). It is worth noting that it is just at the moment of passing from the notion of individual fate (*Schicksal*) to our common destiny (*Geschick*) that Heidegger makes a brief allusion

to the concept of a "generation," encountered as I shall discuss further below in the work of Dilthey: "Dasein's fateful destiny in and with its 'generation' goes to make up the full authentic historicizing of Dasein" (*Being and Time*, p. 436). Heidegger acknowledges this reference to Dilthey in a footnote.

10. In Immanuel Kant, *Perpetual Peace and Other Essays*, trans. Ted Humphrey (Indianapolis: Hackett, 1983), pp. 29–40.

11. Cf. my discussion of his important essay on this topic below, pp. 111–12.

12. Dilthey discusses this problem in a study devoted to the history of the moral and political sciences: "Uber das Studium der Geschichte, der Wissenschaften vom Menschen, der Gesellschaft und dem Staat" (1875), reprinted in Wilhelm Dilthey, *Gesammte Schriften* (Leipzig: B. G. Teubner, 1924) 5:31–73. Only a few pages of this essay are directly related to our topic (pp. 36–41). Among the auxiliary concepts of this history, Dilthey is especially interested in those that constitute "the scaffolding [*das Gerüst*] of the course [*der Verlauf*] of intellectual movements" (ibid., p. 36). One of these is the concept of a generation. Dilthey also made use of this concept in his biography of Schleiermacher, without providing a theoretical justification for it or seeing the difficulties it involves. Mannheim's essay is more thoroughgoing in its analysis: Karl Mannheim, "The Problem of Generations," in idem, *Essays on the Sociology of Knowledge*, ed. Paul Kecskemeti (London: Routledge and Kegan Paul, 1952), pp. 276–322. He also gives a bibliography of the discussion to 1927, when this article was first published.

13. Other thinkers had noted how little individuals in the same age-group were each other's contemporaries, as well as how individuals of different ages could share the same ideals at a given historical moment. In the work of the art historian Pinter, Mannheim finds the notion of the noncontemporaneity of the contemporaneous (*Ungleichzeitigkeit des Gleichzeitigen*) (in "The Problem of Generations," p. 285). Its kinship to the Heideggerian concept of destiny (*Geschick*) is not concealed. Mannheim cites favorably the famous text from *Being and Time* discussed above in chapter 3.

14. Regarding the biological, psychological, cultural, and spiritual aspects of the notion of growing up, the standard work is still Michel Philibert, *L'Echelle des âges* (Paris: Seuil, 1968).

15. Nor does Dilthey make this idea of continuity, which allows for interruptions, steps backward, subsequent renewals, and tranfers from one culture to another, too rigid. What is essential is that the connection between old and new not suffer from total discontinuity. Below (in chapter 9), I shall take up again the discussion of this problem of continuity in history.

16. His source of inspiration in Husserl's work is the fifth *Cartesian Meditation*, in which Husserl attempts to give our knowledge of another person an intuitive status on the same level as that of self-reflection, by means of the analogical appresentation of the phenomenon of "pairing" (*Paarung*). However, unlike Husserl, Schutz takes as hopeless, useless, and even detrimental the enterprise of constituting our experience of the other person within (*in*) and starting from (*aus*) egological consciousness. Experience of the other person for Schutz is as primitive a given as is experience of one's own self, and, it should be added, just as immediate. This immediacy is not so much that of a cognitive operation as of a practical faith. We believe in the existence of the other person because we act upon and with that person, and because we are affected by that person's action. In this sense, Schutz rediscovers Kant's great insight in the *Critique of Practical Reason:* we do not know the other person, but we treat him or her as a person or a thing. The existence of the other is implicitly admitted by the mere fact that we comport ourselves toward this person in one way or another.

17. For Weber, too, "orientation toward the other" is a structure of *sociales Wirken* (cf. *Economy and Society*, ed Günther Roth and Claus Wittich, trans. Ephraim

Fischoff et al. [Berkeley: University of California Press, 1978], §§1 and 2). We practically affect and are affected by the other person.

18. *Ethics*, Part II, def. V, in *The Chief Works of Benedict Spinoza*, trans. R. H. Elwes (New York: Dover Books, 1955), 2:82.

19. It is not that imagination plays no role in those relationships Schutz takes as direct. My own motives already require, if they are to be clarified, a kind of imaginative reenactment. So do my partner's. When I ask you a question, for example, I imagine in the future perfect tense how you will have answered me. In this sense, even an allegedly direct social relationship is already symbolically mediated. The synchrony between two streams of consciousness is assured by the correspondence between the prospective motives of one of them and the explicative motives of the other.

20. "On the contrary, all experience of contemporaries is predicative in nature. It is formed by means of interpretive judgments involving all my knowledge of the social world, although with varying degrees of explicitness" (ibid., p. 183). It is particularly noteworthy that Schutz attributes the phenomenon of "recognition" to this abstract level, in a sense distinct from Hegel's, as "a synthesis of my own interpretations of his experiences" (p. 184). Whence his expression, a "synthesis of recognition" (ibid.).

21. I am following the broad distinction in Schutz's analysis between a we-orientation and a they-orientation, between a direct kind of orientation and an anonymous form based on typifications. Schutz takes great care to nuance this opposition with a careful study (at which he excels) of the degrees of anonymity in the world of contemporaries. The result is a series of figures that warrants the progression toward complete anonymity. For example, certain collective forms—a governing board, a state, a nation, a people, a class—are still close enough to us that we attribute responsible actions to them by analogy. Artificial objects, on the contrary (libraries, for example), are closer to the pole of anonymity.

22. It is even more curious that Schutz says so little about the world of successors. Undoubtedly this was due to the fact that he considers the social phenomenon as something that has already taken shape. This is why it only overlaps time up to the present now. But it is also because he puts too much emphasis on the determined, already accomplished aspect of the past. (This is debatable, insofar as the meaning of the past for us is constantly being reinterpreted.) It is why for Schutz the future has to be completely undetermined and undeterminable (cf. ibid., p. 214). (This too is debatable, insofar as, through our expectations, our fears, our hopes, our predictions, and our plans, the future is at least in part tied to our actions.) That the world of successors is by definition not historical is admissible; that it is therefore absolutely free is contestable as an implication. Below, I shall draw on the reflections of Reinhart Koselleck about our horizon of expectation to forge a more complete and more balanced conception of the world of contemporaries, of predecessors, and of successors. Schutz's major contribution to our problem is his having seen, on the basis of what is still a Husserlian phenomenology of intersubjectivity, the transitional role played by anonymity between private time and public time.

23. Criticism of the testimony of surviving witnesses is more difficult to carry out, due to the inextricable confusion with the quasi-present, remembered as it was experienced at the moment of the event, than is a reconstruction founded only on documents, without even taking into account the distortions inherent in the selection made due to interest—or disinterest—by memory.

24. "Since my knowledge of the world of predecessors comes to me through signs, what these signs signify is anonymous and detached from any stream of consciousness" (ibid., p. 209).

25. Recall our discussion of Braudel's masterpiece, *The Mediterranean and the Mediterranean World in the Age of Philip II*, trans, Siân Reynolds (New York: Harper

and Row, 1972), in volume 1. It is the Mediterranean itself, we said, that is the true hero of this epic that ends when the clash of great powers changed theaters. Who dies in this work? The answer is a tautology: only mortals die. We saw these mortals crossing mountains and plains, along with the nomads and the sheepherders. We saw them navigate over the liquid plains, leading "precarious lives" (ibid., p. 139) on inhospitable islands, laboring along land and sea routes. I said that nowhere in Braudel's immense work did I feel the pain humans suffer as much as in the first part, entitled "The Role of the Environment," for it is there that people are caught closest to living and dying. And could Braudel have called his second part "Collective Destinies and General Trends" if violence, war, and persecution did not ceaselessly refer the reader back from the collective destinies that make up global history to the unique destiny of human beings, each of whom suffers and each of whom dies? The lists of martyrs of those witnessing peoples—the Moors and the Jews—makes the bond between collective destiny and individual fate an indestructible one. This is why, when Braudel, reflecting upon the meaning of his work, asks if in minimizing the role of events and individuals he may have denied the importance of human freedom (ibid., p. 1243), we may ask instead if it is not death that history mishandles even though it is our memory of the dead. It cannot do otherwise inasmuch as death marks the lower bound of that microhistory that the historical reconstruction of the whole seeks to break away from. Yet, surely, it is the whisper of death that keeps Braudel from founding his "structuralism" on "the approach which under the same name is at present causing some confusion in the other human sciences," and that allows him to end by saying, "It does not tend towards the mathematical abstraction of relations expressed as functions, but instead towards the very sources of life in its most concrete, everyday, indestructible and anonymously human expression" (ibid., p. 1244).

26. Cf. François Wahl, "Les ancêtres, ça ne se représente pas," in *L'Interdit de la représentation* (Paris: Seuil, 1984), pp. 31–62.

27. *Perpetual Peace and Other Essays,* p. 30; my emphasis.

28. *Encyclopaedia Universalis* (Paris, 1968), 2:231.

29. *Encyclopaedia Brittanica* (Chicago, 1971), 2:326B.

30. Cf. Stephen Toulmin, *The Uses of Argument* (Cambridge: Cambridge University Press, 1958), pp. 94–145.

31. Regarding the constitution of archives, cf. T. R. Schellenberg, *Modern Archives: Principles and Techniques* (Chicago: University of Chicago Press, 1975); idem, *Management of Archives* (New York: Columbia University Press, 1965).

32. "Documento/Monumento," *Enciclopedia Einaudi* (Turin: Einaudi), 5:38–47.

33. Such a break is suggested by the conclusion to Le Goff's article. "The new document, extended beyond traditional texts—which are themselves transformed insofar as quantitative history is revealed to be possible and pertinent—to data must be treated as a document/monument. Whence the urgency to elaborate a new doctrine capable of transferring these document/monuments from the level of memory to that of historical science" (ibid., p. 47). The underlying assumption here is the opposition, introduced by Michel Foucault in his *The Archeology of Knowledge,* trans. A. M. Sheridan Smith (New York: Pantheon, 1972), between the continuity of memory and the discontinuity of the new documentary history. ("The document is not the fortunate tool of a history that is primarily and fundamentally *memory;* history is one way in which a society recognizes and develops a mass of documentation with which it is inextricably linked" [ibid., p. 6, cited by Le Goff, p. 45].) However, even though Le Goff does accept this opposition between memory, presumed to be continuous, and history, which has become discontinuous, he does not seem to exclude the possibility that the discontinuity of history, far from getting rid of memory, contributes to its enrichment by criticizing it. "The documentary revolution tends to promote a new unit of

information. Instead of the fact that leads to the event and to a linear history, to a progressive memory, the privileged position passes to the datum, which leads to the series and to a discontinuous history. Collective memory reevaluates itself, organizing itself into a cultural patrimony. The new document is stored in data bases and dealt with by means of such structures. A new discipline has arisen, one that is still taking its first steps, and that must respond in contemporary terms to the requirement for calculations as well as to the constantly increasing criticism of its influence on our collective memory" (ibid., p. 42). Foucault's opposition between the continuity of memory and the discontinuity of the history of ideas will be discussed further, within the context of an analysis devoted to the notion of tradition, owing to the place that the notion of discontinuity takes there (cf. below, pp. 142–56).

34. Marc Bloch's *The Historian's Craft,* trans. Peter Putnam (New York: Knopf, 1953), is filled with a number of terms taken to be synonymous with one another: "testimony," "remains," "vestiges," "residues," and finally "traces" (or in the English translation of Bloch's work: "tracks"). What "do we really mean by *document,* if it is not a 'track,' as it were—the mark, perceptible to the senses, which some phenomenon, in itself inaccessible, has left behind?" (p. 55). Everything is said here. But everything is an enigma.

35. Emile Littré, *Dictionaire de la langue française* (Paris, 1965), 7:1164–65.

36. J.-L. Austin, *How to Do Things with Words,* ed. J. O. Urmson (New York: Oxford University Press, 1965).

37. See above, chap. 3, n. 34.

38. *Being and Time,* p. 432.

39. Recall the text cited earlier: "We contend that what is *primarily* historical is Dasein. That which is *secondarily* historical, however, is what we encounter within-the-world [*innerweltlich*]—not only equipment ready-to-hand, in the widest sense, but also the environing *Nature* as the 'very soil of history'" (ibid., p. 433).

40. The remainder of the cited passage directly concerns my own proposal about the trace as one category of historical time: "It belongs to Dasein's average kind of Being, and to that understanding of Being which proximally prevails. Thus proximally and for the most part, even *history* gets understood *publicly* as happening *within-time*" (ibid.; his emphases).

41. The difficulty in pinning down the use of the term *faktisch* in *Being and Time* also bears witness to this fact.

42. Emmanuel Lévinas, "La Trace," in *Humanisme de l'autre homme* (Montpellier: Fata Morgana, 1972), pp. 57–63.

43. As was the case in each of the three works we considered at the end of Part III in volume 2: *Mrs. Dalloway, Der Zauberberg,* and *A la recherche du temps perdu.*

CHAPTER FIVE

1. With few exceptions, the analyses that follow refer without explicitly quoting them to the literary texts analyzed at the end of Part III in volume 2 and the phenomenological theories discussed at the beginning of Part IV in this volume.

2. This method of correlation implies that we be attentive exclusively to the discoveries made by fiction as such and to their philosophical lessons, in contrast to all the attempts, however legitimate these may be in their own order, to spot a philosophical influence at the origin of the literary work under consideration. I have already expressed my reasons for this position on several occasions. Cf. *Time and Narrative,* 2:190, n. 23, and 132–33.

3. Comparing this with the solution contributed by history to the aporias of time calls for considering these aporias in the opposite order to that we encountered in our

aporetics of time. We move in this way from the aporias that phenomenology invents to those it discovers. The didactic advantages of the strategy adopted here are not negligible. First of all, we thereby go straight to the principle underlying the dissymmetry between fiction and history. Next, we avoid the trap of limiting fiction to the exploration of internal time-consciousness, as if the function of fiction, with respect to the antagonism between the rival perspectives on time, were limited to a simple retreat outside the field of conflict. On the contrary, it is up to fiction to explore this very antagonism in its own way, by submitting it to specific variations. Finally, fiction's treatment of the aporias that are constitutive of phenomenological time will take on new relief as a result of being placed against the background of the confrontation, at the heart of fiction, between phenomenological time and cosmic time. The full range of nonlinear aspects of time will, therefore, be unfolded before us.

4. Cf. Husserl, *Ideas*, §111.

5. *Time and Narrative*, 1:87.

6. Cf. J.-P. Vernant, *Myth and Thought among the Greeks* (London: Routledge and Kegan Paul, 1983), pp. 88–91. It is at the stage of personifications of time that fiction renews its relations with myth.

7. On these emblematic expressions in Proust, see Hans-Robert Jauss, *Zeit und Erinnerung in Marcel Prousts A la recherche du temps perdu (Heidelberg: Carl Winter, 1955)*.

8. For this expression borrowed from Dilthey (*Zusammenhang des Lebens*), see above, p. 111. I shall return in the closing pages of this work to the same problem under a new title, that of narrative identity. This notion will crown the union of history and fiction under the aegis of the phenomenology of time.

Chapter Six

1. Karl Heussi, *Die Krisis des Historismus* (Tübingen, J. C. B. Mohr, 1932): "eine zutreffende Entsprechung des im 'Gegenüber' Gewesenen" (p. 48).

2. "Historical conceptions are *Vertretungen* meant to signify [*bedeuten*] what once was [*was . . . einst war*] in a considerably more complicated way open to inexhaustible description" (ibid.). Contrary to Theodor Lessing, for whom history alone confers sense on the nonsensical (the *sinnlos*), this *Gegenüber* imposes a directive and a corrective on historical research, removing it from the arbitrariness that seems to affect the work of selection and organization that the historian performs. Otherwise, how could the work of one historian correct that of another and claim to be closer to what happened (*treffen*)? Heussi also caught sight of those features of the *Gegenüber* that make standing-for such a riddle for historical knowledge, namely (following Troeltsch), the overwhelming richness of this *Gegenüber*, which inclines it toward the side of meaninglessness, along with the multivocal structures of the past, which draw it toward intelligibility. In sum, the past consists of "the plenitude of possible incitations to historical configuration" (*die Fülle der möglichen Anreize zu historischer Gestaltung*) (ibid., p. 49).

3. This term, *représentance,* is found in François Wahl, ed., *Qu'est-ce que le structuralisme?* (Paris: Seuil, 1968), p. 11.

4. In this regard, Bloch's *Historian's Craft* is revealing. He is quite aware of the problem of the trace, which arises for him by way of the notion of a document ("what do we really mean by *document,* if it is not a 'trace,' as it were—the mark, perceptible to the senses, which some phenomenon, in itself inaccessible, has left behind?" [ibid., p. 55; trans. altered]). This enigmatic reference to the trace is immediately attached to the notion of indirect observation familiar to the empirical sciences, insofar as the physicist or the geographer, for example, depend on observations made by others. Of

course, the historian, unlike the physicist, cannot provoke the appearance of the trace. But this infirmity of historical observation is compensated for in two ways: the historian can multiply the number of reports by witnesses and confront them with one another. In this sense, Bloch speaks of evidence converging from "sources of many different kinds" (ibid., p. 67). Above all, he can emphasize those documents that are "witnesses in spite of themselves" (ibid., p. 61), that is, those documents not intended to inform or instruct their contemporaries, much less future historians. However, for a philosophical investigation into the ontological import of the notion of a trace, this concern to indicate how knowledge by means of traces belongs to the realm of observation tends to conceal the enigmatic character of the notion of a trace *of the past*. Authenticated testimony functions like a proxy eyewitness observation. We see through the eyes of someone else. An illusion of contemporaneity is thereby created that allows us to equate knowledge by traces with knowledge by indirect observation. Yet no one has more magnificently underscored the tie between history and time than Marc Bloch has when he defines history as the science "of men in time" (ibid., p. 27).

5. R. G. Collingwood, *The Idea of History* (New York: Oxford University Press, 1956), is a posthumous work first published under the editorship of T. M. Knox in 1946, based on a series of lectures Collingwood wrote in 1936, following his inauguration as Waynflete Professor of Metaphysical Philosophy at Oxford, and then revised up to 1940. The editor has brought together in Part V, entitled "Epilogomena," the most systematic parts of the work finished by Collingwood (ibid., pp. 205–324).

6. In the plan adopted by the editor of *The Idea of History,* the section on "History as Reenactment of Past Experience" (pp. 282–302) expressly follows the section on "The Historical Imagination" (pp. 231–49), which was Collingwood's inaugural lecture at Oxford, and the section on "Historical Evidence," where the concept of human history is opposed to the concept of human nature, and where the concept of reenactment is dealt with directly without passing through reflection upon the imagination. This order of exposition makes sense if reenactment, without constituting the methodological procedure characteristic of history, defines its telos and as such its place in knowledge. To emphasize the philosophical more than the epistemological character of the concept of reenactment, I shall follow the order: documentary evidence, historical imagination, history as the reenactment of past experience.

7. For Collingwood, the question is not so much knowing how history is to be distinguished from the natural sciences as whether there can be another knowledge of man than historical knowledge. He gives a clearly negative answer to this question, for the quite simple reason that the concept of human history comes to occupy the place assigned by Locke and Hume to that of human nature: "the right way of investigating mind is by the methods of history" (ibid., p. 209). "History is what the science of human nature professed to be" (ibid.). "The Science of human mind resolves itself into history" (ibid., p. 220). Collingwood calls the "interpretation of evidence" (ibid., pp. 9–10) what I am here calling documentary proof. (The English word "evidence" rarely can be translated into French by *évidence,* and then principally with reference to juridical matters from which the theory of history borrows it.) In this regard, he says, "evidence is a collective name for things which singly are called documents, and a document is a thing existing here and now, of such a kind that the historian, by thinking about it, can get answers to the questions he asks about past events" (ibid., p. 10).

8. The semiological aspect of the problem is evident, although Collingwood does not use this term. External changes are not what historians consider but what they look through to discern the thought that resides in them (ibid., p. 214). This relationship between outside and inside corresponds to what Dilthey designates as *Ausdruck* (expression).

9. Cf. Elizabeth Anscombe, *Intention* (Oxford: Basil Blackwell, 1957), p. 72.

10. "Philosophy is reflective. . . . thought about thought" (*The Idea of History*, p. 1). On the historical plane the *Gegenüber* of proof is the "past, consisting of particular events in space and time which are no longer happening" (ibid., p. 5). Or, again, "actions of human beings that have been done in the past" (ibid., p. 9). The question is "How do historians know? How do they come to apprehend the past?" (idib., p. 3). The accent on the aspect of the past means that the question can only be dealt with by people qualified in two respects: they must be historians who are experienced in their profession, and they must be philosophers capable of reflecting on this experience.

11. "All thinking is critical thinking; the thought which re-enacts past thoughts, therefore, criticizes them in re-enacting them" (ibid., p. 216). If, in fact, the cause is the inside of the event, only a long effort of interpretation allows us to envisage ourselves in the situation, to think for ourselves what an agent in the past thought it appropriate to do.

12. The relationship between historical evidence and our imagination situates historical research wholly within the logic of questions and answers. This logic was presented in Collingwood's *An Autobiography* (Oxford: Oxford University Press, 1939). Gadamer pays homage to it in his own attempt to make this logic the equivalent of the dialogical method of Plato, following the failure of Hegel. Collingwood, in this regard, is a precursor: "Question and evidence, in history, are correlative. Anything is evidence which enables you to answer your question—the question you are asking now" (*The Idea of History*, p. 281).

13. Collingwood can even appeal to Kant's saying about the imagination, that "blind but indispensable faculty," which "does the entire work of historical construction" (ibid., p. 241). Only the historical imagination has "as its special task to imagine the past" (ibid., p. 242). We are thus at the antipodes of the idea of eyewitness testimony transmitted by authorized sources. "So there are properly speaking no data" (ibid., p. 249). The idealism inherent in this thesis of an a priori imagination breaks out in the concluding lines of the section devoted to it: we have to take the historical imagination as "a self-dependent, self-determining, and self-justifying form of thought" (ibid., p. 249). We must even go so far as a quasi-identification of the work of the historian with that of the novelist to do full justice to the concept of reenactment: "Both the novel and history are self-explanatory, self-justifying, the product of an autonomous or self-authorizing activity; and in both cases this activity is the *a priori* imagination" (ibid., p. 246).

14. In this respect, Rex Martin's proposal, in *Historical Explanation: Reenactment and Practical Inference* (Ithaca: Cornell University Press, 1977), to bring about a rapprochement between reenactment and practical inference constitutes the most fruitful attempt I know to link Collingwood to the philosophy of history of Danto, Walsh, and above all von Wright. Imagination, practical inference, and reenactment have to be thought together.

15. The Roman constitution, or its modification by Augustus, when rethought is no less an eternal object than is a triangle for Whitehead: "The peculiarity which makes it historical is not the fact of its happening in time, but the fact of its becoming known to us by our re-thinking the same thought which created the situation we are investigating, and thus coming to understand that situation" (*The Idea of History*, p. 218).

16. "Thus the historical process is a process in which man creates for himself this or that kind of human nature by re-creating in his own thought the past to which he is heir" (ibid., p. 226). The "historian must re-enact the past in his own mind" (ibid., p. 282). The idea of reenactment thus tends to become substituted completely for testimony, the force of which is to maintain the otherness of the witness and the otherness of what this witness testifies to.

17. *The Idea of History* uses several equivalent expressions: "the subject-matter of history" is not the individual act as it occurred but "the act of thought itself, in its survival and revival at different times and in different persons" (ibid., p. 303). This implies recognizing "the activity of the self as a single activity persisting through the diversity of its own acts" (ibid., p. 306). This object "must be of such a kind that it can revive itself in the historian's mind; the historian's mind must be such as to offer a home for that revival" (ibid., p. 304). "Historical knowledge, then, has for its proper object thought: not things thought about, but the act of thinking itself" (ibid., p. 305).

18. This concern for distanciation is quite strong among French historians. François Furet recommends at the beginning of his book *Interpreting the French Revolution*, trans. Elborg Forster (Cambridge: Cambridge University Press; Paris: Editions de la Maison des Sciences de l'Homme, 1981), that intellectual curiosity break away from the spirit of commemoration or execration. *Un autre Moyen Age*, to use the French title of one of Jacques Le Goff's books—*Time, Work and Culture in the Middle Ages*, trans. Arthur Goldhammer (Chicago: University of Chicago Press, 1980)—is a Middle Ages that is "other" than us. And Paul Veyne, in his *L'Inventaire des Différences* (Paris: Seuil, 1976), says "The Romans existed in a manner both as exotic and as ordinary as that of the Tibetans, for example, or the Mabikwara—nothing more and nothing less—so it becomes impossible any longer to consider them as a sort of leading example" (p. 8).

19. This model was sufficiently seductive to inspire both Raymond Aron and Henri Marrou. The first part of Section II of Aron's *Introduction to the Philosophy of History*, trans. George J. Irwin (Boston: Beacon Press, 1961), entitled "From the Individual to History," proceeds from self-knowledge to knowledge of others, and from there to historical knowledge. In its details, it is true, the argument tends to break up the apparent progression suggested by this plan. But the coincidence of a self with itself being impossible (ibid., p. 56), others constitute the true mediator between me and my self. In turn, our knowledge of others never adds up to a fusion of consciousnesses but always requires the mediation of signs, so that, finally, historical knowledge, founded upon works originating from such consciousnesses, is revealed to be as originary as the knowledge of others and self-knowledge. Consequently, for Aron, "the ideal of resurrection is not so much inaccessible as it is alien to history" (ibid., p. 77). If for Henri Marrou, on the other hand, understanding others remains the basic model for historical knowledge, this is for reasons that have to do with his conjoining of epistemology with ethics in historical knowledge. Understanding others today and understanding people from the past share the same (essentially ethical) dialectic of the Same and the Other. On the one hand, we basically know what resembles us; on the other hand, understanding others demands that we practice an epoché of our own preferences in order to understand the other person as other than ourselves. It is the suspicious temperament of positivist historiography that prevents us from recognizing the identity in the bond of friendship that links us and others today and us and others from earlier times. This bond is more essential than that of curiosity, which, in fact, keeps the other at a distance.

20. Both the approaches referred to in the previous note have often been criticized by analytic philosophy owing to the similar paradoxes they raise for a philosophy that makes empirical knowledge, hence present observation, the ultimate criterion of verification. Their assertions about other people are empirically neither verifiable nor refutable. They also share, to a certain point, the ability of exchanging places, inasmuch as it is principally the actions of human beings like us that history seeks to rejoin in the past, and inasmuch as the knowledge of others contains, even more than does understanding oneself, the same gap between lived experience and retrospection. However, this does not mean that the problem is the same in both cases.

21. Cf. Paul Veyne, "La Conceptualisation historique," in *Faire de l'histoire*, ed. Jacques Le Goff and Pierre Nora (Paris: Gallimard, 1974), 1:62–92. Weber's method of ideal types anticipated this movement of thought. But it is French historiography that has most accentuated the effect of taking a distance tied to historical conceptualization. To conceptualize is to break away from the point of view, the lack of knowledge and illusions, and the whole language of past people. It is already to distance them from ourselves in time. To conceptualize is to adopt the ethnologist's attitude of mere curiosity—if not that of the entomologist.

22. The invariant, declares Veyne, "explains its own historical modifications on the basis of its internal complexity. Beginning from this complexity, it also explains its eventual disappearance" (*L'Inventaire des différences*, p. 24). Thus Roman imperialism, for example, is one of the two great variants of the invariant of a political power's search for security. Instead of seeking such security by means of an equilibrium with other political powers, as in the Greek variant, Roman imperialism seeks it by means of the conquest of the whole human horizon "to its limits, to the sea or to the barbarians, in order finally to be the only one left in the world when everything has been conquered" (p. 17).

23. "Hence the conceptualization of an invariant allows us to explain events. By playing with the variables, we may recreate, on the basis of the invariant, the diversity of historical modifications" (ibid., pp. 18–19). And even more strongly: "only the invariant individualizes" (ibid., p. 19).

24. Veyne will go so far as to say that "the historical facts may be individualized without being set in their place in a spatio-temporal context" (ibid., p. 48). And even that "history does not study humanity in time—it studies human materials subsumed under concepts" (ibid., p. 50). History may be defined at this price as the "science of differences, of individualities" (ibid., p. 52).

25. Cf. "L'Opération historique," in *Faire de l'histoire*, 1:3–41.

26. "To envisage history as an operation will be to attempt . . . to understand it as the relationship between a *place* (a recruiting headquarters, a milieu, a profession, etc.) and some *procedures* of analysis (a discipline)" (ibid., p. 4).

27. This argument will not surprise readers of Horkheimer and Adorno, the great masters of the Frankfurt School, who showed the same will-to-domination to be at work in the rationalism of the Enlightenment. We also find a related form in the early works of Habermas, where the claim of instrumental reason to annex the historical-hermeneutical sciences is denounced. Some of de Certeau's statements go much further in the direction of classical Marxism and suggest a too linear and mechanical relation, to my taste, between historical production and social organization. For example, "from the assembling of the documents to the editing of the book, historical practice is entirely relative to the structure of society" (ibid., p. 13). "Throughout, history remains configured by the system wherein it is elaborated" (ibid., p. 16). On the other hand, what he says about the production of documents and the "redistribution of space" that it implies (ibid., p. 22) is quite illuminating.

28. The rest of this text is quite eloquent: "to take up again an old name which no longer corresponds with its new trajectory, we may say that [research] does not begin from 'rarities' (remains of the past) to arrive at a synthesis (present understanding), but rather it begins from a formalization (a present system) in order to give rise to 'remains' (indices of its limits and in that way a 'past' that is the product of labor)" (ibid., p. 27).

29. With this formula, Ranke defined the ideal of historical objectivity. "History had assigned to it the task of judging the past, of instructing the present for the benefit of ages to come. The present study does not assume such a high office; it wants to show only what actually happened [*Wie es eigentlich gewesen*]" (*Geschichten der ro-*

manischen und germanischen Völker von 1494–1514, in *Fürsten und Völker*, ed. Willy Andreas [Wiesbaden, 1957], p. 4, cited by Leonard Krieger, *Ranke: The Meaning of History* [Chicago: University of Chicago Press, 1977], p. 5.) This well-known Rankean principle does not express the ambition of reaching the past *itself*, with no mediating interpretation, so much as the historian's vow to divest himself of all personal preferences, to "extinguish my own self, as it were, to let the things speak and the mighty forces appear that have arisen in the course of centuries," as Ranke put it in his *Uber die Epochen der neueren Geschichte* (in ibid.).

30. Hayden White, *Metahistory: The Historical Imagination in Nineteenth-Century Europe* (Baltimore: Johns Hopkins University Press, 1973). *The Tropics of Discourse* (Baltimore: Johns Hopkins University Press, 1978) is the title of a collection of his essays that were published between 1966 and 1977. I shall focus on the following essays, which come after *Metahistory:* "The Historical Text as Literary Artifact," "Historicism, History and the Figurative Imagination," and "The Fictions of Factual Representation."

31. "I will consider the historical work as what it most manifestly is—that is to say, a verbal structure in the form of a narrative prose discourse that purports to be a model, or icon, of past structures and processes in the interest of *explaining what they were by representing* them" (*Metahistory*, p. 2; his emphasis). Further on, White repeats that "historical accounts purport to be verbal models, or icons, of specific segments of the historical process" (ibid., p. 30). Similar expressions are also found in the articles subsequent to *Metahistory:* the ambition of choosing "the plot structure that he considers most appropriate for ordering events of that kind so as to make them into a comprehensible story" (*Tropics*, p. 84). The subtlety of the historian lies in "matching up a specific plot structure with the set of events that he wishes to endow with a meaning of a particular kind" (ibid., p. 85). In these two images—most appropriate, matched up—the whole problem of re-presentation of the past is posed along with the operation of emplotment.

32. "This preconceptual linguistic protocol will in turn be—by virtue of its essentially *prefigurative* nature—characterizable in terms of the dominant tropological mode in which it is cast" (*Metahistory*, p. 30; his emphasis). It is not called prefigurative in my sense (mimesis₁), that is, as a structure of human praxis prior to the work of configuration by the historical or the fictional narrative, but in the sense of a linguistic operation unfolding on the level of the as yet unsorted mass of documentary evidence. "By identifying the dominant mode (or modes) of discourse, one penetrates to that level of consciousness on which a world of experience is *constituted* prior to being analyzed" (ibid., p. 33; his emphasis).

33. This is why, in opposition to the binarism in vogue in linguistics and structural anthropology, Hayden White returns to the four tropes of Ramus and Vico. His essay on the "Historical Text as Literary Artifact" presents a detailed criticism of Jakobson's binarism. It is not surprising, in this regard, that *Tropics of Discourse* contains several essays devoted either directly or indirectly to Vico, who is revealed to be White's real master, assisted by Kenneth Burke and his *Grammar of Motives* (Berkeley: University of California Press, 1969). The expression "master-tropes" comes from this latter work.

34. At least, this is how I understand the following assertion, which is disconcerting at first sight: "Irony, Metonomy, and Synecdoche are kinds of Metaphor, but they differ from one another in the kinds of *reductions* or *integrations* they effect on the literal level of their meanings and by the kinds of illuminations they aim at on the figurative level. Metaphor is essentially *representational*, Metonomy is *reductionist*, Synecdoche is *integrative*, and Irony is *negational*" (*Metahistory*, p. 34; his emphases).

35. This problem is taken up again in the essay "Fictions of Factual Representation" (*Tropics*, pp. 122–34). Metaphor emphasizes resemblance, metonomy continuity,

hence the dispersion into mechanical connections (where Burke is responsible for the characterization of dispersion as "reduction"). Synecdoche emphasizes the relation of the part to the whole, hence integration and therefore holistic or organicist interpretations. In irony, finally, its attitude of suspension emphasizing contradiction, we have the aporia that emphasizes the inadequacy of every characterization. White also recalls what he had said in *Metahistory* about the affinity between each trope and a mode of emplotment: metaphor and romance, metonymy and tragedy, etc.

36. The Introduction to *Tropics of Discourse*, "Tropology, Discourse, and Modes of Human Consciousness" (ibid., pp. 1–25), gives a more ambitious function to the "tropical element in all discourse, whether of the realistic or the more imaginative kind" (ibid., pp. 1–2), than that assigned it in *Metahistory*. Tropology now covers every deviation leading from one meaning toward another meaning, "with full credit to the possibility that things might be expressed otherwise" (ibid., p. 2). Its field is no longer confined just to prefiguration of the historical field, it extends to every kind of pre-interpretation. Tropology thus carries the colors of rhetoric against those of logic, especially when understanding endeavors to make the unfamiliar or the alien familiar by means not reducible to logical proof. Its role is so broad and so fundamental that it becomes, progessively, equivalent to a cultural critique with a rhetorical slant in every realm where consciousness, in its cultural praxis, begins to reflect critically upon its setting. Every new encoding is, at some deep level, figurative.

37. "This conception of historical discourse permits us to consider the specific story as an *image* of the events *about which* the story is told, while the generic story-type serves as a *conceptual model* to which the events are to be likened, in order to permit their encodation as elements of a recognizable structure" (ibid., p. 110; his emphases). The division into the rhetoric of tropes and the logic of modes of explanation is substituted for the much too elementary distinction between fact (information) and interpretation (explanation). Conversely, their retroimbrication allows White to reply to Lévi-Strauss's paradox in *The Savage Mind* (Chicago: University of Chicago Press, 1966), where history is to be placed beteween a microlevel, where events are dissolved into aggregates of physical-chemical impulses, and a macrolevel, where history gets lost in the huge cosmologies that mark the ascent and the decline of earlier civilizations. There is thus a rhetorical solution to the paradox that an excess of information prevents understanding and an excess of understanding impoverishes information (*Tropics,* p. 102). To the extent that the work of prefiguration adjusts fact and explanation to each other, it allows history to maintain itself halfway between the extremes accentuated by Lévi-Strauss.

38. This prefiguration means that our histories are limited to mere "metaphorical statements which suggest a relation of similitude between such events and processes and the story types that we conventionally use to endow the events of our lives with culturally sanctioned meanings" (*Tropics,* p. 88).

39. White himself is not unaware of this peril. This is why he wants us to understand "what is fictive in every putatively realistic representation of the world and what is realistic in all manifestly fictive ones" (ibid.). Another passage says the same thing: "In my view, we experience the 'fictionalization' of history as an 'explanation' for the same reason that we experience great fiction as an illumination of a world that we inhabit along with the author. In both we recognize the forms by which consciousness both constitutes and colonizes the world it seeks to inhabit comfortably" (ibid., p. 99). With this declaration, White is not very far from what I shall consider below as the interweaving reference of fiction and history. But since he hardly shows us what is realistic in all fiction, only the fictional side of the purported realistic representation of the world is accentuated.

40. "The implication is that historians *constitute* their subjects as possible objects

of narrative representation by the very language they use to *describe* them" (ibid., p. 95; his emphases).

41. Hayden White quite readily agrees: for him, the novel and history are not just indiscernible as verbal artifacts, both aspire to present a verbal image of reality. The one does not have a vocation of coherence while the other aims at correspondence, both of them aim, in different ways, at both coherence and correspondence. "It is in these twin senses that all written discourse is cognitive in its aims and mimetic in its means" (ibid., p. 122). Similarly, "history is not less a form of fiction than the novel is a form of historical representation" (ibid.).

42. My notion of a debt, applied to our relation to the historical past, has some kinship with the one that runs throughout the work of Michel de Certeau, and which is given a condensed expression in his essay that concludes *L'Ecriture de l'histoire* (Paris: Gallimard, 1975), pp. 312–58. His theme seems limited. It has to do with the relation of Freud to his own people, the Jewish people, as it appears in *Moses and Monotheism.* However, it is the whole fate of historiography that betrays itself there, insofar as, in this late work, Freud wandered into the foreign territory of historians, which thereby became his "Egypt." In so becoming an "Egyptian Moses," Freud repeats in his historical "novel" the twofold relation of contestation and belonging-to, of departing and of a debt, that henceforth characterizes the Jew. If Certeau puts the principal accent on depossession, on the loss of the land of birth, exile to a foreign land, it is the obligation of the debt that dialectizes this loss and this exile, transforming them into a work of mourning, and that becomes the beginning of writing and the book, owing to the impossibility of having a place of one's own. "Debt and departure" (ibid., p. 328) thus become the "no place of a death that binds" (ibid., p. 329). By so linking debt to loss, de Certeau places more emphasis than I do on the "tradition of a death" (ibid., p. 329), and underemphasizes, in my opinion, the positive aspect of the life that has been, in virtue of which life is also the heritage of living potentialities. Nevertheless I rejoin him when I include otherness in this debt. Loss is assuredly a figure of otherness. That the writing of history does more than play a trick on death is already indicated by the close tie between the restitution of this debt and the return of the repressed, in the psychoanalytic sense of this term. We cannot repeat enough that the dead, for whom history mourns, were once living. We shall see, in terms of some reflections on tradition, how expectation turned toward the future and the destitution of everything historical by the untimeliness of the present dialectize this debt, at the same time that this debt dialectizes the loss.

Chapter Seven

1. Hans-Georg Gadamer, *Truth and Method,* trans. and ed. by Garrett Barden and John Cumming (New York: Seabury, 1975).

2. Gadamer willingly refers to the distinction, inherited from biblical hermeneutics during the era of pietism, between three "subtilities": *subtilitas comprehendi, subtilitas explicandi,* and *subtilitas applicandi.* Together these three subtilities constitute interpretation. It is in a sense similar to this that I speak elsewhere of the hermeneutic arch that emerges out of life, crosses through the literary work, and returns to life. Application constitutes the final segment of this arch.

3. See my essay "Appropriation" in Paul Ricoeur, *Hermeneutics and the Human Sciences,* trans. and ed. John B. Thompson (Cambridge: Cambridge University Press; Paris: Editions de la Maison des Sciences de l'homme, 1981), pp. 182–93.

4. In my conclusion I will return to this distinction between "in" and "beyond" reading.

5. See *Time and Narrative,* 1:70.

6. Wayne Booth, *The Rhetoric of Fiction* (Chicago: University of Chicago Press, 1961; 2d. ed., 1981). The second edition contains an important Afterword. This work's objective, we read in the Preface, is to pursue "the author's means of controlling his reader." And further: "My subject is the technique of non-didactic fiction, viewed as the art of communicating with readers—the rhetorical resources available to the writer of epic, novel, or short story as he tries, consciously or unconsciously, to impose his fictional world upon the reader." The psychological analysis of written texts (psychographics) is not, for all that, stripped of all rights; a genuine problem stemming from the psychology of creation remains—that of understanding why and how a real author adopts a particular disguise, this mask rather than that one; in short, why and how the author assumes the "second self" that makes him an "implied author." The problem of the complex relations between the real author and the various official versions he gives of himself fully remains (ibid., p. 71). Cf. also Booth's essay, contemporary with *The Rhetoric of Fiction*, "Distance and Point of View" in *Essays in Criticism* 11 (1961): 60–79.

7. As Booth says, "though the author can to some extent choose his disguises, he can never choose to disappear" (*The Rhetoric of Fiction*, p. 20).

8. The realism of subjectivity is only apparently opposed to naturalistic realism. As realism it stems from the same rhetoric as does its contrary, striving for the apparent effacement of the author.

9. See Jean Pouillon, *Temps et Roman* (Paris: Gallimard, 1946).

10. In this respect Sartre's polemic against Mauriac seems quite pointless. (Jean-Paul Sartre, "François Mauriac and Freedom," in *Literary and Philosophical Essays*, trans. Annette Michelson (New York: Collier Books, 1962), pp. 7–25.) In assuming the raw realism of subjectivity, the novelist takes himself to be God no less than does the omniscient narrator. Sartre grossly underestimates the tacit agreement that confers upon the novelist the right to know what he is attempting to write about. It may be one of the clauses of this contract that the novelist know nothing at all or not be allowed the right to know the mind of a character except through someone else's eyes; but jumping from one viewpoint to another remains a considerable privilege, compared to our resources for knowing other people in so-called "real" life.

11. Whether "an impersonal novelist hides behind a single narrator or observer, the multiple points of view of *Ulysses* or *As I Lay Dying*, or the objective surfaces of *The Awkward Age* or Compton-Burnett's *Parents and Children*, the author's voice is never really silenced. It is, in fact, one of the things we read fiction for" (*The Rhetoric of Fiction*, p. 60).

12. Once again, these considerations do not lead us back to a psychology of the author; what the reader discerns in the markings of the text is the implied author. "We infer [the implied author] as an ideal, literary, created version of the real man; he is the sum of his own choices" (ibid., p. 75). This "second self" is the creation of the work. The author creates an image of himself, just as he does of me, the reader.

13. G. G. Granger, *Essai d'une philosophie du style* (Paris: Armand Colin, 1968).

14. In the opening lines of *The Rhetoric of Fiction*, it is stated that "one of the most obviously artificial devices of the storyteller is the trick of going beneath the surface of the action to obtain a reliable view of a character's mind and heart" (ibid., p. 3). Booth defines this category in the following way. "I have called a narrator *reliable* when he speaks for or acts in accordance with the norms of the work" (ibid., p. 158; his emphasis).

15. According to Booth, a narrative in which the author's voice can no longer be discerned, in which the point of view continually shifts, and in which reliable narrators are impossible to identify, creates a confused vision, and plunges its readers into confusion. After praising Proust for guiding his reader toward an unambiguous illumi-

nation in which author, narrator, and reader join one another on the intellectual level, Booth does not conceal his misgivings about Camus's strategy in *The Fall*. Here the narrator seems to him to draw the reader into Clamence's spiritual collapse. Booth is certainly not mistaken to stress the higher and higher price that has to be paid for a narration that lacks the counsel of a reliable narrator. He may even be justified in fearing that a reader who is thrown into confusion, mystified, puzzled, to the point of being "thrown off balance" will be secretly tempted to give up the task that Erich Auerbach ascribed to narration: "To give meaning and order to our lives" (ibid., p. 371, quoting *Mimesis: The Representation of Reality in Western Literature*, trans. Willard Trask [Princeton: Princeton University Press, 1953], pp. 485–86). The danger is indeed that persuasion will give way to the seduction of perversity. This is the problem posed by the "seductive rogues" who narrate much modern fiction (ibid., p. 379). Above all, however, Booth is right to stress, in contrast to every allegedly neutral aesthetic, that the viewpoint of characters as it is communicated to and imposed upon the reader possesses not only psychological and aesthetic aspects but social and moral ones as well.

His whole polemic centered on the unreliable narrator tends to show that the rhetoric of impartiality, of impassibility, conceals a secret commitment capable of seducing readers and of making them share, for example, an ironic interest in the fate of a character apparently bent on self-destruction. Wayne Booth can thus fear that a great part of contemporary literature goes astray, caught up in a demoralizing operation that is all the more effective in that the rhetoric of persuasion resorts to a more deeply hidden strategy. We may nevertheless wonder who is the judge of what is finally pernicious. If it is true that the ridiculous and odious trial of *Madame Bovary* does not justify *a contrario* every sort of insult to the strict minimum of ethical consensus without which no community could survive, it is also true that even the most pernicious, the most perverse attempt at seduction—the attempt, for instance, to ascribe value to the degradation of women, to cruelty and torture, to racial discrimination, or to advocate disinvolvement, ridicule (in short, ethical divestment), to the exclusion of any broader or higher system of values—can, at the limit, on the level of the imaginary, possess an ethical function: serving as a means of distanciation.

16. Henry James, *The Art of the Novel*, ed. R. P. Blackmur (New York: Charles Schribner's Sons, 1934), pp. 153–54.

17. This is why Booth can only mistrust authors who generate confusion. All his admiration is reserved for those who create not only clarity but worthy universal values as well. His reply to his critics appears in the Afterword to the second edition of *The Rhetoric of Fiction*, "The Rhetoric in Fiction and Fiction as Rhetoric: Twenty-One Years Later" (ibid., pp. 401–57). In another essay, "The Way I Loved George Elliot: Friendship with Books as a Neglected Metaphor," *Kenyon Review* 11:2 (1980): 4–27, he introduces into the dialogical relation between the text and the reader the model of friendship he finds in Aristotelian ethics. He thereby links up with Henri Marrou, who spoke of the relation of the historian to the people of the past. Reading, too, according to Booth can be enriched by the reappearance of a virtue that was so dear to the ancients.

18. "In short, the writer should worry less about whether his *narrators* are realistic than about whether the *image he creates of himself*, his implied author, is one that his most intelligent and perceptive readers can admire" (*The Rhetoric of Fiction*, p. 395; his emphasis). "When human actions are formed to make an art work, the form that is made can never be divorced from the human meanings, including the moral judgments, that are implicit whenever human beings act" (ibid., p. 397).

19. "The author makes his readers. . . . But if he makes them well—that is makes them see what they have never seen before, moves them into a new order of perception

and experience altogether—he finds his reward in the peers he has created" (ibid., pp. 397–98).

20. Michel Charles, *Rhétorique de la lecture* (Paris: Seuil, 1977). "It is a matter of examining how a text presents, even 'theorizes' about, explicitly or not, the reading or readings that we actually do or could do; how it leaves us free (*makes* us free) or how it constrains us" (ibid., p. 9; his emphasis). I will not attempt to draw a full-fledged theory from Charles's work, for he has insisted on preserving the "fragmentary" character of his analysis of reading, which he perceives to be a "massive, enormous, omnipresent object" (ibid., p. 10). Texts that prescribe their own reading and even inscribe it within their own borders constitute an exception rather than a rule. These texts, however, do resemble the limit-case of the absolutely unreliable narrator proposed by Wayne Booth. These limit-cases give rise to a reflection that can itself be said to go to the limit, a reflection that draws an exemplary analysis from exceptional cases. This is the legitimate extrapolation made by Charles when he states as "an essential fact [that] reading belongs to the text, it is inscribed in it" (ibid., p. 9).

21. Concerning the oscillations between reading and reader, cf. ibid., pp. 24–25 (Remarque III). The theory of reading does not escape rhetoric "inasmuch as it presupposes that any reading transforms its reader and inasmuch as it controls this transformation" (ibid., p. 25). In this context, the rhetoric in question is no longer that of the text but that of any and all critical activity.

22. The borderline between reading and reader is not clearly drawn: "At the point where we are, the reader is responsible for this scholarly reading that has been described to us, so that the opposition is now between the frivolousness of the writer and the seriousness of reading" (ibid., p. 48). This statement is counterbalanced by the following one. "The brotherhood of readers and author is obviously an effect of the text. The book presupposes a complicity that it, in fact, constructs out of bits and pieces" (ibid., p. 53). But later we read, concerning the appeal of the text, that "A process is thus set in motion at the end of which, inevitably, the reader (the perfect reader) will be the author of the book" (ibid., p. 57). And further on: "The Prologue describes us, we who read it; it describes us as we are occupied in reading it" (ibid., p. 58).

23. "The postulate of the completeness of the work or of its closure conceals the ordered process of transformation that constitutes the 'text-to-be-read'; the closed work is a work that has been read, which by this token has lost all efficacy and all power" (ibid., p. 61).

24. In saying this, Charles does not allow himself to waver from his thesis that reading is inscribed in the text. "And to assume that decision is free is (again) an effect of the text" (ibid., p. 118). So the notion of an "effect" makes us go outside the text while still remaining within it. This is where I see the limit of Charles's undertaking. His theory of reading never manages to free itself from a theory of writing, when it does not simply turn into one, as is evident in the second part of his book, where Genette, Paulhan, Dumarsais and Fontanier, Bernard Lamy, Claude Fleury, and Cordomoy teach us an art of reading that is totally implicated in the art of writing, speaking, and arguing, on the condition, however, that the design of persuasion remain perceptible. "It is a matter of acting as though the text, writing, are "assimilated" by rhetoric; it is a matter of showing that a rereading of rhetoric is possible on the basis of the experience of the text, of writing" (ibid., p. 211). To be sure, aiming at the receiver does define the rhetorical point of view and is enough to keep it from dissolving into the poetical point of view. But what the receiver does is not taken into consideration here inasmuch as aiming at the receiver is inscribed within the text, is its intention. "To analyse *the* structure of *Adolphe* is therefore to analyze the relation between a text and its interpretation, as neither of these two elements can be treated in isolation; structure

does not designate . . . a principle of order preexisting in the text, but the 'response' of a text to reading" (ibid., p. 215; his emphasis). Here Michel Charles's *Rhétorique de la lecture* overlaps Jauss's *Toward an Aesthetic of Reception,* which we shall discuss below, to the extent that the history of the reception of a text is included in a new reception of it and, in this way, contributes to its current meaning.

25. It is true that Charles takes such pains in rereading classical rhetoric in order to indicate the limits of a normative rhetoric that claims to control its effects. "A rhetoric that did not impose this limit on itself would deliberately 'turn back into' an 'art of reading' in which discourse is conceived of as a function of possible interpretations, its perspective being based on an unknown element: readings yet to come" (ibid., p. 211).

26. Remarque IV returns to this formulation: "The reading of a text is indicated within the text." But a correction follows: "The reading is in the text, but it is not written there; it is the future of the text" (ibid., p. 247).

27. Speaking of "the *infinite* reading that makes Rabelais's work *a text,*" Charles states that "A typology of discourses must be coupled with a typology of readings; a history of genres with a history of reading" (ibid., p. 287; his emphases). This is what we shall do in the pages that follow.

28. Michel Charles both invites us to take this step and forbids us to do so. "In this text by Baudelaire, there are thus elements with a *variable* rhetorical status. This variability produced a *dynamics of reading*" (ibid., p. 254; his emphasis). Only it is not this dynamics that interests Charles here but instead the fact that the interplay of interpretations is finally what constructs the text: "A reflexive text, it reconstructs itself out of the debris of reading" (ibid., p. 254). The reflexivity of reading moves back into the text. This is why his interest in the art of reading is finally always obliterated by his interest in the structure that results from reading. In this sense, the theory of reading remains a variant of a theory of writing for Charles.

29. See *Time and Narrative,* 1:77.

30. Wolfgang Iser, *The Implied Reader: Patterns of Communication in Prose Fiction from Bunyan to Beckett* (Baltimore: Johns Hopkins University Press, 1974), pp.274–94: "The Reading Process: A Phenomenological Approach"; *The Act of Reading: A Theory of Aesthetic Response* (Baltimore: Johns Hopkins University Press, 1978). See also idem, "Indeterminacy as the Reader's Response in Prose Fiction," in *Aspects of Narrative,* ed. J. Hillis Miller (New York: Columbia University Press, 1971), pp. 1–45.

31. Roman Ingarden, *The Literary Work of Art: An Investigation on the Borderlines of Ontology, Logic, and the Theory of Literature,* trans. George G. Grabowicz (Evanston: Northwestern University Press, 1973); *The Cognition of the Literary Work of Art,* trans. Ruth Ann Crowley and Kenneth R. Olson (Evanston: Northwestern University Press, 1973).

32. See *The Act of Reading,* Part III, "Phenomenology of Reading: The Processing of the Literary Text," pp. 105–59. Iser devotes an entire chapter (pp. 135–59) of his systematic work to a reinterpretation of the Husserlian concept of "passive synthesis" in terms of a theory of reading. These passive syntheses take place before the threshold of explicit judgment, on the level of the imaginary. They take as their material the repertoire of signals scattered throughout the text and the variations in "textual perspective," depending on whether the accent is placed on characters, plot, narrative voice, or, finally, on the successive positions ascribed to the reader. To this interplay of perspectives is added the mobility of the wandering viewpoint. In this way, the work of passive synthesis in large part escapes the reading consciousness. These analyses agree perfectly with those of Sartre in his *Imagination,* trans. Forrest Williams (Ann Arbor: University of Michigan Press, 1962), and of Mikel Dufrenne in his *The Phenomenology of Aesthetic Experience,* trans. Edward S. Casey and others (Evanston: North-

western University Press, 1973). An entire phenomenology of image-building consciousness is thus incorporated into the phenomenology of reading. The literary object is, in fact, an imaginary object. What the text offers are schemata for guiding the reader's imagination.

33. The German term is *Wirkung* in the double sense of effect and response. In order to distinguish his own enterprise from that of Jauss, Iser prefers to use the expression *Wirkungstheorie* rather than *Rezeptionstheorie* (*The Act of Reading*, p. x.). But the asserted interaction between the text and the reader implies something more than the unilateral efficacy of the text, as the study of the dialectical aspects of this interaction confirms. Moreover, to the allegation that a theory of reception is more sociological than literary—"A theory of response has its roots in the text; a theory of reception arises from a history of readers' judgments" (ibid.)—we might reply that a theory of literary effects runs the danger of being more psychological than . . . literary.

34. As E. H. Gombrich puts it, "Whenever consistent reading suggests itself . . . illusion takes over" (*Art and Illusion* [Princeton: Princeton University Press, 1961], p. 204; quoted by Iser, *The Act of Reading*, p. 124).

35. Iser quotes this sentence from George Bernard Shaw's *Major Barbara:* "You have learnt something. That always feels at first as if you had lost something" (ibid., p. 291).

36. In this brief study of the activity of reading proposed by Iser, I do not discuss the criticism he levels against efforts to ascribe a referential function to literary works. According to him, this would be to submit a literary work to a ready-made and pre-established meaning; for example, to a catalog of established norms. For a hermeneutic such as ours, which seeks nothing behind the work and which, on the contrary, is attentive to its power of detection and transformation, the assimilation of the referential function to that of the denotation at work in the descriptions of ordinary language and in scientific language, prevents doing justice to the effectiveness of fiction on the very level where the effective action of reading unfolds.

37. Gérard Genette expresses similar reservations in his *Nouveau Discours du récit* (Paris: Seuil, 1983). "Unlike the implied author, who is, in the reader's mind, the idea of a real author, the implied reader, in the head of the real author, is the idea of a possible reader. . . . So perhaps the implied reader should actually be rechristened the *virtual reader*" (ibid., p. 103; his emphasis).

38. On the relation between the implied reader and the actual reader, cf. *The Act of Reading*, pp. 27–38. The category of implied reader serves mainly to reply to the accusations of subjectivism, psychologism, mentalism, or of the "affective fallacy," leveled at a phenomenology of reading. In Iser himself, the implied reader is clearly distinguished from any real reader, to the extent that "the implied reader as a concept has his roots firmly planted in the structure of the text" (ibid., p. 34). "To sum up, then, the concept of implied reader is a transcendental model which makes it possible for the structural effects of literary texts to be described" (ibid., p. 38). In fact, faced with the proliferation of literary categories of "reader," conceived of as heuristic concepts that mutually correct one another, the phenomenology of the act of reading takes a step outside the circle of these heuristic concepts, as can be seen in Part III of *The Act of Reading*, devoted to the dynamic interaction between the text and the real reader.

39. Hans Robert Jauss, *Toward an Aesthetic of Reception*, trans. Timothy Bahti (Minneapolis: University of Minnesota Press, 1982).

40. "Literary History as a Challenge to Literary Theory" (ibid., pp. 3–45). This long essay stems from Jauss's inaugural lecture given in 1967 at the University of Constance.

41. Jauss wants to restore to literary history the dignity and the specificity it has

lost, through a series of misfortunes, owing to the way it continually slips back into psychobiography; owing also to the reduction by Marxist dogmatism of the social effect of literature to a mere reflection of the socioeconomic infrastructure; and owing, finally, to the hostility, in the age of structuralism, of literary theory itself to any consideration extrinsic to the text, set up as a self-sufficient entity; to say nothing of the constant danger that a theory of reception will be reduced to a sociology of taste, paralleling a psychology of reading, which is the fate threatening a phenomenology of reading.

42. The German *dialogische* need not be translated here by "dialectical." The works of Bakhtin and those of Francis Jacques give an unquestionable legitimacy to the term "dialogical." Jauss is to be commended for having connected his dialogical conception of reception to Gaetan Picon's *Introduction à une esthétique de la littérature* (Paris: Gallimard, 1953) and to André Malraux's *The Voices of Silence*, trans. Gilbert Stuart and Francis Price (Garden City, N.Y.: Doubleday, 1967).

43. This concept is borrowed from Husserl, *Ideas I*, §§27 and 82.

44. It is important, in order to distinguish Jauss's enterprise from Iser's, to stress the intersubjective character of the horizon of expectations that founds all individual understanding of a text and the effect that it produces (*Toward an Aesthetic of Reception*, p. 41). Jauss has no doubt that this horizon of expectation can be reconstituted objectively (ibid., pp. 42–43).

45. A comparison is to be made here with the notion of style in Granger's *Essai d'une philosophie du style*. The singular character of a work is the result of the unique solution provided for a set of circumstances, grasped as a singular problem to be solved.

46. "The classical, according to Hegel, 'signifies itself [*Bedeutende*] and interprets itself [*Deutende*]'. . . . What we call 'classical' does not first require the overcoming of historical distance—for in its own constant mediation it achieves this overcoming" (*Truth and Method*, p. 257).

47. Poetik und Hermeneutik, 3 (Munich: Fink, 1968), p. 692, cited by Jauss, *Toward an Aesthetic of Reception*, p. 34.

48. Siegfried Kracauer (discussed by Jauss, pp. 36–37) states that the temporal curves of different cultural phenomena constitute so many "shaped times," resisting all integration. If this is the case, how could one hold, as Jauss does, that "this multiplicity of literary phenomena . . . when seen from the point of view of an aesthetics of reception, coalesces again for the audience that perceives them and relates them to one another as works of *its* present, in the unity of a common horizon of literary expectations, memories, and anticipations that establishes their significance? (ibid., p. 38; his emphasis). It is perhaps too much to ask of the historical effect of works of art that it lend itself to a totalization such as this, if it is true that no teleology governs it. Despite the vigorous criticism leveled at the concept of the "classical" in Gadamer, in which he sees a Platonic or Hegelian residue, Jauss is himself searching for a canonical rule, without which any literary history would perhaps be directionless.

49. Jauss mentions in this respect the sense of parody in Cervantes' *Don Quixote* and in Diderot's *Jacques the Fatalist* (ibid., p. 24).

50. This antinomy parallels that which appeared above with regard to inquiry. Jauss, again here, breaks an arduous path between the extremes of heterogeneous multiplicity and systematic unification. According to him, "it must also be possible . . . to arrange the heterogeneous multiplicity of contemporaneous works in equivalent, opposing, and hierarchical structures, and thereby to discover an overarching system of relationships in the literature of a historical moment" (ibid., p. 36). But if we refuse every Hegelian-type teleology, as well as every Platonic-style archetype, how can we prevent the historicity characteristic of the chain of innovations and receptions from

dissolving into pure multiplicity? Is any integration possible other than that of the last reader (concerning whom Jauss himself says he is the vanishing point but not the goal of the process of evolution? [ibid., p. 34]). Speaking of "the historical dimension of literature," he states that what determines "this historical articulation . . . [is] the history of influence: that which 'results from the event' and which from the perspective of the present constitutes the coherence of literature as the prehistory of its present manifestation" (ibid., p. 39). However, for lack of any conceptually throught-out interconnection, the principle of this organic continuity must perhaps be seen as unnamable.

51. My conception of mimesis, which at one and the same time discovers and transforms, is in perfect agreement with Jauss's critique of the aesthetics of representation, presupposed by both the adversaries and the proponents of the social function of literature.

52. This first distance explains why a work like *Madame Bovary* influenced customs more by its formal innovations (in particular by introducing a narrator who is the "impartial" observer of his heroine) then did the openly moralizing interventions or denunciations so dear to socially committed writers. The absence of any answer to the moral dilemmas of an epoch is perhaps the most effective weapon available to literature to act on social customs and to change praxis. A direct line runs from Flaubert to Brecht. Literature acts only indirectly on social customs by creating what could be called second-order gaps in relation to the first-order gap between imaginary and everyday reality.

53. The final chapter of this section will show how the action of literature on the reading public's horizon of expectation is placed within the more comprehensive dialectic between a horizon of expectation and a space of experience, which we shall use, following Reinhart Koselleck, to characterize historical consciousness in general. The intersection of history and fiction will serve as the privileged instrument for the inclusion of the literary dialectic within an encompassing historical dialectic. And it is indeed through the function of social creation that literary history is integrated, as a particular history, within general history (cf. ibid., pp. 39–45).

54. See Hans Robert Jauss, "Ueberlegungen zur Abgrenzung und Aufgabenstellung einer literarischen Hermeneutik," in *Poetik und Hermeneutik,* 9 (Munich: Fink, 1980), pp. 459–81, translated into French as "Limites et tâches d'une herméneutique littéraire," *Diogène* no. 109 (January–March 1980): 92–119; *Aesthetic Experience and Literary Hermeneutics,* trans. Michael Shaw (Minneapolis: University of Minnesota Press, 1982), pp. 3–188.

55. Michael Riffaterre was one of the first to show the limits of structural analysis and, in general, of mere description of the text in his debate with Jakobson and Lévi-Strauss. Jauss commends him as the one who "introduced the turn from the structural description to the analysis of the reception of the poetic text" (*Toward an Aesthetic of Reception,* p. 141), even if, he adds, Riffaterre is "more interested in the pregiven elements of reception and in the 'rule of actualization' than in the aesthetic activity of the reader who take up or receives the text" (ibid.). Cf. Michael Riffaterre, "The Reader's Perception of Narrative," in *Interpretation of Narrative,* ed. Mario J. Valdes and Owen Miller (Toronto: University of Toronto Press, 1971), pp. 28–37.

56. On the rehabilitation of aesthetic pleasure, cf. Hans Robert Jauss, *Kleine Apologie der aesthetischen Erfahrung* (Constance: Verlaganstalt, 1972). Jauss thus aligns himself with the Platonic doctrine of pure pleasure found in the *Philebus* and with the Kantian doctrine of disinterested aesthetic pleasure and the idea of its universal communicability.

57. The reader is thereby asked to "measure and to broaden the horizon of one's own experience vis-à-vis the experience of the other" (ibid., p. 147).

58. I will not discuss *poiēsis* here. It is nonetheless of importance to the theory of

reading in that reading is also a creative act replying to the poetic act that founded the work. Following Hans Blumenberg, "Nachahmung der Natur! Zur Vorgeschichte des schöpferischen Menschen," *Studium Generale* 10 (1957): 266–83, and Jürgen Mittelstrass, *Neuzeit und Aufklärung. Studium zur Entstehung der neuzeitlichen Wissenschaft und Philosophie* (Berlin and New York: W. de Gruyter, 1970), Jauss retraces the conquest of the creative power freed from every model, from biblical and Hellenic antiquity, by way of the Enlightenment, up to our own day.

59. Remember that in Aristotle's *Poetics* characters are classifed as "better" than, "worse" than, or "like" ourselves; remember, too, that in the discussion of the rhetoric of fiction the strongest reservations expressed by Wayne Booth had to do with the moral effects of the strategy of persuasion in the modern novel.

60. On the translation of catharsis by "clarification" and "purification," cf. my chapter on Aristotle's *Poetics* in volume 1, in particular p. 50.

61. Cf. ibid., p. 49.

62. Hans Robert Jauss, "Limites et tâches d'une herméneutique littéraire," p. 124.

63. In the following chapter, we shall return to this similarity, strengthening it, drawing support form the notion of narrative voice introduced in volume 2, pp. 95–99.

64. I have described elsewhere a comparable dialectic between appropriation and distanciation; see "The Task of Hermeneutics," *Philosophy Today* 17 (1973): 112–24.

65. See *Time and Narrative*, 1:77. No one has better clarified the indissociable relation between communicability and referentiality taken in its broadest generality than has Francis Jacques; cf. *Dialogiques, Recherches logiques sur le dialogue* (Paris: Presses Universitaires de France, 1979) and *Dialogiques II, l'Espace logique de l'interlocution* (Paris: Presses Universitaires de France, 1985).

66. This distinction between reading as stasis or pause and reading as impetus [*envoi*] explains Jauss's oscillations in his estimation of the role of application in literary hermeneutics. As stasis, application tends to be identified with aesthetic understanding; as impetus, it detaches itself from this in rereading and displays its cathartic effects; it then functions as a means of "correcting other applications which continue to be subject to the pressure of situations and to the constraints imposed by decisions to be made concerning direct action;" ("Limites et tâches d'une herméneutique littéraire," p. 133).

CHAPTER EIGHT

1. I will not return again here to the reasons presented above why I prefer to speak of conjoint refiguration or of interweaving rather than of intersecting reference. But this does concern the same problems as those presented in volume 1, pp. 77–82.

2. J. T. Frazer, *The Genesis and Evolution of Time: A Critique of Interpretation in Physics* (Amherst: University of Massachusetts Press, 1982).

3. Cf. my *Rule of Metaphor*, 1st study.

4. See *Time and Narrative*, 1:222.

5. Yosef Hayim Yerushalmi shows in *Zakhor: Jewish History and Jewish Memory* (Seattle: University of Washington Press, 1982) that the Jews were able to do without scholarly historiography for centuries to the very extent that they remained faithful to the call in Deuteronomy—"Remember!"—and that the shift to historical research in the modern period was in large part an effect of the assimilation of gentile culture.

6. Rudolf Otto, *The Idea of the Holy: An Inquiry into the Non-Rational Factor in the Idea of the Divine and Its Relation to the Rational*, trans. John W. Harvey (New York: Oxford University Press, 1958).

7. Cf. *Time and Narrative*, 1:169–74.

8. Once again I rejoin Hannah Arendt's fine analyses on the relation between nar-

rative and action. In the face of the fragility of all things human, narrative uncovers the "who" of action, exposes the agent in the public sphere, confers a coherence deserving to be recounted, and finally assures the immortality of reputation. Hannah Arendt, *The Human Condition* (Chicago: University of Chicago Press, 1958). It is not surprising that Arendt never separated those who suffer history from those who make it, or that she even begins her great chapter on action with this line from Isak Dinesen: "All sorrows can be borne, if you put them into a story or tell a story about them" (ibid., p. 175).

9. Harald Weinrich, *Tempus: Besprochene und erzählte Zeit* (Stuttgart: Kohlhammer, 1964); *Le Temps: le récit et le commentaire*, trans. Michèle Lacoste (Paris: Seuil, 1973).

10. *Time and Narrative*, 2:61–71.

11. For the notion of narrative voice, cf. ibid., pp. 88–99.

12. *Aristotle's Poetics*, trans. James Hutton (New York: W. W. Norton, 1982).

13. I am reserving for my concluding chapter an examination of the notion of narrative identity that, on the level of self-consciousness, crowns the analysis running through the last five chapters and ending here. The reader may wish to refer to this discussion at this point. For my part, I preferred to limit myself to the constitution of human time as such in order to leave open the path that leads to the aporia of the time of history.

CHAPTER NINE

1. I shall refer here to the edition of Hegel's lectures on the philosopy of world history prepared by Johannes Hoffmeister (Hamburg: Felix Meiner, 1955): Georg Wilhelm Friedrich Hegel, *Lectures on the Philosophy of World History: Introduction—Reason in History*, trans. Duncan Forbes (Cambridge: Cambridge University Press, 1975).

2. The inquiry into the "varieties of history writing" (*Arten der Geschichtsschreibung*) that makes up the first draft of the Introduction to the lectures on the philosophy of history has only a didactic purpose. For a public unfamiliar with the philosophical reasons the system establishes for taking freedom as the motive force of a history that is both rational and real, it was necessary to provide an exoteric introduction that leads by degrees toward the idea of a philosophical history of the world which, in truth, is commended only by its own philosophical structure. The movement from "original history" to "reflective history" and then to "philosophical history" repeats the movement from *Vorstsellung*—or from figurative thought—to the Concept, in passing through understanding and judgment. Hegel says that the authors of original history deal with events and institutions they had before their eyes and whose spirit they share. With them, an initial threshold was nevertheless crossed beyond legends and traditions that had been passed on, because the spirit of the nation had already crossed this threshold in inventing politics and writing. History goes along with this real advance by internalizing it. As for reflective history, it too presents forms that are traversed in a certain order and that repeat the hierarchy going from representation to the Concept. It is worth noting that universal history constitutes only the lowest degree of its level, given the lack of a directive idea that would govern the compilation of the abstract summaries and pictures that convey the illusion of lived experience. (The philosophical history of the world will not, therefore, be a universal history in the sense of a synoptic view of national histories set side by side, as on a geographer's map.) The next form to be rejected is "pragmatic history," despite its concern to make both past and present mutually meaningful, for it does so only at the price of a moralizing tendency that places history at the mercy of each particular historian's convictions. (Be-

low, in discussing Reinhart Koselleck's work, I shall return to this important question of *historia magistra vitae*.) Even more surprising is Hegel's harangue against "critical history," the very heart of reflective history, for despite its acuteness in the use of sources, it shares the faults of all thought that is merely critical, wherein are summed up all the resistances to speculative thought, centered upon questions about conditions of possibility and losing contact with the things themselves. It is not surprising therefore that Hegel prefers "specialized history" (the history of art, of science, of religion, etc.), for it at least has the virtue of comprehending one spiritual activity as a function of the forces of the Spirit that give particularity to the spirit of a nation. This is why Hegel puts specialized history at the summit of the modes of reflective history. The passage to philosophical world history nonetheless does constitute a qualitative leap in his traversal of the varieties of history writing.

3. This presupposition has the same epistemological status as does the conviction (*Uberzeugung*) that at the end of chapter 6 of the *Phenomenology of Spirit* is attached to the certitude of self that comes with the agent's becoming one with his intention and his action.

4. Even if we can name several antecedents to the Hegelian enterprise, these arguments that are supposed to reveal its inadequacy are themselves borrowed from the complete system, which has no precedent. Anaxagoras's *Nous*? Plato had already rejected a philosophy for which real causality remained external to the reign of the Spirit. The doctrine of providence? Christians have only understood it in a fragmented way in terms of arbitrary interventions. They have not applied it to the whole history of the world. What is more, in declaring the ways of the Lord hidden, they have fled the task of knowing God. Leibniz's theodicy? Leibniz's categories remain "abstract and indeterminate" (*Lectures,* p. 42) because they have demonstrated historically and not "metaphysically" how historical reality fits with God's plans. His failure to explain evil bears witness to this: "it should enable us to comprehend all the ills of the world, including the existence of evil, so that the thinking spirit may be reconciled with the negative aspects of existence" (ibid., pp. 42–43). So long as evil has not been incorporated into the great plan of the world, the belief in *Nous,* in providence, in a divine plan, is left hanging. As for Hegel's own philosophy of religion, even it is not a sufficient help. Within it there is a strong affirmation that God has revealed himself, but it poses the same problem: how to think through to the end what is only an object of faith? How can we know God rationally? This question sends us back to the determinations of speculative philosophy as a whole.

5. This idea of a double intentionality finds echoes in contemporary thought. I have referred a number of times to Hermann Lübbe's essay "Was aus Handlungen Geschichten macht?" There would be nothing to tell, Lübbe says, if everything happened just as we planned and intended. We only recount what made our simple projects complicated, what made them go wrong, or even become unrecognizable. Typical, in this regard, is the project ruined by the interference of other enterprises. When the produced effect does not agree with the reasons for any of the participants' acts—for example, the inauguration of the stadium at Nuremberg which the architect of the Third Reich planned for the day that was in fact the one when the allies attained their victory—and, even more so, when this effect cannot be attributed to any other third party, we have to narrate how and why things turned out differently than anyone could have foreseen. Hegel takes up this account just where Lübbe leaves off, that is, with the neutral—or ironic, or despairing—admission of the place of chance in history, in Cournot's sense of the term "chance."

6. "The historical fact is essentially irreducible to order: chance is the foundation of history," says Raymond Aron, following Cournot (*Introduction to the Philosophy of History,* p. 16).

7. What I am calling the larger tautology, the one that constitutes the project brought to term by the *Stufengang,* repeats the smaller tautology, the short-circuit, of the famous declaration that "the only thought which philosophy brings with it is the simple idea of *reason*—the idea that reason governs the world, and that world history is therefore a rational process." This affirmation of meaning as given by itself remains Hegel's unshakable philosophical credo, as may be seen on the page following it in Hoffmeister's edition of these lectures: "That world-history is governed by an ultimate design, that it is a rational process—whose rationality is not that of a particular subject, but a divine and absolute reason—this is a proposition whose truth we must assume; its proof lies in the study of world history itself, which is the image and enactment of reason" (ibid., p. 28).

8. This passage was anticipated, as we said above, in special history, wherein we already perceive something of this abolition of narrative in the abstraction of the idea.

9. Let us set aside the political arguments that denounce Hegel as an apologist of the repressive state, or even as a forerunner of totalitarianism. Eric Weil has laid these arguments to rest insofar as they concern Hegel's relation to the states contemporary with him. "Compared to the France of the Restoration or England before the Reform Act of 1832, or Metternich's Austria, Prussia was an advanced state" (*Hegel et l'Etat* [Paris: Vrin, 1950], p. 19). More important, "Hegel justified the sovereign, national state about as much as a physicist justifies the weather" (ibid., p. 78). Nor should we linger over the more tenacious presupposition that Hegel believed that history was fulfilled in that it fully comprehended itself in his philosophy. The marks of the incompleteness of the history of the State are sufficiently numerous and clear in his work that we should stop labeling him with this foolish idea. No State has reached the fullness of meaning that Hegel saw only as a seed and in inchoate forms. Cf. *Hegel's Philosophy of Right,* trans. T. M. Knox (New York: Oxford University Press, 1967), pars. 330–40, pp. 212–16. The philosophy of history comes to occupy precisely that zone of right without law, which the philosophy of right can speak about only in terms of the Kantian language of the essay on perpetual peace (cf. ibid., par. 333, pp. 213–14). The *Stufengang* of the spirits of the nations takes the place of international law, which has not yet reached its maturity in the sphere of actual right. In this sense, the philosophy of history is ahead of the philosophy of right. In return, the philosophy of right, which is capable of completing in its own sphere what the philosophy of history designates as incomplete, may also correct one essential point of the philosophy of history. It is not certain that this time will be one of great men of history, or at least of national heroes in times of peace as well as in times of war (cf. *Hegel et l'Etat,* pp. 81–84). What is still to come is the state that will become, internally, everyone's state and, externally, the world state. Thinking history does not seal up the past, it only comprehends what in it has already taken place, the surpassed past (cf. *Philosophy of Right,* par. 343, p. 216). In this sense, the completion spoken of in the famous passage of the Preface to the *Philosophy of Right* means nothing more that what Eric Weil has seen in it: "one form of life has grown old" (*Hegel et l'Etat,* p. 104). Another form may therefore arise on the horizon. What is important is that the present in which the surpassed past is deposited be sufficiently efficacious so that it does not cease to unfold itself in memory and in anticipation.

10. Cf. Paul Ricoeur, "The Status of *Vorstellung* in Hegel's Philosophy of Religion," in *Meaning, Truth, and God,* ed. Leroy S. Rouner (Notre Dame, Ind.: Notre Dame University Press, 1982), pp. 70–88.

11. What is most astonishing is that we encounter these two currents of anti-Hegelianism in Ranke. On the one hand, the cunning of reason is denounced as "a representation supremely unworthy of God and of humanity [*eine höchst unwürdige Vorstellung von Gott und Menschheit*]" to the benefit of a theology of history without

philosophy: "each age is immediately before God." On the other hand, the historian wants to know the facts and to reach the past such as it really was, to the benefit of a history that also does without any philosophy.

12. What has become unbelievable to us is contained in the following assertion: "the present world and the present form and self-consciousness of the spirit contain [*begreift*] within them all the stages which appear to have occurred earlier in history. These did admittedly take shape independently and in succession; but what the spirit is now, it has always been implicitly, and the difference is merely in the degree to which this implicit character has been developed" (*Lectures on the Philosophy of World History*, p. 150).

13. In fact, in Hegel's text, this transition was already quite weak. Cf. ibid., pp. 52–53.

14. My position here is close to that of Hans-Georg Gadamer. He did not hesitate to begin the second part of his great work *Truth and Method* with the following surprising declaration: "If we are to follow Hegel rather than Schleiermacher, the history of hermeneutics must place its emphases quite differently" (p. 153; cf. also pp. 306–10). For Gadamer, too, we can never refute Hegel with arguments that reproduce moments recognized and surpassed in his speculative enterprise (ibid., p. 307). Given false interpretations and weak refutations, we "have to preserve the truth of Hegel's thought" (ibid.). Hence when Gadamer writes that "to exist historically means that knowledge of onself can never be complete [*Geschichtlichsein heisst, nie im Sichwissen aufgehen*]" (ibid., p. 269), he too abandons Hegel rather than conquering him through criticism. "The Archimedean point from where Hegel's philosophy could be toppled can never be found through reflection" (ibid., p. 308). Gadamer breaks Hegel's "magic spell" (ibid., p. 307) by a confession that has the force of a renunciation. What he renounces is the very idea of an "absolute fusion [*Vermittlung*—mediation] of history and truth" (ibid., p. 306).

CHAPTER TEN

1. Reinhart Koselleck, *Futures Past: The Semantics of Historical Time*, trans. Keith Triber (Cambridge: The MIT Press, 1985). To which disciplines do these two historical categories belong? For Koselleck, they are regulative concepts, having to do with a well-defined enterprise, that of a conceptual semantics applied to the vocabulary of history and the time of history. As semantic, this discipline deals with the meaning of words and of texts rather than with the states of affairs and processes arising out of social history. As a conceptual semantics, it seeks to disentangle the significations of the key words—history, progress, crisis, and so on—that in relation to social history stand as both indicators and factors of change. Indeed, to the extent that these key words bring to language the underlying changes for which social history provides the theory, they contribute to producing, diffusing, and reinforcing the social transformations they name through this very fact of their acceding to the linguistic level. This double relation of conceptual history to social history only appears if we accord to semantics the autonomy of being a distinct discipline.

2. "Experience is the present past [*Gegenwärtige Vergangenheit*] whose events have been incorporated [*einverleibt*] and can be remembered" (ibid., p. 272).

3. Koselleck does not fail to refer to Gadamer's *Truth and Method* (pp. 310–25) as regards the meaning of this term, *Erfahrung*, and its implications for thought about history (ibid., p. 323, n. 4).

4. "As history converged as event and representation [*Darstellung*], the linguistic basis was laid for the transcending turning point leading to the historical philosophy of idealism" (*Futures Past*, pp. 27–28). Koselleck refers to J.-G. Droysen, *Historik*, ed. R. Hübner (Munich and Berlin: R. Oldenbourg, 1943), pp. 325 and 357.

5. I will leave aside here the rapprochements between *Historik* and *Poetik* that stem from this epic quality of history as it is told. Koselleck sees the terms "history" and "novel" as coming close to each other between 1690 and 1750, not as a way of depreciating history but in order to elevate the truth claims of the novel. Reciprocally, Leibniz could speak of history as God's novel. And Kant used the term "novel" metaphorically in the ninth thesis of his "History with a Cosmopolitan Intent" to express the natural unity of general history.

6. "Time becomes a dynamic and historical force in its own right," says Koselleck (ibid., p. 246), and he points to the proliferation between 1770 and 1830 of such constructions as *Zeit-Abschnitt, -Anschauung, -Ansicht, -Aufgabe,* and so on, which evaluate time itself in terms of its historical qualities. *Zeitgeist* is the most striking example from this flowering of terms (cf. ibid., p. 258).

7. This idea of a new time, which has led to our idea of modernity, takes on its full relief if we contrast it with two topoi of previous historical thought that kept this idea from coming to light. It stands out, first of all, against the collapsed background of those political eschatologies whose manifestations Koselleck traces through the sixteenth century. Placed against this horizon of the end of the world, the temporal difference between past events and present ones is inessential. What is more, these events all being in varying ways anticipated "figures" of the end, there circulate among them all those relationships of an analogical symbolization whose density of meaning carries the day over their chronological relations. The second contrast makes understandable the change in the horizon of expectation to which we owe the modern positing of the problem of the relation of the future to the past. It has to do with a famous topos which is even more tenacious: *historia magistra vitae*—history is life's teacher (cf. ibid., pp. 21–38, subtitled "The Dissolution of the Topos into the Perspective of a Modernized Historical Process"). Once reduced to a collection of examples, histories of the past are divested of their original form of temporality which differentiated them from one another, and they become merely the occasion for a learning experience that actualizes them in the present. At this price, these examples become information or monuments. And through their perenniality, they are both the symptom and the reminder of the continuity between past and future. Today, contrary to this neutralizing of historical time through the teaching function of the *exempla,* the conviction of living in new times has, so to speak, "temporalized history" (cf. the section in ibid., pp. 73–155, entitled "Theory and Method in the Historical Determination of Time"). In return, the past, now deprived of its exemplary status, is cast outside our space of experience into the shadows of what no longer exists.

8. Koselleck cites a text from Lessing's *The Education of the Human Race,* where such acceleration is not just acknowledged but also wished for and willed (ibid., p. 18; cf. also p. 297, n. 78). Also this passage from Robespierre: "The time has come to call upon each to realize his own destiny. The progress of human reason has laid the basis for this great Revolution, and the particular duty of hastening it has fallen to you" (ibid., referring to "Sur la Constitution, 10 Mai 1793," *Oeuvres complètes* 9:495). Kant echoes this in his "perpetual Peace," which is "not just an empty idea . . . for we may hope that the periods within which equal amounts of progress are made will become progressively shorter" (ibid.).

9. At the same time, the two previous schemata are reversed. It is from the projected and chosen future that the true eschatologies are born; they are called utopias. They are what, thanks to human action, indicate the horizon of expectation and they are what give the true lessons of history, the ones that teach us the future that is open to us. The power of history, instead of crushing us, exalts us, for it is our own work, even when we do not know what we are doing.

10. Cf. ibid., pp. 198–213: "On the Disposability of History." Another noteworthy expression is the *Machbarkeit der Geschichte* (ibid.).

11. Recall François Furet's remark in his *Interpreting the French Revolution:* "What sets the French Revolution apart is that it was not a transition but a beginning and a haunting vision of that beginning. Its historical importance lies in one trait that was unique to it, especially since this 'unique' trait was to become universal: it was the first experiment with democracy" (ibid., p. 79).

12. Karl Marx, *The Eighteenth Brumaire of Louis Napoleon,* trans. Eden and Cedar Paul (London: Allen and Unwin, 1926), p. 23. This notion of "circumstances" has a considerable scope. I have placed it among the most primitive components of the notion of action at the level of mimesis$_1$. Such circumstances are also what is imitated on the level of mimesis$_2$, within the framework of the plot, as a synthesis of the heterogeneous. In history, too, plot brings together goals, causes, and chance.

13. Koselleck cites this saying from Novalis: if we know how to apprehend history on a broad scale, then we "observe the covert interlinking of the before and after, and learn how to compose history from hope and memory" (ibid., p. 270).

14. "This then is a matter of epistemological categories which assist in the foundation of the possibility of a history. . . . there is no history which could be constituted independently of the experiences and expectations of active human agents" (ibid., p. 269). "Accordingly, these two categories are indicative of a general human condition; one could say that they indicate an anthropological condition without which history is neither possible nor conceivable" (ibid., p. 270).

15. Jürgen Habermas, "La modernité: un projet inachevé," *Critique,* no. 413 (October 1981): 950–69.

16. Jürgen Habermas, *The Theory of Communicative Action,* trans. Thomas McCarthy (Boston: Beacon Press, 1984).

17. Paul Ricoeur, "La raison pratique," in T. F. Geraets, ed., *Rationality Today/La Rationalité aujourd'hui* (Ottawa: University of Ottawa Press, 1979), pp. 225–48.

18. We have already encountered this problem with the polarity between sedimentation and innovation in the traditionality characteristic of the life of the paradigms of emplotment. The same two extremes reappear: servile repetition and schism. And as I have said, I share with Frank Kermode, from whom I borrow this notion of a schism, the visceral refusal of any revision that would transform the criticism of received paradigms into a schism. Cf. *Time and Narrative,* 2:7–28.

19. Koselleck seems to suggest something similar. "Thus it could happen that an old relation once again came into force; the greater the experience the more cautious one is, but also the more open is the future. If this were the case, then the end of *Neuzeit* as optimizing progress would have arrived" (*Futures Past,* p. 288). However, the historian and semanticist of historical concepts will say no more than this.

20. Hans-Georg Gadamer, *Truth and Method,* pp. 267ff. Whether "we are expressly aware of it or not, the power [*Wirkung*] of this effective-history is at work. . . . we see that the power [*Macht*] of effective-history does not depend on its being recognised" (ibid., p. 268).

21. Jean Grondin, "La conscience du travail de l'histoire et le problème de la vérité herméneutique," *Archives de philosophie* 44 (1981): 435–53. There is a precedent to this notion of being-affected by history in the Kantian idea of *Selbstaffektion,* referred to above in my discussion of the aporias of time. We affect ourselves, Kant says, in the second edition of the *Critique of Pure Reason,* by our own acts. By drawing the line, he had already said in the first edition, we produce time, but we have no direct intuition of this productive act, unless it is by way of the representation of objects determined by this synthetic activity. Cf. above, pp. 54–57.

22. Cf. Paul Ricoeur, "Ethics and Culture: Habermas and Gadamer in Dialogue," *Philosophy Today* 17 (1973): 153–65.

23. Cf. above, p. 303 n. 33.

24. He speaks of "the history of thought, of knowledge, of philosophy, of literature . . . seeking, and discovering, more and more discontinuities, whereas history itself appears to be abandoning the irruption of events in favour of stable structures" (*The Archeology of Knowledge*, p. 6).

25. *Time and Narrative*, 1:194–214.

26. Cf. *The Archeology of Knowledge*, pp. 126–31.

27. On this point, the *Archeology of Knowledge* does correct the impression of an overall coherence and a total substitution suggested by *The Order of Things* (New York: Vintage Books, 1973), even though this latter work only considered three epistemological fields, without saying anything about other such fields, and even less about the societies where they took place. "Archeology disarticulates the synchrony of breaks, just as it destroyed the abstract unity of change and event" (*Archeology of Knowledge*, p. 176). To this comment is attached a warning against any overly monolithic interpretation of an episteme, which would quickly lead back to the rule of a sovereign subject (cf. ibid., 191–92). At the limit, if a society were submitted to an overall mutation in every respect, we would find ourselves at that hypothesis of David Hume's, reported by Karl Mannheim, where one generation would completely replace another generation all at once. However, as we have seen, the continuous replacement of generations one after the other contributes to preserving the continuity of the historical fabric.

28. On this point, cf. Victor Goldschmidt, *Temps physique et Temps tragique chez Aristote*, p. 14.

29. Up to the mutation that is currently taking place, according to Foucault, history has been governed by one and the same end: "the reconstitution, on the basis of what the documents say, and sometimes merely hint at, of the past from which they emanate and which has now disappeared far behind them; the document was always treated as the language of a voice since reduced to silence, its fragile, but possibly decipherable trace" (*Archeology*, p. 6). There follows the formula wherein is implied the long-range significance of Foucault's archeology: "The document is not the fortunate tool of a history that is primarily and fundamentally *memory;* history is one way in which a society recognizes and develops a mass of documentation with which it is inextricably linked" (ibid., p. 7; his emphasis).

30. Cf. above, pp. 144–47.

31. Cf. *Time and Narrative*, 2:chap. 1.

32. Ibid., p. 151.

33. Cf. *Truth and Method*, pp. 258–67. "If we are trying to understand a historical phenomenon from the historical distance that is characteristic of our hermeneutical situation, we are always subject to the effects of effective-history" (ibid., p. 267).

34. "The horizon is, rather, something into which we move and that moves with us. Horizons change for a person who is moving. Thus the horizon of the past, out of which all human life lives and which exists in the form of tradition, is always in motion. It is not historical consciousness that first sets the surrounding horizon in motion. But in it this motion becomes aware of itself" (ibid., p. 271). It does not really matter that Gadamer applies the term "horizon" to the dialectic between past and present, whereas Koselleck reserves it for our expectations. We could say that through this term Gadamer describes a constitutive tension of the space of experience. He can do so to the extent that expectation itself is one component of what we are here calling the horizon of the present.

35. Together these worlds "constitute the one great horizon that moves from within and, beyond the frontiers of the present, embraces the historical depths of our self-consciousness" (ibid.).

36. Here the hermeneutics of texts is a good guide: "every encounter with tradition

that takes place within historical consciousness involves the experience of tension between the text and the present. The hermeneutic task consists in not covering up this tension by attempting a naive assimilation but consciously bringing it out. This is why it is part of the hermeneutic approach to project an historical horizon that is different from the horizon of the present" (ibid., p. 273).

37. Eugen Fink, "Bild als 'Fenster' in die Bildwelt," in *Studien zur Phänomenologie (1930–1939)* (The Hague: Nijhoff, 1966), pp. 77–78; *De la Phénoménologie,* trans. Didier Franck (Paris: Minuit, 1974), p. 79).

38. Cf. *Truth and Method,* p. 235.

39. Ibid., pp. 333–41.

40. Cf. ibid., pp. 245–74.

41. Following Heidegger, Gadamer writes, "A person who is trying to understand is exposed to distraction from fore-meanings that are not borne out by the things themselves. The working-out of appropriate projects, anticipatory in nature, to be confirmed 'by the things' themselves is the constant task of understanding. The only 'objectivity' here is the confirmation of a fore-meaning in its being worked out" (ibid., pp. 236–37). Looking for a *homologia* in the very conflict of interpretations bears witness to this: "the goal of all communication [Verständigung] and understanding is agreement [*Einverständnis*] concerning the object" (ibid., p. 260). The anticipation of meaning that governs the understanding of texts is not first private but public (ibid., pp. 261–62).

42. "Our historical consciousness is always filled with a variety of voices in which the echo of the past is heard. It is present only in the multifariousness of such voices: this constitutes the nature of the tradition in which we want to share and have a part. Modern historical research itself is not only research, but the transmission of tradition" (ibid., pp. 252–53).

43. "At any rate understanding in the human sciences shares one fundamental condition with the continuity of traditions, namely, that it lets itself be addressed by tradition" (ibid., p. 251). "Modern historical research itself is not only research, but the transmission of tradition" (ibid., p. 253).

44. "The place between strangeness and familiarity that a transmitted text has for us is that intermediate place between being an historically intended separate object and being part of a tradition. The true home of hermeneutics is in this intermediate area" (ibid., pp. 262–63). This idea should be compared with Hayden White's that history is as much a way of becoming refamiliar with the unfamiliar as of making the familiar unfamiliar.

45. The worm of criticism was already present in the famous text from Heidegger about understanding from which Gadamer's hermeneutical reflection begins: "In the circle [of understanding] is hidden a positive possibility of the most primordial kind of knowing. To be sure, we genuinely take hold of this possibility only when, in our interpretation, we have understood that our first, last, and constant task is never to allow our fore-having, fore-sight, and fore-conception to be presented to us by fancies and popular conceptions, but rather to make the scientific theme secure by working out these fore-structures in terms of the things themselves" (*Being and Time,* p. 195). Heidegger does not say concretely how an interpreter learns to discern an anticipation of meaning "in terms of the things themselves" from fancies and popular conceptions, however.

46. I do not mean to attenuate the conflict between the hermeneutic of traditions and the critique of ideologies. Their "ambition to be universal," to recall the theme of the controversy between Gadamer and Habermas in Karl-Otto Apel et al., *Hermeneutik und Ideologiekritik* (Frankfurt: Suhrkamp, 1971), starts from two different places, the reinterpretation of texts received from tradition, for the one, the critique of systematically distorted forms of communication for the other. This is why we may not

simply superimpose on each other what Gadamer calls a prejudice, which is a favorable prejudice, and what Habermas calls an ideology, which is a systematic distortion of our communicative competence. We can only show that, speaking from two different perspectives, each must integrate a part of the other's argument, as I have attempted to demonstrate in my essay "Ethics and Culture: Habermas and Gadamer in Dialogue," referred to above.

47. For everything concerning the discussion internal to critical theory, I must declare my debt to an unpublished work of J.-M. Ferry, "Ethique de la communication et théorie de la démocratie chez Habermas" (1984).

48. This broad struggle, which occupies the second part of *Truth and Method,* is the same one that was fought in its first part against the claims of aesthetic judgment to set itself up as the tribunal of aesthetic experience, and it is also the one that is carried out in its third part against a similar reduction of language to a merely instrumental function that would conceal the power of speech to bring to language the richness of our integral experience.

49. Cf. Edward W. Said, *Beginnings: Intention and Method* (Baltimore: Johns Hopkins University Press, 1975), chap. 2: "A Meditation on Beginnings," pp. 27–78.

50. Cf. Maurice Merleau-Ponty, *The Visible and the Invisible,* ed. Claude Lefort, trans. Alphonso Lingis (Evanston: Northwestern University Press, 1968), pp. 130–55, 248–51, 254–57, and passim.

51. Cf. *Time and Narrative,* 1:54–55, 136.

52. Ibid., pp. 135–43.

53. Cf. Emile Benveniste, "The Correlations of Tense in the French Verb," in his *Problems in General Linguistics,* trans. Mary Elizabeth Meek (Coral Gables, Florida: University of Miami Press, 1977), pp. 205–15.

54. Cf. Paul Ricoeur, "Les implications de la théorie des actes de langage pour la théorie générale de l'éthique," forthcoming in *Archives de Philosophie du Droit.*

55. Cf. above, pp. 107–9.

56. Cf. above, pp. 113–14.

57. Emmanuel Mounier and Paul Landsberg had already seen in this notion of crisis, beyond the contingent character of the crisis of the 1950s, a permanent element of the notion of a person, one conjoined to those of confrontation and commitment. And in a related sense, Eric Weil characterizes "personality" by its capacity to respond to a challenge perceived as a crisis. Crisis, in this sense, is constitutive of the attitude that organizes the category of "personality." "The personality is always in crisis, that is, at each instant it creates itself in creating its image of what it is to become. It is always in conflict with others, with the past, with inauthenticity" (*Logique de la Philosophie* [Paris: Vrin, 1950], p. 150).

58. Friedrich Nietzsche, *On the Advantage and Disadvantage of History for Life,* trans. Peter Preuss (Indianapolis: Hackett, 1980). "Only so far as history serves life will we serve it: but there is a degree of doing history and an estimation of it which brings with it a withering and degenerating of life: a phenomenon which is now as necessary as it may be painful to bring to consciousness through some remarkable symptoms of our age" (ibid., p. 7). And a bit further on: "These reflections are untimely, because I attempt to understand as a defect, infirmity and shortcoming of the age something of which our age is justifiably proud, its historical education. I even believe that all of us suffer from a consuming historical fever and should at least realize that we suffer from it" (ibid., p. 8).

59. He was preceded in this respect by Jacob Burckhardt in his *Weltgeschichtliche Betrachtungen* (*Force and Freedom: Reflections on History,* trans. James Hastings Nichols [New York: Pantheon, 1943]), where the question of the historical (*das Historische*) is substituted for any inquiry into the systematic principle of universal his-

tory. To the question of what anthropological invariants make human beings historical, Burckhardt responds with his theory of the *Potenzen des Geschichtlichen:* the state, religion, culture, the first two of which constitute principles of stability, the third of which expresses the creative aspect of the spirit. Before Nietzsche did so, Burckhardt emphasized the irrational character of life and of the needs he found at the source of what he called the potentialities for history. He also affirmed the connection between life and crisis. In fact, Schopenhauer's metaphysics of the will lies as a common background to both Nietzsche and Burckhardt. But because Burckhardt remained faithful to the concept of *Geist,* he could not accept the brutal simplification Nietzsche brought about in his essay, emphasizing life alone, and the relations between these two friends deteriorated seriously following its publication. A more detailed comparison of Nietzsche and Burckhardt may be found in Herbert Schnädelback, *Geschichtsphilosophie nach Hegel: Die Probleme des Historismus* (Freiburg and Munich: Karl Alber, 1974), pp. 48–89.

60. This limiting use of the term "horizon" should be noted, in contrast to the connotations of openness that appeared in my two preceding analyses. For Nietzsche, "horizon" has instead the sense of an encompassing setting. "The unhistorical resembles an enveloping atmosphere in which alone life is generated only to disappear again with the destruction of this atmosphere. . . . with an excess of history man ceases again, and without that cloak of the unhistorical he would never have begun and dared to begin" (*Advantage and Disadvantage of History,* p. 11).

61. We might say that Nietzsche's own excess in this text is his refusal to distinguish the genealogical critique of historical culture from the critique in the epistemological sense of history as a science. It is precisely this excess, this refusal to distinguish between these two critiques, that is the sovereign indication of the untimely. Nietzsche is well aware that he was skirting another form of sickness insofar as the unhistorical was close to a superhistorical point of view, like the one a historian such as B. G. Niebuhr could claim to attain as a knowing being. However, to the extent that the unhistorical is a work of life, to the same extent the superhistorical is a fruit of wisdom . . . and of nausea. The unhistorical has no other function than to teach us how better to "do history [*Historie zu trieben*] for the sake of life" (ibid., p. 14).

62. We rediscover here the topos of *historia magistra vitae* referred to above.

63. Here again we may refer to what was said above about the contrast between reenactment of the Same and the "inventory of differences."

64. Nietzsche's attack against the separation of interior and exterior, against the emphasis on interiority, against the opposition between form and content, recalls a similar struggle, carried out in the name of "substance," *Sittlichkeit,* in Hegel's *Phenomenology of Spirit,* then in the name of the *Volksgeist* in his philosophy of history. Hegel's phantom springs up again and again in Nietzsche's work.

65. It is worth noting that here the expression "to make history," which I discussed above, appears: "it is a matter of indifference what you do as long as history itself is preserved nice and 'objective,' namely by those who can never themselves make history" (*Advantage and Disadvantage of History,* p. 31).

66. Hegel is supposed not only to have announced the end of history but to have brought it about by writing it down. He thereby inculcated the belief in the "old age of mankind" (ibid., p. 44) and sealed humanity, which was ready for the last judgment, a bit more within the *momento mori* that Christianity has taught without respite. Following Hegel, human beings could only be successors without any descendants, latecomers, epigoni—in short, there is room only for the antiquarian vision of history.

67. He carries the scandal to the point of farce. Hegel is said to have seen "the apex and terminus of world history . . . in his own Berlin existence"! (ibid., p. 47).

68. Taking up the image of a "republic of geniuses," inherited from Schopenhauer,

Nietzsche sees such giants as escaping the process (*Prozess*) of history to "live in timeless simultaneity [*zeitlos-gleichzeitig*], thanks to history, which permits such cooperation" (ibid., p. 53). Another sense of the present appears here, coming from the contemporaneity of the noncontemporaneous, which we have already considered in speaking of the concept of a generation.

69. The whole conclusion of Nietzsche's broadside is an appeal to youth, that at times approaches the level of demagogy, against the history of scholars born with gray hairs. "Thinking of *youth* at this point I cry land ho! land ho!" (ibid., p. 58; his emphasis).

70. We too may say, "And yet!" Nowhere does Nietzsche really appeal to an intuition stemming just from life. His antidotes, his counterpoisons are also interpretations. The unhistorical, or worse the superhistorical, are not returns to the animal indifference referred to at the beginning but a moment of ironical nostalgia. Of course, in other works, Nietzsche does call for rumination. But a culture based on forgetting demands more, a greater culture. Even when Nietzsche speaks of life "alone," we must not forget the genealogical status—that is, the philological and symptomatic status—of all his "concepts" relative to life, to emotions, and to the body. After all, what would a great culture be if not the rediscovery of the good use of history, even it were as such only the good use of a form of sickness, as one of Nietzsche's most detested predecessors put it? Are we to save history along with its three ways, monumental, antiquarian, and critical? Are we to return history to its function of serving life? How can we do this unless we discern in the past its unaccomplished promises, its cut-off possibilities of actualization, rather than its successes? If not, how are we to make sense of the fact that his book ends with one last appeal to the Greek idea of culture? What greater irony, for a Hegel, than this communion in the great dream of German philosophical Romanticism! Hence Nietzsche's "Untimely" discourse invites us to reread the philosophy of tradition in light of its *strebende Hoffnung,* a rereading guided not by the fait accompli of the present but by its "force."

Conclusions

1. These conclusions might have been called a Postscript. Indeed, they are the result of a rereading undertaken almost a year after finishing the manuscript of this third volume of *Time and Narrative.* Their composition is contemporary with the final revisions to that manuscript.

2. Cf. Hannah Arendt, *The Human Condition.* See also *Being and Time,* §25 ("An Approach to the Existential Question of the "Who" of Dasein"), pp. 150–53, and §64 ("Care and Selfhood"), pp. 364–70.

3. On these concepts of cohesion ("the connectedness of life"), "movement" (*Bewegtheit*), and "self-constancy," cf. *Being and Time,* §72, pp. 424–29.

4. Marcel Proust, *Remembrance of Things Past,* 3:1089.

5. See *Time and Narrative,* 1:261, n. 16.

6. Ibid., pp. 71–76.

7. The figuration of time by a line reinforces the assumption of the oneness of time. It is in virtue of this representation that time can be said to be linear.

8. Cf. the phrase "the *immanent time* of the flow of consciousness" (*Phenomenology of Internal Time-Consciousness,* p. 23).

9. For this difficult argument, see the texts of Husserl cited above, pp. 41–43.

10. Edmund Husserl, *Cartesian Meditations: An Introduction to Phenomenology,* trans. Dorian Cairns (The Hague: Nijhoff, 1960), pp. 120–28.

11. This enclosure is especially prepared for from the early stages of the analytic of Dasein. If, in fact, Dasein is capable of receiving an existential characterization, it is

in virtue of its relation to existence, where existence means that Dasein "has its Being to be, and has it as its own [*dass es je sein Sein als seiniges zu sein hat*]" (*Being and Time*, p. 33). By so emphasizing the "each time" (*je* in German) of existence, Heidegger opens the way at the very beginning for an analysis of Care leading to the phenomenon where "each time" is brought to its fulfilment: Being-towards-death. Indeed, that one Dasein cannot be "represented" (*Vertretbarkeit*) by another means that "no one can take [*abnehmen*] the Other's dying from him:" (ibid., p. 284). So it is not surprising that time, for Heidegger, fragments into mortal time, historical time, and cosmic time.

12. If, at the end of our periplus, we find ourselves once again on Augustinian ground, it may be because the problematic of temporality does not radically change its frame of reference in passing from Augustine's *animus* to Heidegger's Dasein, in passing through Husserl's innermost consciousness.The distributive aspect of the existential, the "each time" referred to above, imposes a residual subjective tone on an analysis that means however to be deliberately ontological. This is undoubtedly one of the reasons why the first part of *Being and Time* was left without a sequel.

13. These comments focussed on Heidegger do not exclude our seeking other correlations with Husserl's analyses. For example, between the retentions of retentions and traditionality. We explored this direction in our chapter on fiction and its imaginative variations.

14. M. Gauchet, *Le Désenchantement du monde. Une histoire politique de la religion* (Paris: Gallimard, 1985).

15. Even if a kind of thinking of a different order, that of a theology of history, which is not taken into account here, proposes to link a Genesis to an Apocalypse, it certainly does not propose to do so by introducing a plot of all plots that this thinking could set in relation to the beginning and end of all things. The simple fact that we have four Gospels to recount the event held to be the turning point of history in the confession of the early Christian church suffices to prevent theological thinking from proceeding on the basis of a univocal superplot.

16. The case of ancient Israel, referred to above with regard to the notion of narrative identity, is particularly striking. Gerhard von Rad was able to devote the first volume of his *Theology of the Old Testament*, trans. D. M. G. Stalker (New York: Harper and Row, 1962–65), to a "theology of traditions" constituted by the progressive integration of narratives of different origins into one continuous narrative that finds its initial dimensions, structure, and contours in the work of the Jahwist. To this core were added other narratives that prolonged this narration beyond the founding of the Davidic monarchy, as can be seen in the Deuteronomistic history. The case of ancient Israel is especially interesting for our thesis insofar as the narrative medium is revealed to be the principal vehicle of the confession of faith bearing on the relations of a covenant between a people and its God. It is also interesting in another way. It might be objected that this theology of traditions includes nonnarrative sections, especially the laws, which turn this part of the Hebraic Bible into a kind of teaching, a Torah. To this we may respond that the mass of legislation subsequently added to the emblematic figure of Moses could be integrated into the theology of traditions only at the price of a narrativization of the legislative moment itself. The giving of the law is turned into an event worthy of being recounted and integrated into the overall narrative. So it is relatively easy to posit the equation between tradition and narrative. As for the conjunction between narrative and nonnarrative, I shall return to this below. Cf. Paul Ricoeur, "Temps biblique," *Archivio di Filosofia* 53 (1985): 29–35.

17. See Time and Narrative, 2:88–93.

18. For example, the Jews who survived the Babylonian Exile projected their vision of new times in terms of a new Exodus, a new wilderness, a new Zion, a new Davidic kingship.

19. This is the meaning Greimas retains in his narrative semiotics. In a neighboring sense, Claude Chabrol, in his dissertation, "Eléments de psycho-sociologie du langage," uses the term "narrative schema" to designate the course covered by such complex acts as Gift, Aggression, Exchange, etc., which are both interactions and interlocutions at the same time, and which receive an appropriate expression in speech acts such as commissions and orders. So another categorization than that of genres can be applied to such narrative schemas, that of speech acts.

20. Goldschmidt, p. 76.

21. This opening to an abyss of meaning rejoins that other opening, also encountered in our commentary on Aristotle (pp. 16f.), the invincible obscurity of the definition of movement itself as the entelechy of what is as such possible (*Physics*, II, 201a10–11).

22. In this respect, I am also reminded of considerations of a more existentiell kind circulating around the expression "being in time" which the philosophical story of the *Timaeus* led us to.

23. See Clémence Ramnoux, "La notion d'Archaïsme en philosophie," *Etudes présocratiques* (Paris: Klincksieck, 1970), pp. 27–36.

24. Hermann Diels, *Ancilla to the Pre-Socratic Philosophers*, trans. Kathleen Freeman (Oxford: Basil Blackwell, 1948), p. 19, fragment B1.

25. In Mircea Eliade, *The Myth of the Eternal Return, or Cosmos and History*, trans. Willard Trask (Princeton: Princeton University Press, 1954), we find a typology of the relations between our time and the founding elements that appeared *in illo tempore*, with a special emphasis on the "terror of history" that results from the antinomical relations between the time of origins and everyday time.

26. *Myth and Thought among the Greeks*, p. 88.

27. This is the correlation that guides Vernant's analyses (see ibid., pp. 88–95) aimed at reconstituting the mental activity of ancient Greeks through a historical psychology.

28. See *Time and Narrative*, 1:22–30.

29. Let us recall this passage from Augustine: "in eternity nothing moves into the past: all is present. Time, on the other hand, is never all present at once" (*Confessions*, 11:13). Also: "Your years are completely present to you all at once, because they are at a permanent standstill [simul stant]" (ibid., 13:16). Cf. *Time and Narrative*, 1:236, n. 35, regarding the question of which term is positive and which negative.

30. Any exegesis of Exodus 3:14 must take into account the declaration that follows it. "And he said, 'Say this to the people of Israel, "I am has sent me to you."' God also said to Moses, 'Say this to the people of Israel, "The Lord, the God of your fathers, the God of Abraham, the God of Isaac, and the God of Jacob, has sent me to you": this is my name forever, and thus I am to be remembered throughout the generations'" (3:14b–15).

31. The unpronounceable name of JHWH designates the vanishing point common to the suprahistorical and the intrahistorical. Accompanied by the prohibition against graven images, this "name" preserves the inscrutable and sets it at a distance from its own historical figures.

32. These questions are given considerable development and a new orientation in Heidegger's *Kant and the Problem of Metaphysics*, trans. James S. Churchill (Bloomington: Indiana University Press, 1962), particularly in §§9, 10, and 32–34. See also *The Basic Problems of Phenomenology*, §§7–9 and 21, and *Interprétation phénoménologique de la "Critique de la Raison pure" de Kant*, trans. E. Martineau (Paris: Gallimard, 1982), from volume 25 of the *Gesamtausgabe*.

33. See *The Basic Problems of Phenomenology*, §§19–22, pp. 229–330.

34. In this work, we need not take a stand concerning Heidegger's ambition, stated at the end of *The Basic Problems of Phenomenology*, to ground a scientific ontology on

the new a priori that Temporality henceforth constitutes (ibid., p. 327). In any case, Heidegger's intention not to allow this science to turn into a new form of hermeticism is strongly underscored in the closing pages of his lectures (which were not completed) where he takes up for his own use the opposition Kant makes in the short manuscript "Von einem neuerdings erhobenen vornehmen Ton in der Philosophie" (1796) between the sobriety of the Plato of the *Letters* and the supposedly intoxicated Plato of the Academy, a mystagogue in spite of himself.

35. See *Time and Narrative,* 1:175–225.

36. The word "magic" falls from Proust's pen when he speaks of the moribund figures at the dinner of death's-heads that follows the Visitation scene. "These were puppets bathed in the immaterial colours of the years, puppets which exteriorized Time, Time which by Habit is made invisible and to become visible seeks bodies, which wherever it finds it seizes, to display its magic lantern upon them" (3:967).

37. The first intersection characterizes the Pentateuch. With the Jahwist document, narrative and laws are interwoven. In this way the immemorial aspect of narrative, turned toward what went before by the prefaces to the prefaces that precede the narratives of the covenant and deliverance, intersects with the immemorial aspect of the Law, condensed into the Revelation at Sinai. Other significant interweavings can be added to this one. The prophetic openness to time provokes, as a kind of recoil effect, an overturning of the theology of traditions developed by the Pentateuch. In turn, the historicity common to both traditions and prophets, which is retrospective as well as prospective, is confronted by that other form of the immemorial, wisdom, gathered into the wisdom writings of Proverbs, the book of Job, and Ecclesiastes. Finally, all these figures of the immemorial are reactualized in the laments and praises found in the Psalms. So it is by a chain of nonnarrative mediations that, in the Bible, narrative is brought to the stage of a confessional narrative (see above, p. 200 n. 16).

38. Cf. Käte Hamburger, *The Logic of Literature,* 2nd. rev. ed., trans. Marilyn J. Rose (Bloomington: Indiana University Press, 1973), discussed in *Time and Narrative,* 2:65–66.

Bibliography

Alexander, J. *The Venture of Form in the Novels of Virginia Woolf.* Port Washington, New York: Kennikat Press, 1974.

Alter, Robert. *Partial Magic: The Novel as a Self-Conscious Genre.* Berkeley: University of California Press, 1975.

Anscombe, Elizabeth. *Intention.* Oxford: Basil Blackwell, 1957.

Apel, Karl-Otto et al. *Hermeneutik und Ideologiekritik.* Frankfurt: Suhrkamp, 1971.

Arendt, Hannah. *The Human Condition.* Chicago: University of Chicago Press, 1958.

Ariès, Philippe. *The Hour of Our Death.* Trans. Helen Weaver. New York: Knopf, 1981.

Aristotle. *The Complete Works of Aristotle.* Ed. Jonathan Barnes. Princeton: Princeton University Press, 1984, 2 volumes.

———. *La Poétique.* Texte, traduction, notes par Roselyne Dupont-Roc et Jean Lallot. Paris: Seuil, 1980.

———. *La Poétique.* Texte établi et traduit par J. Hardy. Paris: Les Belles Lettres, 1969.

———. *Poetics.* Introduction, commentary, and appendices by Frank L. Lucas. New York: Oxford University Press, 1968.

———. *Poetics.* Trans., with an introduction and notes, James Hutton. New York: W. W. Norton, 1982.

Aron, Raymond. *Introduction to the Philosophy of History: An Essay on the Limits of Historical Objectivity.* Trans. George J. Irwin. Boston: Beacon Press, 1961.

———. *La Philosophie critique de l'histoire: essai sur une théorie allemand de l'histoire.* Paris: Vrin, 1969.

———. "Comment l'historien écrit l'épistémologie: à propos du livre de Paul Veyne." *Annales,* no. 6 (November–December 1971): 1319–54.

Auerbach, Erich. *Mimesis: The Representation of Reality in Western Literature.* Trans. Willard R. Trask. Princeton: Princeton University Press, 1953.

Augustine. *Confessions.* Trans. E. Tréhorel and G. Bouissou. Translation based on the text of M. Skutella (Stuttgart: Teubner, 1934), with an introduction and notes by A. Solignac. Paris: Desclée de Brouwer, 1962.

———. *Confessions.* Trans. R. S. Pine-Coffin. New York: Penguin Books, 1961.

Austin, J. L. *How to Do Things with Words.* Ed. J. O. Urmson. New York: Oxford University Press, 1965.

Bakhtin, Mihail. *The Dialogic Imagination: Four Essays.* Ed. Michael Holquist. Trans. Caryl Emerson and Michael Holquist. Austin: University of Texas Press, 1981.

———. *Problems of Dostoevski's Poetics.* Trans. R. W. Rotsel. Ann Arbor: Ardis Publications, 1973.

Balas, David L. "Eternity and Time in Gregory of Nyssa's *Contra Eunomium*." In H. Dorrie, M. Altenburger, and U. Sinryhe, eds., *Gregory von Nyssa und die Philosophie*. Leiden: E. J. Brill, 1972, pp. 128–53.

Barreau, Hervé. *La Construction de la notion de temps*. Strasbourg: Atelier du Département de Physique, VLP, 1985.

Barthes, Roland. "Introduction to the Structural Analysis of Narrative." In *A Roland Barthes Reader*, ed. Susan Sontag. New York: Hill and Wang, 1982, pp. 251–95.

———. *Poétique du récit*. Paris: Seuil, 1977.

———. *Writing Degree Zero and Elements of Semiology*. Trans. Annette Lavers and Colin Smith. Boston: Beacon Press, 1976.

Beierwaltes, W. *Plotin über Ewigkeit und Zeit: Enneade III 7*. Frankfurt: Klostermann, 1967.

Benjamin, Walter. "The Storyteller." In *Illuminations*, ed. Hannah Arendt, trans. Harry Zohn. New York: Schocken Books, 1969, pp. 83–109.

Benveniste, Emile. *Problèmes de linguistique générale*, volume 2. Paris: Gallimard, 1974.

———. *Problems in General Linguistics*. Trans. Mary Elizabeth Meek. Coral Gables: University of Miami Press, 1977.

Bergson, Henri. *Time and Free Will: An Essay on the Immediate Data of Consciousness*. Trans. F. L. Pogson. New York: Macmillan, 1912.

Berlin, Isaiah. "Historical Inevitability." In *Four Essays on Liberty*. London: Oxford University Press, 1969. Also in Gardiner, ed., *Theories of History*, pp. 161–86.

Bernet, R. "Die ungegenwärtige Gegenwart. Anwesenheit und Abwesenheit in Husserls Analyse des Zeitbewusstseins." In E. W. Orth, ed., *Zeit und Zeitlichkeit bei Husserl und Heidegger*. Freiberg and Munich, 1983, pp. 16–57.

———. "La présence du passé dans l'analyse husserlienne de la conscience du temps." *Revue de métaphysique et de morale* 88 (1983): 178–98.

Berr, H. *L'Histoire traditionnelle et la Synthèse historique*. Paris: Alcan, 1921.

Bersani, L. "Déguisement du moi et art fragmentaire." In Roland Barthes et al., *Recherche de Proust*. Paris: Seuil, 1980, pp. 13–33.

Bloch, Marc. *The Historian's Craft*. Trans. Peter Putnam. New York: Knopf, 1953.

Blumenberg, H. "Nachahmung der Natur! Zur Vorgeschichte der schöpferischer Menschen." *Studium Generale* 10 (1957): 266–83.

Booth, Wayne. *The Rhetoric of Fiction*. Chicago: University of Chicago Press, 1961, ²1981.

———. "Distance and Point of View." *Essays in Criticism* 11 (1961): 60–79.

———. "The Way I Loved George Eliot: Friendship with Books as a Neglected Metaphor." *Kenyon Review* 11, no. 2 (1980): 4–27.

Boros, Stanislas. "Les Catégories de la temporalité chez saint Augustin." *Archives de Philosophie* 21 (1958): 323–85.

Braudel, Fernand. *Civilization & Capitalism: 15th-18 Century*. Trans. Siân Reynolds. New York: Harper and Row, 1981–84. Volume 1: *The Structures of Everyday Life: The Limits of the Possible*. Volume 2: *The Wheels of Commerce*. Volume 3: *The Perspective of the World*.

———. *The Mediterranean and the Mediterranean World in the Age of Philip II*. Trans. Siân Reynolds (New York: Harper & Row, 1972–74, 2 volumes.

———. *On History*. Trans. Sarah Matthews. Chicago: University of Chicago Press, 1980.

Bremond, Claude. "The Logic of Narrative Possibilities." *New Literary History* 11 (1980): 387–411.

———. *La Logique du récit*. Paris: Seuil, 1973.

Brisson, Luc. *Le Même et l'Autre dans la structure ontologique du Timée de Platon: un commentaire systématique de Timée du Platon*. Paris: Klincksieck, 1974.

Bibliography

Burckhardt, Jacob. *Force and Freedom: Reflections on History.* Trans. James Hastings Nichols. New York: Pantheon, 1943.
Burke, Kenneth. *A Grammar of Motives.* Berkeley: University of California Press, 1969.
―――. *Language as Symbolic Action: Essays on Life, Literature, and Method.* Berkeley: University of California Press, 1966.
Callahan, John C. *Four Views of Time in Ancient Philosophy.* Cambridge: Harvard University Press, 1948.
―――. "Gregory of Nyssa and the Psychological View of Time." *Acts of the Twelfth International Congress of Philosophy.* Florence, 1960, p. 59.
―――. "Basil of Caesarea: A New Source for Augustine's Theory of Time." *Harvard Studies in Classical Philology* 63 (1958): 437–54.
Canary, R., and Kozicki, M. *The Writing of History: Literary Form and Historical Understanding.* Madison: University of Wisconsin Press, 1978.
Certeau, Michel de. *L'Ecriture de l'histoire.* Paris: Gallimard, 1975.
―――. "L'opération historique." In Le Goff and Nora, eds., *Faire de l'histoire,* pp. 3–41.
Chabrol, Claude. "Eléments de psycho-sociologie du langage." Dissertation.
Charles, Michel. *Rhétorique de la lecture.* Paris: Seuil, 1977.
Chatman, Seymour. *Story and Discourse: Narrative Structure in Fiction.* Ithaca: Cornell University Press, 1978.
―――. "The Structure of Narrative Transmission." In Fowler, ed., *Style and Structure in Literature,* pp. 213–57.
Chaunu, Huguette, and Chaunu, Pierre. *Séville et l'Atlantique: 1504–1650.* Paris: SEPVEN, 1955–60, 12 volumes.
Chaunu, Pierre. *Histoire quantitative—Histoire sérielle.* Paris: Armand Colin, 1978.
―――. *La Mort à Paris, XVIᵉ, XVIIᵉ, XVIIIᵉ siècles.* Paris: Fayard, 1978.
Cohn, Dorit. *Transparent Minds: Narrative Modes for Presenting Consciousness in Fiction.* Princeton: Princeton University Press, 1978.
Collingwood, R. G. *An Autobiography.* Oxford: Oxford University Press, 1939.
―――. *An Essay on Metaphysics.* Oxford: Clarendon Press, 1948.
―――. *The Idea of History.* Ed. T. M. Knox. Oxford: Oxford University Press, 1946.
Conen, P. F. *Die Zeittheorie des Aristoteles.* Munich: C. H. Beck, 1964.
Cornford, F. M. *Plato's Cosmology: The Timaeus of Plato translated with a running commentary.* New York: The Liberal Arts Press, 1957.
Costa de Beauregard, O. *La Notion de temps. Equivalence avec l'espace.* Paris: Hermann, 1953.
―――. "Two Lectures on the Direction of Time." *Synthèse* 35 (1977): 129–54.
Couderc, P. *Le Calendrier.* Paris: Presses Universitaires de France, 1961.
Courcelle, P. *Recherches sur les Confessions de saint Augustin.* Paris: de Boccard, 1950.
―――. "Traditions néo-platoniciennes et traditions chrétiennes de la région de dissemblance." *Archives d'Histoire Littéraire et Doctrinale du Moyen Age* 24 (1927): 5–33. Reprinted as an appendix to *Recherches sur les Confessions de saint Augustin.*
Culler, Jonathan. "Defining Narrative Units." In Fowler, ed., *Style and Structure in Literature,* pp. 123–42.
Dagognet, François. *Ecriture et Iconographie.* Paris: Vrin, 1973.
Daiches, David. *The Novel and the Modern World.* Chicago: University of Chicago Press, 1939; revised edition, 1960.
―――. *Virginia Woolf.* Norfolk, Conn.: New Directions, 1942; revised edition, 1963.
Danto, Arthur. "What Can We Do?" *The Journal of Philosophy* 60 (1963): 435–45.
―――. "Basic Actions." *American Philosophical Quarterly* 2 (1965): 141–48. Re-

printed in Alan R. White, ed., *The Philosophy of Action*. New York: Oxford University Press, 1968, pp. 43–58.

———. *Analytical Philosophy of History*. New York: Cambridge University Press, 1965.

———. *Analytical Philosophy of Action*. New York: Cambridge University Press, 1973.

Deleuze, Gilles. *Proust and Signs*. Trans. Richard Howard. New York: George Braziller, 1972.

Derrida, Jacques. *Speech and Phenomena*. Trans. David B. Allison. Evanston: Northwestern University Press, 1973.

———. "Ousia and Gramme: Note on a Note from *Being and Time*." In *Margins of Philosophy*. Trans. Alan Bass. Chicago: University of Chicago Press, 1982, pp. 29–67.

Diels, Hermann. *Ancilla to the Pre-Socratic Philosophers*. Trans. Kathleen Freeman. Oxford, Basil Blackwell, 1948.

Dilthey. Wilhelm. "Ueber der Studium des Geschichte, der Wissenschaften vom Menschen, der Gesellschaft und dem Staat" (1875). In *Gesammelte Schriften:* Leipzig: B. G. Teubner, 1924, 5:31–73.

Doležel, L. *Narrative Modes in Czech Literature*. Toronto: University of Toronto Press, 1973.

———. "The Typology of the Narrator: Point of View in Fiction." In *To Honor Roman Jakobson,* volume 1. The Hague: Mouton, 1967, pp. 541–52.

Dray, William. *Laws and Explanations in History*. London: Oxford University Press, 1957.

———, ed. *Philosophical Analysis and History*. New York: Harper & Row, 1966.

Droysen, J.-G. *Historik*. Ed. R. Hübner. Munich and Berlin: R. Oldenbourg, 1943.

Duby, Georges. Préface. In Marc Bloch, *Apologie pour l'histoire ou Métier d'historien*. Paris, 1974.

———. "Histoire sociale et idéologie des sociétés." In Le Goff and Nora, eds., *Faire de l'histoire,* 1:147–68.

———. *The Three Orders: Feudal Society Imagined*. Trans. Arthur Goldhammer. Chicago: University of Chicago Press, 1980.

Dufrenne, Mikel. *The Phenomenology of Aesthetic Experience*. Trans. Edward S. Casey and others. Evanston: Northwestern University Press, 1973.

Duhem, Pierre. *Le Système du monde,* volume 1. Paris: A. Hermann, 1913.

Dumézil, G. *Les Dieux souverains des Indo-Européens*. Paris: Gallimard, 1977.

———. "Temps et mythe." *Recherches philosophiques* 5 (1935–36): 235–51.

Durkheim, Emile. *The Elementary Forms of Religious Life*. Trans. Joseph Ward Swain. New York: The Free Press, 1965.

Eliade, Mircea. *The Myth of the Eternal Return, or Cosmos and History*. Trans. Willard Trask. Princeton: Princeton University Press, 1954.

Else, G. F. *Aristotle's Poetics: The Argument*. Cambridge: Harvard University Press, 1957.

Escande, Jacques. *Le Récepteur face à l'Acte persuasif. Contribution a la théorie de l'interprétation (à partir de l'analyse de textes évangéliques)*. Thèse de 3ᵉ cycle en sémantique générale dirigée par A.-J. Greimas. Paris: EPHESS, 1979.

Febvre, Lucien. *Combats pour l'histoire*. Paris: Armand Colin, 1953.

Ferry, J.-M. "Ethique de la communication et Théorie de la démocratie chez Habermas." Dissertation, 1984.

Fessard, G. *La Philosophie historique de Raymond Aron*. Paris: Julliard, 1980.

Findlay, J. N. *Kant and the Transcendental Object: A Hermeneutic Study*. Oxford: Clarendon Press, 1981.

Bibliography

Fink, Eugen. "Vergegenwärtigen und Bild: Beiträge zur Phänomenologie der Unwirklichkeit." In *Studien zur Phänomenologie (1930–1939)*. The Hague: M. Nijhoff, 1966, pp. 1–78. *De la Phénoménologie*, trans. Didier Franck. Paris: Minuit, 1975, pp. 15–93.

Florival, G. *Le Désir chez Proust*. Louvain and Paris: Nauwelaerts, 1971.

Focillon, Henri. *The Life of Forms in Art*. Trans. Charles Beecher Hogan and George Keebler. New Haven: Yale University Press, 1942.

Foucault, Michel. *The Archeology of Knowledge*. Trans. A. M. Sheridan Smith. New York: Pantheon, 1972.

———. *The Order of Things*. New York: Vintage Books, 1973.

Fowler, Roger, ed. *Style and Structure in Literature: Essays in the New Stylistics*. Ithaca: Cornell University Press, 1975.

Fraisse, Paul. *The Psychology of Time*. New York: Harper and Row, 1963.

———. *Psychologie du rythme*. Paris: Presses Universitaires de France, 1974.

Frankel, C. "Explanation and Interpretation in History." *Philosophy of Science* 24 (1957): 137–55. Reprinted in Gardiner, ed., *Theories of History*, pp. 408–27.

Frazer, J. T. *The Genesis and Evolution of Time: A Critique of Interpretation in Physics*. Amherst: University of Massachusetts Press, 1982.

Friedemann, K. *Die Rolle des Erzählers im Epik*. Leipzig, 1910.

Frye, Northrop. *Anatomy of Criticism: Four Essays*. Princeton: Princeton University Press, 1957.

———. "New Directions from Old." In *Fables of Identity: Studies in Poetic Mythology*. New York: Harcourt Brace and World, 1963, pp. 52–66.

Furet, François. *Interpreting the French Revolution*. Trans. Elborg Forster. Cambridge: Cambridge University Press; Paris: Editions de la Maison des Sciences de l'Homme, 1981.

Gadamer, Hans-Georg. *Truth and Method*. Trans. and ed. Garrett Barden and John Cumming. New York: Seabury Press, 1975.

Gallie. W. B. *Philosophy and the Historical Understanding*. New York: Schocken Books, 1964.

Gambel, Isabel. "Clarissa Dalloway's Double." In Jacqueline E. M. Latham, ed., *Critics on Virginia Woolf*. Coral Gables: University of Miami Press, 1970, pp. 52–55.

Gardiner, Patrick. *The Nature of Historical Explanation*. Oxford: Clarendon Press, 1952.

———, ed. *The Philosophy of History*. New York: Oxford University Press, 1974.

———, ed. *Theories of History*. New York: The Free Press, 1959.

Garelli, Jacques. *Le Recel et la Dispersion: Essai sur le champ de lecture poétique*. Paris: Gallimard, 1978.

Gauchet, M. *Le Désenchantement du monde. Une histoire politique de la religion*. Paris: Gallimard, 1985.

Geertz, Clifford. *The Interpretation of Cultures*. New York: Basic Books, 1973.

Genette, Gérard. "Frontiers of Narrative." In *Figures of Literary Discourse*. Trans. Alan Sheridan. New York: Columbia University Press, 1982, pp. 127–44.

———. *Narrative Discourse: An Essay in Method*. Trans. Jane E. Lewin. Ithaca: Cornell University Press, 1980.

———. *Nouveau Discours du récit*. Paris: Seuil, 1983.

———. "La question de l'écriture." In Roland Barthes et al., *Recherche de Proust*. Paris: Seuil, 1980, pp. 7–12.

Gilson, Etienne. "Notes sur l'être et le temps chez saint Augustin." *Recherches augustiniennes* 2 (1962): 204–23.

———. *Philosophie et Incarnation chez saint Augustin*. Montreal: Institut d'études médiévales, 1947.

————. "*Regio dissimilitudinis* de Platon à saint Bernard de Clairvaux." *Medieval Studies* 9 (1947): 108–30.

Goethe, J. W. "Uber epische und dramatische Dichtung" (1797). In *Sämtliche Werke.* Stuttgart and Berlin: Jubiläums-Ausgabe, 1902–7, volume 36, pp. 149–52.

Golden, Leon. "Catharsis." In *Proceedings of the American Philological Association* 43 (1962): 51–60.

Golden, L., and Hardison, O. B. *Aristotle's Poetics: A Translation and Commentary for Students of Literature.* Englewood Cliffs, N. J.: Prentice-Hall, 1968.

Goldman, A. I. *A Theory of Human Action.* Englewood Cliffs, N. J.: Prentice-Hall, 1970.

Goldschmidt, Victor. *Le Système stoïcien et l'Idée de Temps.* Paris: Vrin, 1953.

————. *Temps physique et Temps tragique chez Aristote.* Paris: Vrin, 1982.

Gombrich. E. H. *Art and Illusion.* Princeton: Princeton University Press, 1961.

Goodfield, Jane, and Toulmin, Stephen. *The Discovery of Time.* Chicago: University of Chicago Press, 1977.

Goodman, Nelson. *The Languages of Art: An Approach to a Theory of Symbols.* Indianapolis: Hackett, 1968.

Gorman, Bernard S., and Wessman, Alden, eds. *The Personal Experience of Time.* New York: Plenum Press, 1977.

Goubert, P. *Bouvais et le Beauvaisis de 1600 à 1730.* Paris: SEVPEN, 1960. Reprinted as *Cent Mille Provinciaux au XVIIe siècle.* Paris: Flammarion, 1968.

Gouhier, Henri. *Antonin Artaud et l'essence du théâtre.* Paris: Vrin, 1974.

————. *Le Théâtre et l'existence.* Paris: Aubier-Montaigne, 1952.

Graham, John. "Time in the Novels of Virginia Woolf." *University of Toronto Quarterly* 18 (1949): 186–201. Reprinted in Latham, ed., *Critics on Virginia Woolf,* pp. 28–35.

Granel, Gérard. *Le Sens du temps et de la perception chez E. Husserl.* Paris: Gallimard, 1958.

Granger, G. G. *Essai d'un philosophie de style.* Paris: Armand Colin, 1968.

Granier, Jean. *Discours du monde.* Paris: Seuil, 1977.

Greimas, A.-J. *Du Sens: Essais sémiotiques.* Paris: Seuil, 1970.

————. *Du Sens II.* Paris: Seuil, 1983.

————. "Eléments d'une grammaire narrative." *L'Homme* 9:3 (1963): 71–92.

————. "The Interaction of Semiotic Constraints." *Yale French Studies* 41 (1968): 86–105.

————. *Maupassant. La sémiotique du texte: exercices pratiques.* Paris: Seuil, 1976.

————. *Structural Semantics: An Attempt at a Method.* Trans. Daniele McDowell, Ronald Schleifer, Alan Velie. Lincoln: University of Nebraska Press, 1983.

Greimas, A.-J., and Courtés, J. *Semiotics and Language: An Analytical Dictionary.* Trans. Larry Christ, Daniel Patte, et al. Bloomington: Indiana University Press, 1982.

Grondin, J. "La conscience du travail de l'histoire et le problème de la vérité herméneutique." *Archives de philosophie* 44 (1981): 435–53.

Grünbaum, Adolf. *Philosophical Problems of Space and Time.* Dordrecht and Boston: D. Reidel, 1973, ²1974.

Guiguet, J. *Virginia Woolf and Her Works.* London: The Hogarth Press, 1965.

Guillaume, G. *Temps et Verbe.* Paris: Champion, 1929, 1965.

Guitton, J. *Le Temps et l'Eternité chez Plotin et saint Augustin.* Paris: Vrin, 1933, 1971.

Gurvitch, George. *The Spectrum of Social Time.* Trans. and ed. Myrtle Korenbaum assisted by Phillip Bosserman. Dordrecht: D. Reidel, 1964.

Habermas, Jürgen. "La modernité: un projet inachevé." *Critique,* no. 413 (1981): 950–69.

———. *The Theory of Communicative Action.* Trans. Thomas McCarthy. Boston: Beacon Press, 1984.

Hafley, J. *The Glass Roof: Virginia Woolf as Novelist.* Berkeley: University of California Press, 1954.

Halbwachs, Maurice. *Les Cadres sociaux de la mémoire.* Paris: Alcan, 1925.

———. *The Collective Memory.* Trans. Francis J. Ditter and Vida Uzadi Ditter. New York: Harper and Row, 1980.

Hamburger, Käte. *The Logic of Literature.* 2nd rev. ed., trans. Marilynn J. Rose. Bloomington: Indiana University Press, 1973.

Hart, H. L. A. "The Ascription of Responsibility and Rights." *Proceedings of the Aristotelian Society* 49 (1948): 171–94.

Hart, H. L. A., and Honoré, A. M. *Causation in the Law.* Oxford: Clarendon Press, 1959.

Hegel, G. W. F. *Lectures on the Philosopy of World History: Introduction—Reason in History.* Trans. Duncan Forbes. Cambridge: Cambridge University Press, 1975.

———. *The Phenomenology of Spirit.* Trans. A. V. Miller. Oxford: Clarendon Press, 1977.

———. *Philosophy of Right.* Trans. T. M. Knox. New York: Oxford University Press, 1967.

Heidegger, Martin. *Being and Time.* Trans. John Macquarrie and Edward Robinson. New York: Harper and Row, 1962.

———. *The Basic Problems of Phenomenology.* Trans. Albert Hofstadter. Bloomington: Indiana Unviersity Press, 1982.

———. "Ce qu' est et comment se détermine la *Physis.*" In *Questions II,* trans. F. Fédier. Paris: Gallimard, 1968, pp. 165–276.

———. *Interprétation phénoménologique de la "Critique de la Raison pure" de Kant.* Trans. E. Martineau. Paris: Gallimard, 1982.

———. *Kant and the Problem of Metaphysics.* Trans. James S. Churchill. Bloomington: Indiana University Press, 1962.

Hempel, Carl G. "The Function of General Laws in History." *The Journal of Philosophy* 39 (1942): 35–48. Reprinted in Gardiner, ed., *Theories of History,* pp. 344–56.

Henry, A. *Proust romancier: le tombeau égyptien.* Paris: Flammarion, 1983.

Heussi, Karl. *Die Krisis des Historismus.* Tübingen: J. C. B. Mohr, 1932.

Hubert, René. "Etude sommaire de la représentation du temps dans la religion et la magie." In *Mélanges d'histoire des religions.* Paris, Alcan, 1909.

Husserl, Edmund. *The Crisis of the European Sciences and Transcendental Philosophy.* Trans. David Carr. Evanston: Northwestern University Press, 1970.

———. *Cartesian Meditations: An Introduction to Phenomenology.* Trans. Dorian Cairns. The Hague: Martinus Nijhoff, 1960.

———. *Ideas Pertaining to a Pure Phenomenology and to a Phenomenological Philosophy. First Book: General Introduction to a Pure Phenomenology.* Trans. F. Kersten. The Hague: Martinus Nijhoff, 1982.

———. *The Phenomenology of Internal Time-Consciousness.* Trans. James S. Churchill with an introduction by Calvin O. Schrag. Bloomington: Indiana University Press, 1964.

———. *Zur Phänomenologie des inneren Zeitbewusstseins (1893–1917).* Ed. Rudolf Boehme. *Husserliana,* volume 10. The Hague: Martinus Nijhoff, 1966.

Ingarden, Roman. *Cognition of the Literary Work of Art.* Trans. Ruth Ann Crowley and Kenneth R. Olson. Evanston: Northwestern University Press, 1973.

————. *The Literary Work of Art: An Investigation on the Borderlines of Ontology, Logic, and Theory of Literature*. Trans. George G. Grabowicz. Evanston: Northwestern University Press, 1974.

Iser, Wolfgang. *The Act of Reading: A Theory of Aesthetic Response*. Baltimore: Johns Hopkins University Press, 1978.

————. *The Implied Reader: Patterns of Communication in Prose Fiction from Bunyan to Beckett*. Baltimore: Johns Hopkins University Press, 1974.

————. "Indeterminacy as the Reader's Response in Prose Fiction." In J. Hillis Miller, ed. *Aspects of Narrative*. New York: Columbia University Press, 1971, pp. 1–45.

Jacob, André. *Temps et Langage: Essai sur les structures du sujet parlant*. Paris: Armand Colin, 1967.

Jacques, F. *Dialogiques, Recherches logiques sur le dialogue*. Paris: Presses Universitaires de France, 1979.

————. *Dialogiques II, l'Espace logique de l'interlocution*. Paris: Presses Universitaires de France, 1985.

James, Henry. "Preface to *The Portrait of a Lady*." In *The Art of the Novel*, ed. R. P. Blackmur. New York: Charles Scribner's Sons, 1934, pp. 42–48.

Janet, Pierre. *Le Développement de la mémoire et de la notion de temps*. Paris: A. Chahine, 1928.

Jauss, Hans Robert. *Aesthetic Experience and Literary Hermeneutics*. Trans. Michael Shaw. Minneapolis: University of Minnesota Press, 1982.

————. *Kleine Apologie der aesthetischen Erfahrung*. Constance: Verlaganstalt, 1972.

————. "Ueberlegungen zur Abgrenzung und Aufgabenstellung einer literarischen Hermeneutik." *Poetik und Hermeneutik* 9 (Munich: Fink, 1980), pp. 459–81. "Limites et tâches d'une herméneutique littéraire." *Diogène* no. 109 (January–March 1980): 92–119.

————. *Toward an Aesthetic of Reception*. Trans. Timothy Bahti. Minneapolis: University of Minnesota Press, 1982.

————. *Zeit und Erinnerung in Marcel Prousts A la recherche du temps perdu*. Heidelberg: Carl Winter, 1955.

Kant, Immanuel. *Critique of Judgment*. Trans. J. H. Bernard. New York: Hafner, 1966.

————. *Critique of Practical Reason*. Trans. Lewis White Beck. Indianapolis: Library of the Liberal Arts, 1956.

————. *Critique of Pure Reason*. Trans. Norman Kemp Smith. New York: St. Martin's Press, 1965.

————. "On the Form and Principles of the Sensible and Intelligible World." In *Kant: Selected Precritical Writings and Correspondence with Beck*, trans. G. B. Kerferd and D. E. Walford. New York: Barnes and Noble, 1968, pp. 45–92.

————. "History from a Cosmopolitan Point of View." In *Perpetual Peace and Other Essays*, trans. Ted Humphrey. Indianapolis: Hackett, 1983, pp. 29–49.

————. "Perpetual Peace." In *Perpetual Peace and Other Essays*, trans. Ted Humphrey. Indianapolis: Hackett, 1983, pp. 107–43.

————. *Versuch, den Begriff der negativen Grossen in die Weltweisheit einzuführen*, 1763.

Kenny, Anthony. *Action, Emotion and Will*. London: Routledge and Kegan Paul, 1963.

Kermode, Frank. *The Genesis of Secrecy: On the Interpretation of Narrative*. Cambridge: Harvard University Press, 1979.

————. *The Sense of an Ending: Studies in the Theory of Fiction*. New York: Oxford University Press, 1966.

Koselleck, Reinhart. *Futures Past: The Semantics of Historical Time.* Trans. Keith Tribe. Cambridge: The MIT Press, 1985.

Kracauer, S. "Time and History." In *Zeugnisse. Theodor Adorno zum 60. Geburtstag.* Frankfurt: Suhrkamp, 1963, pp. 50–64.

Krieger, Leonard, ed. *Ranke: The Meaning of History.* Chicago: University of Chicago Press, 1977.

Kucich, John. "Action in the Dickens Ending: *Bleak House* and *Great Expectations.*" *Nineteenth Century Fiction* (1978): 88–109.

Lacombe, P. *De l'histoire considérée comme une science.* Paris: Hachette, 1894.

Langlois, Charles Victor, and Seignobos, Charles. *Introduction to the Study of History.* Trans. G. G. Berry. New York: Henry Holt, 1908.

Latham, Jacqueline E. M., ed. *Critics on Virginia Woolf.* Coral Gables: University of Miami Press, 1970.

Le Goff, Jacques. "Documento/Monumento." *Enciclopedia Einaudi.* Turin: Einaudi, 5:38–48.

———. *Time, Work, and Culture in the Middle Ages.* Trans. Arthur Goldhammer. Chicago: University of Chicago Press, 1980.

Le Goff, Jacques; Chartier, Roger; and Revel, Jacques. *La Nouvelle Histoire.* Paris: Retz-CEPL, 1978.

Le Goff, Jacques, and Nora, Pierre, eds., *Faire de l'histoire.* Paris: Gallimard, 1974, 3 volumes.

Lejeune, P. *Le Pacte autobiographique.* Paris: Seuil, 1975.

Le Roy Ladurie, Emmanuel. *Carnival in Romans.* Trans. Mary Feeney. New York: G. Braziller, 1979.

———. *Montaillou: The Promised Land of Error.* Trans. Barbara Bray. New York: G. Braziller, 1978.

———. *The Peasants of Languedoc.* Trans. John Day. Urbana: University of Illinois Press, 1974.

———. *Times of Feast, Times of Famine: A History of Climate since the Year 1000.* Trans. Barbara Bray. Garden City, N. Y.: Doubleday, 1971.

———. *The Territory of the Historian.* Trans. Ben Reynolds and Siân Reynolds. Chicago: University of Chicago Press, 1979.

Lévinas, Emmanuel. "La Trace." In *Humanisme de l'autre homme.* Montpellier: Fata Morgana, 1972, pp. 57–63.

Lévi-Strauss, Claude. *The Savage Mind.* Chicago: University of Chicago Press, 1966.

———. "The Story of Asdiwal." In *Structural Anthropology.* Trans. Monique Layton. New York: Basic Books, 1976, 2:146–97.

———. "The Structural Study of Myth." In *Structural Anthropology.* Trans. Claire Jacobson and Brooke Grundfest. New York: Basic Books, 1963, pp. 206–31.

Lotman, Juri. *The Structure of the Artistic Text.* Trans. Ronald Vronn. Ann Arbor: University of Michigan Press, 1977.

Love, J. O. *Worlds in Consciousness: Mythopoetic Thought in the Novels of Virginia Woolf.* Berkeley: University of California Press, 1970.

Lubac, Henri de. *Exégèse médiévale. Les quatre sens de l'Ecriture.* Paris: Aubier, 1959–64, 4 volumes.

Lübbe, H. "Was aus Handlungen Geschichten macht: Handlungsinterferenz; Heterogonie der Zwecke; Widerfahrnis; Handlungsgemengeladen; Zufall." In Jürgen Mittelstrass and Manfred Reidel, eds., *Vernünftiges Denken, Studien zur prakitschen Philosophie und Wissenschaftstheorie.* Berlin and New York: W. De Gruyter, 1978, pp. 237–68.

Mackie. J. L. *The Cement of the Universe: A Study of Causation.* Oxford: Clarendon Press, 1974.

Malraux, André. *The Voices of Silence.* Trans. Gilbert Stuart and Francis Price. Garden City, N. Y.: Doubleday, 1967.

Mandelbaum, Maurice. *The Anatomy of Historical Knowledge.* Baltimore: Johns Hopkins University Press, 1977.

———. *The Problem of Historical Knowledge.* New York: Liveright, 1938.

Mann, Thomas. *The Magic Mountain.* Trans. H. T. Lowe-Porter. New York: Alfred A. Knopf, 1927; Vintage Books, 1969.

Mannheim, Karl. "The Problem of Generations." In *Essays on the Sociology of Knowledge,* ed. Paul Kecskemeti. London: Routledge and Kegan Paul, 1952, pp. 276–322.

Marrou, Henri I. *The Meaning of History.* Trans. Robert J. Olson. Baltimore: Helicon, 1966.

Martin, Gottfried. *Kant's Metaphysics and Theory of Science.* Trans. P. G. Lucas. Manchester University Press, 1955.

Martin, Rex. *Historical Explanation: Reenactment and Practical Inference.* Ithaca: Cornell University Press, 1977.

Martineau, E. "Conception vulgaire et conception aristotélicienne du temps. Notes sur *Grundprobleme der Phänomenologie* de Heidegger." *Archives de philosophie* 43 (1980): 99–120.

Marx, Karl. *The Eighteenth Brumaire of Louis Napoleon.* Trans. Eden and Cedar Paul. London: Allen and Unwin, 1926.

Maupassant, Guy de. "Two Friends." In *Selected Short Stories.* Trans. Roger Colet. New York: Penguin, 1971, pp. 147–56.

Meijering, E. P. *Augustin über Schöpfung, Ewigkeit und Zeit. Das elfte Buch der Bekenntnisse.* Leiden: E. J. Brill, 1979.

Mendilow, A. A. *Time and the Novel.* London: Peter Nevill, 1952; 2d ed., New York: Humanities Press, 1972.

Merleau-Ponty, Maurice. *Phenomenology of Perception.* Trans. Colin Smith. New York: Humanities Press, 1962.

———. *The Visible and the Invisible.* Ed. Claude Lefort. Trans. Alphonso Lingis. Evanston: Northwestern University Press, 1968.

Meyer, E. *Zur Theorie und Methodik der Geschichte.* Halle, 1901.

Meyer, Hans. *Thomas Mann.* Frankfurt: Suhrkamp, 1980.

Michel, H. "La notion de l'heure dans l'antiquité." *Janus* 57 (1970): 115–24.

Miller, J. Hillis. "The Problematic of Ending in Narrative." *Nineteenth Century Fiction* 33 (1978): 3–7.

Mink, Louis O. "The Autonomy of Historical Understanding." *History and Theory* 5 (1965): 24–47. Reprinted, with minor changes, in Dray, ed., *Philosophical Analysis and History,* pp. 160–92.

———. "History and Fiction as Modes of Comprehension." *New Literary History* 1 (1970): 541–58.

———. "Philosophical Analysis and Historical Understanding." *Review of Metaphysics* 20 (1968): 667–98.

Mittelstrass, Jürgen. *Neuzeit und Aufklärung. Studium zur Entstehung der neuzeitlichen Wissenschaft und Philosophie.* Berlin and New York: W. de Gruyter, 1970.

Momigliano, A. *Essays in Ancient and Modern Historiography.* Oxford: Basil Blackwell, 1977.

Moody, A. D. "Mrs. Dalloway as a Comedy." In Latham, ed., *Critics on Virginia Woolf,* pp. 48–58.

Moreau, Joseph. *L'Espace et le Temps selon Aristote.* Padua: Editions Antenore, 1965.

Müller, Günter. *Morphologische Poetik*. Ed. Elena Müller. Tübingen: M. Niemeyer, 1968.

Nabert, Jean. "L'expérience interne chez Kant." *Revue de métaphysique et de morale* 31 (1924): 205–68.

Nagel, Ernst. "Some Issues in the Logic of Historical Analysis." *Scientific Monthly* 74 (1952): 162–69. Reprinted in Gardiner, ed., *Theories of History*, pp. 373–86.

Nef, Frédéric, et al. *Structures élémentaires de la signification*. Brussels: Complexe, 1976.

Nietzsche, Friedrich. *On The Advantage and Disadvantage of History for Life*. Trans. Peter Preuss. Indianapolis: Hackett, 1980.

Otto, Rudolf. *The Idea of the Holy: An Inquiry into the Non-Rational in the Idea of the Divine and Its Relation to the Rational*. Trans. John W. Harvey. New York: Oxford University Press, 1958.

Pariente, J.-C. *Le Langage et l'Individuel*. Paris: Armand Colin, 1973.

Pepper, Stephen. *World Hypotheses: A Study in Evidence*. Berkeley: University of California Press, 1942.

Petit, J.-L. "La Narrativité et le concept de l'explication en histoire." In Tiffeneau, ed., *La Narrativité*, pp. 187–201.

Philibert, Michel. *L'Echelle des âges*. Paris: Seuil, 1968.

Piaget, Jean. *The Child's Conception of Time*. Trans. A. J. Pomerans. New York: Basic Books, 1970.

Picon, Gaéton. *Introduction à une esthétique de la littérature*. Paris: Gallimard, 1953.

Plato. *Timaeus*. In *The Collected Dialogues of Plato*, ed. Edith Hamilton and Huntington Cairns. Princeton: Princeton University Press, 1961.

Popper, Karl. *The Open Society and Its Enemies*. London: Routledge and Kegan Paul, 1952.

Pouillon, J. *Temps et Roman*. Paris: Gallimard, 1946.

Poulet, G. *Etudes sur le temps humain*. Paris: Plon and Ed. du Rocher, 1952–58, volumes 1 and 4.

———. *Proustian Space*. Trans. Elliot Coleman. Baltimore: Johns Hopkins University Press, 1977.

Prince, G. *Narratology: The Form and Function of Narrative*. The Hague: Mouton, 1982.

Propp, Vladimir. *Morphology of the Folktale*. 1st edition, trans. Laurence Scott, 2d edition rev. and ed. Louis A. Wagner. Austin: University of Texas Press, 1968.

———. "Les transformations du conte merveilleux." In *Théorie de la littérature. Textes des formalistes russes,* ed. T. Todorov. Paris: Seuil, 1965, pp. 234–62.

Proust, Marcel. *Jean Santeuil*. Trans. Gerard Hopkins. Longon: Weidenfeld and Nicolson, 1955.

———. *Remembrance of Things Past*. Trans. C. K. Scott Moncrieff, Terence Kilmartin, and Andreas Mayor. New York: Random House, 1981, 3 volumes.

Rad, Gerhard von. *Theology of the Old Testament*. Trans. D. M. G. Stalker. New York: Harper and Row, 1962–65, 2 volumes.

Ramnoux, Clémence. *La notion d'Archaïsme en philosophie*. Etudes présocratiques. Paris: Klincksieck, 1970, pp. 27–36.

Ranke, Ludwig. *Fürsten und Völker: Geschichten der romanischen und germanischen Völker von 1494–1514*. Wiesbaden: Willy Andreas, 1957.

———. *Ueber die Epochen der neueren Geschichte*. Ed. Hans Herzfeld, Schloss Laupheim. In *Aus Werke und Nachlass*. Ed. Th. Schieder and H. Berding. Munich, 1964–75, volume 2.

Redfield, James M. *Nature and Culture in the Iliad: The Tragedy of Hector.* Chicago: University of Chicago Press, 1975.

Reichenbach, Hans. *The Philosophy of Space and Time.* Trans. John Freund. New York: Dover Books, 1957.

Ricoeur, Paul. "Appropriation." In *Hermeneutics and the Human Sciences,* trans. and ed. John B. Thompson. Cambridge: Cambridge University Press; Paris: Editions de la Maison des Sciences de l'homme, 1981, pp. 182–93.

———. *The Contribution of French Historiography to the Theory of History.* The Zaharoff Lecture for 1978–79. Oxford: Clarendon Press, 1980.

———. "Le discours de l'action," In Ricoeur, Paul, and le Centre de Phénoménologie. *La Sémantique de l'action.* Paris: Editions du Centre National de la Recherche Scientifique, 1977, pp. 3–137.

———. "Ethics and Culture: Habermas and Gadamer in Dialogue." *Philosophy Today* 17 (1973): 153–65.

———. "Explanation and Understanding." In *The Philosophy of Paul Ricoeur: An Anthology of His Work,* ed. Charles E. Reagan and David Stewart. Boston: Beacon Press, 1978, pp. 149–66.

———. "La grammaire narrative de Greimas." *Documents de recherches sémio-linguistiques de l'Institute de la langue française,* no. 15 (1980): 5–35.

———. "L'imagination dans le discours et l'action." In *Savoir, faire, espérer: les limites de la raison.* Brussels: Publications des Facultés Universitaires Saint-Louis, 1976, 1:207–28.

———. "Les implications de la théorie des actes, de langage pour la théorie générale de l'éthique." *Archives de Philosophie du Droit.*

———. *Interpretation Theory: Discourse and the Surplus of Meaning.* Fort Worth: Texas Christian University Press, 1976.

———. "Jenseits von Husserl und Heidegger." In Bernard Waldenfels, ed., *Leibhaftige Vernunft. Spüren von Merleau-Ponty's Denken.* Munich: Fink, 1986, pp. 56–63.

———. "The Metaphorical Process as Cognition, Imagination, and Feeling." *Critical Inquiry* 5 (1978): 143–59.

———. "The Model of the Text: Meaningful Action Considered as a Text." *Social Research* 38 (1971): 529–62.

———. "The Question of Proof in Psychoanalysis." *Journal of the American Psychoanalytic Association* 25 (1977): 835–72. Reprinted in *The Philosophy of Paul Ricoeur: An Anthology of His Work,* ed. Charles E. Reagan and David Stewart. Boston: Beacon Press, 1978, pp. 184–210.

———. "La raison pratique." In T. F. Geraets, ed., *Rationality Today/La Rationalité aujourd'hui.* Ottawa: University of Ottawa Press, 1979, pp. 225–48.

———. *The Rule of Metaphor: Multidisciplinary Studies of the Creation of Meaning in Language.* Trans. Robert Czerny with Kathleen McLaughlin and John Costello, S.J. Toronto: University of Toronto Press, 1977.

———. "The Status of *Vorstellung* in Hegel's Philosophy of Religion." In Leroy S. Rouner, ed., *Meaning, Truth, and God.* Notre Dame, Ind.: Notre Dame University Press, 1982, pp. 70–88.

———. "La Structure symbolique de l'action." In *Symbolism,* Acts of the 14th International Conference on Sociology of Religion, Strasbourg, 1977. Paris: Editions du Centre National de la Recherche Scientifique, n. d., pp. 31–50.

———. "The Task of Hermeneutics." *Philosophy Today* 17 (1973): 112–24.

———. "Temps biblique." *Archivio di Filosofia* 53 (1985): 29–35.

Riegel, Klaus F., ed. *The Psychology of Development and History.* New York: Plenum Press, 1976.

Riffaterre, Michel. "The Reader's Perception of Narrative." In Mario Valdes and Owen Miller, eds., *Interpretation of Narrative*.Toronto: University of Toronto Press, 1971, pp. 28–37.

Rimmon-Kenan, Shlomith. *Narrative Fiction: Contemporary Poetics*. New York: Methuen, 1983.

Ross, W. D. *Aristotle's Physics, a Revised Text with Introduction and Commentary*. Oxford: Oxford University Press, 1936.

Rossum-Guyon, Françoise van. "Point de vue ou perspective narrative." *Poétique*, no. 4 (1970): 476–97.

Russell, Bertrand. "On the Notion of Cause." *Proceedings of the Aristotelian Society* 13 (1912–13): 1–26.

Ryle, Gilbert. *The Concept of Mind*. New York: Barnes and Noble, 1949.

Said, Edward. *Beginnings: Intention and Method*. Baltimore: Johns Hopkins University Press, 1975.

———. "Molestation and Authority in Narrative Fiction." In J. Hillis Miller, ed., *Aspects of Narrative*. New York: Columbia University Press, 1971, pp. 47–68.

Sartre, Jean-Paul. "François Mauriac and Freedom." In *Literary and Philosophical Essays*, trans. Annette Michelson. New York: Collier Books, 1962, pp. 7–25.

———. *Imagination*. Trans. Forrest Williams. Ann Arbor: University of Michigan Press, 1962.

Schafer, Roy. *Language and Insight*. New Haven: Yale University Press, 1978.

———. "Narration in the Psychoanalytic Dialogue." *Critical Inquiry* 7 (1980): 29–53.

———. *A New Language for Psychoanalysis*. New Haven: Yale University Press, 1976.

Schapp, W. *In Geschichten verstrickt*. Wiesbaden: B. Heymann, 1976.

Schellenberg, T. R. *Management of Archives*. New York: Columbia University Press, 1965.

———. *Modern Archives: Principles and Techniques*. Chicago: University of Chicago Press, 1975.

Schelling. F. W. J. *The System of Transcendental Idealism* (1800). Trans. Peter Heath. Charlottesville: University of Virginia Press, 1978.

Schnädelbach, Herbert. *Geschichtsphilosophie nach Hegel: Die Probleme des Historismus*. Freiburg and Munich: Karl Alber, 1974.

Schneider, Monique. "Le temps du conte." In Tiffeneau, ed., *La Narrativité*, pp. 85–123.

Scholes, Robert, and Kellogg, Robert. *The Nature of Narrative*. New York: Oxford University Press, 1966.

Schopenhauer, Arthur. *The World as Will and Representation*. Trans. E. F. J. Payne. New York: Dover Books, 1966, 2 volumes.

Schutz, Alfred. *The Phenomenology of the Social World*. Trans. George Walsh and Frederick Lehnert. Evanston: Northwestern University Press, 1967.

Segre, Cesare. *Structures and Time: Narration, Poetry, Models*. Trans. John Meddemmen. Chicago: University of Chicago Press, 1979.

Shattuck, Roger. *Proust's Binoculars: A Study of Memory, Time, and Recognition* in A la recherche du temps perdu. New York: Random House, 1963.

Simiand, François. "Méthode historique et science sociale." *Revue de synthèse historique* 6 (1903): 1–22, 129–57.

———. "Introduction générale" to *La Crise de l'économie française à la fin de l'Ancien Régime et au début de la Révolution française*. Paris: Presses Universitaires de France, 1944.

Smith, Barbara Herrnstein. *Poetic Closure: A Study of How Poems End*. Chicago: University of Chicago Press, 1968.

Souche-Dagues, D. *Le Développement de l'intentionnalité dans la phénoménologie husserlienne*. The Hague: Martinus Nijhoff, 1972.

———. "Une exégèse heideggerienne: le temps chez Hegel d'après le §82 de Sein und Zeit." *Revue de métaphysique et de morale* 84 (1979): 101–20.

Souriau, Etienne. *Les Deux Cent Mille Situations Dramatiques*. Paris: Flammarion, 1950.

Spinoza, Benedict. *The Chief Works of Benedict Spinoza*. Trans. R. H. Elwes. New York: Dover Books, 1955.

Stanzel, Franz. *Narrative Situations in the Novel: Tom Jones, Moby-Dick, The Ambassadors, Ulysses*. Trans. James P. Pusack. Bloomington: Indiana University Press, 1971.

———. *Theorie des Erzählens*. Göttingen: Van den Hoeck & Ruprecht, 1979.

Stevens, Wallace. "Notes Toward a Supreme Fiction." In *The Collected Poems of Wallace Stevens*. New York: Knopf, 1977, pp. 380–407.

Strawson, Peter F. *Individuals: An Essay in Descriptive Metaphysics*. London: Methuen, 1959.

Taylor, Charles. *The Explanation of Behavior*. London: Routledge and Kegan Paul, 1964.

Thieberger, Richard. *Der Begriff der Zeit bei Thomas Mann, vom Zauberberg zum Joseph*. Baden-Baden: Verlag für Kunst und Wissenschaft, 1962.

Tiffeneau, Dorian, ed. *La Narrativité*. Paris: Centre National de la Recherche Scientifique, 1980.

Todorov, Tzvetan. *The Fantastic: A Structural Approach to a Literary Genre*. Trans. Richard Howard. Ithaca: Cornell University Press, 1973.

———. "Langage et littérature." In *Poétique de la prose*. Paris: Seuil, 1971.

———. *Mikhaïl Bakhtine: le principe dialogique*, with *Ecrits du Cercle de Bakhtine*. Paris: Seuil, 1981.

———. "La notion de littérature." In *Les Genres du discours*. Paris: Seuil, 1978, pp. 13–26.

———. "L'origine des genres." In *Les Genres du discours*, pp. 44–60.

———. *Poetics of Prose*. Trans. Richard Howard. Ithaca: Cornell University Press, 1977.

Toulmin, Stephen. *The Uses of Argument*. Cambridge: Cambridge University Press, 1958.

Toulmin, Stephen, and Goodfield, June. *The Discovery of Time*. Chicago: University of Chicago Press, 1972.

Uspensky, Boris. *A Poetics of Composition: The Structure of the Artistic Text and a Typology of Compositional Forms*. Trans. Valentina Zavanin and Susan Wittig. Berkeley: University of California Press, 1973.

Valdés, Mario. *Shadows in the Cave: A Phenomenological Approach to Literary Criticism Based on Hispanic Texts*. Toronto: University of Toronto Press, 1982.

Verghese, P. T. "Diastema and Diastasis in Gregory of Nyssa: Introduction to a Concept and the Posing of a Concept." In H. Dorrie, M. Altenburger, and U. Sinryhe, eds., *Gregory von Nyssa und die Philosophie*. Leiden: E. J. Brill, 1976, pp. 243–58.

Vernant, J.-P. *Myth and Thought among the Greeks*. London: Routledge and Kegan Paul, 1983.

Veyne, Paul. *Comment on écrit l'histoire,* augmented with "Foucault révolutionne l'histoire." Paris: Seuil, 1971.

———. "L'histoire conceptualisante." In Le Goff and Nora, eds., *Faire de l'histoire*, 1:62–94.

———. *L'Inventaire des différences*. Paris: Seuil, 1976.

Vleeschauwer, Herman de. *La Déduction transcendentale dans l'oeuvre de Kant.* Paris: E. Leroux/The Hague: Martinus Nijhoff, 1934–37, 3 volumes.

Vovelle, M.: *Piété baroque et déchristianisation en Provence au xviii* siècle: les attitudes devant la mort d'après les clauses des testaments.* Paris: Plon, 1979.

———. "L'histoire et la longue durée." In Jacques Le Goff, Roger Chartier, Jacques Revel, eds., *La Nouvelle Histoire.* Paris: Retz-CEPL, 1978, pp. 316–43.

Wahl, François, ed. *Qu'est-ce que le structuralisme?* Paris: Seuil, 1968.

———. "Les ancêtres, ça ne se représente pas." In *L'Interdit de la représentation.* Paris: Seuil, 1984, pp. 31–64.

Watt, Ian. *The Rise of the Novel: Studies in Defoe, Richardson, and Fielding.* Berkeley: University of California Press, 1957.

Weber, Max. *Economy and Society: An Outline of Interpretive Sociology.* Ed. Günther Roth and Claus Wittich. Trans. Ephraim Fischoff et al. New York: Bedminster Press, 1968; reprint, Berkeley: University of California Press, 1978.

———. "Critical Studies in the Logic of the Cultural Sciences." In *The Methodology of the Social Sciences,* trans. Edward Shils and Henry A. Finch. Glencoe, Ill.: The Free Press, 1949, pp. 113–88.

———. *The Protestant Ethic and the Spirit of Capitalism.* Trans. Talcott Parsons. New York: Charles Scribner's Sons, 1958.

Weigand, H. J. *The Magic Mountain.* New York: D. Appleton-Century, 1933; reprint, Chapel Hill: The University of North Carolina Press, 1964.

Weil, Eric. *Hegel et l'Etat.* Paris: Vrin, 1950.

———. *Logique de la philosophie.* Paris: Vrin, 1950.

Weinrich, Harald. *Tempus: Besprochene und erzählte Zeit.* Stuttgart: W. Kohlhammer, 1964. *Le Temps. Le récit et le commentaire.* Trans. Michèle Lacoste. Paris: Seuil, 1973.

Weizsäcker, C. F. von. "Zeit, Physik, Metaphysik." In Christian Link, ed., *Die Erfahrung der Zeit. Gedenkschrift für Georg Picht.* Stuttgart: Klett-Cotta, 1984, pp. 22–24.

White, Hayden. *Metahistory: The Historical Imagination in Nineteenth-Century Europe.* Baltimore: Johns Hopkins University Press, 1973.

———. The Structure of Historical Narrative." *Clio* 1 (1972): 5–19.

———. *The Tropics of Discourse.* Baltimore: Johns Hopkins University Press, 1978.

White, Morton. *Foundations of Historical Knowledge.* New York: Harper and Row, 1965.

Winch, Peter. *The Idea of a Social Science and Its Relation to Philosophy.* London: Routledge and Kegan Paul, 1958.

Windelband, Wilhelm. "Geschichte und Naturwissenschaft," Strassburg Rektorrede, 1894. In *Präludien: Aufsätze und Reden zur Philosophie und ihrer Geschichte.* Tübingen: J. C. B. Mohr, 1921, 2:136–60.

Woolf, Virginia. *The Common Reader.* London: The Hogarth Press, 1925–32, 2 volumes.

———. *Mrs. Dalloway.* London: Hogarth Press, 1924; reprint, New York: Harcourt Brace Jovanovich, 1953.

———. *A Writer's Diary.* Ed. Leonard Woolf. London: Hogarth Press, 1959.

Wright, G. H. von. *An Essay in Deontic Logic and the General Theory of Action.* Amsterdam: North Holland, 1968.

———. *Explanation and Understanding.* Ithaca: Cornell University Press, 1971.

———. *Norm and Action.* London: Routledge and Kegan Paul, 1963.

Yerushalmi, Y. H. *Zakhor: Jewish History and Jewish Memory.* Seattle: University of Washington Press, 1982.

Index

351

Index

353

Index

Ricoeur, Paul, 275, 312, 323, 326, 329
Riegel, Klaus F., 275
Riffaterre, Michael, 319
Robespierre, M., 325
Ross, W. D., 279

Said, Edward, 329
Sartre, J.-P., 67, 254, 313, 316
Saussure, Ferdinand de, 150
Schellenberg, T. R., 303
Schematism, 48, 49, 183, 226
Schiller, F. von, 198
Schleiermacher, F. E. D., 301
Schnädelback, Herbert, 330
Schopenhauer, A., 330
Schutz, Alfred, 109, 112, 113, 234, 257, 300, 301, 302
Searle, John, 232
Seeing-as, 155, 156, 159, 181, 185, 186
Shaw, George Bernard, 317
Simiand, François, 5
Socrates, 247
Solignac, A., 276
Souche-Dagues, Denise, 283, 298
Spinoza, B., 113, 302
Standing-for, 100, 129, 142, 143, 144, 151, 154, 155, 156, 157–59, 177, 178, 180, 184, 186, 188, 190, 202, 245, 305
Stein, Edith, 279
Style, 153, 162, 170
Symbolic function, 116, 221

Testimony, 91, 114, 117, 118, 248
Thales, 111
Theodicy, 187, 198
Time, anonymous, 114; astral, 120; calendar, 108, 120, 122, 138, 229, 245; chronicle, 106, 108, 109; chronological, 131, 255; common, 130; cosmic, 88, 99, 100, 105, 112, 115, 127, 130, 136, 156, 180, 244, 245; hierarchy of, 63, 71, 80, 135, 140, 245; historical, 99, 104–26, 127, 138, 245; human, 180, 192; linguistic, 109; lived, 99, 100, 107, 109, 130; monumental, 130; mortal, 105, 115, 130, 136, 141; mythic, 105, 106; objective, 38, 244, 252, oneness of, 6, 102, 103, 193, 242–43, 249–61; ordinary, 120, 124, 131; phenomenological, 112, 115, 127, 156, 180, 244, 245; physical, 107, 108, 109; psychological, 108; private, 113, 114; public, 113, 114, 115, 124, 136, 141; unrepre-

sentable, 243, 261–74; world, 141, 245
Tolstoy, L., 186
Toulmin, Stephen, 89, 298, 303
Trace, 78, 79, 99, 100, 104, 114, 116, 117, 118, 119–26, 143, 144, 146, 147, 155–56, 183–84, 202, 229, 256, 283, 294, 305, 327
Tradition, 103, 110, 147, 207, 211, 216, 217, 219, 221, 222–24, 226, 227, 228, 229, 234, 235, 237, 256, 312, 326, 328; traditionality, 219, 220, 221, 227, 228, 230, 256, 258, 259, 326, 332
Tréhorel, E., 276
Troeltsch, E., 305
Truth, 5, 35, 186, 221, 222, 223, 224, 225, 226, 227, 236, 238, 285

Understanding, 63, 148, 158, 174, 175, 206, 222, 224, 225, 226, 227, 308, 311, 328
Utopia, 176, 213, 215, 226, 228, 235, 258, 260, 325

van Gogh, V., 177
Verisimilitude, 190
Vernant, Jean-Pierre, 263, 305, 333
Veyne, Paul, 149, 150, 188, 189, 308, 309
Vico, G., 310
Vleeschauwer, Herman de, 288–89
Voice, narrative, 134, 137, 160, 161, 162, 170, 186, 190, 191, 192, 260, 313, 316
von Wright, Georg H., 231, 307

Wahl, François, 303, 305
Waldenfels, Bernard, 284
Weber, Max, 112, 113, 258, 301, 309
Weil, Eric, 323, 329
Weinrich, Harald, 189–90, 191, 321
Weizsäcker, C. F. von, 298
Wessman, Alden, 275
White, Hayden, 148, 152–54, 181, 185, 310, 311, 312, 328
Whitehead, A. N., 307
Wittgenstein, Ludwig, 205
Woolf, Virginia, 129, 130, 133–34, 136, 137, 274
World of the text, 6, 101, 142, 158, 159, 178, 179, 180, 245

Yerushalmi, Yosef Haymin, 320
Yorck von Wartenburg, Paul Graf, 294

Zeno, 219